Gender and Jewish Difference from Paul to Shakespeare

THE MIDDLE AGES SERIES

Ruth Mazo Karras, Series Editor

Edward Peters, Founding Editor

A complete list of books in the series
is available from the publisher.

Gender and Jewish Difference from Paul to Shakespeare

Lisa Lampert

PENN

UNIVERSITY OF PENNSYLVANIA PRESS

Philadelphia

10 9 8 7 6 5 4 3 2 1

Published by
University of Pennsylvania Press
Philadelphia, Pennsylvania 19104-4011

Library of Congress Cataloging-in-Publication Data

Lampert, Lisa.
    Gender and Jewish difference from Paul to Shakespeare / Lisa Lampert.
       p. cm. — (The Middle Ages series)
    Includes bibliographical references and index.
    ISBN 0-8122-3775-7 (cloth : alk. paper)
    1. English literature—Middle English, 1100–1500—History and criticism. 2. Jews in
literature. 3. Christian drama, English—England—East Anglia—History and criticism.
4. Shakespeare, William, 1564–1616. Merchant of Venice. 5. Paul, the Apostle, Saint—
Relations with Jews. 6. Chaucer, Geoffrey, d. 1400. Prioress's tale. 7. English drama—To
1500—History and criticism. 8. Difference (Psychology) in literature. 9. Sex role in literature.
I. Title. II. Series.

PR151.J5L36 2004
820.9'8924—dc22   2003066570

In memory of
Howard Victor Lampert (1937–1994)

Contents

1. INTRODUCTION: MADE, NOT BORN   1

2. THE HERMENEUTICS OF DIFFERENCE   21

3. REPRIORITIZING THE *PRIORESS'S TALE*   58

4. CREATING THE CHRISTIAN IN LATE MEDIEVAL
EAST ANGLIAN DRAMA   101

5. "O WHAT A GOODLY OUTSIDE FALSEHOOD HATH!"
EXEGESIS AND IDENTITY IN *THE MERCHANT
OF VENICE*   138

CONCLUSION   168

LIST OF ABBREVIATIONS   173

NOTES   175

BIBLIOGRAPHY   235

INDEX   265

ACKNOWLEDGMENTS   275

I

Introduction: Made, Not Born

One is not born, but rather becomes, a woman.
—Simone de Beauvoir, *The Second Sex*[1]

Fiunt, non nascuntur Christiani.
—Jerome, *Epistles* 107, 1[2]

REPRESENTATIONS OF MEDIEVAL Christians and Christianity, although obviously the objects of intensive study, are rarely subject to the same types of scholarly scrutiny as representations of Jews and Judaism. "The Christian," however, is as constructed a term, category, or identity as "the Jew." Moreover, Christian perspectives dominate in the literatures and cultures of the Western European Middle Ages and also in many approaches to defining, delineating, and explaining medieval texts and contexts even in today's postsecular age. In attempting to de-center Christianity from a normative position, this book simultaneously attempts to aid in releasing the study of medieval representations of Jews and Judaism from a restricted economy of particularism. In doing so, I hope to illuminate how these representations are not simply representations of the "Other" in early English texts but are implicated in the fundamental understandings of reading, interpretation, and identity that these texts engage.

My exploration is not the description of a unified pattern of meaning but rather a study of the production of Christian meaning or, more accurately, Christian meanings. Christians are, in Jerome's words, "made not born." The texts examined in this project acknowledge, either explicitly or implicitly, that Christian identity is neither static nor fixed. Christian authors created complex and sometimes contradictory notions of Christian identity through strategic use of opposition to and identification with representations of Jews that are shaped through Christian self-definition. Even as they attempt to present Christian identity as complete and whole, Christian authors also acknowledge it to be fragile, created, and tenuous, representing Christianity and the Christian community as simultaneously universal and vulnerable. And it is at moments of the most profound instability—such as that of conversion—or in relation to theological controversies—such as those surrounding transubstantiation or the Incarnation—that representations of Christians and Jews alike are often most extreme, even violent.

My initial interest in this project was sparked by observation of a parallel between the ways in which medieval texts depict both Jews and women. Medieval representations of Jews and women tend to split into halves. Idealized Jewish patriarchs contrast sharply with demonized contemporary Jews; likewise, virgin and whore regard each other across a conceptual chasm. Current scholarship tends to examine these bifurcations separately, but I see them as related complications of an exegetical tradition that links the spiritual, masculine, and Christian and defines them in opposition to the carnal, feminine, and Jewish.

Women and Jews, however, are not simply the Other for the Christian exegetical tradition; they also represent sources of origin. One cannot conceive (of) men without women or (of) Christianity without Judaism. To accommodate these paradoxes, paradigms shift and splinter. These tensions within Christian self-definition are crucial to anti-Semitism on the one hand, to misogyny on the other, and to the entangled and conflicted relationships between them. As Simone de Beauvoir so brilliantly asserted in *The Second Sex*, the figure of woman, like that of the Jew, holds a paradoxical and conflicted place in relation to the universal in Western thought.[3] The bifurcated representations of woman and Jew found in the literature of the Middle Ages and beyond reflect the uneasy figurations of women and Jews as both insiders and outsiders to Christian society. By examining together relationships between representations of women and Jews I hope to convey how they function not only as discrete identity categories but also at times as intersecting ones. Perhaps most importantly, I also wish to suggest how they are implicated in questions of meaning and identity that extend well beyond the limiting parameters of "the Jewish question" or "the Woman question."

My approach is influenced by one of the most important advances in the field of academic feminist theory during the 1980s and 1990s, the acknowledgment and exploration of the ways in which the category of gender inflects and is inflected by the category of race.[4] Theorists such as Gloria Anzaldúa, bell hooks, Trinh T. Minh-ha, Cherríe Moraga, and Barbara Smith have been among the foremost thinkers and writers on these issues, challenging a normative whiteness assumed by many academic feminists and feminist institutions.[5] Such work has created a more inclusive and more sophisticated set of theoretical tools for feminist scholars to use in conjunction with the insights of other critical approaches, among them postcolonial theory, critical race theory, queer theory, and cultural studies.[6] As Anne McClintock argues, the categories of "race, gender and class are not distinct realms of experience, existing in splendid isolation from each other; nor can they be simply yoked together retrospectively like armatures of Lego. Rather they come into existence *in and through* relation to each other—if in contradictory and conflictual ways. In this sense, gender, race and class can be called articulated categories."[7] To describe this set of interrelationships, Kimberlé Crenshaw has introduced the term "intersectionality," which refers to the complex ways in which race and gender impact one another in the realms of experience, politics, and representation.[8]

Theoretical perspectives that foreground the intersectionality of the categories of race, gender, class, and sexuality have often been grounded in examination of nineteenth- and twentieth-century contexts, but their insights have been used to stunning effect by scholars of the English early modern period, such as Ania Loomba and Kim Hall.[9] Despite an efflorescence of research on gender and a recent flurry of publications on representations of Jews and of the Other in Middle English literature, however, investigations of the connections between Jewishness and gender difference in Middle English literature has been less in evidence.[10] Important work has been done on the intersectionality of gender and other types of difference, including Jewish difference, in Middle English texts, including innovative studies of Middle English texts by Steven F. Kruger, Denise Despres, and Geraldine Heng, but there has been to date no book-length examination of the intersection of gender with Jewish difference in medieval English texts.[11] *Gender and Jewish Difference from Paul to Shakespeare* addresses this lacuna in the scholarship by examining the connections between gender and Jewish difference in Geoffrey Chaucer's *Canterbury Tales*, the Croxton *Play of the Sacrament*, and the N-Town plays. The book concludes, for reasons that will follow, with a chapter on William Shakespeare's *The Merchant of Venice*.

In its aim to show how interconnected representations of women and Jews function in literary texts beyond the limiting economies of particularism, this book also attempts to address recent debates on the impact of the growth of "identity politics" and "multiculturalism" on political thought. Scholars committed to radical democratic ideals have questioned whether or not political and theoretical focus on particularized identities has led to paralyzing fragmentation, rendering it impossible to rally disparate groups around common goals.[12] Among the most compelling of the accounts of universalism that has emerged from "the return of universalism" is Ernesto Laclau's *Emancipation(s)*.[13] Building upon his earlier work with Chantal Mouffe in *Hegemony and Socialist Strategy*, he responds to debates over multiculturalism and the limits of postmodern theory for political thought in the wake of communism's collapse.[14] Laclau argues that positing a social system of absolute differences replicates a vision of identity and society that "lies at the root of apartheid."[15] But neither does he advocate for a universalism that is a "quest for Truth or a true Subject."[16]

Laclau's universal is an "empty place" that is never reducible or equivalent to any particular or particulars. This universality is, however, always imbricated with particularity. Particular identities within a social system are each related to and defined through each other, as "each identity is what it is only through its differences from all the others."[17] The universal is an "empty signifier" that is not separate from or opposite to but derives meaning from a particular or particulars:

Precisely because the community as such is not a purely differential space of an objective identity but an absent fullness, it cannot have any form of representation of its own, and has to borrow the latter from some entity constituted within the equivalential space—in the same way as gold is a particular use value which assumes, as well, the function of representing value in general.[18]

Laclau's model allows for description of the way in which one particular identity can come to assume the place of the universal, although this placeholding is never a stable or permanent state but a continual process of negotiation, as the universal is a type of "absent fullness" that assumes its value from the community, the system as a whole.

It is a gold standard of value for the universal that feminist critic Naomi Schor has critiqued with reference to Laclau's account. She argues that a relationship between the universal and the particular such as Laclau posits is a "synedoche masquerading as a metaphor. The false universal passes itself off as a whole (Mankind) standing for all its constitutive parts (Women, Children, Blacks, Queers), rather than recognizing that it is a mere fragment of the whole."[19] Schor sees this universal as an "inflated particular," but as Linda Zerilli points out, and Schor herself acknowledges, a "false" universalism would imply the possibility of a "true" one.[20] Further, the relationship between the universal and the particular that Laclau describes, which he defines as one of hegemony, is characterized by negotiation and struggle rather than a simple inflation or a type of fixity. As Judith Butler notes, the theory of hegemony, like the theory of performativity, stresses "the way in which the social world is made—and new social possibilities emerge—at various levels of social action through a collaborative relation with power."[21]

Not every particular can or will come to assume the place of the universal. The way in which one "particular content becomes the signifier of the absent communitarian fullness is exactly what we call a *hegemonic relationship*."[22] It is not a "realization of a shared essence" but a "process of mediation through which antagonistic struggles articulate common social objectives and political strategies."[23] As Laclau asserts, "[I]n a society (and this is finally the case of *any* society) in which its fullness—the moment of its universality—is unachievable, the relation between the universal and the particular is a hegemonic relation."[24] Laclau's model takes into account "the unevenness of the social" and acknowledges that "[n]ot any position in society, not any struggle is equally capable of transforming its own contents in a nodal point that becomes an empty signifier."[25]

Zerilli identifies a new political philosophy of mediation between the particular and the universal based on Laclau. This recognition of the universal as something that is not an "ossified rule" is an enabling model for future political strategizing.[26] And because this model can accommodate varied temporal and cultural contexts, it also can serve to provide interpretive tools with which to examine earlier representations of relationships between identities. The conceptional relationship between the universal and particular that Laclau posits is adaptable to understandings of communities that differ in time and geography precisely because the model of the hegemonic relationship is "unstable and undecidable."[27]

Many of the texts examined in this book provide representations of the Christian community as whole and complete. At the same time, however, these texts explicitly and implicitly acknowledge that Christian identity can never be entirely stable, much less monolithic. The Pauline texts so central to later understandings of the relationship between Judaism and Christianity, such as Romans and 2 Corinthians, are themselves addressed to communities that were not unified but divided in belief, practice, and background. Likewise, early interpreters of Paul and the New Testament wrote in situations of theological and political negotiation between competing sets of beliefs and practices. Augustine, for example, formulated many of his ideas about Jews and the Old Testament as he challenged perspectives he viewed as heretical, such as Manichaeism.[28] Christianity and Christian identity are then objects of contention among individuals and groups, even as they may be negotiated through traditional terms, symbols, and analogies.

Although his focus is secular, Laclau's discussion does consider universalism in relation to Christianity.[29] He differentiates his notion of the universal from that of "classical ancient philosophy," which holds that "there is no possible mediation between universality and particularity: the particular can only *corrupt* the universal."[30] These two forms of universalism differ from the eschatological orientation of Christianity where the particular and the universal are mediated by the divine through a relationship of incarnation.[31] According to Laclau, in the Christian model, the particular and the universal are not, as they are in classical philosophy, related as content is to form but through a temporal relationship that I would characterize as typological, as a particular order of events is realized in a universal one.

In Laclau's brief history of universalisms, this model is superseded by a third approach, in which God is replaced by Reason as the mark of universality. The break between the second and the third modes, which seems to correspond to a transition between medieval/early modern thinking and that of the Enlightenment, is, however, not a complete one. Laclau writes of the transition from a universalism mediated through the divine to one that elevates reason:

A subtle logic destined to have a profound influence on our intellectual tradition was started in this way: that of the *privileged agent of history*, the agent whose particular body was the expression of a universality transcending it. The modern idea of a "universal class" and the various forms of Eurocentrism are nothing but the distant historical effects of the logic of incarnation.[32]

Laclau here seems to draw a connection between a premodern incarnational universalism and the missionizing univeralism associated with colonial imperialism. The comments of Schor resonate with Laclau's as she points to the origin of French universalism in the Catholic Church, which she reminds us is "from the Greek *Katholikos*, 'universal.' "[33] Her assertion that "[t]he history of universalism in France is then a history of the transvaluation of a fundamental religious belief into a prime means of desacralizing society" further indicates the importance of medieval traditions to current understandings of universalism.[34]

Despite their references to Christianity in relation to the history of the concept of universalism, Laclau's and Schor's discussions of pre-Enlightenment paradigms are evocative, dense, and tantalizingly brief. Taking such glimpses as substitutes for full accounts would be inaccurate and might serve to replicate the very types of supersessionist treatments of the Middle Ages that Kathleen Biddick has so insightfully critiqued.[35] And, indeed, in *Hegemony and Socialist Strategy*, Laclau and Mouffe's reference to medieval peasant communities as an exclusionary limit for the concept of hegemony replicates the traditional use of the Middle Ages as the originary Other from and against which the modern is constituted.[36] These brief reflections on theological universalisms, however, reveal the necessity for discussion of medieval and early modern contexts in relation to the universalist-particularist debate and indicate the need to investigate more closely the influence of Christian theological paradigms on later universalisms, looking beyond the traditional periodization boundary that curtains off the medieval period from serious consideration.

I have therefore treated the "return of universalism" at some length not because I think Laclau's discussion of the hegemonic relationship provides some kind of ideal template for understanding medieval texts. That is clearly not the case. Rather I have tried to detail some of the elements in the universalist-particularist debate to present a theoretical framework and vocabulary that I find useful for investigating the roles of two particular identities—Jew and woman—in relation to conceptions of the universal. Contemporary theoretical approaches can indeed illuminate underexamined dimensions of medieval representations of Jewish-Christian relations or of the place of woman in medieval cultures. Just as important, however, are the ways in which medieval texts and contexts can both broaden and sharpen our understandings of contemporary debates. When Laclau and Schor mention the Christian heritage of modern universalisms, they are cracking open a door, beyond which lies an entire tradition of Christian writing and thought. This book attempts to peer in at that tradition, opening the door a little wider by using the tools of literary analysis to examine the role of two particular identities—that of the Jew and the woman—within early contributions to that tradition. My readings, I hope, will not only invite further discussion of questions of universalism among scholars of early literature but will also illuminate to nonspecialists just what kinds of insights and connections we forfeit when we close the door on medieval texts. Because I believe so much is lost when this foreclosure occurs, I hope through this book to encourage those engaged with modern and postmodern universalisms to consider the crucial longer tradition of what they discuss, especially in relation to the association between Jews and particularism that endures to this day.

I suggest that we can better understand the intellectual tradition that posits an "absolute human type" as masculine and Christian by investigating early representations of the hegemonic relationships that posited a Christian universality standing in supersessionary relationship to the particular identities of both Jews and women.[37] By attending to medieval and early modern contexts, which is a "blind spot" in current theoretical discussion of universalism, I hope to help to address another "blind spot" in some feminist investigations of the universal: that of racial and religious differences.[38]

Feminist inquiry has continually exposed the problems inherent in universalist thought. Joan Scott, tracing back the history of French feminist movement into the eighteenth century, has shown how the relationship of women to the universal has always been paradoxical, because as women made claims for recognition of their universal rights they had of necessity to do so through acknowledging their difference. As Scott puts it, "This paradox—the need both to accept *and* refuse 'sexual difference' as a condition of inclusion in the universal—was the constitutive condition of feminism as a political movement throughout its long history."[39] Beauvoir's famous exploration of this paradox began with classical and biblical antecedents, and, as we will see in the next chapter, her early work has been followed by an impressive body of feminist investigations of the figure of woman in theological and philosophical understandings of the universal that long preexisted feminism as a distinct political movement.

Although the situation of women and Jews or their place in Western symbolic economies are by no means identical, the role that Jews and Judaism have played in the development of Western European universalisms is also of great significance. Adam Sutcliffe has recently demonstrated how Enlightenment thinkers, most notably Voltaire, who contributed so significantly to the development of a philosophical understanding of the universal and related ideas such as tolerance and universal human rights, shaped their notions of universality and reason against and through an attitude of profound ambivalence toward Jews and Judaism. Certainly the Enlightenment was a time of political gains for Jews, and Enlightenment writings contained some positive attitudes toward Jews and Judaism, but at the same time the Jews were also identified with an archaic, superstitious, and backward particularity and, indeed, with particularity itself and, crucially, with a stifling and exclusionary particularity.

Sutcliffe draws upon imagery of weaving and knots to describe the intricate way in which Jews and Judaism have to be understood not simply as discrete objects of consideration by Enlightenment thinkers. They were rather elements interwoven into the very fabric of Enlightenment intellectual life, incorporated into its texture in ways that well exceeded ideas and issues created by actual contact between Jews and non-Jews. "Judaism," Sutcliffe argues, "was thus profoundly ensnared in the relationship between the Enlightenment and the Christian worldview from and against which it emerged."[40] Even as Enlightenment thinkers "desacralized" society, as Schor's account puts it, replacing the divine with reason, as Laclau asserts, they relied on representations of Jews and Judaism that drew from Christian writers of the patristic, medieval, and early modern periods where the figure of the Jew was part of the very warp and weft of Christian thought.[41]

Crucial patterns in this pre-Enlightenment tradition have recently been charted and analyzed in Jeremy Cohen's important *Living Letters of the Law: Ideas of the Jew in Medieval Christianity*, which investigates the history of representations of Jews and Judaism in patristic and medieval Christian texts. Cohen traces the development of what he calls the "hermeneutical Jew," a complex, shifting, and not purely negative figure "crafted" in the interests of Christian "self-definition."[42] In the terms of the debates over universalism in recent years, the "hermeneutical Jew" can be seen as a conceptual tool through which Christian thinkers can claim Christianity as a universal faith. Because of its "protean" nature the figure of the hermeneutical Jew functions differently depending on the context in which the figure is deployed, but these varied uses by Christian writers have generated a continuous and complicated tradition.[43] As Denise Despres has recently asserted, we cannot overlook the "distinctive place" of the Jews in the Christian cultures of medieval Europe.[44] This distinctiveness, it is clear throughout the tradition both before and after the medieval period, often functioned in relation to other particular identities, such as that of heretics, but is not equivalent to them.[45]

The hermeneutical Jew is an ideological construction created not as a reflection of actual reality but as a tool of Christian theology.[46] Part of the crucial importance of Cohen's analysis lies in the fact that it illuminates how these hermeneutical constructions, influential far beyond theology, art, and literature, were part of Christian "self-definition and propagation."[47] As Cohen discusses through reference to Foucault, the figure of the hermeneutical Jew needs to be examined as part of "the experience of order and of its modes of being" in Latin Christendom.[48] So too, I would add, does the figure of woman, which, drawing upon recent feminist scholarship on early and medieval Christian theological treatments, can aptly be called "the hermeneutical Woman." Both figures play important roles in the ways that Christian writers pose questions of understanding, meaning, and being.

Central to these questions is that "analogy of analogies" introduced by Paul in 2 Corinthians 3:6—"the letter kills, but the spirit gives life."[49] This dictum became linked in the exegetical tradition to an understanding of the superseded Jewish law and with Jews and Judaism in general, as they became associated with a way of reading and interpretation that was seen not to be reading or interpretation at all, as it refused to recognize Christian supersession. Drawing upon Paul's references to Moses veiled at Sinai in 2 Corinthians, Jews were regarded as blinded by the veil of the letter, doomed to carnal understandings of their Scriptures and of the world around them. At every turn the relationship between Christians and Jews is figured through the relationship between the "New" and "Old" testaments, and therefore, at some level, all Christian depictions of Jewish-Christian relations reference hermeneutical paradigms, indelibly linking the difference between Jewish and Christian identities to questions of interpretation.[50] Analyzing the figure of the veil and the paradigm of the letter and the spirit, Carolyn Dinshaw powerfully demonstrated how Christian hermeneutic paradigms are marked by gender. In the next chapter, I will explore the important intersection of Jewish and gender difference in relation to Christian hermeneutics and specifically to the question of supersession.

Christian hermeneutics rely upon a supersessionist understanding of Jewish scripture and of Jews and Judaism that figures Jewish particularity as both origin and stubborn remainder. This view of Jews and Judaism references not only a specific people with specific history and traditions but also a mode of understanding and being that is figured as inherently deficient and likened to blindness. Jewish particularity becomes transformed into a conception of Jewish particularism.[51] It is because Jews and Judaism not only come to signify a people but also become synonymous with a devalued hermeneutical practice (as little as this signification has to do with actual Jewish practice) that intra-Christian disputes and charges of heresy can be so readily figured as questions of "judaizing." Anti-Semitism and actual persecution and violence against Jews stem from complex political, economic, and social causes specific to each location and incidence. Nevertheless, the fact that Christian understandings of Jews and Judaism are so completely imbricated in Christian universalism and Christian self-understanding renders more understandable "anti-Semitism without Jews." All of the texts examined in this book were created during a time when Jews were officially banished from England, but this did not, as these texts clearly show, keep the figure of the Jew from leading a powerful life within Christian imaginations.

This representational life often features images of graphic and even gruesome embodiment. Formulations of supersession are not limited to exegetical abstraction but are also grounded in symbolism of the body as hermeneutical paradigms are "made flesh." At the moment of the Incarnation, the Word becomes Flesh, and Christian understanding is seen as freed from the tyranny of the letter. The Incarnation itself therefore stands as a central premise of Christian understanding of the relationship between the letter and the spirit. This moment of spiritual awakening is also a profoundly embodied one, taking place through the body of a woman who is both virgin and mother, Christian and Jew.

To analyze these symbolic bodies I will draw upon anthropologist Mary Douglas's classic study of the body as a symbol of society. Of special interest is her argument that the boundaries of the symbolic body "can represent any boundaries which are threatened or precarious" and that representations of bodily orifices, bodily margins, and the matter that they excrete are symbolic of the boundaries of society itself.[52] The contested boundaries of Mary's body become symbolic of the contact between Judaism and Christianity and come to represent the limits of Christian ideology and of Christian identity. The types of embodied tensions played out in debates over the body of the Virgin extend well beyond theological texts. At moments of ambiguity and instability, late medieval English literature often graphically and violently literalizes the exegetical boundaries between masculine and feminine and between Christian and Jewish. Out of the torn and bleeding bodies that litter these works emerge striking images of Christian wholeness, impermeability, and purity, most significantly the Eucharist and Mary's womb. It is around such symbols that Christian identities are constructed through iterative practices, such as the Mass, and through stories of defilement, such as Chaucer's *Prioress's Tale*.

The third, fourth, and fifth chapters of this book present literary readings that treat the relationships between these symbolic bodies and the hermeneutical paradigms that they engage. Chapter 3 presents readings of sections of Chaucer's *The Canterbury Tales* in an attempt to extend study of representations of Jews in Chaucer beyond the obsessive focus on Chaucer's possible anti-Semitism that has dominated criticism for more than fifty years. I begin by investigating how the Host's reference to Lollards in the *Man of Law's Endlink* opens a space for negotiation about faith, piety, and religious authority among the pilgrims. Chaucer's two nuns, the Prioress and the Second Nun, create competing models of idealized Christian identity that engage with the radical splits between the masculine and the feminine enabled by Christian hermeneutics. I read the Prioress's engagement with these hermeneutical models as a direct reaction to the *Shipman's Tale*, in which moral chaos stems from an unspoken sin, the tale's hidden usury. The Prioress brings this usury out into the open, connecting it specifically with the Jews. And, in contrast to the Shipman's lack of moral distinctions, the Prioress presents a world in which the lines between good and evil are clear-cut, with their contours conforming to the difference between Christian and Jew. Asked to follow a tale in which a wife prostitutes herself with a monk, the Prioress depicts pious male and female Christians coming together around a martyred boy and against the demonized Jews who murdered him. This picture of Christian unity is of particular significance given the Prioress's own situation. Speaking as a woman of authority surrounded almost entirely by men, she attempts to redeem the integrity of the feminine and the Christian through her portrayal of the Virgin and her assertion of the importance of a Marian-centered and femininized affective piety within the traditional framework of male-dominated ecclesiastical institutions.

The *Prioress's Tale*, however, not only valorizes feminized piety but also infantilizes it. The Second Nun reacts to the Prioress's implicit devaluation of learning with her tale of Saint Cecelia, an active female martyr who converts others to Christianity through education and understanding. The Second Nun's definition of the Christian draws upon Pauline models of universal inclusion that demonstrate the ways in which the actions of a female martyr were instrumental to the very founding of the ecclesiastical institutions that the Prioress depicts. The Second Nun does not, however, attack the Prioress's method, which creates a model of the Christian through a demonization of the Jew that precludes the possibility of conversion (often a feature of the Miracle of the Virgin genre from which the *Prioress's Tale* derives). Although the *Second Nun's Tale* relies primarily on an inclusive model of conversion, she still draws upon the exclusionary opposition inherent in the universalism of Pauline texts such as Galatians. Through her use of the dichotomies between blindness and insight, and pagan and Christian, the Second Nun invokes an opposition to Jewish perfidy that draws power from the *Prioress's Tale*. Her tale also draws on the Pauline definition of the Christian as one who has the capacity to "read" the spiritual, thereby engaging with Wycliffite discourses concerning representation in ways that have implications for the entire *Canterbury Tales* and for the study of Lollardy that is currently so prominent in Middle English studies. Through examination of the relationship between these two tales and their place in Fragments VII and VIII, I show how the category of the Jewish informs Chaucer's representations of the feminine, the pagan, and the Lollard and how the interarticulations of these terms contribute to a notion of Christianity that comprises difference and fractures. Christianity is then continually negotiated and renegotiated among the pilgrims beyond the *Prioress's Tale* into Chaucer's own "self-presentation" in the Thopas/Melibee sequence and his "Retraction" and into the penitential guide for the construction of the Christian self that is the *Parson's Tale*.

In Chapter 4 I turn to two fifteenth-century East Anglian dramas, the Croxton *Play of the Sacrament* and the N-Town cycle, specifically the N-Town "Nativity" and "Assumption." My focus is on moments of crossing: conversion, transubstantiation, incarnation, and their relationship to comedy and dramatic representations of conversion and difference. I examine how these crossings are inflected by Pauline formulations of the feminine and the Jewish and how, in turn, these inflections structure the plays' overall forms, which are arguably comic, as well as their critically contentious risible moments. In these plays the hermeneutical Jew and the hermeneutical Woman are linked in the physicality of their representations through the topos of the stricken hand.[53] In the N-town "Nativity," Salomé the midwife insists on examining Mary to test her virginity. As punishment her hand is rendered shriveled and useless until she is restored to physical wholeness through belief. In the Croxton play, Jonathas the Jew and his men torture the host to test the truth of transubstantiation. As part of these trials, Jonathas attempts to hurl it into a pot of boiling oil, but the host remains attached to his hand. He tries frantically to detach it, but his arm is severed and, like Salomé's, is only restored upon his conversion.

I argue that these two liminal figures, the midwife and the doubting Jew, represent particular types of doubters. Because of the originary relationship of Judaism to Christianity, Jewish doubt threatens to destabilize Christian claims to religious truth. Likewise the midwife, a "woman on top" in the feminine realm of the birthing chamber, poses a challenge to an otherwise male-dominated society. These figures are presented as doubters who are converted through faith, as supersession is literally inscribed into their very bodies. But despite their endings in conversion, these narratives do not find easy closure. They are instead sites of potential laughter and even disruption among audience members, as we know was the case in the now missing York version of the Virgin's Assumption.[54]

Disruptive potential is generated because the play gives the audience opportunity not only to gape at the doubting sinner in horror but also to identify with him or her. The constructed nature of the Christian is foregrounded in these dramas because each invites the audience to assume the place of the doubter who understands only literally and carnally (the desecrating Jew and Salomé, the skeptical midwife). The difficult comic moments that ensue stem from realizations of the fragility of Christian identity. Even miraculous conversion to Christianity must be accompanied by the performative rituals of confession, penance, and communion, which increasingly came to shape the orthodox Christian in late medieval England. These Christian rituals perform the hermeneutical paradigms that shape the Christian in the exegetical tradition. Christianity is therefore under construction, a fragile edifice that existed alongside, and yet in contrast to, Christian ideals of wholeness such as the Eucharist. These plays show that the exegetical model of supersession sometimes has difficulty negotiating the hermeneutical Jew and the hermeneutical Woman, whose "residues" also stubbornly challenge the transformative Christian paradigm. In the context of medieval drama, ribald and risible moments provide the audience with an opportunity to strengthen their faith through exploration of their doubts.

In Chapter 5, I read the "Renaissance" comedy *The Merchant of Venice* in light of the patristic and medieval Christian hermeneutics explored in earlier chapters. What distinguishes my reading is that I regard Bassanio and Portia not only as the play's main pair of lovers but as its master exegetes. Taking Portia's query "Which is the Merchant here? and which the Jew?" as the play's central question, I show how the characters grapple with challenges to who and what define "the Venetian" (and, by extension for Shakespeare's audience, the "English").[55] These issues, I argue, are centered around Christian hermeneutical paradigms, with the key question of the proper relationship between the literal and the spiritual climaxing in the famous trial scene of Act IV. There the cross-dressed Portia interprets the law so literally as to "out-Jew" Shylock, calling into question the "superiority" of Christian Venetians such as Portia and Antonio. This moment of indeterminacy also marks the culmination of the play's concern with the corrosive effects of trade and exploration on Christian discourse. *Merchant* shows how the Venetians' desire for profit undermines the possibility of creating stable identity; when even human flesh is assigned a cash value, all units of meaning are thereby reduced to fungible signs, a problematic that refigures the Eucharistic questions I discuss in relation to medieval texts.

Key moments in *Merchant* are framed in terms of a central tension between inner and outer meanings that is marked by difference in religion and in "race," as emblematized by the challenge of the three caskets. Portia is not, however, the only prize available to a man who can see beneath exteriors. Shylock's daughter Jessica, Launcelot's Moorish mistress, and the alluring and dangerous "Indian beauty" evoked by Bassanio are each figured in terms of the dichotomy of inner and outer meaning that underlies Christian exegetical practice. Although seemingly a Christian fantasy of Jewish conversion, Jessica's situation actually calls this very fantasy into question. In Jessica's uneasiness and her continual doubts that she can escape a Jewish essence, the play most clearly reveals its concerns about the fragility of Christian and Venetian identities. Exotic females such as Jessica, made available to the Christian male through commercial "intercourse," threaten the commonwealth with miscegenation that will further complicate any attempt to distinguish between Christian Venetian and Other. Shakespeare's play explores the question of whether trade, which brought about contact with all sorts of "aliens," would ultimately destabilize a Christian England. The play's emphasis on the making and unmaking of Christians suggests that to be a Christian is not a static state but an identity to be performed and enacted. Although the play's Venetian characters seem to assume a direct and uncomplicated equality between Venetian and ideal Christian identity, their actions show that although one may be born Venetian or Jewish, Christians are paradoxically both born *and* made, a process still understood by Shakespeare very much in terms of the Christian hermeneutical paradigms of patristic and medieval authors.

The choice to conclude with a chapter on a Shakespearean text merits further explanation. My goal is not to create a telos toward the wisdom of the Bard but rather to read *Merchant* in light of the medieval exegetical tradition that so shapes it and the figurations of the Jewish and the feminine that it explores. A glimpse into the early modern period is also called for to demonstrate the ways in which categories of race and gender destabilize traditional periodization schemes. In her study of the woman writer as a central figure in the creation of English literary history, Jennifer Summit draws upon the classic work of Joan Kelly, arguing that feminist scholarship has already demonstrated that "the Burckhardtian schemes of 'medieval' and 'Renaissance' were never relevant to the history of women."[56] Similarly, I would argue, the figure of the Jew also confounds a tidy master narrative that posits all that is modern, including the category of race, as having a distinctly postmedieval origin.[57]

The question of whether we can discuss the Jews in terms of the category of "race" and whether or not we can therefore consider anti-Semitism to be a type of racism is highly contested; equally contested is the use of terms such as "race" and "anti-Semitism" in relation to medieval contexts.[58] Medieval representations of Jews are nevertheless undeniably important to the history of Western European prejudice and to an understanding of the development of the category of race,[59] and discussions of the history of prejudice against the Jews are, in literary historical contexts at least, still powerfully influenced by the periodization categories of "Middle Ages" and "Renaissance."[60] An influential article by Jerome Friedman, for example, locates the origin of the modern concept of race in the early modern period, specifically in the infamous Spanish blood laws, and one sees the impact of such ideas in the usage of the term "race" by scholars of early modern literature.[61] Further, the periodicity model impacts more general discussions of race as well. In his essay entitled "Race" in the guide *Critical Terms for Literary Study*, Kwame Anthony Appiah, an important scholar and theorist in the field of African American studies, avoids the medieval-early modern divide by avoiding the "Middle Ages" altogether, examining the "long process of transition from the views of the ancient world" to "racialism" through reference to early modern drama.[62] Although Appiah steers around the Burckhardtian medieval-Renaissance divide by emphasizing the importance of theological models to Elizabethan ideas of race, he ends up redrawing the familiar contours of theories of the development of the idea of race by simply placing the shift from "theological" to "biological" later in time.[63] I suggest that these two sets of binaries commonly used to discuss the history of the concept of race are of very limited use. This book focuses on theological paradigms in literary contexts, with a goal of generating deeper understandings of the relationships between Jewish and gender difference that might be of use to those investigating the concept of race and the problems of racism.

Of course, in the Middle Ages, the Elizabethan theological ideas to which Appiah gives such weight also had major importance, and these ideas were by no means unified or monolithic over time or region.[64] Attempts to understand the history of medieval prejudice against Jews and to deduce causes for its various shifts and changes have been undertaken by numerous historians, among them Anna Abulafia, Jeremy Cohen, Amos Funkenstein, Gavin Langmuir, Lester Little, and R. I. Moore. Each has pointed to some kind of change in the nature of prejudice against Jews in either the twelfth or the thirteenth centuries.[65] Focusing on the question of Jewish conversion to Christianity, Robert Stacey has argued that "[b]y the middle of the thirteenth century in England, there was clearly an irreducible element to Jewish identity in the eyes of many Christians, which no amount of baptismal water could entirely eradicate, at least from a layman. Through baptism, converts from Judaism became Christians, but this did not mean that they had entirely ceased to be Jews in the eyes of their brothers and sisters in Christ."[66]

As Yosef Yerushalmi points out, this is a perspective that might also be at play in notorious incidents such as the conflict over the Jewish ancestry of the controversial Pope Anaclet II, whom Bernard of Clairvaux denounced during the Schism crisis of 1130.[67] Peter Biller presents evidence of "ethnographic" thought from the twelfth century that also muddies the waters of terminology, because in early writers such as Caesarius of Heisterbach we find elements that are "disturbingly, very like the constituent elements of vulgar racial stereotypes in the modern world."[68] Such evidence confounds any easy assertions that "race" as a concept emerged in the early modern or modern eras. Recently, Robert Bartlett has provided a complex and nuanced examination of the terms "race" and "ethnicity" in medieval contexts, demonstrating that the corresponding medieval terminology, such as the Latin terms *gens* and *natio*, were "no more straightforward than our own."[69] Medieval authors considered not only genealogy in considering how to categorize human groups but also elements of "environmental influence," ultimately placing the greatest importance upon "the cultural and social component of ethnic identity."[70] For Bartlett, the idea of "race" in the medieval period would appear to be synonymous with "ethnic group," a categorization that places emphasis on linguistic, legal, political, and cultural affinities, emphasizing them over somatic difference as a marker of "racial" difference.

These terms and examples point to the extremely thorny problem of discussing the history of prejudice against Jews in the West, because even the basic terminology available, both medieval and modern, is difficult to define and to employ. Furthermore, scholarship about Jews in any historical period must, for the time being at least, still acknowledge the long shadow that the Holocaust casts upon theory and historiography.[71] In the introduction to *Communities of Violence: Persecution of Minorities in the Middle Ages,* David Nirenberg analyzes the different historiographic schools engaged with this question and shows the pitfalls of attempting to read for the "origins of European intolerance" in a "teleology leading, more or less explicitly, to the Holocaust."[72] According to Nirenberg, the characteristic objects of study for historians of the "longue durée" of the history of intolerance are "collective images, representations, and stereotypes of the 'other.' "[73]

I have found Nirenberg's overview of this historiographic problem extremely valuable, and I agree that we must reject distorting models that create an understanding of anti-Semitism as naturalized and therefore eternal, as Hannah Arendt cautioned in 1951.[74] But as a literary critic interested in two interrelated figures, the hermeneutical Woman and the hermeneutical Jew, I find my focus squarely fixed on images and representations that, having common roots in the Christian exegetical tradition, do form a kind of overarching discourse from which medieval and early modern authors drew. Although this tradition clearly manifests itself differently not only within different localities and communities but also within each individual literary work, there are nevertheless points of connection. It is inaccurate and anachronistic to paint unreflectively the history of prejudice against Jews with one broad brush of the term "anti-Semitism," thereby creating a direct connection between medieval hostilities toward Jews and the atrocities of the Holocaust.[75] I want to avoid that kind of polemical connection.[76] At the same time, however, I believe that it is equally problematic to sidestep the issue of the connections between medieval, early modern, and modern prejudice against Jews by prohibiting the use of key terminology, such as the terms "anti-Semitism" and "race/racial," or by avoiding modern theoretical paradigms developed from studies of modern texts and contexts.[77] Such tactics impede research both within and outside of medieval studies. Drawing boundaries between medieval and early modern prejudice through emphasis on a distinction between theological and secular forms only serves to replicate the clearly problematic periodization boundaries between the Middle Ages and the Renaissance. With all of these considerations in mind, I will employ the terms "anti-Judaism" and "anti-Semitism" in this book. I reserve the use of "anti-Semitism" for those moments when I believe that the text or situation indicates a representation of or belief in a Jewish essence that, to borrow from Stacey's formulation, no baptismal water seemed able to wash away. The term "race" comes up only rarely in my discussions, but when it does prove useful to refer to this concept in my readings of medieval and early modern texts, I will use the term in quotation marks to indicate both its evolving historical nature and its contested status among medievalists and modern theorists alike.[78] In analyzing the use of scare quotes around the term "ethnic" in a United Kingdom census report, Bartlett notes astutely that this punctuation "warn[s] that the author wishes simultaneously to assert something and to retract it."[79] One can detect a similarly double gesture in my usage, but I wish to retain crucial terms that necessarily come into play in the undergraduate classroom, while at the same time, I wish to foreground the historical and constructed nature of these terms in order to de-naturalize such categories for scholars and for their students.[80] For, finally, as Anne McClintock argues, "To dispute the notion that race is a fixed and transcendent essence, unchanged through the ages, does not mean that 'all talk of "race" must cease,' nor does it mean that the baroque inventions of racial difference had no tangible or terrible effects. On the contrary, it is precisely the inventedness of historical hierarchies that renders attention to social power and violence so much more urgent."[81]

An awareness of the problems that this discussion of periodization and terminology poses for both research and teaching figures into my choice of texts for this project. Two of my chapters focus on major canonical authors, Chaucer and Shakespeare, in the hope of reaching an audience not only of medievalists but of early modern scholars as well. My choice to discuss medieval drama in Chapter 4 also reflects this intention, because I hoped that these texts might be familiar to early modernists as part of training in "pre-Shakespearean" drama. Despite the many problems with the idea and enforcement of a "canon," *The Canterbury Tales* and *The Merchant of Venice* are currently very much part of a common language among literary scholars, and Chaucer and Shakespeare are authors that many undergraduates study and that nonspecialists frequently teach. Moreover, these texts are not only part of a literary canon but also a part of a canon of texts central to formation of ideas of "Jewishness."

Finally, I also wish to encourage further dialogue between medievalists, early modernists, and modernists by using the issues of gender and Jewish difference, which defy periodization boundaries, to facilitate this discussion. Using the tools of literary analysis, this book examines the creation of Christian identities within specific literary contexts, but it also seeks to suggest the key importance of the hermeneutical Jew and the hermeneutical Woman within an extended literary tradition. No simple transhistorical trajectory can account for the relationship between these figures into the modern period, and I attempt here to situate my readings within the specific moments in which the texts in question were created. But to understand more fully the existing connections between these categories over time, we must acknowledge the vital importance of relatively neglected medieval paradigms to formulations of not only gender and religious difference but national and racial difference as well. This book attempts to illuminate crucial theological elements in these formulations in the hope of encouraging scholars of later periods to explore the effects of these Christian hermeneutics as they were rearticulated into the modern age.

2

The Hermeneutics of Difference

Hör Jud, so merk dir und verstee
Dass alle Geschicht der alten Ee
Und aller Propheten Red gemein
Ein Figur der neuen Ee ist allein
—Hans Folz[1]

The discourse of man is in the metaphor of woman.
—Gayatri Spivak[2]

ON APRIL 12, 1933, Cardinal Saliège of Toulouse expressed solidarity with persecuted German Jews, explaining why he felt compelled to speak out against their ill treatment:

I could not forget that the staff of Jesse has flowered in Israel and has given there its fruit. The Virgin, Christ, the first disciples were of the Jewish race. How could I not feel bound to Israel like a branch to the trunk that has borne it!

Moreover, I recognize only one morality, one that is universal, and in every man I see I respect the eminent dignity of human nature. Catholicism cannot agree that belonging to a specific race places men in a position of inferior rights. It proclaims the essential equality of all races and all individuals. Any difference in the scale of human values based on the sole principle of blood, or race, is unknown in a universal religion like Catholicism. "He is of another race; I am permitted anything against him": we condemn this principle of violence, of injustice, this morality of sovereign force, destructive of the rights and duties of the human person. . . . And now, to sum up my deepest thought, I take the words of a great Jew who became a great Christian: "There is among you now neither pagan nor Jew, neither Scythian nor barbarian; all are but one in Jesus Christ."[3]

Speaking in the wake of the infamous German boycott against Jewish merchants, which had begun on April 1, 1933, Saliège challenges racism through passages from the Pauline Epistles that directly address questions of differences between human beings and the relationship of different groups to each other and to God.[4] Saliège draws upon the vision of life in Christ in Colossians 3:11: "Here there cannot be Greek and Jew, circumcised and uncircumcised, barbarian, Scythian, slave, free man, but Christ is all, and in all," itself drawn from the baptismal formulation in Galatians 3:28: "There is neither Jew nor Greek, there is neither slave nor free, there is neither male nor female; for you are all one in Christ Jesus."[5] Saliège combines this Pauline universalism with post-Enlightenment language of rights, equality, and human dignity, stressing a tradition linking the *Katholikus* of the Church and the principles of universal human rights in resistance to an ideology in which the ideas of universality have collapsed into the absolute and savage particularism of National Socialism.[6]

The passage also alludes to elements in the Pauline corpus that have been used not only to express unity between Jews and non-Jews but also to stress division between them. In declaring himself bound to Israel like a "branch to the trunk that has borne it," Saliège draws upon the metaphor of the relationship between the people of Israel and the Gentiles in Romans 11:16–24:

If the root is holy, so are the branches. But if some of the branches were broken off, and you, a wild olive shoot, were grafted in their place to share the richness of the olive tree, do not boast over the branches. If you do boast, remember it is not you that support the root, but the root that supports you. You will say, "Branches were broken off so that I might be grafted in." That is true. They were broken off because of their unbelief, but you stand fast only through faith. So do not become proud, but stand in awe. . . . And even the others, if they do not persist in their unbelief, will be grafted in, for God has the power to graft them in again. For if you have been cut from what is by nature a wild olive tree, and grafted, contrary to nature, into a cultivated olive tree, how much more will these natural branches be grafted back into their own olive tree.

In Romans, Paul addresses a church in a city with a large and well-established Jewish community, where Gentiles also were in attendance at synagogues. Paul was not addressing "Christians," because that identity was still in development. His audience were those Jews and Gentiles in the "Jesus movement." Their community has been described as one in transition, as they negotiated their identity through and against influences from the Roman state, varying perspectives from within the Jewish community and differing beliefs and practices among Gentile groups.[7]

Paul's analogy draws upon prophetic images of Israel as an olive tree such as that found in Jeremiah 11:16, in which Israel's flourishing in faith is linked to a healthy tree in full growth; faithlessness threatens the tree with destruction.[8] Addressing his audience in the second person, emphasizing that they are not outside observers to this analogy but part of it, Paul depicts an organic relationship between Jews and Gentiles and stresses their mutual relationship to God through the idea of the broken and grafted branches, with God himself as the horticulturist.[9] Branches are part of the tree not by virtue of what type of branches they are (cultivated or wild olive), but through faith, just as Jew and Gentile respectively are joined to the tree through faith, not by birth. Those grafted in are not to feel superior to the others, because they too can be broken away, just as the broken branches can be regrafted onto the tree.

As it was received and interpreted through the centuries, this crucial analogy came to be understood not only as an expression of an organic unity of particular groups joined in Christ but also alternatively as an expression of relations between Christians and Jews that regarded them as separate and indeed mutually exclusive groups. Brief examination of just a few of the influential early Christian exegetes of Romans reveals a broad range of interpretation. Origen's exegesis stresses the organic nature of the tree, noting that a tree is not born, but rather grows and develops; it must be cultivated, and so must Christians grow and develop, exercising their free will, lest they too end up broken away from the tree.[10] Moving away from a fluid model of process to take a more divisive stance, John Chrysostom reads Paul as making strong attacks against the Jews in Romans, even as he attempts to win them to the faith.[11]

The extremely influential writings of Augustine also treat Romans 9–11 in various works. The late work *Tractatus Adversus Iudaeos* begins and ends with the image of the olive tree, using it to stress how Jewish nonbelievers are broken away from the root of the patriarchs and exhorting believers to continue to preach to the Jews, even if that preaching is received with stubborn scorn.[12] In other works Augustine's treatment of Roman's olive tree links this image of communal relationships to an understanding of the relationship between the Old and New Testaments. In *Contra Faustum*, the fluid and contested communities that Paul addressed in the Roman Church are seen now as divided camps, and Paul's conversion itself is figured as a transition from broken to grafted branch. Asserting the importance of the Old Testament to the New against Manichaean objections, Augustine also likens the Manichaeans themselves to the broken branch.[13] The argument, focused on the relationship of sacred texts, links Christian identity to reading and understanding, a way of interpreting texts and the world that becomes key in Christian figurations of the Christian relationship to Judaism.

In *Enarrationes in Psalmos,* Augustine notes that the grafting of the wild olive onto the cultivated plant is an inversion of the typical horticultural process, by which the cultivated plant is usually grafted onto the wild. As a result of this atypical grafting, the fruit comes from the graft, rather than the root; the product of the tree therefore derives from Christians rather than what is identified as a Jewish root.[14] This horticultural supersession parallels the relationship that Augustine posits between the Old Testament and the New. This connection between the parts of the grafted tree and the Old and New Testaments is illustrative of a point well made recently by Lisa Freinkel, that one of the key oppositions between believers and nonbelievers for Augustine can be seen as a difference between "legere" and "intellegere." The Jews, Augustine argues, read the Old Testament, but they do not understand it, and hence, through this lack of understanding and faith, they are broken away from the tree.[15]

For Augustine, the olive tree image delineates the relationship between Christian and Jew and between Christianity and its Jewish origin. Judaism may be Christianity's root, but Christianity has superseded Judaism. The analogy of the broken branch permits re-union, but the image of the broken branches, cut away from the tree, represents a radical break between those Jews who refuse to believe and the universal salvation represented by the entire tree. The paradox of supersession is apparent here. Jews are both roots and broken branches. They represent particular identities radically cut off from universal salvation, but they have played a role in salvation history and can never be completely extricated from it.

My goal here is not to provide an exhaustive catalogue of interpretations of what one scholar has called a "test case in Pauline exegesis."[16] A striking example from one of Augustine's most important medieval interpreters, Bernard of Clairvaux, however, provides an influential example of Romans exegesis that follows Augustine in depicting Christians and Jews as divided and that figures Christian priority through supersession. In his *Sermones super Cantica Canticorum,* Bernard of Clairvaux takes up Paul's olive tree image in Sermon 79, in which he figures the Jews as rivals to a magnanimous Church that continues to offer them salvation despite their stubborn disbelief:

Great is the charity of the Church, who does not grudge her delights even to her rival, the Synagogue. What could be kinder than to be willing to share with her enemy him whom her soul loves? But it is not surprising, because "salvation is from the Jews." The Saviour returned to the place from which he had come, so that the remnant of Israel might be saved. Let not the branches be ungrateful to the root, nor sons to their mother; let not the branches grudge the roots the sap they took from it, nor the sons grudge their mother the milk they sucked from her breast. Let the Church hold fast the salvation which the Jews lost; she holds it until the fulness of the Gentiles comes, and so all Israel may be saved.[17]

For Bernard, Christians are both metaphoric branches drawing sap from a Jewish root and metaphoric sons sucking milk from the breasts of their mothers. Bernard acknowledges Judaism's role as Christianity's origin, but Judaism's temporal priority is superseded by Christianity's claims to truth. Bernard depicts Jews as Christianity's root, but Christians drain this root's sap just as sons take milk from their mothers' breasts. One might well think of mothers giving milk to their children in a nurturing way, as Bernard does when he tells his monks that in correcting subordinates they should be gentle like mothers: "Let your bosoms expand with milk, not swell with passion."[18] But here the branch/son/Christian actively takes from the root/mother/Jew much as one might argue that the Christian exegete draws from the Old Testament. The familial metaphor reinforces a sense of Christian inheritance: the future generation of sons nourishes itself with mothers' milk. Bernard creates the sense that a vital spiritual essence has been drained from its Jewish source to be more properly used by Christians.

As Friedrich Lotter argues in his discussion of early Cistercian writings, the views of Bernard and other early Cistercians, such as William of St. Thierry, are by no means purely negative but reflect ambivalent and sometimes paradoxical views.[19] However one finally decides to balance or weigh the ultimately unresolvable issue of the "negativity" or "positivity" of Romans exegesis, it is clear that supersession is at the core of the wide range of post-Pauline interpretations of Romans. Christianity is figured as the universal religion that has superseded its roots. Jews can be seen as originary figures, part of the tree, or as separated figures, broken branches, who can be transformed and regrafted into the Christian whole. Unconverted contemporary Jews are never fully excised from the picture; they are problematically residual, stubborn particulars who are both part of and separate from the universal. In keeping with this view, we find Christian writers treating Jews as a lingering, atavistic group that exists as living proof of Christian origins, as in Augustine's doctrine of Jewish witness.[20] There is a promise of future salvation, of regrafting and re-union for the

Jewish people, as Christian thinkers assert that "a remnant will be saved" or "all Israel will be saved," but this promise lies in the future. It also requires that Jewish particularity be finally completely subsumed into the universal as these remaining Jews convert to Christianity.

The figure of the olive tree represents complex and fluid relationships between particular groups—Jews who accept Christ as the Messiah and Gentiles who believe the same and Jews who do not. The tree is at once a unified organic image and also one that contains strife, negotiation, and development. The Jews represented by the broken branches are both part of this tree, literally of it, and yet severed from it. In Romans 11:25–26, Paul stresses universal salvation, when even the hardened remnant will be saved, but at the present moment, those Jews who do not believe remain cut off. Paul declares, "I want you to understand this mystery; brethren: a hardening has come upon part of Israel, until the full number of the Gentiles come in, and so all Israel will be saved." Daniel Boyarin has characterized the tree metaphor as an example of a "particular universalism." Of the analogy of the olive tree, Boyarin writes,

The story of Israel in the Hebrew Bible is essentially a myth of tribal identity, not entirely unlike other tribal myths of origin and identity. The appropriation of the story of a particular tribe, with all that marks it as such, as the story of all humanity would inevitably lead to paradox and even contradiction. If one olive tree among all the others has come to be the all-in-all, then any others become necessarily only so much dead wood. It is in this ambivalent symbol, then, that there begins a certain logic of exclusion by inclusion, or "particular universalism" that would characterize Christian discourse historically.[21]

Although, clearly, these ideas are not themselves, as Boyarin stresses, "anti-Judaic," the paradoxes inherent in "the nascent Pauline doctrine of supersession" that Boyarin illuminates loom large in the subsequent Christian tradition of Pauline exegesis.[22] I now turn to how some of these paradoxes play out in patristic and medieval exegetical texts and how they intersect with questions of gender, particularly with the paradoxical role that the hermeneutical Woman plays in Christian theology.

In his analysis of the Pauline corpus, Boyarin has made the important and provocative assertion in relation to the Western tradition that " 'the Jew' has been constructed analogously to 'Woman' within the culture and by a very similar historical vector."[23] I consider here some points along this trajectory of ideas present in examples from patristic and medieval exegetical texts, considering specifically the parallel dynamics of supersession by which the believing Christian subject is posited as normatively masculine. Through these dynamics a believing woman is figured as transcending her sex as she achieves salvation. For the Jew, such partaking in the universal can only come through another type of transcendence, conversion, abandoning Jewish particularity to become subsumed within the Christian universal. Considering these dynamics of supersession reveals the creation of a Christian universal that has distinct but related relationships to two particulars, Jews and women, represented in Christian exegesis through the figures of the hermeneutical Jew and the hermeneutical Woman. Both of these particulars are, as the model of the hegemonic relationship would suggest, inextricably linked to the universal, which also, crucially, draws meaning from them. Yet at the same time, the limits of the Christian community are defined through and against these particulars.

The Christian community in Galatians is defined as a universal one. This universal union is in Christ, but in this world it is never complete and differences do therefore have meaning.[24] For Augustine, for example, the vision of fulfillment and union proclaimed in Galatians 3:28 is a vision of the future, not the present:

Such difference of race or social rank or sex has already been removed by the unity of faith, but it remains in the mortal condition and is prescribed by the apostles as normative for the path of this life. They also transmit most salutary rules, how Jews and Greeks may live among themselves in accordance with their different race, masters and slaves in accordance with their unequal social rank, and men and wives in accordance with their sexual disparity. Similar rules apply to parallel circumstances. And God himself said this earlier, "Give to Caesar what belongs to Caesar, and to God what belongs to God."[25]

Galatian's final consummation promises "neither Jew nor Greek . . . neither male nor female" in Christ, but for Augustine this egalitarian future is deferred and subsumed by the hierarchical exigencies of a corrupted present, which places spiritual over carnal, masculine over feminine, Christian over Jew. Within these hierarchical relationships, the nature of Christian identity is defined through these differences, as one term is superseded by the other.

We can conceive of supersession as the crossing of what James Samuel Preus calls the "hermeneutical divide."[26] The location and contours of this divide are complex and shifting. For Origen, for example, the divisions between letter and spirit and Old and New Testament apply to the "anthropological hierarchy of body and soul or mind."[27] For Augustine, the hermeneutical divide between Old and New Testaments can be understood in different ways based on differing notions of the concept of promise. If one sees promise as temporal, then the Old Testament contains mere shadows of the New. But if the Old Testament is read through the "Promise of Christ," then it can be understood as a *figura* in a prophetic sense, a foretelling of the story of Christ and Christian faith.[28] Viewed in this way, both the Old Testament and the New always lead to the same conclusion of fulfillment in Christ.[29] As Boyarin's analysis would imply, however, this unity, what Henri de Lubac refers to as the "harmonization" of the relationship between the two Testaments, is also, despite its complex manifestations, a type of homogenization.[30] Christian exegesis, resting on a foundation laid by Pauline formulations, has the potential to enable a theology of inclusion, like that expounded by Saliège, one in which every human shares the possibility for salvation. At the same time, Paul's allegorical method can be seen as standing at the "origins of western anti-Judaism and misogyny."[31] This allegorical method, which draws greatly upon traditions of Neoplatonism and Hellenistic Judaism, including the thought of Philo, is built on a system of binaries that posits oppositional relationships between "external and internal realities."[32] As Boyarin explains, in this schema, "language itself is understood as an outer, physical shell, and meaning is construed as the invisible, ideal, and spiritual reality that lies behind or is trapped within the body of language."[33]

These figurations of supersession have specific grounding in Christian hermeneutics. Clearly a central point of contact between Jews and Christians is the so-called Old Testament, sacred to both Judaism and Christianity, but interpreted so differently by each. From the Christian perspective, the critical and foundational relationship between the two faiths is mediated through this sacred text, which must be read in a new way, according "to the spirit," in order to be properly understood within the new order. This hermeneutical relationship between Christianity and Judaism intersects in Christian exegetical texts with the gendered hierarchy of hermeneutical meaning revealed by Carolyn Dinshaw in *Chaucer's Sexual Poetics*. Just as texts and textual meaning can be marked as feminine in Christian exegesis, so does a certain type of reading, literal reading, become figured in relation to a hierarchy of method in which Christian hermeneutics are considered superior to Jewish literal ones. Jews become associated with a profitless way of reading and are figured as blind readers who read without comprehension. The Jews are figured as mere custodians of the Old Testament, indeed they become linked to the literal text itself. Just as the Christian reader's masculine identity is constructed in relation to a figuration of a feminized text or textual truth, so too is his Christian identity constructed through relation to a text that is marked as either pagan or Jewish.

The hermeneutical Woman and the hermeneutical Jew both become associated with veiled knowledge, a clouded seeing, and, of course, with carnality and the body itself. Both become figured as embodied particulars in relation to a universal that transcends embodiment. Yet Christian universality is an incarnational universality as the Word is made Flesh. This chapter will conclude with an examination of the Virgin Mother, the Jewish Christian, whose body is the site of the Incarnation and, as the critical site of contact between the two faiths, an embodiment of the paradoxes posed by the figures of both woman and Jew.

She Will Become Male

Although the feminine sometimes represents for Christian writers, as Jean Leclercq put it, "all that is best in themselves and all mankind," there is an important strain of Christian thought that genders spiritual transcendence as masculine, thereby ultimately gendering Christian identity itself as normatively masculine.[34] Some key tensions that stem from the relationship between the sexes presented in Genesis emerge as well in the Pauline Epistles. On the one hand, within the Epistles stands the universalizing formula of Galatians 3:28 and, on the other, are the statements in 1 Corinthians 11:2–16, which seem to reverse the assertion that there is "no male or female" in Christ and to assert gender hierarchy. Indeed the repetition of the Galatians baptismal formula in 1 Corinthians 12:13 omits reference to gender. It seems unsatisfactory simply to attribute this discrepancy to the fact that Paul faced varied situations and contingencies, following perhaps his assertion in 1 Corinthians 9:19–23 that he became many things to many different types of people in order to preach the gospel.[35] Boyarin argues, convincingly in my opinion, that Paul distinguishes between the future egalitarian vision of Galatians and his instructions to the Corinthians, which stress the symbolic hierarchies of a world prior to the Parousia.[36]

Whether or not one accepts this view, there is strong consensus that the androgynous vision of Galatians 3:28 is neither sexless nor neuter but rather must be understood as masculine.[37] Here we have the association between the universal, the universal in Christ, and the normative masculine universal subject that Simone de Beauvoir's analysis reveals. This split, as Boyarin points to through reference to Judith Butler's important analysis of Beauvoir, renders an association between the female with the body and the male with a disembodied universality. Butler argues that Beauvoir is not simply writing of the "right of women," but that she makes a

fundamental critique of the very disembodiment of the abstract masculine epistemological subject. That subject is abstract to the extent that it disavows its socially marked embodiment and, further, projects that disavowed and disparaged embodiment on to the feminine sphere, effectively renaming the body as female. This association of the body with the female works along magical relations of reciprocity whereby the female sex becomes restricted to its body, and the male body, fully disavowed, becomes, paradoxically, the incorporeal instrument of an ostensibly radical freedom.[38]

In early Christian writings we find such figurations of masculine disembodiment. Women can believe as Christians, but when they do so, they leave behind their womanhood, marked by their body, and become men. Ambrose, for example, writes, "She who does not believe is a woman and is still designated by the name of her bodily sex, whereas she who believes progresses to complete manhood, to the measure of the adulthood of Christ."[39]

Here woman is linked to the body and to a type of spiritual immaturity that must be outgrown. The split between the feminine and the masculine then comes to parallel a posited philosophical opposition between spirit and body that preexists the Christian tradition and is present in authors such as Philo, who also genders this dichotomy.[40] Within this scheme, a woman can remain tied to her sex, or she can transcend it. Ambrose's formulations are echoed by Jerome: "As long as woman is for birth and children, she is as different from man as body is from soul. But if she wishes to serve Christ more than the world, then she will cease to be a woman and will be called man."[41]

Here we find Jerome explicitly linking through analogy two related binaries: woman is to man as body is to soul. By choosing between the options of another opposition, serving Christ or serving the world, a woman may transcend her bodily sex, explicitly associated in this passage with her reproductive capacities. In embracing the spirit, such a woman earns the name of man.[42] The movement of supersession therefore shapes a Christian understanding of gender difference. If a woman, associated with the body and the carnal, wishes to become truly Christian, she must transcend her body. The result is not an androgynous state to which men could also aspire through the shedding of their male bodies but rather a shedding of feminine difference that renders the woman masculine.

Augustine wrestles with the question of the believing woman, resorting to a model that draws upon Neoplatonic elements to portray the relationship of man to woman in analogy to the faculties of the human mind. Augustine makes distinctions between how gender is to be understood in this temporal world and the contrasting way it is to be understood in relationship to the *imago Dei*, which is beyond gender.[43] In *De Trinitate*, Augustine questions how we are to understand gender hierarchy in explicit relation to the declaration in Galatians that there is "neither male nor female" in Christ:

'For whoever of you have been baptized in Christ, you have put on Christ. There is neither Jew nor Greek, there is neither male nor female. For are you not all of you one in Christ Jesus.' Have the believing women, therefore, lost their bodily sex? But because they are renewed there to the image of God, where there is no sex, man [*homo*] is made there to the image of God, where there is no sex, namely in the spirit of his mind. Why, then, is the man [*vir*] on that account not bound to cover his head because he is the image and glory of God, but the woman must cover it because she is the glory of the man, just as if the woman were not renewed in the spirit of her mind, who is renewed unto the knowledge of God according to the image of Him who created him? But because she differs from the man by her bodily sex, that part of the reason which is turned aside to regulate temporal things, could be properly symbolized by her corporeal veil; so that the image of God does not remain except in that part of the human mind in which it clings to the contemplation and consideration of the eternal reasons, which, as is evident, not only men, but also women possess.[44]

Explaining the hierarchy between the sexes through a model of the human mind, Augustine argues that both men and women have the capacity to draw upon "that part of the human mind in which it clings to the contemplation and inspiration of eternal reasons (*rationes*)." That part of the mind reflects the *imago Dei*, which, according to Augustine's model, is gendered masculine even as both sexes have access to it.[45] Distinguishing between woman as *homo* and woman as *femina* or *mulier*, Augustine argues that, as *homo*, woman is formed in the image of God, but as *femina*, different from man (*vir*) in respect to her corporeality, she is unlike the image of God and "subordinate."[46] He argues that "in their minds a common nature is recognized; but in their bodies the division of this one mind itself is symbolized."[47] Augustine is not declaring the spiritual inferiority of women to men. Genevieve Lloyd argues, however, that although Augustine's treatment of the figure of woman "can be seen as an upgrading" from earlier thinkers such as Philo, in spite of Augustine's "good intentions, his own symbolism pulls against his explicit doctrine of sexual equality with respect to the possession of Reason."[48]

Even as he acknowledges woman as a spiritual being, Augustine links woman to the body, even likening Adam's dominion over Eve in the Garden to the order by which the soul has control over the body like a master over a servant.[49] No transcendence of the male body is necessary for *vir*, but woman is incomplete without man and subject to him, a state of subordination symbolized by her covering her head.[50] Addressing Paul's instructions in 1 Corinthians, Augustine writes,

In what sense, therefore, are we to understand the Apostle, that the man is the image of God, and consequently is forbidden to cover his head, but the woman is not, and on this account is commanded to do so? The solution lies, I think, in what I already said when discussing the nature of the human mind, namely, that the woman together with her husband is the image of God, so that that whole substance is one image. But when she is assigned as a help-mate, a function that pertains to her alone, then she is not the image of God; but as far as the man alone is concerned, he is by himself alone the image of God, just as fully and completely as when he and the woman are joined together into one. As we said of the nature of the human mind, both that if as a whole it contemplates the truth, it is the image of God; and also when its functions are divided and something of it is diverted with a certain purpose to the handling of temporal things, nevertheless that part from which the mind consults the truth is the image of God, but that other part, from which the mind is directed to the handling of inferior things, is not the image of God.[51]

In Augustine's scheme then, man alone can be the image of God, but woman cannot. Augustine, like Paul, would neither deny women's "religious subjectivity" nor their potential for salvation, beliefs very much in keeping with the experiences both had with pious Christian women during their lifetimes.[52] Within symbolic economies, however, woman is defined by her body and marked by corporeality in a way that man is not. Woman is not by any means cut off from the universal in Christian thought, but she, in her particularity as a woman, is marked by her sex and cannot represent the universal. Her salvation can come only through transcending her sex.

The Elder Will Serve the Younger

These early formulations go to the very heart of the questions feminism poses to universalism. In the past three decades, feminist scholars of religious and philosophical thought such as Allen, Børresen, Boyarin, Clark, Lloyd, and Ruether have made huge strides in tracing and clarifying the paradoxical relationship of woman to the universal, whether this universal is tied to Christian salvation or to an idea of Reason. What has not been explored, however, is the way in which these gendered dynamics are mirrored in some important ways by the relationship of supersession posited between Judaism and Christianity.[53] Augustine's characterization of the relationship of the Old Testament to the New, like the relationship of *mulier* to *vir*, is posited as one of fundamental deficiency: one side of a binary opposition can only find wholeness and completion in its superseding term. In *De Civitate Dei*, Augustine writes, "For although the Old Testament is prior in time, the New Testament is to be put before the Old in order of importance, since the Old Testament is the herald of the New."[54] The Old Testament cannot stand independently; it can only be fulfilled and understood in light of the New Testament, which supersedes it. This relationship is figured through a wide variety of analogies, including that of harmonization, the figure of a wheel within a wheel, the water that Christ turns to wine at Cana,[55] and often powerfully through biblical stories in which a younger brother takes precedence over an older one, read in accordance with Roman 9:12: "the elder will serve the younger." Jill Robbins has shown how through exegesis of fraternal narratives, those of Cain and Abel, Esau and Jacob, Ishmael and Isaac, and the story of the prodigal son, Augustine develops an understanding of the relationship of supersession between the Old Testament and the New and between Jews and Christians. In these stories Christians always represent the younger brother who takes precedence over the older one, a configuration that, as we will see, plays a role in the way that Jews are represented in *The Canterbury Tales* as well as in *The Merchant of Venice*.[56]

The Jews become linked to the Old Testament not as the inheritors of its message but as mere caretakers who bear and read the text without understanding its true meaning.[57] Augustine writes,

Therefore in what does the reproach of the Jews consist? The Jew carries a book, from which a Christian may believe. They have been made our librarians, just as it is customary for servants to carry books behind their masters, so that those who carry faint and those who read profit. And the reproach of the Jews consists in this; and that which was so long ago foretold is fulfilled: "He hath given unto reproach those that trampled on me." So what kind of reproach is it, brothers, when they read this verse and they who are themselves blind turn toward their own mirror? The appearance of the Jews in the holy scripture which they carry is just like the face of a blind man in a mirror; he is seen by others, by himself not seen. "He hath given unto reproach those that trampled on me."[58]

As those studying the doctrine of "Augustinian toleration" have shown, the Jews become bearers of the Law, living reminders of the Old Testament's truth against challenges to it, such as those presented by heretical groups concerning the truth of the Old Testament as an essential precursor to Christian truth, against challenges to both the Old Testament and to Christianity.[59]

Because of their role as witness the Jews are not to be harmed but instead should be preserved in order to act as custodians of the Book until their eventual conversion.[60] The Jew becomes linked with carnality not only through an association with literal and carnal meaning as opposed to spiritual meaning but through a bodily relationship to the Book as its literal bearer. Indeed, the Jew becomes the letter of the text itself in the Bernardine formulation from which Jeremy Cohen takes the title of his study; for Bernard, Jews are "*vivi . . . apices,*" living letters of Scripture.[61] The Jew can only reach a state beyond this intellectual and spiritual imprisonment in the letter by turning to the spirit and converting to Christianity. In this way the Jew becomes an embodied particular identity, associated with a literal book, a tablet of stone, the letter devoid of meaning, empty of spirit.

In parallel ways, then, the figure of the woman and the Jew are incomplete. Woman becomes complete by transcending her sex. The Jew also exists in a state characterized by the carnal and the literal and will only reach fulfillment through conversion, by becoming Christian. Rabanus Maurus highlights the notion of Christian transcendence as a masculine state in his exegesis of Numbers 7, in which a wide variety of offerings is brought to the tabernacle. Seeing the variety of offerings and suppliants, Rabanus comments on their variety through a series of oppositions: some suppliants are wise, some are foolish, some are rich, some are poor, some are firm of mind, others infirm. For Rabanus, these parallels are analogous with the Jewish and Christian peoples: "Then the rough and uncultivated Jewish people had to be polished into shape, dwelling under the shadow of the law; now the Christian people, seeing the law's mysteries explained in the truth of the Gospel, must be nourished into perfect manhood."[62]

The Jewish people stand on the side of the foolish, the poor, and the mentally infirm, needing to be polished into shape; Christians are not shadowed by the law: as the new and true Israel, they are being molded to a higher perfection through the New Testament, a perfection that, drawing on the language of Ephesians 4:13, is characterized as "virum," manhood.[63]

Hermeneutic Polarities

Both the hermeneutical Woman and the hermeneutical Jew have paradoxical relationships to Christian notions of universality and to a normative Christian identity that, as we have seen, is figured as masculine. It is these paradoxical tensions, the way in which these two particularities are superseded by a Christian universal that may well account for the striking cleavages we find in representations of Jews and women, with their polarizations into virgin and whore, patriarch and Christ-killer.[64] As Elisa Narin van Court has recently shown in relation to representations of Jews, "the conceptual space between the binary oppositions of exemplary Scriptural Jew and perfidious historical Jew is actively occupied by diverse and often contradictory representations."[65] The same can be noted of representations of women, and although it would therefore be a distortion to assert that polarizations are the only extant types, polarizing representations are so prevalent and so influential that they are more than simply the limits of representational extremes. Rather, their polarized ambiguities are generated, I would argue, from the tensions that these two particular identities create in respect to Christian universalisms.[66]

The famous Eva/Ave anagram epitomizes the polarization found in the hermeneutical Woman. We find it in the antiphon from the Office of the Virgin, *Ave Maris Stella*:

Sumens illud Ave	Receiving that Ave
Gabrielis ore,	From the lips of Gabriel,
Funda nos in pace,	Establish us in peace,
Mutans nomen Evae.	Changing Eva's name.[67]

Eve, the mother of humanity, through willful disobedience, is the cause of all sin and woe; the Virgin, mother of Christ, through humble obedience, makes possible the birth of the Redeemer. This polarization is not limited to the figures of Eve and Mary and did not originate in the Middle Ages. Neither are representations of woman limited to these dualisms but instead present a rich variety that cannot be adequately described by over-simplified "positive and negative" images. Nevertheless the split that Eileen Power has characterized as being between "a pit and a pedestal," although not totalizing, is significant in its influence and pervasiveness and has been remarked upon by scholars of patristic and medieval texts from a wide range of disciplines and critical orientations.[68] Elizabeth Clark notes in patristic texts an "extreme ambivalence on the topic of womanhood."[69] She asserts that there is a continual "dual evaluation of woman by the church fathers as the 'devil's gateway' and 'the bride of Christ.' The fathers' alternate condemnation and exaltation of the female sex is both striking and baffling."[70] Rosemary Ruether is not so puzzled by this phenomenon, arguing that the "ambivalence between misogynism and the praise of the virginal woman is not accidental. One view is not more 'characteristic' than the other. Both stand together as two sides of a dualistic psychology that was the basis of the patristic doctrine of man," a doctrine based on a hierarchical valuation of the masculine over the feminine.[71] In his controversial *Medieval Misogyny*, R. Howard Bloch goes so far as to posit that the very attempt to categorize woman through the polarizing strategies of either denigration or praise is inherently misogynist.[72] It is highly debatable whether the act of defining woman is the essence of misogyny, because such a definition gives undue emphasis to the power of speech over other types of power, notably physical violence. The dualism that Bloch points to, however, as the observations of so many other scholars also indicate, is an essential undergirding to the structure of the hermeneutical Woman.

Similar polarizing tendencies appear in representations of Jews.[73] We find this sort of cleavage in the New Testament in Romans 11:28–29: "As regards the gospel they are enemies of God, for your sake; but as regards election they are beloved for the sake of their forefathers." Because of the patriarchs, prophets, and heros, the Jews are beloved. These ancestors, who came before the time of Christ (but who are often portrayed as believing in him), are viewed positively. Those Jews who lived at the time of Christ or after and who refused to accept him as the messiah and Son of God are, in contrast, the object of rejection and scorn.[74] This polarized view of Jews also characterizes the Augustinian doctrine of relative toleration, in which the Jews were tolerated among Christians as a living reminder of the prophecies of Christ and the truth of the Old Testament. The Jews were seen as being preserved in punishment in order to play their appointed role in the Christian salvational scheme.[75] For example, in writing about true desire for God in the second of his *Sermones super Cantica Canticorum*, Bernard of Clairvaux praises what he calls the Jewish patriarchs' "burning desire" for Christ, which puts to shame the "lukewarmness, the frigid unconcern of these miserable times."[76] But despite this praise for the patriarchs as Christians *avant la lettre*, Bernard elsewhere heaps scorn upon contemporary Jews as stiff-necked unbelievers. Drawing on Pauline and Augustinian writings in Sermon 14, Bernard describes the Jews as stubbornly and blindly tied to the literal, refusing to understand the grace of the Spirit.[77] Within the *Sermones* then, we find a very common paradoxical situation: biblical Jews, the patriarchs, are praised as proto-Christians who longed for a Christ who is, of course, Jesus Christ. At the same time, Jews living after the Crucifixion who refuse to recognize this savior are heaped with condemnation.

This bifurcated view of the Jew is not limited to exegetical texts. It is, for example, made graphically literal in the twelfth-century Christmas Play of Benediktbeuern, *Ludus de Nativitate*. The play opens with Augustine at the front of the church, probably on a platform. To his right stand a line of prophets: Isaiah, Daniel, the Sibyl, Aaron, Balaam; facing them on the left stand Archisynagogus and his Jews. The prophets come forward foretelling the Virgin birth, which Archisynagogus and his Jews vehemently deny, claiming it to be "simplicitas," as foolish as to declare that a camel would descend from a cow.[78] The prophets, both Hebrew and pagan, are represented as calm and dignified. They declare in measured verse the coming of Christ through the Virgin birth. The stage directions at one point call specifically for their leader, Augustine, to speak in a voice that is "sobria and discreta."[79] Archisynagogus and crew are, in stark contrast, loud and obnoxious. Archisynagogus, according to the stage directions, is meant to be portrayed in a way that deliberately parodies "Jewish" mannerisms, yelling and shaking: "Let Archisynagogus with his Jews, having heard the prophecies, make an excessive clamor; and, shoving forward his comrade, agitating his head and his entire body and striking the ground with his foot, and imitating with his sceptre the mannerisms of a Jew in all ways, with his companions let him say indignantly."[80] The Israelite prophets are revered and bring news of Christian truth; contemporary Jews are characterized as blindly unbelieving and ridiculous, traits that manifest themselves onto their very bodies, as we will see occurring as well in later dramatic representations of unbelievers, such as the Croxton *Play of the Sacrament* and the N-Town "Nativity."[81] Archisynagogus, with "the mannerisms of a Jew," shakes, yells, and laughs immoderately, acting out his spiritual perversions in what could be seen as a combination of the humorous and the terrifying. We find a bifurcation in representations of Jewish figures in later drama as well through the presentation of the *Ordo Prophetarum*.[82] In such representations, the prophets and other Jewish figures who lived before the time of Christ are revered ancestors, who would have believed in Christ if they could have and, indeed, did believe in their own way. In contrast, Jews who lived at the time of the Crucifixion or after it are obstinate disbelievers, ignorant, or even malicious.

Non Litterae, Sed Spiritus

Not that we are sufficient of ourselves to claim anything as coming from us; our sufficiency is from God, who has qualified us to be ministers of a new covenant, not in a written code but in the Spirit; for the written code kills, but the Spirit gives life.
  —2 Corinthians 3:5–6

Here, as Paul defends his ministry against his opponents with the community at Corinth, he compares his ministry to that of Moses, figuring his new purpose in supersessionary relationship to the old. The triumph of the Spirit over the written code (literally "not of letter but of spirit")[83] and what this formulation means in terms of the status of this "written code," linked to "the Law," has been open to the same type of intense interpretive scrutiny over the centuries as the analogy of the relationship between Jews and Gentiles in Romans.[84]

    This opposition between letter and spirit becomes central to formulations of Christian hermeneutic practice. We find this clearly in Augustine's comments on spiritual reading in his guide to Christian reading, *De Doctrina Christiana*: "when that which is said figuratively is taken as though it were literal, it is understood carnally. Nor can anything more appropriately be called the death of the soul than that condition in which the thing which distinguishes us from beasts, which is the understanding, is subjected to the flesh in the pursuit of the letter."[85] Augustine here defines a way of reading in which, to borrow from Boyarin's formulation, "hermeneutics becomes anthropology."[86] To read according to the spirit is what distinguishes the human, and this humanity is linked to the soul, in opposition to the flesh, which is tied to the literal. To read and interpret a text or a sign for its own sake rather than in charity, out of love for God, is nothing less than spiritual death. Further, the exegetical process is not simply limited to the task of reading, it is the task of building the Christian self, the transcendence of the death of the letter. After the coming of Christ, Jewish stubborn refusal to change their way of reading texts and events created the division between Christians and Jews. The difference between Christian and Jew is then very much marked by a difference in ways of reading. For Augustine, to read with maturity, through the spirit, is to read as a Christian.[87] In *Augustine the Reader*, Brian Stock argues that the experience of Christian reading was, for Augustine, the process of creating a Christian self: "Encouraged by the allegories of Ambrose, he came to understand that the reader could distinguish between what Paul called the 'spirit' and the 'letter' as a parallel to the 'inner' and 'outer' self. Texts and selves interpenetrated; it became possible to look upon the building of a new self as an exegetical and interpretive process."[88] Stock speaks of Augustine becoming a "Christian reader" who joined his "spiritual progress to his ability to read and interpret biblical texts," a view of the Christian exegetical project that makes hermeneutics the engine of the creation of the self.[89]

At the heart of this way of reading lies the assumption that textual meaning is layered and that these layers have hierarchically differing values. Dinshaw has traced the classical and patristic origins of Western Christian hermeneutics, illuminating the gender politics of the relationship between exegete and text. She demonstrates how the figure of the exegetical veil functions in two different models, both of which represent as feminine either the text or the veil covering it. In the first model, the text and its truth are like a woman who must be unveiled. In the second, the feminine is associated with the decorative veil that covers the text—its pleasing narrative. To reveal the text's truth, this decoration must be stripped away. In her discussion of these two basic models and their variations, Dinshaw notes that "the value of the feminine (and the letter) is thus shifting and contradictory in exegetical tradition, ranging from Jerome's apparent nurturing of the feminine to Gregory's drastic reduction. But the hermeneutic paradigm itself remains resolutely patriarchal."[90] In whatever ways the relationships between veil, text, and truth are configured, the gendered hierarchy of reader and text remains consistent. In one model, the feminine is associated with the textual truth whose meaning must be revealed by the exegete. In the other model, the feminine is associated with the superficial decorative layer of the text that the exegete must remove in order to find the text's spiritual importance. In both cases, the exegete who uncovers this spiritual meaning is gendered masculine, and the text he reads is gendered feminine.

One of the most striking examples that Dinshaw analyzes is Jerome's creation of a Christian model for reading pagan texts through the figure of the captured foreign bride of Deuteronomy 21:10–13. The Deuteronomy passage deals with the situation of a Hebrew warrior who wishes to take to wife a non-Israelite woman captured in war. This bride, beautiful and seductive, is to be taken into the home and purified through the shaving of her head, the paring of her nails, and the removal of all of her old garments.[91] After a month of mourning for her family, she is then considered a suitable wife. Jerome, famously tempted by pagan literature, compares these seductive texts to Deuteronomy's alluring prize of war: "Is it surprising that I, too, admiring the grace of her eloquence and the fairness of her form, desire to make that secular wisdom, which is my captive and handmaid, a matron of the true Israel? Or that cutting away and shaving off all in her that is dead whether this be idolatry, pleasure, error, or lust, I take her to myself clean and pure and beget by her servants for the Lord of Sabaoth?"[92] As Dinshaw observes in her analysis of this passage, the distracting ornaments of the pagan text must be stripped away in order to make it useful to the Christian reader.[93] However, in referring to those things that the bride must strip away as "dead," Jerome is not drawing on the language of the Deuteronomy passage itself but rather as Dinshaw shows, pointing to a "Pauline deadness."[94] The Deuteronomy passage does refer to giving the woman a period of mourning for her family, but there is no linguistic cue in the Hebrew Bible or the Septuagint or Vulgate translations that evokes a sense of death connected to the woman and her body itself. Jerome alludes instead to that central Pauline formulation of Christian reading, the "letter kills and the spirit gives life," and to the "dispensation of death" of 2 Corinthians 3.[95] In this way, Jerome evokes the very process of interpreting the Old Testament according to the spirit, which is, of course, what he is attempting to do in his use of the Deuteronomy passage to discuss the judicious use of texts. In utilizing this passage, Jerome not only reads it according to the spirit but also appropriates the role of the conquering Hebrew soldier. The Christian reader therefore comes not only to assume the role of the conquering male warrior who transforms his captive bride but also to assume the name of the warrior's people. Christians, through their reading practices, become the true Israel according to the spirit.

The supersession of the Hebrew text is even clearer in an earlier source of Jerome's analogy. Jerome's passage derives from Origen, who is not only writing about the uses and dangers of interpretation but doing so in the context of his *Homilies on Leviticus*.[96] As Charlotte Fonrobert posits, seen from a Christian perspective, Leviticus may well be "the most Jewish" portion of the Hebrew Bible.[97] In Homily 7, Origen interprets Leviticus 11:3–7, which deals with animals that are impure because they are partially clean (they chew their cud) and partially unclean (they have cloven hooves). In Origen's interpretation, these two attributes of animals become like ways of reading. Those who "chew the cud" have the word of God in their mouths, reading "the letter according to the spiritual sense." Those who "part the hoof" are preparing their "deeds for the coming age." Origen translates the distinctions used for categorizing animals in Leviticus into categorization of heretics. These heretics, who learn from (presumably pagan) philosophers, do not "chew the cud," that is, they do not read the Bible according to the spirit, and they are therefore unclean. Failing to "chew the cud" is death, the spiritual death of 2 Corinthians 3.

To explain this situation further, Origen turns to the example of Deuteronomy's foreign captive:

But nevertheless, I also frequently "have gone out to war against my enemies and I saw there" in the plunder "a woman with a beautiful figure." For whatever we find said well and reasonably among our enemies, or we read anything said among them wisely and knowingly, we must cleanse it also from the knowledge which is among them, remove and cut off all that is dead and worthless—namely all the hairs of the head and the nails of the woman taken from the spoils of the enemy—and so, at last make her your wife when she has nothing of the things that are called dead through infidelity; when she has nothing dead on her head or in her hand that might introduce something unclean or dead into her thoughts or deeds; then finally we must make her our wife. For the women of our enemies possess nothing pure, because there is no wisdom in them that does not have some admixture of uncleanness.[98]

Here is the imaginative precedent for Jerome's appropriation of the role of the conquering Hebrew warrior. Origen analogizes the process of making the captive a suitable bride with the way a Christian exegete should approach a text. By invoking infidelity, Origen links the dead and worthless elements of the text with transgressive sexuality. By stripping the bride and stripping the text, there is no chance that either will pose a threat to purity.

Origen is here focused on interpretation of the Hebrew Bible. He explicitly expresses a wish to ask the Jews for further clarification on their laws, simultaneously referring to the Deuteronomy passage and the book of Leviticus that is the subject of his Homily: "Yet, I wish that the Jews would tell me how these things are preserved among them. What is the cause? Why is the woman "to be shaved bald" and "her nails removed"? Let us suppose, for example, that the one who is said to have found her should find that she has neither hair nor nails. What did she have that he ought to remove according to the Law?"[99] Origen distinguishes between an actual warrior and a spiritual one. The "we" are not soldiers, but exegetes, and the captive is explicitly a text. Christian reading then, becomes a form of spiritual conquest, a battle for spiritual Life:

> But we, whose combat is spiritual and whose "arms are not carnal but power from God to destroy arguments," if "a beautiful" woman had been found among our enemies and some reasonable doctrine, we will purify her in the way that we said above. Therefore, it is necessary for him who is pure not only "to part the hoof" and to distinguish between the deeds and works of the present age and of the future age, but also "to produce hoofs" or, as we have read elsewhere, "to cast them out" so that, "purifying ourselves from dead works," we may remain in life.[100]

By purifying himself from "dead works," the Christian exegete ensures that the spirit triumphs over the letter. Origen, focusing on the Pauline trope of the letter and the spirit throughout his Homily, imports the idea of the woman's hair and nails as both impure and "dead" in the sense of 2 Corinthians 3:7, linking the instructions of the Deuteronomy text to Christian reading practice. Finally, the analogy of the purification of the foreign bride is melded to the explication of the parted hoof, as the Christian reader becomes not just one who discerns the mark of the hoof, but one who creates a hoof himself, generating a text in the spirit that will be of use in preparing the Christian for the future age "in life."

In both Origen's and Jerome's uses of the figure of the beautiful foreign captive, the Christian reader is figured as masculine, dominating and domesticating a feminine text. As Dinshaw's reading powerfully shows, the gender of the implied Christian reader seems clear: to read according to the spirit is to read like a man. A woman may also read like a man, but when she does so she leaves her feminine nature behind, "progressing to manhood."[101] Rita Copeland, building on Dinshaw's analysis, succinctly encapsulates the gendering of Christian hermeneutic practice:

Good reading is tantamount to good faith, and to read as a woman is to read with a gross carnality, resistant to the spiritual sense. Individual women can of course learn how to read spiritually and become believers, as Ambrose indicates; but in so doing they leave their carnal feminine natures behind, assuming a chaste, "masculine" spirituality. Thus on the terms of this metaphysical law, women are hermeneutically handicapped; or we might say that reading is gendered, such that good, productive, spiritual reading that leads to faith is identified with a masculine essence, and perverse reading, which is literal and self-interested, is associated with a feminine principle of carnality.[102]

This description of women as "hermeneutically handicapped," unable to read spiritually, parallels the view of the Jew as interpreter prevalent in Christian exegesis. Woman and Jew read with spiritual impediments. This impeded ability to read is tied to the profound embodiment with which Woman and Jew are associated. They are weighed down, prevented from universal understanding through their limited particularities. Their spiritual state is analogous to a crippled flesh in a way that recalls Archisynagogus, whose spiritual perversion manifests itself unto his physical being. This leads to the most prevalent charge leveled by Christian writers against the Jews: that they are blind.[103]

Blinded by the Veil of the Letter

In his *Adversus Iudaeorum inveteratam duritiem*, Peter the Venerable exhorts the Jews to overcome their "hermeneutical handicaps": "Open your eyes at last, open your ears, and be ashamed that you are clearly the only blind people in the world, the only deaf people to remain."[104] As with Augustine, who likens the Jew to the blind man looking in a mirror, for Peter to read like a Jew is, in essence, not to read at all. The Jew is spiritually blind and deaf, unable to understand and interpret, an accusation with roots in the New Testament.[105] In John 9, Jesus cures a man born blind, but the Pharisees are spiritually blind to his identity. Similarly, in John 12, the blindness and deafness of Isaiah 6:9–10 is read as Jewish blindness to Christ.[106] Jewish blindness is figured through the influential image of the veil in 2 Corinthians 3:15–18: "Yet to this day whenever Moses is read a veil lies over their minds; but when a man turns to the Lord the veil is removed. Now the Lord is the Spirit, and where the Spirit of the Lord is, there is freedom. And we all, with unveiled face, beholding the glory of the Lord, are being changed into his likeness from one degree of glory to another; for this comes from the Lord who is the Spirit."[107] A veil covers the eyes of the Jews, hardening their hearts and leaving them blind to the true word of God, an accusation that echoes through countless permutations in patristic and medieval Christian texts.[108] The veil also appears in figurations of the relationship between the Old dispensation and the New. The time of the Old dispensation is figured as veiled, and the coming of the New is represented by a lifting of that veil, which acts as a kind of curtain between an epoch of blindness and one of understanding.[109]

Accusations of blindness are often directed at the Jewish people as a group, and we will see this accusation shaping representations of Jews in each of the texts examined in subsequent chapters. A popular mode of representing Jewish blindness is through the allegorical figure of Synagoga, which in numerous visual and written examples is presented in contrast to her superseding opposite, Ecclesia. The Synagoga figure appears to have origins in Lamentations, in which Jerusalem, daughter of Zion, is portrayed as a fallen queen.[110] We find non-Jewish examples of an allegorized female figure to represent Judea or Jerusalem dating back to the Roman period, and the figure of Synagoga was common among early Christian writers.[111] Although gender is clearly important in this representation, a precursor to the figure of the "beautiful Jewess" that we will examine in Chapter 5, this is not a "feminization" of the Jew of the type prevalent in nineteenth- and twentieth-century stereotypes of the emasculated male Jew.[112]

Rather, what we find is an overlay of certain opposing values onto two female allegorical figures. Their bifurcation is clear in the numerous graphic representations of Ecclesia and Synagoga, such as the famous statues from Strasbourg Cathedral.[113] There both figures are represented as noble and graceful women, but in contrast to the crowned Ecclesia, the Strasbourg Synagoga has lost her crown and stands supported by a broken lance, her eyes blindfolded and face downcast to represent her fall. These physical signs of falseness are crucial in both the textual and graphic representations of Synagoga as she comes to be pictured as blind, defeated, and sometimes sinful, through complex associations with fallen and adulterous women and even with prostitutes.[114] Through these connections with fallen women, negative and carnal traits are thereby symbolically attributed to the Jewish people, who are seen as feminine not in the sense of effeminacy, but in the sense that they become marked by the carnality that we have seen associated with the feminine and figured as antithetical to a state of Christian spiritual salvation.[115] In contrast, Ecclesia, though also feminine, is associated with the triumphant, virtuous Spirit.

Such an association with carnality and sexuality is clear as Jerome compares Synagoga to the harlot brides of Hosea: "A prostitute is one who copulates with many; an adulteress is one who deserts one man to join with another. Synagogue is both these things. If she should continue in a state of fornication and adultery, God will take away from her the clothing and ornaments that he gave to her."[116] In *Moralia in Job*, Gregory the Great figures the Synagogue as the mother of the Redeemer, who brings forth God but nevertheless refuses to acknowledge his divinity:

The Redeemer's mother after the flesh was the Synagogue, from whom he came forth to us, made manifest by a body. But she kept him to herself, veiled under cover of the letter, when she neglected to open the eyes of understanding to his spiritual significance. Because he veiled himself with the flesh of a human body, she [the Synagogue] refused to see God, as if she scorned to behold him naked in his divinity. But he "came naked out of his mother's womb," for when he came forth from the flesh of the Synagogue, he came openly manifest to the gentiles.[117]

Because God was veiled in human flesh, Synagoga refused to see him but was instead blinded by this covering. Yet, although Christ was covered and hidden from the Jews, he was fully exposed and naked to the Gentiles, who perceived his divinity despite his human form. Christ's human form is like a garment, and it is through this garment that Gregory links the Synagogue to the would-be adulteress, Potiphar's wife.

Christ is figured as Joseph, who left his cloak behind as he fled the advances of his master's wife: "For when the adulterous woman would have used him to no good end, he fled from the house, leaving his cloak behind him; because when the Synagogue would have bound him as it were in an adulterous embrace, thinking the Lord to be simply man, he left the covering of the letter to her eyes, and, to make known the might of his divinity, he showed himself undisguised to the gentiles."[118] Because the Synagogue resembles Potiphar's wife, the actions of the Jews become like the sin of adultery, but their sin stems from an inability to perceive Christ's divinity. Like Potiphar's wife, the Jews are left holding a covering; it is the Gentiles who perceive God unveiled in his Divinity. Gregory then links this Jewish blindness to 2 Corinthians:

So too Paul says: "Even to this day when Moses is read, a veil is over their hearts." That is to say, because the adulteress kept her cloak in her hands, but him whom she had wickedly taken hold of, she let go naked. He then who coming from the Synagogue plainly revealed himself to the faith of the gentiles, "came naked from his mother's womb." But does he completely forsake her? What about that which the prophet declares: "For though your people Israel be as the sand of the sea, yet a remnant shall be saved." Where is that which is written: "Until the fulness of the gentiles come in, and so all Israel shall be saved"? This, therefore, will be when he appears clearly to the Synagogue as well. This will doubtless be at the world's end, when he will make himself known, even as he is God, to the remnant of his people.[119]

Here the Synagogue takes on a role parallel to the Virgin Mary's in the Incarnation. The Synagogue is the mother of Christ, the source from which he springs. But just as Mary wrapped Christ in human flesh, the Synagogue wraps him in the veil of the letter.[120] Just as they are blind to the true meaning of the word of Moses, the Jewish people remain blind to Christ's divinity, veiled in flesh. The veil is linked to carnality, adultery, and deceit through the figure of Potiphar's wife. Christ appears like Joseph, leaving the veil behind him, which is picked up and used in the hands of the Synagogue, who becomes the adulterous wife, rightly refused. The Synagogue is not wholly spurned, however, because at the end of the world, Israel will also be saved. The veil of the letter will finally be rent and Jewish blindness overcome.

A similar vision of a Synagogue who is blind until the removal of the veil of the letter is found in Sermon 14 of Bernard of Clairvaux's *Sermones super Cantica Canticorum*, which contrasts the blind and fallen Synagogue with a woman famously fallen and redeemed, the reformed harlot, Mary Magdalene:

"God is renowned in Judah, his name is great in Israel." The pagan people who walked in darkness have seen a great light, a light that shone in Judah and Israel, and filled them with longing to draw near and be enlightened. Those who once were not a people at all would now be formed into a people, and the two, converging like walls, would be joined as one by the one corner-stone. This union's fruit is peace.

For confidence was imparted in the very utterance of the invitation already proclaimed: "Rejoice, pagans, with his people." Hence their desire to draw near; but the synagogue stood in their way, insisting that a church gathered from among the pagans would be both unclean and unworthy, taunting them as idolaters of the lowest type, blinded by the darkness of ignorance. "By what right do you come here?" the Jews challenged. "Do not touch me." "Why?" asked the pagans. "Is God the God of the Jews alone and not of the pagans too?"[121]

Bernard envisions a Church attempting to unite people in the purest sense of the universal salvation of Galatians 3:28. The Jews, attempting to thwart such a union, ironically utter Jesus's words to Mary Magdalene: "Noli me tangere." Here it is the pagans who are represented by the figure of a fallen woman, but she is, of course, a fallen woman redeemed. Ironic reversal echoes throughout the passage as the Jews accuse the Church of groping blindly in the "darkness of ignorance," a state Bernard associates with the Jews themselves throughout the rest of the sermon. Binaries abound: blindness *versus* insight, Synagogue *versus* Church, light *versus* darkness. Each figures the conflict between Jews and Christians through opposition. Sermon 14 continues this strategy of definition through opposition with a long series of accusations against the Jews and their resistance to Christianity: the Jews are blind, quarrelsome, and ungrateful. Rather than recognize the new reign of grace given to them by Christ, they remain tied to the Law.

Continuing in a passage echoing 2 Corinthians 3:14–18, Bernard links the Jews' failings to their way of reading, finally describing the spiritual triumph of Christianity itself as a type of interpretation: "When the veil of the written letter that brings death is torn in two at the death of the crucified Word, the Church, led by the Spirit of liberty, daringly penetrates to his inmost depths, acknowledges and takes delight in him, occupies the place of her rival to become his bride, to enjoy the embraces of his newly-emptied arms."[122] The Jews' reading of Scripture is superficial; Christian readings penetrate Scripture to its core. The passage's use of the present tense allows Bernard to recall the Crucifixion but also implies that any reading according to the spirit, any tearing of the "veil of the written letter" evokes simultaneously Christ's sacrifice on the cross, the spiritual marriage represented by the figure of the bridegroom and the bride of the Song of Songs, and the final union promised when Christ returns. If the Crucifixion is seen as a critical transition point between Judaism and Christianity, then every act of reading through the Spirit, as opposed to reading only the Letter, reenacts this transition, that moment when the Synagogue loses her crown, the full realization of the supersession of Judaism by Christianity.

The Word Made Flesh

The figure of the Synagogue comes to embody the dynamic of Christian supersession. She personifies the subjugation of the Jewish people, her blindfold symbolizing a stinted, inferior mode of seeing and interpreting both signifier and signified. The Synagogue is an important element in medieval representations of Jews and Judaism, but it is the figure of Mary that affords us fuller insight into how the figures of woman and Jew come together within Christian hermeneutical paradigms. Mary, after all, is the Jewish woman whose body is the site of the critical turn in the Christian narrative of supersession, the Incarnation, when the Word is made Flesh. Origen opens his *Homilies on Leviticus* with a focus on the Incarnation. Distinguishing between seeing and understanding, he posits that to see is to perceive only the surface, to understand is to penetrate the obscuring veil of either the flesh or the letter and to comprehend the divine hidden beneath. Just as Mary clothed Christ in flesh, so too when the Word of God was given to the Israelites through Moses and the Prophets it was also clothed—clothed in the veil of the letter.[123] Origen argues that it is with these analogies of the veil in mind that the Christian reader must approach Leviticus:

Such, then, is what we now find as we go through the book of Leviticus, in which the sacrificial rites, the diversity of offerings, and even the ministries of the priests are described. But maybe the worthy and the unworthy see and hear these things according to the letter, which is, as it were, the flesh of the Word of God and the clothing of its divinity. But "blessed are those eyes" which inwardly see the divine spirit that is concealed in the veil of the letter; and blessed are they who bring clean ears of the inner person to hear those things. Yet, they will perceive openly "the letter which kills" in these words.[124]

Origen reads Leviticus, a book of detailed Jewish ritual and law, not as he believes that the Jews do, according to the killing letter, but like a Christian, according to the spirit. The veil of the letter is analogous to the veil of the flesh; the letter is, in a sense, "the flesh of the Word of God and the clothing of its divinity." The Word "takes form in the Prophets and Lawgiver," with these Jewish figures thereby becoming a kind of fleshly, human instrument to carry divine truth, a role not unlike that Augustine saw for post-Crucifixion Jews as textual custodians or even the Bernardine vision of the Jew as the letter incarnate.[125]

Of course, none of the hermeneutical analogies we have examined makes sense without the aid of another Jewish body, that of Mary, who clothes in flesh the Word itself, giving the exegetical relationships we have been examining a corporeal reality. As Tertullian insists, it is not only allegory or metaphor that are at stake in Christian interpretation. Christians are dealing with a truth that also exists in the realm of the corporeal: "Now all things are not pictures, but are also truths, nor are all things shadows, but are bodies as well, such that all the more remarkable facts concerning the Lord himself were preached more clearly than light. For the Virgin did not conceive in the womb figuratively, nor did she bear Emmanuel, 'God with us,' indirectly."[126] Tertullian lists the Incarnation as the first in a long series of events that culminates in the violence of the Crucifixion. He also forges a clear link between Christian reading practice and the reality of the corporeal, specifically those sacred bodies involved in the Incarnation and those who foretold it, the bodies and voices of the prophets. Biblical events are not figurative but have in Tertullian's argument a concrete, historical reality of which the Incarnation is a part.

Of the elements we have examined so far—polarized representations of women, the division in representations of pre- and post-Crucifixion Jews, the dichotomy between letter and spirit, and the Incarnation—each play a role in medieval representations of Mary, a figure at the center of multiple paradoxes. At the moment of the Incarnation, the Word is made Flesh, and Christian understanding is seen as freed from the tyranny of the letter, marking the dawn of a new era of Christian spiritual understanding. The Incarnation itself, therefore, stands as a central premise of Christian understanding of the relation between letter and spirit.[127] The nature of this virginal body and the question of its purity, issues with such profound importance to the Christian faith, were, not surprisingly, the objects of controversy. The dogma of the Virgin Birth was accepted as early as the fourth century, but the question of the Immaculate Conception, for example, was vigorously contested until 1854, when Pope Pius IX proclaimed the Virgin Mary "free from all stain of original sin."[128] As Charles Wood has shown, medieval theologians also debated whether or not the Virgin Mary menstruated, a question that is not only concerned with Mary's singularity among women but also with the boundaries of her body and its excretions.[129] And the debates surrounding Mary were not limited to Christian interpreters. The Virgin and her body, sometimes represented and discussed as a type of bordered space, were the subject of intense Jewish-Christian polemic and debate.

Medieval Jewish polemics against Christianity and Christian doctrines such as the Incarnation and transubstantiation were complex and various, often relying on sophisticated philosophical method to make their case. Important among the arguments of Jewish polemicists was the crucial premise that God was incorporeal and could therefore not be "encom-

passed by a woman's womb or by Jesus' body," a principle that Joseph
ben Shem Tov, for example, used Aristotelian principles to support.[130]
Alongside these philosophical objections to the Incarnation we find what
Daniel Lasker characterizes as "the standard Ashkenazic vulgar reference
to the place of incarnation," focused on the impurity of the womb and
impossibility of God's confinement within it.[131] The charge of the impurity
of Mary's womb seems related to the *Toledot Yeshu* tradition, which recounts the story of Jesus's conception not only as one of adultery between
an unwitting Mary and a soldier, but as the product of a sexual union that
occurred during Mary's menstruation, a time of ritual impurity.[132] About
the idea that God would descend into Mary's womb, Joseph Kimḥi writes
in the twelfth century, "[H]ow shall I believe that this great inaccessible
Deus absconditus needlessly entered the womb of a woman, the filthy, foul
bowels of a female, compelling the living God to be born of a woman, a
child without knowledge or understanding, senseless, unable to distinguish between his right hand and his left, defecating and urinating, sucking his mother's breasts from hunger and thirst, crying when he is thirsty
so that his mother will have compassion on him."[133] Kimḥi lingers with
disgust on the detailed implications of God's humanity, encompassed
within two human bodies, that of Mary and of Jesus, and subject to all
the limitations, functions, and impurities of both. Another Jewish author,
probably Menachem ben Jacob Shalem, contends of Christian believers:
"They posit that God Himself, may He be blessed and exalted, changed
Himself, made His spirit corporeal, and lowered His holiness into the
most filthy and polluted impurity in the menstrual blood of an impure
woman. May His name and mention be blessed and exalted greatly beyond the imagination of these idolatrous and impure fools!"[134] According
to Robert Chazan, Jewish objections to the doctrine of Incarnation such
as this one not only exist on a philosophical level but "involved profound
emotional revulsion at the notion of a deity born incarnate to a woman,
living the life of flesh and blood, and eventually perishing in what Jews
saw as humiliation upon the cross."[135] The Jewish polemics generate a
sense of claustrophobia and squeamishness that appears to stem not from
an inherent revulsion with the female womb but from a revulsion with the
idea of the divine descending into the flesh—a flesh moreover made impure through menstruation. The claustrophobia evoked seems in concert
with the rabbinic idea of the womb as a type of chambered room, a room
into which God, who exists beyond all human limitations, could not con-
ceivably be sandwiched.[136]

Christians responded to these Jewish attacks, and in the twelfth century a series of authors, including Anselm of Canterbury, Odo of Tournai, Guibert of Nogent, and Gilbert Crispin, addressed the question of the Incarnation and Mary's womb in writings that draw upon reasoned arguments and debate formats and that also focus notably on issues of embodiment, the very element that Chazan links to Jewish "revulsion" at the notion of Incarnation and upon which authors such as Tertullian also insist. To defend the Incarnation, Christian theologians must defend the intactness and impermeability of Mary's virginal womb. To do so, they often draw upon metaphors from nature such as that of light passing through glass in order to transcend a notion of a purely embodied God trapped in the prisonlike space of a human body.[137] This metaphor generates a sense of openness and a certain antiseptic quality that contrast sharply with the Jewish writings. The Christian apologists, however, also evoke in their responses the revulsion conveyed in Jewish attack, sometimes augmenting it in order to counter it.

Anselm's *Cur Deus Homo*, which arguably influenced both Odo of Tournai and Guibert of Nogent, examines the causes of the Incarnation in relation to the question of redemption. In the text's dialogue, Boso, who acts as the mouthpiece of the *infideles* or unbelievers, charges, "Unbelievers, ridiculing our simplicity, accuse us of offending and dishonoring God when we assert that He had descended into the womb of a woman, was born of a female body, that He grew up, nourished by milk and human foods, and—not to mention many other things which do not seem fitting for God—that he endured fatigue, hunger, thirst, scourging and crucifixion and death between thieves."[138] It is open to debate whether or not Anselm is directly addressing Jews (and perhaps also Muslims) in *Cur Deus Homo*, although it seems clear that Jewish objection to the doctrine of the Incarnation plays some role.[139] These objections defend the distinction between the divine and the human, arguing that this boundary cannot be crossed and that Anselm's redemptive "God-Man" cannot therefore exist.[140] What is most interesting here is the content of the debate itself. As Steven Kruger has shown, bodily imagery is central to Christian constructions of self and Other in these debates.[141] The debate highlights issues of embodiment, particularly the types of embodiment involved in maternity and birth, questions that, as Anna Abulafia has shown, become the objects of ever-increasing theological attention in the twelfth century.[142] Christ has taken on a human body through the body of a woman, and the nature of both bodies is very much at the center of debate, as well as piety.[143]

According to its author, Odo of Tournai, the *Disputatio contra Judaeum Leonem nomine de adventu Christi filii Dei* represents an actual encounter in Poitiers in 1100 between the author and a Jew of Senlis, Leo. After a dialogue about issues such as the messiah, sin, and redemption, Leo the Jew is presented as making his final point: "In one thing especially we laugh at you and think that you are crazy. You say that God was enclosed in maternal bowels, in the vile prison of a fetid womb, and suffered enclosure for nine months, when finally, in the tenth month, he emerged from her private parts (who is not embarrassed by such a scene!). Thus you attribute to God what is most unbecoming, which we would not do without great embarrassment."[144] Through explicit and vivid language, the Virgin's womb is depicted as vile, filled with foul fluid. This is embodiment at its extreme, a carnality portrayed in a way that seems designed to promote both disgust and outrage. This sort of rhetoric sharpens the debate and shows how Christian theological claims depend on an understanding of and an opposition to this vision of embodiment as inherently degrading.

Odo responds to Leo with an appeal to reason. Our sense, Odo explains, "despises our genitalia, viscera, and excrement, and judges them unclean. Reason, however, judges nothing unclean but sin, because God created all things good."[145] Therefore, Odo posits, it is only reliance on the senses that would lead one to the mistaken view of Mary's womb as a place of filth and disgust. On the contrary, he argues, using reason, one realizes that Mary is the site of glory: "[H]er sex was filled with glory, her womb was filled with glory, her organs were filled with glory, the whole of her was filled with glory, because the whole of her was filled with grace."[146] Odo shows the superiority of reason through a series of interesting examples. A peasant, he says, would prefer a rock to a snake, because "the sight of a serpent is horrible but the sight of a rock is not horrible."[147] A peasant prefers coins to beasts and shrubs to stars, because the peasant can only focus on what he perceives with his senses. He does not have access to reason, which would help him make superior, abstract choices. Here, implicitly, Odo links the Jew to the senses and also to the peasant who cannot use reason, even if the tone of the debate is relatively civil and calm.

In his considerably more heated *Tractatus de Incarnatione contra Judaeos,* Guibert of Nogent portrays the Jews as almost pathologically unable to see the truth of the Incarnation, their "murmurings" against Mary are part of their very nature.[148] Like Anselm and Odo, Guibert also has a Jew pose a question similar to that of Jewish writers such as Kimḥi, asking how God could have succumbed to the horror of descending into the womb.[149] He also focuses on the question of Christ's embodiment, painting a very graphic picture of the more sordid aspects of the human condition: "Ask, most stinking and worthless one, concerning our Lord, whether he spit, whether he wiped his nose, whether he drew out the phlegm of his eyes and ears with his fingers, and understand that since he performed these higher [actions] with such honesty, he also thus carried through the rest [of his bodily functions]. . . . I tremble violently while I dispute such things; but you, sons of the devil, drive me to it."[150] Here Guibert focuses obsessively on the orifices of Christ's body and the excretions that they, as with all other human bodies, produced, writing using, as Kruger has aptly phrased it, a "rhetoric of repugance."[151] As with Odo, Guibert defends this corporeality through recourse to the essential goodness of all human bodies, but he carries the questions implied by Jewish commentators to a logical and literal extreme. And, in addressing these graphic images of Christ at his most human toward "stinking and worthless" sons of the devil who make his own body shake, Guibert conjures images not only of the holy bodies in question but of the bodies of the Christians and Jews involved in the debate as well.[152] Indeed, in the tract, the mouths of the Jews become actual sites of pollution, in contrast to the defamed, but holy, bodies of the Virgin and Christ.[153] The body of Christ debated between Christians and Jews comes to stand, in Guibert's argument, for their own bodies, and more importantly, the margins of Christ's body come to represent the site of debate between believers and nonbelievers.

These debates over Mary and her body provide for us a conceptual link for the abstract relationships between the Jewish, the feminine, the carnal, and the literal within Christian hermeneutical paradigms and the more graphic and corporeal representations of these relationships that we find in the medieval and early modern literary texts to which we will now turn. The graphic polemics over Mary's body may seem far removed from the abstraction of hermeneutical supersession, but it is the Incarnation, that moment that the Word becomes flesh in Mary's womb, that marks the movement of supersession, that shift from Jewish to Christian. Mary's body, not unlike the body of Archisynagogus, acts as a symbol for the relationships between Jews and Christians within the framework of Chris-

tian theology. It is therefore no accident within that text that Archisynagogus appears at the very moment when the Incarnation is being portrayed.

In his account of Christianity's framing between the universal and the
particular, Laclau argues that Christianity has at its center the notion of
incarnation, "its distinctive feature being that between the universal and
the body incarnating it there is no rational connection whatsoever. God is
the only and absolute mediator."[154] His brief discussion, however, is never
specific about any instance of particularity in the Christian system. It seems
clear, however, that divine incarnation of the universal must take into account the bodies of Christ and Mary. In the debates over the boundaries
of Mary's body we find unease generated by the paradoxes inherent in
Mary's role. Within Christian thinking there is, of course, an inclusive universalism, but this universalism is incarnated in two Jewish bodies, and
these bodies, which are both marked by their Jewishness and, in the case
of Mary, by their gender, transcend these particularities, yet never completely, due to the marked nature of these very categories. Mary is exceptional among women, her sex still marked within a hierarchy of value. In
this way, then, when we consider Laclau's argument that the "subtle
logic" of Christian universalism bequeathed to modern universalisms the
idea of a "privileged agent of history," we must remember that the particular identities of Jew and woman each have relations to this universal that
will always be grounded in the Christian account of salvation history,
based on a specific supersessionist view of the relationship between Judaism and Christianity.

Finally, though, an analysis of these figures through these more abstract formulations of the universal and the particular cannot account for
the extreme disgust, "the rhetoric of repugnance" that we find in the
debates over the Virgin and that will appear, mixed with violence, in texts
such as *The Prioress's Tale* and *Merchant.* To begin to understand these
elements, we need an account of the human body as symbol, such as that
developed by Mary Douglas. The bodies of Archisynagogus and the Virgin
Mary symbolize elements of the relationship posited between Christianity
and Judaism in Christian theology. In *Purity and Danger*, Douglas argues
that the boundaries of the symbolic body can "represent any boundaries
which are threatened or precarious":

All margins are dangerous. If they are pulled this way or that the shape of fundamental experience is altered. Any structure of ideas is vulnerable at its margins. We
should expect the orifices of the body to symbolise its specially vulnerable points.

Matter issuing from them is marginal stuff of the most obvious kind. Spittle, blood, milk, urine, faeces or tears by simply issuing forth have traversed the boundary of the body. So also have bodily parings, skin, nail, hair clippings and sweat. The mistake is to treat bodily margins in isolation from all other margins.[155]

Here we have, as it were, an anthropologist's answer to Origen's wishful query to the Jews about Deuteronomy's beautiful captive. Following Douglas's analysis, the boundaries of these bodies and the products of these boundaries are symbolic of contact between two cultures. The bodies of Mary, Archisynagogus, and the beautiful captive each comes to represent contact between human structures of belief. In the case of Guibert's vivid conjuring of images of Christ's excretions, we can see him stressing precisely points of contention between Christians and Jews and questions that were also logical and important among Christians. The boundaries of the bodies of Christ and the Virgin, then, come to represent the boundaries of Christian ideology and Christian identity. As Theresa Coletti has convincingly argued, Mary is not simply "one term of a binary opposition of good women and bad; rather representations of the Virgin and, more specifically, representations of her body, become the sites in which cultural tensions are negotiated.[156] And, as Douglas's analysis would suggest, it is often the margins of Mary's body, specifically the boundaries of her womb, that are locations of anxiety and the subject of contested representation.

Also useful in understanding these extreme images of Christian and Jew is the concept of abjection, which was developed by Julia Kristeva by incorporating Douglas's model into a psychoanalytic framework in *Powers of Horror*.[157] Extending the concept of abjection beyond a model of an individual psyche, Butler discusses the abject in terms of an understanding of relations between groups of individuals and the different cultural categories of gender, racial, and sexual identities. Butler speaks of abjection and the uncanny in terms of a "zone of uninhabitability" that "will constitute that site of dreaded identification against which—and by virtue of which—the domain of the subject will circumscribe its own claim to autonomy and to life. In this sense, then, the subject is constituted through the force of exclusion and abjection, one which produces a constitutive outside to the subject, an abjected outside, which is, after all, 'inside' the subject as its own founding repudiation."[158] What is so abhorrent in the abject Other is its uncanny relation to the self, an originary relationship that illuminates the paradoxical roles of Jews and women in the texts we will explore. And, as Kristeva notes, it is at moments of ambiguity that the abject appears.[159] In the readings that follow, I will focus on contested moments, moments when it is difficult to discern "which is the Christian here and which the Jew," and when there is instability in gender hierarchy as power is contested between men and women. It is at these moments, often connected to important moments of religious transition, such as conversion, Incarnation, and transubstantiation, that the boundaries of Christian identity are explored through representations of bodies that are sometimes gems of gleaming wholeness and sometimes abject pieces of broken flesh.

Jews and women are simultaneously marginalized and central, and the ways in which they are represented are explorations of the "zone of uninhabitability"; representations of Christians are created within the text in relation to this zone. The vital, inextricable connection that the abjected other has to the "inside" of the subject is what makes the conception of abjection so useful in exploring the dynamics by which medieval and early modern authors constructed idealized Christian identities. The authors whose writings are examined in this book use representations of women and Jews to create models for the Christian through fluid strategies of association and opposition. An important element in the Butlerian model of abjection is that it, in keeping with theories of performativity, describes process, not stasis. This emphasis on process and negotiation is something that the concept of the "zone of uninhabitability" shares with the concept of the hegemonic relationship: both capture a sense of negotiation and making. Butler notes this connection on a broader scale: "The theory of performativity is not far from the theory of hegemony in this respect: both emphasize the way in which the social world is made—and new social possibilities emerge—at various levels of social action through a collabora-tive relation with power."[160]

In the chapters that follow, I will examine representations of women and Jews that are part of literary representations of Christian communities. The authors creating these representations write from within actual Chris-tian communities characterized by division, negotiation, and controversy, and these authors deploy the figures of the hermeneutical Woman and the hermeneutical Jew as part of this negotiation. As I have attempted to show by examining the ways in which Christian theology creates a normative masculine Christian universal that supersedes the particular identities of the Jew and the woman, these two particularities each have specific and highly charged relationships to Christian notions of universality and to the very way that Christian theology approaches not only questions of reading and interpreting texts, but questions of reading and interpreting the world itself and of managing the social order that governs that world. As we examine these figures in the *Canterbury Tales*, the Croxton *Play of the Sacrament* and N-Town plays, and *Merchant of Venice* we will see that they are not simply representations of the Other, but that, due to their specific positions within the Christian tradition, the woman and the Jew become imbricated into what are usually considered broader and more universal patterns of meaning.

3

Reprioritizing the *Prioress's Tale*

THROUGH RESEARCH RANGING FROM STUDIES of individual works and characters to examinations of questions of authorship and the nature of poetic meaning, recent feminist scholarship has shown the centrality of issues of gender to the Chaucerian corpus.[1] In contrast, studies of Jewish difference, although they have flourished of late, have tended to focus narrowly on a single piece of Chaucer's writing, the *Prioress's Tale*.[2] Some critics have examined the intersectionality of gender and Jewish difference within this tale, but these studies have tended to remain bounded by its ghetto, leaving relatively unexamined the importance of Jews and Judaism outside its gates. This chapter attempts to encourage a new way of seeing the Jew in Chaucer's writings, one that looks beyond demonizing representations such as those found in the *Prioress's Tale* to examine how representations of Jews and Judaism inform some important sequences in the *Canterbury Tales* as a whole. The "Jewish question" is clearly not a Chaucerian preoccupation of the same order as that of "the Woman question," but, I would argue, within the *Tales*, the hermeneutical Jew is implicated in the broader engagement of the *Tales* with questions of meaning, understanding, and authority, as well as with the issue of gender itself.

This is not to say that the questions of anti-Semitism that have so long preoccupied critics of the *Prioress's Tale* should now be ignored; L. O. Aranye Fradenburg's important 1989 essay definitively established the importance of these issues to Chaucer scholarship. Furthermore, one need only type "ritual murder" or "Simon of Trent" into any internet search engine to see the power that these anti-Semitic myths seem to hold for some even today. Nevertheless, representations of Jews and Judaism now also need to be addressed in contexts beyond moments of traumatic representation.[3] As we have seen, the hermeneutical Jew is firmly woven into the pattern of Christian hermeneutics.[4] The critical relationship that Christianity posits between the Old and New Testaments comes into play either implicitly or explicitly, for example, when the "analogy of analogies" of the letter and the spirit is evoked, as it is in relation to the questions of "sentence" that are of such great significance to the *Canterbury Tales* project and the Chaucerian corpus.[5] This chapter then will look for the figure of the hermeneutical Jew beyond the ghetto of the *Prioress's Tale*, focusing on Fragments VII and VIII of the *Tales*, where representations of Jews, women, and pagans intersect around issues of learning, faith, and understanding, which were very much at the center of intellectual and religious controversy in late fourteenth-century England.

I begin my reading by investigating how the Host's reference to Lollards in the *Man of Law's Endlink* opens a space for negotiation about Christian ideals and Christian community among the pilgrims, exploring the ways in which Jews and Judaism are evoked in contemporary debates about hermeneutics, translation, and textual authority. I then turn to the ways in which these issues inflect questions of gender in the figures of Chaucer's two nuns, the Prioress and the Second Nun. The Prioress's tale presents a model of piety that is unlearned and childlike; the Second Nun presents a much more learned and mature ideal Christian. Both nuns are engaging with the paradigm of the hermeneutical Woman, challenging the model of woman as deficient through figures that align piety with different models of Christian understanding. Through these figures the tales draw upon the opposition between the spirit and the letter, linked in the exegetical tradition, as we have seen, to notions of Jewish carnality and spiritual blindness. Through this focus on spiritual understanding, their tales present competing models of idealized Christian identity that engage not simply with issues of a feminine or feminized piety, but also with questions of meaning and interpretation that are inflected by the controversy generated by Wycliffite dissent.

The *Canterbury Tales*, as we find it in handsome volumes such as *The Riverside Chaucer*, is itself, of course, a type of construction. Because Chaucer did not complete this work, questions concerning its composition, particularly the order of the tales, have engaged generations of scholars. Tales from Fragment VII, which are at the center of consideration in this chapter, are also central to the *Tales*' "most volatile" textual ordering controversy, that concerning the Bradshaw shift, which proposes an alternative to the standard Ellesmere order that would solve the geographical inconsistencies arising from it. The Bradshaw shift places Fragment VII to follow the *Man of Law's Introduction, Prologue, Tale*, and *Endlink*.[6] I find the evidence supporting the idea of the Bradshaw shift unconvincing, but

I do think that one of the textual foci of the ordering controversy, the *Man of Law's Endlink*, helps to illuminate questions of Jewish particularity in relation to Christian identity within the *Tales*. Many scholars believe that the *Man of Law's Endlink*—present in only thirty-five extant *Canterbury Tales* manuscripts—was part of an early version of the *Tales*. They conjecture that the Man of Law was originally assigned the *Tale of Melibee* and that this tale was to be followed by the *Shipman's Tale* and the rest of Fragment VII, with the *Endlink* acting as a bridge. I find this early textual possibility highly plausible and think it is valuable to consider the reference to Lollardy in the *Man of Law's Endlink* in relation to Fragment VII and to the *Tales* as a whole.[7] This juxtaposition highlights issues of Christian identity and interpretation in late fourteenth-century England and may reveal to us the genesis of the exchange between the Shipman and the Prioress.

The question of Lollardy arises when the Man of Law has finished his tale. Harry Bailley then asks the Parson for his tale, but the Parson objects to the swearing in the Host's request. His objections imply a type of attention to the power of words themselves; such swearing, the Parson believes, inflicts a wound unto the very body of Christ. The Host responds by accusing the Parson of Lollardy ("I smelle a Lollere in the wynd" [II.1173]) but continues to request the tale. The Shipman protests vigorously against the possibility of hearing the Gospel glossed by the Parson (II.1180). He argues that all present believe in God and that the Parson will sprinkle "cokkel in our clene corn," implying perhaps that the Parson will provide renegade interpretations that threaten to contaminate Pauline grain with chaff and also invoking a common pun on Lollard, which played with the Latin for weed, *lollium*.[8] The Host and the Shipman seem misinformed about Lollards, who, for example, objected to pilgrimages.[9] The Parson ultimately ends the *Canterbury Tales* by telling a highly orthodox tale and advocating a most orthodox reading practice, further refuting the Lollardy charge. Patricia J. Eberle notes that "Lollard" was a common term of abuse for "religious zealots of whatever persuasion."[10] Despite the loose and inappropriate nature of the charge, however, the Shipman's punning reiteration of it keeps it in play among the pilgrims, making the issue of Lollardy frame whatever tales would follow.

My provisional wording, that the *Man of Law's Endlink* creates a frame for "whatever" tales "would follow," is a necessary one, considering that the *Endlink* seems a vestige of an early version of the *Canterbury Tales*. I will not here diverge into the many permutations of interpretive possibilities opened by the wide variety of sequences that could be generated by its inclusion, both with and without the Bradshaw shift.[11] What is important to my argument about representations of Jews in Fragment VII is that the *Endlink*, in raising the issue of the Lollard heresy, presents a crack in the edifice of Christian identity and opens a literary space in which Christian beliefs can be debated. Kantik Ghosh has recently made a powerful case for the ways in which Wycliffite ideas, including those about religious authority and reception of Scripture, as they moved from the university into the broader realm of vernacular discourse "radically problematised issues fundamental to the very definition of Christianity, and to the perceived validity of the social, political and intellectual discourses traditionally enjoying its sanction."[12] As John Ganim observed in *Chaucerian Theatricality*, Lollardy can be seen as "the most intellectually visible and perhaps relatively restrained version of a range of unorthodox attitudes and popular pietistic trends" and Chaucer's writings engage with this vital intellectual ferment.[13] Clearly, the *Canterbury Tales* is a Christian poem whose central frame is a pilgrimage, but just exactly what "Christian" means within the community of pilgrims is not static—it is, rather, continually debated and renegotiated, in large part through reference to other particular identities such as "Lollard," "Jewish," "pagan," and "woman."

Christianity can be seen as assuming the "empty space" of the universal in this textual representation, as it not only traces a pilgrimage to Canterbury but also implies that greater pilgrimage to the heavenly Jerusalem. But this state of things is neither static nor complete; it is continually under debate through the variety of pilgrims' voices. In Paul's preaching to the varied and conflicted nascent Christian communities addressed in his Epistles and in Augustine's refutations of heretical challenge, Jewish particularity is inextricably woven into the fabric of how Christian writers express Christian truths. Chaucer is not here preaching or creating polemic, but he too is engaged in a tradition of Christian writers. In representing Christianity, writers must negotiate its past relationships to gentile pagans and believing and disbelieving Jews, and indeed, this past is a fertile means for treating issues raised by dissent among Christians, such as that presented in Chaucer's time by the Wycliffite heresy. These particularities are imbricated in representations of Christianity in the *Canterbury Tales*, contributing to a vision of Christian universality that, even as it searches for a vision of truth, is never a stable or permanent state but a continual process of negotiation. This universal is a type of "absent fullness" that assumes its value from the community, the system as a whole, a system that experienced varying episodes of debate and upheaval.

Inherent in these debates are questions of universality, specifically in relation to universal salvation. Who is included in the community of the faithful? What are its limits? These questions, integral to Paul's vision in Romans, are continual sources of discussion and debate for Christians, and late medieval English Christians were no exception. This context has recently been illuminated by Nicholas Watson, who argues that questions of universal salvation were intimately linked to the issue of vernacularity in late medieval England and that use of the English vernacular could imply a "nonhierarchic" universality that could "challenge" the "mode of universality" associated with Latin. Latin also represented a universal language, but one associated with the hierarchical authority of "high culture" and the church.[14] He shows how a range of vernacular texts, including *Mandeville's Travels*, *Piers Plowman*, Julian of Norwich's *Showings*, and Walter Hilton's *Scale of Perfection* engaged with questions of salvation, including whether or not Jews and Saracens could be included among the saved. Watson remarks upon the "irony" that "a relative tolerance" toward the Jews found in some late medieval English texts might have been in part facilitated by the fact that they had been expelled from England in 1290. As Watson observes, "[I]nclusiveness itself can surreptitiously depend on acts of exclusion—as is especially true of what still sometimes seems to scholars of Christianity that most inclusive category of *Christianitas* itself."[15] These insights have resonance with Daniel Boyarin's analysis of Christianity's "particular universalism" and the "certain logic of exclusion by inclusion" that it entails.[16] There is, of course, no single Christian universalism. Watson stresses the heterogeneity of the "forms of vernacular universalism" that he investigates in late medieval English texts.[17] This heterogeneity reveals once again elements of negotiation, difference, and dissent so prominent in late medieval English thought. Yet this antagonistic limit, the expulsion of actual Jews coupled with the powerful afterlife of medieval English anti-Jewish representation, brings into focus the specific dynamics of the hegemonic relationship between Jewish particularity and Christian universalism, a dynamic always tempered by and through questions of hermeneutics. Jewish particularity is always part of Christian universalism but, at the same time, marks its limits. The Jew is both root and broken branch, and this specific paradox within the Christian tradition distinguishes Jewish particularity from other types, even as it intersects with them.

The specific intersection between Jewish and Lollard particularities is one that merits closer examination in relation to two distinct bodies of new research both on Lollardy and on conceptions of Jews in late medieval England. Why, for example, did Margery Kempe's contemporaries not only accuse her being a Lollard but also ask her "whedyr sche wer a Cristen woman er a Iewe"?[18] It seems reasonable to assume that since Kempe's actions and appearance confounded attempts to fit her into the categories traditionally available to fifteenth-century Englishwomen, people around her tried to categorize her as belonging outside the orthodox Christian community and as opposed to it. But the terms of abuse chosen for Kempe were not merely placeholders to designate a "zealot" of any persuasion; the labels of "Lollard" and "Jew" had particular interrelated ramifications in the religious and political climate of late medieval England.

Even a brief survey of the flood of new research on the impact of the Wycliffite movement in late medieval England reveals an intense engagement with the questions of interpretation and authority raised by this movement that is found well beyond texts that directly engage the controversy. At issue are some of the same hermeneutical formulations present in Christian conceptions of the relationship between Judaism and Christianity. Lollardy is very much concerned with not only how sacred texts are interpreted but who has the right to access these texts in the first place.[19] A central tenet of Wycliffite belief is that everyone should have access to the word of God. This goal required translation of the Bible into English in order to make it universally accessible. In a tract on the Function of the Secular Ruler, the author argues, "Sythen witte stondis not in langage but in groundynge of treuthe, for þo same witte is in Laten þat is in Grew or Ebrew, and trouthe schuld be openly knowen to alle manere of folke, trowthe moueþ mony men to speke sentencis in Yngelysche þat þai han gedirid in Latyne, and herfore bene men holden heretikis. For wele I wote þat trouthe is an vnspecte, and no man schulde schame of trouthe as no man schulde schame of God."[20] The Lollard author posits a truth that is outside language and that therefore has the same meaning in any language, be it Latin, Greek, or Hebrew. This same meaning should be "open" to everyone, regardless of what language medium they can grasp, and Scripture should therefore be allowed to be translated into English and made available to a wider audience. And, indeed, the author calls upon scriptural precedence for this. Christ, he argues, citing John 18:20–21, taught "openly." This concept of "openness" is a particular one in Lollard thought. In the terms of the *General Prologue* to the Wycliffite Bible, what makes scripture "open" to lay readers is the way that the translated Bible provides the literal sense straightforwardly in English.[21] Furthermore, Paul "wrote in mony langagys, as to Romaynys he wrot in Latyne, ande to Ebrewys in Ebrew, for þo sentence schulde be more knowen and lyȝter to þo peple."[22] Drawing upon this not uncommon medieval misconception about Pauline preaching, the author attempts to provide further precedence for vernacularity. We also find the *General Prologue* to the Wycliffite Bible advocating translation from Latin into English to facilitate understanding of Scriptural "sentence," citing other instances of translation into various vernaculars, such as French, to justify this English translation.[23]

These perspectives on translation take on the question of language as medium and the problem of conveying important truths despite linguistic variation. The writings of John Wyclif himself provide insight into the philosophical underpinnings of such translation theories. Aware of the "destabilizing" effects of "human eloquence" and of the presence of figurative language in Scripture, Wyclif saw "the language of Scripture to be a singular system, governed by its own particular linguistic logic, which he calls the *vis* (or *virtus*) *sermonis*."[24] Wyclif places Scriptural language in its own realm, outside that of human language:

Quod ista est vera de virtute sermonis secundum quamlibet eius partem et quod professores scripture sacre debent sequi eam in modo loquendi quoad eloquenciam et logicam plus quam aliquam alienam scripturam gentilium.

On account of the *virtus sermonis* Scripture is true in each and all of its parts, and the exponents of sacred Scripture ought to follow its particular mode of speaking, insofar as eloquence and logic are concerned, more than any pagan writing.[25]

Wyclif's notion of Scriptural text blurs the traditional split between the literal and the spiritual in Scripture, where the literal can be figurative and the figurative literal.[26] The normal rules of textual explication simply do not apply to the word of God, allowing greater freedom to the translator and the exegete. These interpreters must attempt to focus not on *how* Scripture speaks, but on its "sentence," and upon capturing and conveying this "sentence" for as large an audience as possible. Wyclif's theology, from which Lollardy drew its basic tenets, attempts to grapple with the orthodox Church and its hierarchical and exclusionary approach to learning through a blurring of the distinction between literal and spiritual in the *virtus sermonis*, presenting English and Latin as equal vernaculars because they are both mediums of translation of the Bible's original Hebrew and Greek. A focus on Latin's status as a medium of translation, rather than as a holy language, gives English a status that equally authorizes it as the language of Holy Writ, an assertion directly combated by Arundel's Constitution of 1407, which figured meaning as tied to the language through which this meaning is conveyed.[27]

As Mary Dove has argued, Wycliffite focus on the intent of the Bible's original, true meaning makes the "Old Testament" Jews and their access to and understanding of Scripture important to the Lollards. Dove points to the central importance of Jewish Scripture to the Wycliffite project, arguing that Wycliffite translators "paid more exact attention to the text and meaning of Jewish Scripture than did any other scholars in England in Chaucer's lifetime, for their project involved editorial, hermeneutic, and linguistic biblical scholarship."[28] An important part of what this translation project put at issue is the status of the literal sense. As Rita Copeland has shown, the literal had multiple and shifting status within intersecting and competing discourses of theology, education, and politics in late medieval England.[29] Tracing the roots of some of these issues back into classical pedagogy, Copeland unravels different traditions of the literal sense. An important strand of thought about the literal sense is the reevaluation of the literal as a privileged point of access to scriptural truth in learned circles (and for learned readers) in the thirteenth and fourteenth centuries, as exemplified by the thought of Aquinas, Lyre, and Fitzralph and drawn upon by Wyclif, part of the tradition engaging Jewish scripture to which Dove points.[30] Distinct from this tradition is a pedagogical one in which the literal sense is associated with childhood and a stage in learning that is preparatory and inferior to adult apprehension. Just as Ghosh has shown the radical potential of Wycliffite ideas as they moved from academic circles into broader vernacular discourses beyond these settings, Copeland demonstrates how the politics of the literal sense takes on complex new political meaning and urgency as the Wycliffite movement advocates providing all believers with access to scripture in the vernacular as a means for comprehending divine meaning and intention. Although the different understandings of the literal sense that Copeland elucidates cannot be conflated with the slaying letter of 2 Corinthians, the differing traditions of the literal sense also point to the essential question inherent in the Pauline formulation. What is divine truth, how can it be legitimately and accurately comprehended, and, most importantly, who has the ability and the right to determine this truth? What particular types of individuals or groups merit this access and should have the power to regulate it?

These questions are clearly not only theological but political in na-

ture. The political question of particular identity and access has been approached by scholars from a variety of avenues. Notably, Ruth Nissé has
explored the question of how "Englishness" figures in Lollard writings,
for example, in the *General Prologue* to the Wycliffite Bible:

Also Crist seith of the Jewis that crieden Osanna to him in the temple, that thouȝ
thei weren stille stoonis schulen crie, and bi stoonis he vndirstondith hethen men,
that worshipiden stoonis for her goddis. And we Englische men ben comen of
hethen men, therfore we ben vndirstonden bi thes stonis, that schulden crie hooly
writ, and as Jewis, interpretid knowlechinge, singnefien clerkis, that schulden
knouleche to God, bi repentaunce of synnes, and bi vois of Goddis heriyng, so
oure lewide men, suynge the corner ston Crist, mowen be singnefied bi stonis,
that ben harde and abydinge in the foundement; for thouȝ couetouse clerkis ben
woode by simonie, eresie, and manye othere synnes, and dispisen and stoppen holi
writ, as myche as thei moun, ȝit the lewid puple crieth aftir holi writ, to kunne it,
and kepe it, with greet cost and peril of here lif.[31]

In her reading of this complicated passage, Nissé shows how the Lollard
author carves out a specifically English inheritance of biblical tradition.
Drawing on the pagan past of the English, the author builds their former
worship of idols into a signification of their future Christianity, a Christianity that stands in contrast to interpreted knowledge and to the belief
of the Jewish priests, who opposed Christ.[32] This emphasis on the priests
is in keeping with the split in representations of the hermeneutical Jew
between those "innocent," often idealized Jews who lived before Christ's
coming and those stubborn, disbelieving Jews who refused to accept
Christ as the Son of God. These vilified Jewish clerks are not the same as
the Israelites of Moses' time but are instead the proud and obstinate Jews
of anti-Jewish polemic. The Lollard author argues that the English, who
wish to understand and worship in their vernacular and risk death to do
so, are the true inheritors of the biblical tradition, in contrast to the corrupt clerics of the orthodox church.[33]

   We find similar identifications between Jews and corrupt clerics in a
Wycliffite sermon that reads the two sons of Matthew 21:28–32 as "two
folc, þe Iewis and heþene men."[34] The heathens are the first son, who
refuses to serve God, who is represented by the father who asks his sons
to serve in the vineyard. The second son, representing the Jews, does serve
for a time through "many patriarkis," but by the time of Christ, this son,
the Jews, had fallen away from faith, whereas heathen men had become
the followers of Christ. The sermon then continues through a further analogy to the present day situation of the church:

And þus may men parte þe chirche in seculer men and in clerkis. Seculer men ben þe firste sone, and clerkis ben þe toþer sone. Clerkis and prestis lyueden first wel, and specialy in Cristis tyme, for Crist and his apostelis also were boþe prestis and clerkis; and þei traueliden most in þe chirche, and maden it large and florischinge, siþ þat Crist bouȝte his chirche and tok it into heuene wiþ hym. But nou ben þes two sones turnyd, for feiþ and good religioun stonden in seculer men, and in prestis/ben wordis wiþoute good dede. Prestis seyen þei suen Crist, and kepen nexst þe lif of hym, siþ in hem stondiþ holy chirche, as mannus lif stondiþ in his soule. And men þat knowen þe worldis stat seyen þat popis and cardinalis, bischops and religious ben most fer fro Cristis lif. And so þis parable of Crist dampneþ hem for her falsed. But take we all þis witt of Crist, for we þat biheten to serue Crist and gon abac as false sones maken ussilf þe secound sone.[35]

This analogy creates what we might call double supersession. Just as the Jews and Judaism have been superseded, so now do secular men supersede the corrupt church hierarchy. As with other formulations of supersession, a complex shift in temporality operates here. The heathen, now secular men, who were indeed truly prior to the Jews all along, take over the place of true believers, with the corrupt clerks and institutions of the church becoming not only like the second son, but also like the Jews, who served for a time, but eventually fell away from belief to become "false" and "noyous to holy chirche."[36] Arranging various particular identities against an idealized Christian purity in Christ, the sermon uses a complicated association with believed Jewish corruption and lack of belief, which was present in Christ's time and which continues, to attack corruption within the church.

In her analysis of the tract *The Tretise of Miraclis Pleyinge*, Nissé not only demonstrates how Lollard authors drew upon the traditional accusation that Jewish exegesis is stunted by its carnal ties to the letter to attack the dramatization of scripture but also demonstrates how orthodox opponents of the Lollards turned this same accusation by association against them. Nissé shows how the Dominican Thomas Palmer "associates the Lollard translators, in their insufficient understanding of Scripture, with the 'carnal' and stubbornly literal understanding of the Jews."[37] We find a similar tactic enduring in slightly modified form decades later in the mid-fifteenth century polemic of Reginald Pecock, who portrays the Lollards as, like the Jews in Paul's time, placing too much exclusive emphasis on scriptural text: "Forwhi in the daies of Seint Poul Iewis and tho that weren conuertid fro Iewis lawe into Cristenhode magnifieden ouermiche the Oold Testament."[38] Drawing upon the distinctions between gentiles and

Jews found in Romans, Pecock claims for the opponents of the Lollards an affinity with the newly grafted Gentiles, whereas the Lollards are linked to a boastful reliance on prowess or "kunnying" in the reading Scripture, an arrogance that resembles that of the Jews.[39]

The debate over the vernacular reached into nonbiblical translation projects. Trevisa's "Dialogus inter dominum et clericum," attached to his English translation of the *Polychronicon*, presents multiple arguments in favor of "good and neodful" English translation, including that scripture itself was created from translations of Hebrew and Greek into Latin and then French. He questions why it should not also be translated into English and draws upon the native translation precedents of Alfred, Caedmon, and Bede.[40] As both Dove and Andrew Cole have recently shown, Chaucer engages the terms of these translation debates in the prologue to his *Treatise on the Astrolabe*, composed in "lighte Englissh" for his son, Lewis Chaucer.[41] Noting that the "trewe conclusions" of the treatise have been expressed to Greeks in Greek, Arabs in Arabic, Jews in Hebrew, and to those who spoke Latin in their own native tongue, Chaucer concludes that "God woot that in alle these langages and in many moo han these conclusions ben suffisantly lerned and taught, and yit by diverse reules; right as diverse pathes leden diverse folk the righte way to Rome."[42] Chaucer's concern is to make the critical ideas conveyed in the treatise available to one who is still at an early stage of understanding but who can still benefit from the truths that the astrolabe reveals. The echoes of Wycliffite assertions of the importance and appropriateness of vernacular translation ring clearly here, even if definitive assertions of influence will likely always prove elusive. Cole concludes his important essay on these questions with the provocative statement that "[t]he gentry in Chaucer's circle were reading Wycliffite texts with interest—Chaucer included."[43] This assertion is bound to provoke controversy, but recent research makes clear the essential importance of this context for Chaucer studies.

Other Chaucerian texts engage with the terms of these debates over translation and over the ways and means through which "trewe conclusions" may be conveyed, debates which engage not only questions of language but the issue of right interpretation and understanding itself. Taking this intellectual ferment into account can reprioritize the *Prioress's Tale*, indicating the role of the hermeneutical Jew as it is deployed in broader symbolic economies and used not only to define the limits of the Christian community but to reveal its internal struggles.

*   *   *

The Shipman presents a world in which it is difficult to make clear moral distinctions and judgments because each of the tale's main characters—the merchant, his wife, and daun John—is corrupt. The merchant's usury is especially interesting because his livelihood depends upon blurring the boundary between honest trade and usury, a boundary that also traditionally separated Christian merchants from Jews, who were considered the prime perpetrators of usurious activity. This boundary blurring is enacted in the tale itself; it brims with realistic details, many of which, such as the mention of Bruges and the Lombards, point to the world of foreign exchange; but despite this very high level of detail, we never learn specifically what this merchant trades but are told instead only of his "bagges" and "reckonings" and "his need for liquid assets."[44] In a very convincing reading of the tale, Thomas Hahn argues that although the merchant is not specifically called a usurer, his financial dealings have links to usurious activity. Showing the merchant to be a fourteenth-century "financial entrepreneur," Hahn connects him to usury, arguing that currency traders such as the merchant went to great lengths to ensure that their monetary dealings would not be labeled usurious.[45] These machinations did not, however, alter the fact that currency traders were creating money from money.[46] That it is "unnatural" to create money from money, a sterile substance, was an important component of both Aristotelian and scholastic condemnations of usury.[47] Aquinas explains, "A birth of sorts occurs when money grows from money. And therefore, acquisition of money in this way is especially contrary to nature, because it is in accord with nature that money should grow from natural things and not from money itself."[48] According to this sort of analysis, usurers engage in a sterile and unnatural reproduction, creating money from itself in a self-reproductive process at odds both with "nature" and with a society built on principles of natural law.[49]

The merchant himself likens his financial dealings to a type of reproduction when he tells his friend "moneie" is the merchant's "plogh" (VII.288). That usury uses money as a tool for profit harkens precisely to the scholastic critique of it—profit should be made not from monetary manipulations but from "natural" forms of creation, such as growing actual crops with actual plows. In the context of his wife's adultery and her depiction of her husband's lack of financial and sexual largesse, the merchant's words also bring into play connotations of sexual reproduction. The association between plowing and sexual intercourse appears as well in other medieval texts, such as the *Roman de la Rose*, in which Genius urges,

"Arez, pour Deu, baron, arez, / E voz lignages reparez; / Se ne pensez forment d'arer / N'est riens qui les puist reparer."[50]

The merchant's practice of making money from money, the catalyst for all the rest of the "unnatural" dealings in the tale, is portrayed as an obsessive activity that cuts him off from family and friends.[51] His wife resents the time her husband devotes to his financial dealings, a practice that interferes with the normal running of the household, eating, and showing proper hospitality to daun John. After making her agreement with daun John, she rouses her husband:

> Up to hir housbonde is this wyf ygon,
> And knokketh at his countour boldely.
>   "*Quy la?*" quod he. "Peter! it am I,"
> Quod she; "What, sire, how longe wol ye faste?
> How longe tyme wol ye rekene and caste
> Youre sommes, and youre bookes, and youre thynges?
> The devel have part on alle swiche rekenynges!
> Ye have ynough, pardee, of Goddes sonde;
> Com doun to-day, and lat youre bagges stonde.
> Ne be ye nat ashamed that daun John
> Shal fasting al this day alenge goon?
> What, let us heere a messe, and go we dyne." (VII.212–20)

The mood is comic as the wife marches up to her husband's counting house door to chide and cajole him. Her scolding reveals not only her own bold hypocrisy but also her evident frustrations with her husband's preoccupations. This frustrated tone is reinforced by her repetition of "how long" and her stressing that the dealings of the counting house are exclusively his: "your sommes, and youre bookes, and youre thynges." Even if his wealth helps to maintain her, the wife consigns her husband's dealings to the devil. Her words could simply indicate her disgust, but their formulation also hints at the darker, usurious side of the merchant's work. The wife's frustrations seem to stem from the fact that the merchant's financial "reproductions" also keep him from fulfilling his sexual obligations. The end of the tale, which portrays the merchant as actively amorous, shows that he is capable of performing sexually for his wife but that he is very often too wholly absorbed in his financial dealings to attend to anything else.[52] It is only after he secures his large profit that the merchant turns, at the tale's end, to paying the "marriage debt."[53] With its neat series of sexual and financial exchanges, some critics remark upon the smooth ending of this tale, which is full of trickery but free of retribution.[54] The tale does create a sense of generative excess, however, through its exponential growth in coins—the merchant earns 1,000 francs in his transactions—and in sins—the breaking of marital and monastic vows, lying, cheating, and the transformation of marriage into prostitution. At the root of these transgressions is the merchant's usury, which can be seen as supplying both opportunity and motivation for all the other sinful acts in the tale.[55]

The merchant cannot, of course, be held solely responsible for the corruption of his marriage. The tale presents a more flagrant violation by the wife, who conducts the illicit trade of her body. The comic effect of the tale's portrayal of her actions stems in large part from an anxiety over the danger of female agency and independent female sexual prerogative. We have seen the comic effect of the wife's bold reproaches to her husband; her score it on "my taille" is a matching punch line to the Shipman's conclusion. She is neither "afered nor affrayed" when her husband asks her about the hundred franc debt, and although the tale does not provide definitive insight into her feelings and desires, it is clear that she, like her husband, knows how to deal and how to make the best of changing "markets." By commodifying her own "joly body," the wife threatens social order not only by prostituting marriage but by risking an illegitimate child. Although Harry Bailley declares that both merchant and wife are made "apes," and the wife is surely tricked, she manages to stay "on top" of things, eluding detection and punishment with an effrontery that recalls the ticklish situation of May in the *Merchant's Tale*. It is, in fact, the sheer effrontery of these female characters that accounts for much of the tales' comic impact; the humor they create stems from the fact that such female behavior could not be sanctioned outside the realm of the fiction. Paralleling the economic usury in the tale is what Marc Shell, writing about *The Merchant of Venice*, calls a kind of "verbal usury," a profligate multiplication of meanings occurring through "punning and flattering," which is deemed "unnatural" by the Church fathers."[56] The Shipman concludes with a blasphemous prayer—"Thus endeth my tale, and God us sende / Taillynge ynough unto oure lyves ende. Amen" (VII.433–34)—thereby conflating financial credit, sexual intercourse, and tale-telling.[57] It refers to the bold retort of the merchant's wife, "score it upon my taille" (VII.416), which invites her husband to both place her debt "on her tab" and to collect it through intercourse with her, transforming marriage into prostitution. This double meaning resonates with the merchant's usurious activities, which both create an unnatural reproduction through usury and corrupt the sanctioned reproductive function of his marriage.

As a reference to tale-telling, the Shipman's pun also has very specific implications within the context of the Canterbury pilgrimage. The Shipman's pun connects the pilgrimage contest to the licentious deeds of his tale, an inference that by itself lands the next teller, the Prioress, in a socially awkward situation. Harry Bailley asks her to follow a tale that is not only an extended dirty joke, but one that rhetorically implicates all tale-tellers in illicit sexual deeds, deeds measured in the same terms used to measure usury.[58]

*   *   *

The Prioress responds to the moral chaos of the *Shipman's Tale* by presenting a tale with much more clear-cut distinctions. Her reference to usury, emphasized by its placement in the opening of her tale and unique to Chaucer's version of the little clergeon story, makes usury explicitly and exclusively Jewish:[59]

> Ther was in Asye, in a greet citee,
> Amonges Cristene folk a Jewerye,
> Sustened by a lord of that contree
> For foule usure and lucre of vileynye,
> Hateful to Crist and to his compaignye. (VII.488–91)

As opposed to the morally confusing situations of the *Shipman's Tale*, the *Prioress's Tale* depicts a world where boundaries are much more readily discerned; the poor Christians of the tale are a small island of believers in a sea of the godless. The Prioress draws out the usury in the *Shipman's Tale*, making the implicit explicit.[60] I argue that her reference to usury is in part an attempt to counteract the effect of the sins of the *Shipman's Tale*—to remind her audience that it is not only the bold wife and wily monk who sin, but also the husband. The implication of the *Shipman's Tale*, that the religious orders are hopelessly corrupt and that only sin can ensue from female agency, puts the Prioress in a delicate position, because she is, after all, a woman who wields a degree of authority. Although scholars remain divided on the exact nature and scope of the Prioress's power, it is clear that she has privilege. Eileen Power argues, "Socially in all cases, and politically when their houses were large and rich, abbots and abbesses, priors and prioresses, ranked among the great folk of the countryside. They enjoyed the same prestige as the lords of the neighboring manors and some extra deference on account of their religion. It was natural that the Prioress of a nunnery should be 'holden digne of reverence.'[61] Responding to a strain of criticism that dismisses the Prioress as frivolous and ineffectual, Hardy Long Frank emphasizes the many responsibilities of a prioress, asserting, "The 'little lady' whom we dismiss so airily was in fact an estate manager."[62] Hahn also demonstrates the prestige associated with the Prioress's position but reminds us that this position depends upon the approval of men.[63] Because she is living within a male-dominated culture, whatever power the Prioress does possess carries the potential to generate anxiety and conflict; one could read the Nun's Priest's ironic tale of a rooster among hens as an indication of this.[64] When we remind ourselves that the audience of pilgrims is composed almost exclusively of men, it seems fitting that the Prioress tells a tale about an active, powerful, female figure, the Virgin, who plays a crucial role but who is eventually contained and controlled within the Church's male-dominated hierarchy. The Prioress asserts the importance of a feminized, affective piety centered on Mary, showing the complementary nature of this piety within masculinized institutions.

The Prioress "quites" the Shipman's "unnatural" proliferation of money, meaning, and sin and the anxieties they generate through her focus on the most holy and significant of reproductions—the Incarnation. The Incarnation is that moment when the Word becomes flesh, creating a transition to a stabilized production of meaning. At the Incarnation of the Word, endless "taillying" is shut down, all meaning is ultimately subsumed in "oure doctrine," an act accomplished through the pure body of a willing woman.[65] In contrast to the Shipman's punning "prayer," the *Prioress's Prologue* is in earnest, imploring Mary's aid through a focus on Mary's role as mediator and participant in the Incarnation:

> O mooder Mayde, O mayde Mooder free!
> O bussh unbrent, brennynge in Moyses sighte,
> That ravyshedest doun fro the Deitee,
> Thurgh thyn humblesse, the Goost that in th'alighte,
> Of whos vertu, whan he thyn herte lighte,
> Conceyved was the Fadres sapience,
> Help me to telle it in thy reverence! (VII.467–73)

The Prioress's depiction of the Annunciation makes Mary notably active; her humbleness ravishes the Holy Ghost down from God, a description that blends the erotic and the pious.[66] The Virgin offers her body in a reproductive act that transcends mortal sexuality and that stands as a polar opposite to the prostitution of the wife in the *Shipman's Tale*. In volunteering to be the mother of God, Mary actively "cuckolds" Joseph to redeem another kind of debt, human sin.

The Prioress's portrayal of an active Mary extends beyond her Prologue and into her tale of a little schoolboy murdered by Jews as he passes through the Jewry and sings the *Alma Redemptoris Mater*. In another erotically, spiritually charged description, the Virgin's sweetness pierces the clergeon's heart, and the boy cannot help but sing her praises:

> The swetnesse his herte perced so
> Of Cristes mooder that, to hire to preye,
> He kan nat stynte of syngyng by the weye. (VII.555–57)

To honor Mary, the child vows to learn the *Alma* even though he knows that he risks being beaten "thries in a houre" for ignoring his regular lessons (VII.542). His devotion is something actively encouraged by his actual and his spiritual mothers; the threat of punishment sets up a tension between the demands of masculinized ecclesiastical institutions and a feminized piety associated with home and mothers.

The tale depicts maternal bonds not only as powerful but as in fact interfering with the little boy's schooling, a process that takes place within a male-dominated educational institution. Historians of medieval English education identify the little clergeon as a participant in a medieval English "song school." Although there is evidence that these schools were open to girls, they were clearly primarily schools for boys, run by men.[67] The boy goes back and forth daily between the world of women and the world of men, from the maternally run home of his mother to the school, where he learns "swich manere doctrine as men used there" (VII.499). The tale emphasizes the back-and-forth nature of the boy's learning process through the singsong, childlike doubling prevalent in the passages describing the boy's learning the *Alma:* the doubling verbally echoes the boy's travels back and forth between school and home. The Prioress says that the boy learns "day to day"; he learns the *Alma* "word to word," he sings it "twice a day" as he passes "to and fro" through the Jewry. The boy's trips between two worlds of pious learning, reinforced by this pairing dic-tion, create a tension between his formal schooling within the ecclesiastical educational structure and his feminized devotion to Mary.[68] This situation of split devotional loyalties leads, rather directly, to his gruesome murder. It is as if the boy remains vulnerable until the feminized piety of home and the masculinized institutional worship of school are brought together.

It is the coming together of male and female figures that solves the murder. The Virgin's intervention keeps the boy singing in the privy, but after the murder is "out," male figures associated with the Church, Jesus and the Abbot, intervene. Although Christ is mentioned early in the tale, male Christian figures become truly active agents only after the Jews have killed the boy. At that point, the males' actions become very significant, even dominant. The widow pleads for Mary's help in finding her child, but it is Jesus who leads her to him:

> . . . but Jhesu of his grace
> Yaf in hir thoght inwith a litel space
> That in that place after hir sone she cryde,
> Where he was casten in a pit bisyde. (VII.603–6)

Mary's grain plays an important role in the solving of the murder, but the Abbot has arrived to intervene and interpret. The grain itself and the manner in which it lies upon the boy's tongue recall the eucharist, which could be administered only by priests.[69] Although Mary has placed the grain in the clergeon's mouth, we learn of this act indirectly; the Virgin's activity is mediated through the boy's telling. It is the male Abbot who finally withdraws the grain, resolving the action. The boy himself notes,

> But Jesu Crist, as ye in bookes fynde,
> Wil that his glorie laste and be in mynde,
> And for the worship of his Mooder deere
> Yet may I synge *O Alma* loude and cleere. (VII.652–55)

Here, as in the tale's closing lines, the action is performed by Christ for Mary's sake. Devotion to Mary remains an important object of the tale, but Mary's own active ravishing and piercing have faded to the background. As Sumner Ferris has argued, the tale demonstrates Mary's place in the theological hierarchy; she is revered yet firmly subordinated to God and Christ.[70] I add that now the relationship between the boy and the Virgin, which once caused the boy to risk the balance between masculinized and feminized devotion, becomes finite. It cannot gain further strength but is, rather, contained, like the boy's body, within the walls of the Church. The martyrdom unites the Christian community behind the boy and against the Jews, strengthening a sense of Christian community and identity at the same time that it contains and checks the maternal powers of the Virgin, harnessing those for use by the Church. Feminine forces are subsumed within the universal Church, controlled by men.

It is crucially important that the act that disrupts this maternal bond—the murder—is enacted not by the male agents of the Church but by satanically inspired Jews. The Jews carry out the punishment that the school had only threatened. Instead of being beaten thrice hourly, the clergeon is slaughtered in an act that recalls the Crucifixion.[71] Robert Hanning links this threat of punishment to the murder, reading the incident as an attack by the Prioress on the male-dominated educational system: "The response of the Jews to the 'clergeon's' song, while much more extreme in violence, is perhaps not so different in kind from the imagined response of his Christian teacher. When Mary frustrates the malice of the Jews by granting continued power of song to her devotee, the Prioress strikes a muffled blow at the system of male-dominated education and authority."[72] I would also stress, however, the very muffled nature of the "blow" that the Prioress aims at the system of Church education. Because the Jews kill the boy, the bond between the clergeon and Mary is disrupted without implicating the male Christian ecclesiasts who are spiritually bound to venerate the Virgin.[73] Instead, the murder is carried out by Mary's enemies, the Jews. Through her description, the Prioress places the boy's murder in a constellation of common medieval accusations against the Jews. Although the murder in the tale is not a ritual murder in the strict sense of that terminology, the scenario closely resembles ritual murder in various accusations.[74] The details of the murder, particularly that of the privy, echo the accusation surrounding the death of the famous child martyr Hugh of Lincoln, who was recorded in ballads and songs as being thrown into a well by Jewish murderers.[75] The Prioress later cements this association with her closing reference to little Hugh. Boyd argues that the Prioress "cites Hugh of Lincoln in the context of the slain clergeon as a further instance of Jewish incorrigibility with regard to child murder," thereby linking this tale to stories of ritual murder.[76]

After recounting that the Jews fling the boy into a privy, the Prioress calls them "O cursed folk of Herodes al newe," invoking the Massacre of the Innocents (VII.574). Elements of the tale allude to Childermas, the

Feast of the Holy Innocents, observed on December 28th.[77] Although it
is debatable whether Chaucer had the liturgy for this feast in mind when
composing the tale, the Prioress's allusion to the murder of the Innocents
does add an additional layer of association with child murder onto her
telling. It also further links the murder of the clergeon to the Crucifixion,
because the Innocents not only are part of the story of the life of Jesus but
are "types of Christ."[78] The ritual murder accusation is, of course, modeled on the idea that the Jews crucified Christ. Each new act of alleged
violence by Jews invokes this central act, reminding the audience of what
they consider to be the Jews' most heinous crime. The murder and its
heavy weight of symbolic associations rip through the tale, severing its
earlier focus on the boy's devotion to the Virgin. One thread, however,
remains intact in its fabric—the murder shifts the audience's full attention
onto the Jews and recalls the Prioress's opening mention of usury. If one
reads the Prioress's reference to usury as a response to the trickery of the
monk and the wife in the *Shipman's Tale*, this seems well accomplished by
the power of the ritual murder accusation. This accusation draws attention
away from any aspersion cast at female agency, whether this is directed at
wanton women such as the merchant's wife or at the pure yet perhaps
overwhelmingly powerful Virgin. The tale's opening reference reveals an
underlying anxiety over the close coexistence of Jews and Christians, a
coexistence that fosters this sin of usury. The effect of the murder is to
absorb and engulf any anxiety generated over the power of the maternal
and over the violence used to disrupt this power.[79] The force of exclusion
and the limits of the community are defined through opposition to a
demonized Jewry, all other types of particularities are absorbed within the
community of the faithful.

The tale's violence, then, can be read as a response to ambiguity, a
disturbance in order and in clear-cut definitions of identity that are at the
root of abjection. The glib moral ambiguity of the *Shipman's Tale* becomes manifest in the topography of the great Asian city, where Christians
and Jews live cheek to jowl for the purpose of usurious profit. Of the
Jewish quarter the Prioress notes that "thurgh the strete men myghte ride
or wende, / For it was free and open at eyther end" (VII. 492–94). Any-
one can ride or pass through this Jewry, precisely the action that imperils
the little clergeon. It is as if a danger were posed simply by interacting
with or being in the midst of the Jews. This anxiety emerges not only in
this text but in numerous contemporary Christian laws, which made Jews
wear distinctive clothing and which prohibited certain types of interaction,

notably sexual intercourse, between Christians and Jews.[80] This process of separating Christians and Jews is an important one, because it is precisely by claiming its difference from Judaism, and from Jews, that Christianity claims its identity.

The tale also plays out its anxieties about the maternal and about Jews through its negative preoccupation with "permeable" boundaries.[81] The bond between Mary and the little clergeon involves a breaking and cross-ing of boundaries; the boy's devotion to the Virgin compels him to break with the normal course of study; the boundaries of his heart are pierced by her sweetness. After his praises for the Virgin "pass through" the boy's throat (VII.547), the Jews slit it open when he passes through the Jewish quarter. Each of these ruptures is, of course, quite different, but each pro-vokes anxiety and each connects to the grisly murder. The murder occurs within the Jewry, a separate yet permeable space within the city. This space is quite literally a "zone of uninhabitability" for Christians, but the boy ventures into this space anyway—with disastrous results:[82]

> This cursed Jew him hente, and heeld hym faste,
> And kitte his throte, and in a pit hym caste.
> I seye that in a wardrobe thy hym threwe
> Where as thise Jewes purgen hire entraille. (VII.570–73)

With her emphatic "I seye," the Prioress stresses the gruesome detail that the boy's body is flung into a filthy privy. This description calls attention to the Jews' bodies and to their excretions, emphasizing that, like their section of town, their bodies are "free and open at eyther end" (VII.494).[83] The human body, specifically the Jewish body, becomes a model for societal disorder.

The openness and filth of the Jews' bodies contrast sharply with the impermeability displayed by the little clergeon's body after his murder. The boy is likened to hard jewels, in contrast to the denigrated, vulnerable bodies of the Jews.[84] These references to jewels also specifically associate the little clergeon's wholeness with sexual purity; he is a "gemme of chas-tite, this emeraude, / And eek of martirdom the ruby bright" (VII.609–10). The Prioress has already lauded the boy's virgin status in an earlier stanza:

> O martir, sowded to virginitee,
> Now maystow syngen, folwynge evere in oon

The white Lamb celestial—quod she—
Of which the grete evaungelist, Seint John,
In Pathmos wroot, which seith that they goon
Biforn this Lamb and synge a song al newe,
That nevere, flesshly, wommen they ne knewe. (VII.579–85)

The Prioress emphasizes not the clergeon's devotion, but his sexual purity.[85] Stephen Spector has noted the connection between the body of the little boy and the ideal of bodily chastity for a nun such as the Prioress; the Jews represent the antithesis of this spotlessness.[86]

This ideal of bodily chastity and wholeness applies most of all, as we have seen in the debates over Mary's womb, to the body of the Virgin herself. Marina Warner remarks, "The virgin body was not only pristine, however; it was also whole. The biblical images the Fathers applied to the birth of Christ reveal that they conceived of a virgin's body as seamless, unbroken, a literal epiphany of integrity. The Virgin Mary is a 'closed gate,' a 'spring shut up,' a 'fountain sealed.' Her physical virginity *post partum* was as important a part of orthodoxy in the early Church as her virginal conception by the power of the Holy Ghost."[87] Christians must depict Mary as absolutely virginal, an intact and immaculate vessel. Like the body of the little clergeon, and in contrast to the bodies of the Jews in the *Prioress's Tale*, her body is intact, her womb free from the stain of sexual intercourse and impervious to assaults from Jewish detractors. This sealed womb contrasts strikingly to typical wombs, the female origin from which every human springs. In the rhetorical and philosophical attacks posed by Jews and then reiterated by Christians in order to be refuted, we are confronted with a representation of a womb that is foul and filthy— rather like the privy into which the murdered clergeon is cast. The tale's description of the murder scene, "in an aleye" that "hadde a privee place" (VII.568), invites the observation that the boy's devotion to the Virgin lands him in a place resembling that from which he first emerged.[88] Only at the tale's closing is he finally transferred to "a tombe of marbul stones cleere" (VII.681)—his body out of the hands of mothers and of Jews, enclosed in an impermeable resting place within the walls of the Church.

The disgust over where the boy is thrown (and by extension over the place from which he emerged) is transferred onto the bodies of the Jews as the audience's attention shifts from mothers to murder. The Jews' bodies are associated with permeability and filth and are ultimately ripped apart—drawn by wild horses. As Steven Kruger argues in his reading of this tale and as part of his development of a broader understanding of the representations of both Jewish and Christian bodies in medieval texts, the boy's body and, by extension, Christian bodies and the Christian community are made to seem comparatively intact, whole and clean, very different and distinct from the womblike privy and from the Jews. Kruger writes, "At the heart of The Prioress's Tale is an opposition between the Christian body, attacked but preserved, and the Jewish body, foul ('purging its entraille' [573]), attacking innocence, justly destroyed."[89] To look at Kruger's analysis from the perspective of Douglas's discussions of bodily symbolics, if the Jewish body represents societal order in chaos, the boy's comes to represent the Christian community in order and unity, just as in the controversies surrounding the status of her womb, Mary's body becomes a metaphor for an ideal of the origins of Christian identity. And notably, in this story, the Jews, longtime enemies of the Virgin, are literally ripped apart, the degraded representation of their filthy, mortal bodies elevating the representation of her intact, immortal, and immaculate one. The tale's representation of Jewish and Christian bodies implies that the Christian community may be attacked but remains impermeable; the Jewish community, in contrast, is easily torn asunder.

Through her depiction of the Virgin's immaculate power, the Prioress attempts to recuperate women from the blows they are dealt in the ambiguous, freewheeling world of the *Shipman's Tale*. She shows, through her focus on the most holy example of Christian femininity, the Virgin, how the affective feminized piety that characterizes the clergeon's Marian devotion complements the masculinized religious institutions that formally sanction his martyrdom. Through the tale's shift to a focus on male figures, however, the Prioress acknowledges that feminized piety operates within the bounds of masculine religious institutions even as she stresses its importance. The *Prioress's Tale* averts attention from the potential conflict between masculine and feminine styles of worship by deflecting any possible anxieties over female agency and power onto the tale's murderous Jews. This movement toward order and harmony is physically represented through the tale's graphic representations of whole, intact, Christian bodies and filthy, fragmented, Jewish ones.[90] In this way the difference of gender is trumped by the difference between Jew and Christian.

*   *   *

We find then, in the Prioress's response to the Shipman's tale, a world of clear-cut distinctions, literally embodied by the bodies of Christians and

Jews. The Prioress's response is also notable, however, not only for its graphic violence, but also for the violence of its pathos. Carolyn Collette has argued that the Prioress's highly emotional, irrational brand of religious devotion is characteristic of late fourteenth-century fashionable piety.[91] The Prioress praises such urgent piety, opposing it to learned understanding:

> O Lord, oure Lord, thy name how merveillous
> Is in this large world ysprad—quod she—
> For noght oonly thy laude precious
> Parfouned is by men of dignitee,
> But by the mouth of children thy bountee
> Parfourned is, for on the brest soukynge
> Somtyme shewen they thyn heriynge. (VII.453–59)

Focusing on the performance of praise rather than its content, the Prioress shows that this important work is done not only by "men of dignitee," adult men in positions of power, but by infants, the most innocent and powerless of human beings. Through the image of babes at the breast, the Prioress presents a model of Christian piety that is specifically unlettered and unlearned, associated with children in a time before speech itself.[92] As Shulamith Shahar explains, before seven years, the medieval *annis discretionis*, a child was considered *infans*, not because he is incapable of utterance, but because at this stage he speaks in imitation of adult speech without true comprehension.[93] Despite the fact that he has reached the age of seven, a lack of comprehension certainly characterizes the little clergeon. We know specifically that neither he nor his older schoolmate understand the Latin words of the *Alma*, a detail unique to Chaucer's version of the story.[94]

> This litel child, his litel book lernynge,
> As he sat in the scole at his prymer,
> He *Alma redemptoris* herde synge,
> As children lerned hire antiphoner;
> And as he dorste, he drough hym ner and ner,
> And herkned ay the wordes and the noote,
> Til he the firste vers koude al by rote.
>
> Noght wiste he what this Latyn was to seye,
> For he so yong and tendre was of age.

> But on a day his felawe gan he preye
> T'expounden hym this song in his langage,
> Or telle hym why this song was in usage;
> This preyde he hym to construe and declare
> Ful often tyme upon his knowes bare.
>
> His felawe, which that elder was than he,
> Answerde hym thus: "This song, I have herd seye,
> Was maked of our blisful Lady free,
> Hire to salue, and eek hire for to preye
> To been oure help and socour whan we deye.
> I kan namoore expounde in this mateere,
> I lerne song; I kan but smal grammeere." (VII.516–36)

It is, ironically, the Jews who understand both the literal meaning of the *Alma* and its spiritual impact, which they do not accept, yet comprehend well enough to kill the boy.[95] In depicting this situation, the Prioress creates an odd twist on the usual Christian accusation of Jewish slavish belief in the literal: the tale's Jews understand the literal meaning of the *Alma* but fail to comprehend its spiritual importance, a circumstance that leads to the boy's death in literal enactment of "the letter kills but the spirit gives life." The tale's infantilized hero, on the other hand, feels the call of the spirit without comprehension of the letter. Although he understands spiritual import, he does not have a full understanding of his situation. The Prioress implicates herself in this lack of understanding, because she has, in her Invocation, likened herself to the clergeon through her self-portrayal as a babe at the breast:

> My konnyng is so wayk, O blisful Queene,
> For to declare thy grete worthynesse
> That I ne may the weighte nat susteene;
> But as a child of twelf month oold, or lesse,
> That kan unnethes any word expresse,
> Right so fare I, and therfore I yow preye,
> Gydeth my song that I shal of yow seye. (VII.481–87)

Aligning herself against learned "men of dignitee" and with a model of childlike devotion, the Prioress asks to become a vessel of praise rather like the clergeon's corpse. She depicts her inspiration as moving through her rather than being generated by her own understanding.

The Prioress's brand of piety, however fashionable, was not without its critics. Through the model of Saint Cecelia, the Second Nun responds to the lack of understanding that the Prioress implicitly valorizes. There are many features of these two rhyme royal tales that indicate the connections between them.[96] Both tellers belong to the same convent, both begin by invoking Mary, and it has been convincingly argued that the *Prioress's Prologue* is an adaptation of the Second Nun's.[97] Both tales tell of a martyr who challenges institutions and conventions: the little clergeon's devotion to Mary leads him away from his normal course of studies, whereas St. Cecelia remains a virgin in marriage, preaches, and refuses to honor Roman gods. Finally, both martyrs meet gruesome fates with striking visual resemblances. The clergeon lies in the privy with his throat slashed, yet still sings the *Alma Redemptoris Mater*; St. Cecelia has her throat cut and yet remains alive in a tub of boiling water for three days, preaching and converting until the moment of her death.

There are, of course, also some important differences between these martyrdom tales. Generically, the *Prioress's Tale* is a Miracle of the Virgin and, as such, the tale hinges on the direct intervention of Mary, and, as we have seen, of Jesus. The clergeon is essentially a passive martyr, murdered by the Jews during his innocent trips through the Jewry. As the Second Nun explicitly indicates, her tale is a "legende" (VIII.25), a saint's life in the tradition of Jacobus a Voragine's *Legenda Aurea*.[98] Like so many early Christian female martyrs, St. Cecelia plays a very active role in her own salvation. She understands fully the worldly risks and heavenly rewards of martyrdom and uses this understanding to convert others. It is precisely through this difference between the two martyrs' activities and agency that we can understand the ways in which the Second Nun's tale responds to the Prioress's by presenting an alternative model of ideal Christian identity that also valorizes a pious woman. Both tales challenge the inferior position of women in relation to a normatively masculine Christian subject by presenting models of exceptional piety that are enacted or inspired by women. Saint Cecelia's story, however, focuses not on the divine intervention of a specific figure but upon a human martyr's activity. Although Mary is invoked and God's power certainly enables Cecelia, particularly in the tale's last scene, it is her own passion, courage, and learning that drive the tale. The Second Nun takes an active adult female piety out of the realm of the divine and places it in the world of humans.

We find in the figure of the Second Nun herself a type of piety that differs markedly from the Prioress's. We do not know much about the Second Nun, but it is not, despite the assertions of some critics, impossible to say anything about her.[99] In the *General Prologue*, the narrator finishes describing the Prioress and adds: "Another NONNE with hire hadde she, / That was hir chapeleyne, and preestes thre" (I.163–64). The *Middle English Dictionary* (*MED*) defines a *chapeleyne* as a "nun who serves as private secretary and assistant to the abbess or prioress of a convent." Eileen Power tells us that the "chapeleyne" was also meant to act as an ever-present witness to the head of the nunnery, helping to protect her good name.[100] Because a nun acting as chapeleyne was also supposed to aid the prioress with written tasks, it is reasonable to assume that the Second Nun is acquainted with learning, despite the generally very low levels of education among fourteenth-century English nuns.[101] The Second Nun's prologue, in fact, highlights erudition. The bilingual emphasis of her very first lines, "The ministre and the norice unto vices, / Which that men clepe in Englissh Ydelnesse" (VIII.1–2), brings into focus immediately the translated nature of her tale and her own awareness of linguistic difference. She refers again explicitly to the act of translating by explaining it as a guard against idleness:

> And for to putte us fro swich ydelnesse,
> That cause is of so greet confusioun,
> I have heer doon my feithful bisynesse
> After the legende in translacioun
> Right of thy glorious lif and passioun,
> Thou with thy gerland wroght with rose and lilie—
> Thee meene I, mayde and martyr, Seint Cecilie. (VIII.22–28)

As opposed to the *Prioress's Prologue*, which reworks sections of the liturgy, the *Second Nun's Prologue* celebrates and displays more advanced learning, calling to attention, for example, her knowledge of Saint Bernard's Marian devotions and of Macrobius. Even the Second Nun's humility topos is sophisticated; she is no nursing baby, but an adult translator:

> Yet preye I yow that reden that I write,
> Foryeve me that I do no diligence
> This ilke storie subtilly to endite,
> For bothe have I the wordes and sentence

Of hym that at the seintes reverence
The storie wroot, and folwen hire legende,
And pray yow that ye wole my werk amende. (VIII.78–84)

The Second Nun's self-presentation focuses on her work within a literary context, a world of words. The third portion of her invocation, the etymology of Cecelia's name, reveals an interest in language itself, a desire to get at its inner meaning. Rather than portraying herself as outside of language, the Second Nun splits words like atoms, harnessing every particle of semantic energy. Her approach to understanding Saint Cecelia through her name demonstrates a desire for a full, learned understanding. The Second Nun has both "wordes and sentence" at her disposal. If the Prioress attempted to shut down the proliferation of meaning created by the Shipman's pun, the Second Nun demonstrates an ability to create a proliferation of holy meanings, much as her protagonist performs a kind of "spiritual procreation" through her powers to convert.[102] Like the Second Nun, her protagonist, Saint Cecelia, has been educated as a Christian:

This mayden bright Cecilie, as hir lif seith,
Was comen of Romayns and of noble kynde,
And from hir cradel up fostred in the feith
Of Crist, and bar his gospel in hir mynde.
She nevere cessed, as I writen fynde,
Of hir preyere and God to love and drede,
Bisekynge hym to kepe hir maydenhede. (VIII.119–26)

Saint Cecelia is raised from the cradle to bear the gospel in her mind. In its emphasis on this very typical hagiographic feature of childhood devotion, Cecelia's upbringing resembles that of the little clergeon, but is notably more cognitive. With the gospel "in mind," as Cecelia's (written and translated) story shows, she understands fully the terms of her faith and its rewards and risks; she combines belief with understanding. When Tiburce voices his fears of being burned alive for worshiping a god "yhid in hevene pryvely," Cecelia convinces him of the rightness of martyrdom, outlining for him its heavenly rewards:

"Men myghten dreden wel and skilfully
This lyf to lese, myn owene deere brother,
If this were lyvynge oonly and noon oother.

"But ther is bettre lif in oother place,
That nevere shal be lost, ne drede thee noght,
Which Goddes Sone us tolde thurgh his grace.
That Fadres Sone hath alle thyng ywroght,
And al that wroght is with a skilful thoght;
The Goost, that fro the Fader gan procede,
Hath sowled hem, withouten any drede.

"By word and by myracle heigh Goddes Sone,
Whan he was in this world, declared heere
That ther was oother lyf ther men may wone." (VIII.320–32)

Cecelia converts Tiburce through an argument that focuses on cognitive faculties and thought rather than on emotional appeal—"al that wroght is with a skilful thoght." She next explains to him the Trinity through analogy to the human faculties of memory, imagination, and judgment. Preaching and teaching doctrine, Cecelia converts the very guards who come to fetch her for trial, and she continues "to teche and to preche" until the very moment of her death.

I disagree with Gail Berkeley Sherman's assessment that Cecelia is "a speaking body," a mere vessel for the Word.[103] On the contrary, even when lying mutilated in a tub of boiling water, Cecelia's last gestures are still active and self-initiated. She wills her possessions to Urban to aid in the founding of a Church, telling him that she has asked God for the three days that she remains in the boiling tub, hanging between life and death, but still preaching:

". . . I axed this of hevene kyng,
To han respit thre dayes and namo
To recomende to yow, er that I go,
Thise soules, lo, and that I myghte do werche
Heere of myn hous perpetuelly a cherche." (VIII.542–46)

The Second Nun and the Prioress present two opposing models of ideal Christian identity, approached in strikingly different ways. In Saint Cecelia, the Second Nun presents a model for the ideal Christian that is full of understanding and learning, a woman who converts through preaching and teaching until her very last hour.[104] The *Second Nun's Tale* focuses on a model of ideal Christian identity that defies prohibitions against women's preaching and teaching and presents a world in which men and women play not only complementary but equally important roles in salvation history. The story of Saint Cecelia depicts a woman who exhibits bravery, fortitude, and understanding. Saint Cecelia's active preaching and teaching, and the conversions they bring about, are what generates her power as a saint. In contrast to depicting a feminized piety that is ultimately subordinated to masculinized institutions, the Second Nun recounts a woman's involvement in the beginnings of the Church itself. The Second Nun depicts a female saint who is driven by what she describes as reasoned belief to create, with male fellow believers such as Urban, the foundations of the Church. Saint Cecelia accomplishes this both figuratively and quite literally through willing her home as the site for an actual church. Critics have struggled over the Second Nun's statement that she is an "unworthy sone of Eve" (VIII.62), and it seems likely that it is an incomplete revision of the tale's earlier version, composed before the Canterbury frame. This explanation is certainly plausible, but it is interesting that Mary herself is addressed as a "sonne" in the Prologue, "thou, that art the sonne of excellence" (VIII.52). Scholars have suggested that "sonne" here might be ambiguous in gender or refer to Mary as the Sun, but the confluence of gender-ambiguous terms is suggestive, and I read these textual "anomalies" as reinforcements of the egalitarian thrust of the tale.

Although the Second Nun creates in her legend a model of Christian identity that draws primarily on positive example, she also uses, as does the Prioress, a technique of opposition to an unbelieving Other to define the "Christian" through contrast. In the *Second Nun's Tale*, the unbelieving Other is a pagan, and her depiction of pagan disbelief draws upon the contrast between blindness and insight. Saint Cecelia's crusade against spiritual blindness is exemplified in her speech to Almachius. He demands that she worship idols and she responds,

> "Ther lakketh no thyng to thyne outter yen
> That thou n'art blynd; for thyng that we seen alle
> That it is stoon—that men may wel espyen—
> That ilke stoon a god thow wolt it calle.
> I rede thee, lay thyn hand upon it falle
> And taste it wel, and stoon thou shalt it fynde,
> Syn that thou seest nat with thyne eyen blynde." (VIII.498–504)

Creating a Platonic contrast between inner and outer sight, Cecelia charges that Almachius sees the stone but fails to recognize that it signifies no more than what it literally is. For Saint Cecelia, Christian identity goes beyond seeing the spiritual in the literal; it is being able to discern the true spiritual meaning of the physical world. Just as the Jews in the *Prioress's Tale* were deaf to the spiritual meaning of the *Alma*, Almachius and the Romans attribute meaning to the idols when none is there.

Because of the Pauline basis of her argument, Jewish blindness informs Saint Cecelia's accusations to Almachius as well. Both Saint Cecelia and the little clergeon are murdered by those who refuse to accept Christian truth—who can hear the words of the *Alma* but refuse to believe them, or who see a stone, mistake it for a god, and murder all those who refuse to worship it. The murders of the clergeon and St. Cecelia enact the Pauline dictum "the letter kills and the spirit gives life," but both stories modify the traditional association of the hermeneutical Woman with the literal and the carnal by presenting a female saint and a feminized clergeon as champions of Christianity and its spiritual meanings. The striking iconographic parallels in the way in which the two martyrdoms are depicted reinforce the parallels between the blindness of their murderers.

The particular identities—Christian, Jewish, pagan, female, and male—are mapped out on the bodies of the characters in the tales of the Second Nun and the Prioress. Jocelyn Wogan-Browne, in a discussion of virgin martyr stories that includes the Katherine group and selected *Canterbury Tales*, has argued that "the boundaries of Christian polity are policed on the bodies of virgins: represented bodily integrity serves an exclusionary definition of Christian community asserted against the 'pagan.' The figure of the pagan in this way encodes contemporary anxieties about heresy and, very pointedly in the Katherine Group as in *Ancrene Wisse*, contemporary anti-Semitism. The female audiences of these texts are encouraged to define themselves against 'the envious Jews,' especially in calibrating the refinement and ardour of their feeling for Christ."[105]

St. Cecelia's body, resilient to axe and boiling water, becomes a metaphor for an intact Christian community; this metaphor parallels the jewel-like integrity of the similarly violated little clergeon and his relation to the Christian community. In both stories, a celebration of feminine piety is enabled by opposition to an Other, as it is in Wogan-Browne's descriptions of the Katherine group texts.

In arguing that the hermeneutical Jew and the topos of Jewish blindness inform the *Second Nun's Tale*, I do not wish to imply that representations of pagans and Jews are identical or interchangeable, or that the latter can be subsumed by the former. Rather, I would argue that representations of pagans, insofar as they are tools through which Christian authors construct representations of Christians, function in a parallel fashion to the way in which we have seen Christian authors use Jews as oppositional figures. A fundamental difference between the two terms is that Christianity sees itself as the fulfillment of the Jewish religion, not of any pagan one. To be sure, Christianity developed within a Roman context and the lives of the early saints, such as that of St. Cecelia, depict martyrs to tyrannical Roman oppression. But Christianity did not draw upon Roman culture for its theological basis in the same basic way as it relied (and continues to rely) on the Hebrew Bible. Furthermore, Rome later became Christian and we cannot think of Romans continuing to live as a minority within Christendom as the Jews did. Jewish particularity and its hegemonic relationship to a Christian universal is always tempered by Judaism's specific historical relationship to Christianity. In the context of the Prioress's and Second Nun's tales, representations of Jewish particularity in the *Prioress's Tale* inform the depictions of pagans in St. Cecelia's story, and the two representations then serve to reinforce each other and an idealized notion of Christian identity that is opposed to them and linked to ideas of fulfilled understanding, spirituality, and holiness.

Finally, the consideration of Lollardy brought into play by the *Man of Law's Endlink* can help us to understand better the context of the *Second Nun's Tale* and contemporary intersections of the terms "pagan," "Lollard," and "Jew." The Second Nun presents, within a thoroughly orthodox context, many of the same issues raised by the Wycliffite heresy. In contrast to the unlettered understanding valorized by the Prioress, the Second Nun stresses a learned and sophisticated understanding that is at odds with Lollard rhetoric of "lewd" folk but that shares their zeal for conversion and true access to the word of God. But the relationship of the *Second Nun's Tale* to Lollard controversy may be even more specific than this, because the Second Nun's depiction of pagan worship taps into contemporary debates over idolatry, an issue (as we have already seen) hotly contested by Lollards and their opponents. Wyclif condemned idolatry, which he took to mean the worshiping of an image itself, rather than what that idol signified. Wyclif attacked those, for example, who would address images of the Virgin as though they really were the mother of God. As W. R. Jones explains, Wyclif, in his *De mandatis divinis*, links "the heathen, the sorcerer, the Jew, the Saracen, and the heretic—all of whom worshiped false gods," arguing that this prohibition applies to all Christians as well.[106] The Lollards, following Wyclif, attacked what they saw as the worship of elaborate and costly religious images and statuary rather than the worship of the spirit of God. Jones notes that the "kindest thing that Lollards could say about images was that they were mere 'blynde stockys' and 'dede stoyns,' possessed of no marvelous power and, therefore, incapable of the wonders attributed to them by popular credulity."[107] One Lollard sermon argues, "And now men shulden be more gostly and take lesse hede to siche sensible signes, as dyden the apostlis of Crist, that by schort tyme and rewlis of goddis hestis and charite ledden men to hevene with-outen siche new peyntynges schewid by manes craft. For oure lord god dwellis by grace in gode mennes soulis, and, with-oute comparesone, bettere than all ymagis made of man in erthe, and bettere than alle bodies of seyntis, be the bones of hem never so gloriously shreynyd in gold."[108] This disregard for images is reminiscent of St. Cecelia's attack on Almachius. Like St. Cecelia, Lollards ask Christians to look upon the material world with discernment and understanding, separating the literal, dead, and cold from the living spirit. Again, I do not propose Lollard texts as direct sources for the *Second Nun's Tale*, but rather I suggest that we begin to see Lollard discourse as an essential component of our understanding of the debates over idolatry in which the categories and terms "pagan," "Lollard," and "Jew" each played important, interrelated roles. As Lynn Staley asserts of Cecelia in her excellent reading of this tale in the context of Wycliffism, "In effect, she tells Almachius that he must redefine his system of reality; she asserts a sharp division between the systems and codes of earth and heaven. . . . Her argument, which affirms the reality of the incorporeal and the blindness and folly of those who find a reality in what is mutable and unreal, suggests an unresolvable tension between the church and the world."[109] Staley's remarks demonstrate how Cecelia's sanctity intersects with discourses of reform, as we have seen in Lollard polemic that associates corrupt clergy with wicked Jewish clerks. As Christian writers of all different perspectives attempt to define the future path of the true church, they draw upon its past, engaging with Jewish and heathen particularities that a Christian universalism aims to subsume. The controversies over the use of religious imagery, like the debates over vernacular translation and its implications for exegesis, are at their core debates over the nature of representation and the relationship between signifier and signified, the letter and the spirit. How one interprets signs, be they written words or

religious statues, determines the nature of one's Christian identity—
"hermeneutics becomes anthropology."[110]

* * *

The *Shipman's Tale* presents a type of antihermeneutics. Its blurry moral
boundaries make it difficult to discern its "sentence," a problem stemming
from the tale's ambiguous usury. And, like a type of usury (or a translation
run amok), the Shipman's closing pun advocates a proliferation of tales/
tails and interpretations. The Prioress responds to the Shipman's excesses,
pinpointing the Jews as culprits. She draws upon a dichotomy between
Christian and Jew to make her point, even as she revises the dichotomy
between masculine and feminine within a Christian context. The Second
Nun further responds to the Prioress's portrayal of feminine piety, adjust-
ing to accommodate a more active, adult view of a Christianity in which
women play a founding role, but also drawing upon an opposition to Jewish blindness.

The ways in which these tales engage with the figure of the hermeneutical Jew are part of their tellers' self-presentation. Through the figure
of the Virgin and the scapegoating of the Jews, the Prioress presents a tale
that shows the important, albeit subsidiary, role of the feminine in Christian piety, a depiction important to her own standing among the pilgrims.
The Second Nun proposes a more radically egalitarian model of gender in
Christianity, one that also challenges an important element of the Prioress's self-presentation, her depiction of herself as unlearned.[111] The Second
Nun does, however, still draw upon an opposition to non-Christian blindness (and hence to Jewishness) in order to define Christian identity. The
Second Nun ultimately shows the compatibility of the feminine with
Christian understanding through her tale's protagonist and her own role
as learned translator. At stake for her is how religious women are perceived, and she makes clear her definition of the place of women in Christianity by emulating the work of St. Cecelia through her own "bisy"
translating of a story that is meant to instruct and to provide a Christian
role model.

The differences between the Prioress's and the Second Nun's depictions of ideal Christians show one way in which gender and Christian identity are negotiated within the *Tales* as a whole and also reveal a significant
crack in the edifice of a stable definition of Christianity created by the
reference to Lollards in the *Man of Law's Endlink*. Further implications of

this exchange and its manipulation of Pauline paradigms can be found in
the two tales that immediately follow the *Prioress's Tale*, those told by
"Chaucer," *Sir Thopas* and the *Melibee*, where questions of self-presentation, identity, and the stability of a Christian way of interpretation are
most fully highlighted. When the Prioress finishes her tale, the pilgrims
are somber and silent until Harry Bailley turns for the first time to Chaucer
and questions his identity directly, "What man artow?" (VII.695). The
Host requests a "tale of myrthe," but he implies that Chaucer's tale will
also be a confirmation of character, helping to identify Chaucer to the
other pilgrims. Judging from his "cheere," Harry Bailley expects "som
deyntee thyng" from Chaucer (VII.711). Chaucer then presents *Sir Thopas*, a tale so rambling and superficial that even the most determined of
exegetes would be hard-pressed to separate the grain from the chaff.[112]
Indeed, after attempting to listen to it, Harry Bailley finds the tale to be
simply excrement, a "drasty speche" (VII.923). Before offering another
tale, Chaucer provides his audience with a guide to interpretation:

> "Gladly," quod I, "by Goddes sweete pyne!
> I wol yow telle a litel thyng in prose
> That oghte liken yow, as I suppose,
> Or elles, certes, ye been to daungerous.
> It is a moral tale vertuous,
> Al be it told somtyme in sondry wyse
> Of sondry folk, as I shal yow devyse.
>   "As thus: ye woot that every Evaungelist
> That telleth us the peyne of Jhesu Crist
> Ne seith nat alle thyng as his felawe dooth;
> But nathelees hir sentence is al sooth,
> And alle acorden as in hire sentence,
> Al be ther in hir tellyng difference.
> For somme of hem seyn moore, and somme seyn lesse,
> Whan they his pitous passioun expresse—
> I meene of Mark, Mathew, Luc, and John—
> But douteless hir sentence is al oon.
> Therfore, lordynges alle, I yow biseche,
> If that you thynke I varie as in my speche,
> As thus, though that I telle somwhat moore
> Of proverbes than ye han herd bifoore
> Comprehended in this litel tretys heere,

> To enforce with th'effect of my mateere;
> And though I nat the same wordes seye
> As ye han herd, yet to yow alle I preye
> Blameth me nat; for, as in my sentence,
> Shul ye nowher fynden difference
> Fro the sentence of this tretys lyte
> After the which this murye tale I write.
> And therfore herkneth what that I shal seye,
> And lat me tellen al my tale, I preye." (VII.936–66)

The passage explains that the moral treatise that will be told, the "litel thyng in prose," has been told before, in "sondry wyse / Of sondry folk." Nevertheless the passage stresses the value of this retelling, which can be read as a reply to the Host's attack on *Sir Thopas*, a critical appraisal that focuses exclusively on form, ignoring, for better or for worse, narrative content. To illustrate a triumph of content over form, Chaucer chooses a serious and sacred example—the retelling of the Crucifixion, the "peyne of Jhesu Crist," by the various Evangelists, Mark, Matthew, Luke, and John. This example seems to refer to the retelling of earlier material, in this case, a retelling of the *Livre de Melibée et de Dame Prudence* by Renaud de Louens, itself a reworking of *Liber consolationis et consilii* of Albertanus of Brescia.[113]

Just as there is only one "sentence" that can be derived from the Passion, despite different Gospel versions of the event, so too will Chaucer's version of this tale, although not using the same words, express the same meaning and have the same value. In analogizing this retelling of the *Melibee* to the Gospel accounts of such a central Christian event, the Passion, larger issues of representation and truth are brought into play. This position understands representation as something that is at once superficial to inherent truth, the truth of the Passion, yet at the same time able to communicate that truth to an audience. Although the framing of the problem differs somewhat from the debates over vernacular translation examined earlier, the issue of representation is similar. The *Thopas/Melibee* link presents a firm belief in a central, holy truth, a "sentence" that can be conveyed by human beings through language and that remains unchanged by this medium. A similarity, then, between this view and a defense of vernacular translation like that found in the General Prologue to the Wycliffite Bible is that the medium, be it the choice of language or the course of narrative, is not the message—the message, the "sentence," has the potential and power to shine through no matter how it is conveyed.

Although I do not wish to argue that this link presents a "Lollard" view of representation, it clearly engages with issues raised by the debates over vernacular translation of the Bible, a context that the example of the Passion, so central to Christian identity and meaning, only serves to reinforce. The question of "sentence," then, is also, in somewhat altered terms and contexts, at the center of the debates over vernacular translation and literal meaning, which call into question the nature of Christian meaning itself, the best ways of conveying and understanding it, and which ultimately question who has the authority to control this meaning. The way that these questions of meaning are articulated in the *Canterbury Tales* is illuminated by Lee Patterson's powerful reading of the *Thopas/Melibee* sequence, which characterizes Chaucer's authorial self-presentation as that of a "child with a difference," a gesture through which Chaucer locates himself "outside" the "social whole."[114] Patterson pinpoints reflections on childhood and the child as a central thematic link between the two self-assigned tales, reading *Sir Thopas* as a "puerile" presentation of childhood and the *Melibee* as an example of pedagogical literature "that features as its narrative object an absent child."[115] Throughout the *Canterbury Tales*, Patterson argues, Chaucer "uses childhood to stage a problematic central to the act of writing."[116] Chaucer's representations of children function as representations of "a form of consciousness that is at the center of Chaucer's kind of poetry" and that is most fully developed in Fragment VII.[117] Given the problem of interpretation as framed in the *Thopas/Melibee* link, this has to do not only with writing in the sense of authorial creation, but also with the questions of interpretation and Christian understanding we have been exploring. I believe we can use Patterson's important insight into the role of the child figure in Fragment VII and in the *Canterbury Tales* as a whole to understand better the impact of the *Prioress's Tale*, as well as its representations of Jews, beyond the context of the tale and the Second Nun's response to it. In Patterson's reading, the Prioress's little clergeon comes to represent "psychological integrity, moral innocence, and ontological fullness," a figure that stands in opposition to "childishness as puerility, instability and mockery" as represented by the Prioress herself.[118] The little clergeon is the most fully developed of the child figures in Fragment VII. Like Sophie in the *Melibee* and the children of Ugolino of Pisa in the *Monk's Tale*, the clergeon is a victim, but he is also a central figure, a bright jewel gleaming in the heart of the dark and menacing Asian city, whose actions and desires are the most fully expressed and chronicled of the children depicted. In this way we could see the clergeon as the central figure of Christian childhood in Fragment VII, against which the other figurations are compared and contrasted. We have seen that the exalted figure of childhood represented by the clergeon is one of innocence that can nevertheless intuitively grasp "sentence." The little clergeon does not understand the words of the *Alma*, but he does understand their meaning on a fundamental level that transcends language. This spiritual understanding represents the triumph of pure Christian youth over the forces of evil, the devil, and the Jews.

Late medieval figurations of the child and childhood, of which Patterson provides numerous examples, include the Christ child and related representations of children under threat, figures of sacrifice and types of Christ, as in the Massacre of the Innocents, alluded to in the *Prioress's Tale* and linked there and elsewhere to ritual murder accusation narrative.[119] The movement of this triumph of youth echoes the movement of supersession, where the younger triumphs over the elder as Christianity triumphs over Judaism.[120] This supersession is encapsulated in the reference to the clergeon's mother as the "new Rachel," an allusion to Matthew's account of the Massacre of the Innocents at the hands of Herod (2:16–18), which includes in it the Jeremiah 31:15 description of Rachel weeping for her children as an example of inconsolable maternal grief. In Jeremiah, of course, this grieving figure is offered consolation directly from God in the next verse; her children, Israel, will be restored. Within the context of Jeremiah, Rachel takes on significance as a figure for the people of Israel as they struggle through a difficult moment in their history. Within Christian readings of Matthew, this crisis is used to illustrate a traumatic moment in the salvational history of the new Israel, understood to medieval Christian readers as the Christians, seen as the true inheritors of Jewish prophesy. In the Prioress's allusion, we have a Rachel who is doubly new, because Rachel is a type of the grieving mothers of the massacred Innocents, whereas the mother of the clergeon is another of her avatars. These Christian mothers are also offered divine consolation; through the power of Christ and through his sacrifice, their loss will also ultimately be restored, and in receiving this final consolation, they become new Rachels and, with their Christian children, the new Israel within this city in "Asie." In this way the allusion to Rachel is not a kind of ironic or disjunctive moment but is exactly in keeping with a narrative of supersession.[121] Rachel is not a post-Crucifixion Jew; she is an honored matriarch, a type of Christian motherhood. And through this figure and the figure of the divine mother, Mary, all Christians become children, the youthful inheritors of an outdated, superseded Jewish past, mourned for in their fallen state and restored through Christ.

The child becomes an important emblem of Christian identity in a dynamic in which the younger (the Christian) always takes precedence over the elder (the Jew). This dynamic informs the discourse of ritual murder accusation as a whole. If we consider somewhat later visual representations of ritual murder, such as those from the fifteenth and sixteenth centuries depicting the infamous case of Simon of Trent, we find the figures of young boys, naked or nearly naked, vulnerable, and often posed in a way that imitates Christ on the cross. The boy is surrounded by Jews, who use instruments of torture to reenact the Crucifixion, not only upon him, but figuratively upon every Christian. The Christian viewer is not simply drawn into the scene of ritual murder voyeuristically, but he or she is also called upon to identify with this suffering child, to feel him- or herself equally vulnerable to such evil and protected only by faith.[122] These visual representations make graphic the dynamic of the ritual murder accusation played out in the *Prioress's Tale*, where the assaulted child, a figure for Christ, comes to represent the entire Christian community as well. This symbolism is created not only through images of purity and impurity but through associations with notions of Christian understanding. Chaucerian fictional self-presentation as a child can be seen then as a response to the *Prioress's Tale* that is similar to the Second Nun's in that it avoids the Prioress's sentimentality while still celebrating the clergeon as a figure for the triumph of youthful Christian understanding and while still accepting the tale's account of demonized Jews who make the child a martyr.

*　*　*

By contrasting Christianity with an older, superseded Judaism, Christian writers create an important association between Christianity and youth, which in Fragment VII is inflected through representations of Christian understanding as youthful through the *Prioress's Tale*. These questions of understanding and "sentence" thread through Fragment VII, which Alan Gaylord has called "the literature group" because of the "thematic significance" of questions of "sentence" and "solaas" within it.[123] The fragment coheres not only through the broad theme of "the art of storytelling" that Gaylord suggests, but through the related themes of reading and interpretation in a Christian mode.[124] The Monk's endless repetition of the same tragic plot, for example, could be seen as revealing a failed model of the Christian reader who cannot see beyond these tragic patterns to the redemptive ascent of Christian comedy, the joy and consolation of Boethius. The Nun's Priest concludes his presentation of a fable world with an expression of unified doctrine: "For Seint Paul seith that al that writen is, / To oure doctrine it is ywrite, ywis" (VII.3441–42). This statement, echoed in Chaucer's "Retraction," has affinities to the *Thopas/Melibee* link. Admittedly, these thematics can be found throughout the *Tales*, but this fact does not undermine their significance in Fragment VII, but rather points to ways in which Fragment VII can be analyzed in relation to the *Tales* as a whole. The idea that all that is written is written for Christian doctrine appeals to the same type of understanding of an actual Christian truth that unifies a multitude of tales, just as the various accounts of the Passion in the gospels present the same "sentence."

The multiple layers of implication for the entire *Tales* of the exploration of "sentence" in Fragment VII is signaled by a moment in the *Thopas/Melibee* link whose meaning is contested by Chaucer scholars. What happens, for example, if following Robertson and Huppé, we read "tretys" in the link to stand not simply for the *Melibee*, but for the whole of the *Canterbury Tales*, as it does in Chaucer's *Retraction*? Even though this reading is extremely controversial, its implications for the question of "sentence" in the *Tales* are worth considering. By portraying himself as a pilgrim, Chaucer blurs the lines between fiction and "reality," foregrounding the fictional nature of the Canterbury frame and the complexity of its levels of meaning. If we read Chaucer's reference to "sondry folk" speaking in "sondry wyse" as applying not only to other tellers of the *Melibee* but also to the diverse voices of the pilgrims, then they become like the Evangelists, each of whom tells the story of Christ in different ways with "one sentence."[125] My point here is not simply to reproduce a Robertsonian reading of the *Tales*. I don't believe that a unified Christian meaning is produced or recommended here. Rather, it is the production of Christian meanings that is being explored and called into question. This questioning is explored through evocation of particular identities that are traditionally figured as threats to Christianity itself, such as heretics (here Lollards) and Jews, who are continually implicated in the representation of Christianity through a negotiation of self and Other. It is the sense of negotiation that is most important here; these figures are not simply outsiders, they become signs of internal dissent as well.

In addition, we can see this type of shaping negotiation in what has been read as the most orthodox and Christian of all the *Tales*, the *Parson's Tale*. Figuring prominently in that tale is the central event used to discuss the unity of "sentence" in the *Thopas/Melibee* link—the Passion—an event in which, in medieval representations including the *Parson's Tale*, the Jews play important implicit and explicit roles.[126] The *Parson's Tale* can be read as a guide to the making of a Christian; it is a step-by-step discussion of Penitence and draws from the penitential handbook form, even if most critics refer to the tale generically as a sermon.[127] One main inspiration for contrition, one of three "bihovely and necessarie" elements of Penitence, is the memory of the Passion: "The fifthe thyng that oghte moeve a man to contricioun is remembrance of the passioun that oure Lord Jhesu Crist suffred for oure synnes" (X.255). This focus on the Passion appears to be one of two instances when Chaucer departed significantly from one of his principal sources, Pennaforte's *Summa*.[128] The Parson details the Passion, through which Christ suffered for human sin, which the Parson figures as a rebellion against order in the human soul. Patterson has argued that this vision of the nature of sin, understood "ontologically, as a derangement of the divine order," is a characteristic that distinguishes Chaucer's tale.[129] In the *Parson's Tale*, the subordination of reason to sensuality is the essence of sin, a kind of disorder or "up-so-doun" that evokes the conditions of disorder through which the Christian self is undone.[130] The Parson describes this turmoil in the human soul, declaring, "For this disordinaunce of synful man was Jhesu Crist first bitraysed, and after that was he bounde, that cam for to unbynden us of synne and peyne. / Thanne was he byscorned, that oonly sholde han been honoured in alle thynges and of all thynges. / Thanne was his visage, that oghte be desired to be seyn of al mankynde, in which visage aungels desiren to looke, vileynsly bispet. / Thanne was he scourged, that no thynge hadde agilt; and finally, thanne was he crucified and slayn" (X.276–80).

These sins, which invert human order and pervert the human spirit, mirror the shocking topsy-turvy between how Christ should have been treated and the violence he suffered. If human sins and the disorder they create are the cause of the Passion, then the Jews, the alleged perpetrators of Christ's suffering, are embodiments of this sin, emblems of the disordered soul and agents of disorder. The Jews figure prominently in the late medieval meditations on the Passion, which Thomas Bestul has convincingly shown to be another generic influence on the tale.[131] The Parson repeats descriptions of attacks on the body of Christ, sometimes explicitly naming the Jews, sometimes only implying the actions against Jesus so often attributed to them. The Jews are mentioned explicitly, for example, at X.598, when the Parson asserts that those who swear despise the body of Christ "moore booldely than dide the cursede Jewes or elles the devel," exactly the sin that the Parson objects to in the *Man of Law's Endlink*. In X.276–80, he details the scorn, blows, and spit that Jesus endured before he was crucified but does not name the agents of these deeds as Jews, as he does in reference to their scorn in X.663.

Because of the strong accusation against the Jews as the killers of Christ, Jews are present not only in those moments when the Parson refers to them directly, but throughout his tale. As the ultimate agents of disorder and sin, they are the force against which the tale itself, a narrative of ordering and redemption, is shaped. If sin is explored on an "ontological" level in the tale, a specific understanding of Jewish particularity is a fundamental, indeed foundational, element of that ontology. The *Parson's Tale* dissects the disordered soul element by element and offers discrete and ordered remedy to create a saved, ordered, Christian soul. Reference to Jewish particularity is a crucial part of what shapes this desired model of Christian identity. The Parson ends the sermon with a vision of a whole, strong, Christian body that resembles the intact Christian body in the *Prioress's Tale*. In "the endelees blisse of hevene," which is the "fruyt of penaunce . . . the body of man, that whilom was foul and derk, is moore cleer than the sonne . . . the body, that whilom was syk, freele, and fieble, and mortal, is inmortal, and so strong and so hool that ther may no thyng aperyren it" (X.1076–8). These bodies are like the bodies of the martyrs, the clergeon and Saint Cecelia, whole and intact, preserved through faith against the ravages of disbelieving pagans and murderous Jews, a wholeness reflected in the resurrected body of Christ. The Jews, when seen as the agents of Christ's death, come therefore to shape an eternal, malevolent presence against which this vision of the Christian is created. They are disbelief and disorder, brought to order through Christianity, just as the books of the Bible, the Old and New Testaments, are brought to harmony and order through Christian doctrine.[132] It is this order that ends the Canterbury pilgrimage and that gives a guide to life itself as pilgrimage, the journey to "Jerusalem celestial," the goal of orthodox and heterodox Christians alike (X.51). The heavenly Jerusalem is the supersessionary culmination of the Christian narrative as the old, earthly Jerusalem of the Jews is transformed and redeemed. When Christian doctrine is fulfilled, then the Jews too will be "brought to order"—converted to Christianity.

In the *Parson's Tale*, then, where Jewish presence is important even when it is not explicitly named, we find a situation that is analogous to that of the *Tales* as a whole. Such notions of Jews and Judaism need to be taken more fully into account when examining late medieval English representations not only of Lollardy but of sin, of pagan culture, and of childhood, to name some examples discussed here. Feminist scholarship and queer theory have shown us the ways in which medieval (and modern) discourses of reading, writing, and other elements of the production of meaning are marked in crucial and complex ways by gender and sexuality. What I suggest through this chapter is that the hermeneutical Jew is also a presence that deserves more consistent and widespread examination beyond the ghetto walls. When we think of that "analogy of analogies," the analogy of the letter and the spirit—we need to take into account not only religious unity, or even questions of heresy, but Jewish difference, which relates to and inflects "other differences."[133]

To speak of the letter and the spirit or of questions of meaning without at least considering this element is to ignore the importance of the hermeneutical Jew in the history of Christian thought. The importance of the hermeneutical Jew to the *Canterbury Tales*, and in fourteenth-century English literature more generally, is not limited to those moments when demonized Jews leap out from beyond the ghetto walls with murderous intent. By breaking out of the ghetto, once and for all overcoming an obsession with Chaucer's own ultimately unknowable "anti-Semitic" or "philo-Semitic" views to analyze how notions of Jews and Judaism inflected key discourses in fourteenth-century English life and thought, shaping not only ideas about good and evil but about the very nature of meaning and being. The representation of Jews in the *Prioress's Tale* cannot be dismissed as isolated or ironic; rather, it shapes the contours of the entire Canterbury project, because it is in relation to Jews and Judaism that Christians continually negotiate what it means to be Christian.

4

Creating the Christian in Late Medieval East Anglian Drama

IN MEDIEVAL DRAMA, the Word is literally made flesh by human actors who bring moments in Christian history into the present. The drama provides particularly fertile ground to examine the roles of the hermeneutical Jew and the hermeneutical Woman in Christian self-definition because the drama is not simply a mimetic microcosm of a community but is itself a communal endeavor and site of cultural negotiation. Further, the dramatic medium highlights the constructed nature of identity as individuals depict actions and characters on the stage. Not only were female figures portrayed by men or boys in "drag," but the Jews represented were, of course, played by Christians in Jews' clothing, an illusion that calls attention to the construction of Christian identity itself.[1] This chapter presents readings of two late medieval East Anglian texts, the Croxton *Play of the Sacrament* and the N-Town "Nativity," focusing on the liminal dramatic figures of Jonathas the Jew and Salomé the midwife as representative types of the hermeneutical Jew and the hermeneutical Woman. Both *Croxton* and N-Town can be seen as presenting visions of Christian universality. *Croxton* enacts conversion, as doubting Jews and their corrupt Christian accomplices are brought to belief through miracles of the host. The N-Town cycle presents Christian history on a grand scale beginning with Creation and ending with Judgement Day. The visions presented in both plays, however, are neither static nor fixed. Their presentations of Christian truths depict Christian identity as made, not born. The representations of paradigmatic doubters, Jew and woman, are particular identities through and against which a vision of Christian identity is created.

Presentations of the hermeneutical Woman and the hermeneutical Jew in the drama differ from the nondramatic instances we have already considered because of the ways in which Christian truths and identities become "embodied" in the drama and the ways in which, in Ruth Evan's formulation, "The modes of address of staged bodies construct identities for their audiences."[2] Gail McMurray Gibson explains this in theological terms: "The Incarnation as vehicle of transcendence was for Paul the central Christian mystery; medieval biblical drama was likewise incarnate *mysterium*. The Word made flesh was both dramatic theory and theological justification of these biblical plays—plays by which, as Phillipe de Mézières explained, the mind stirred by visible signs and actions 'may be enabled to arrive at knowledge of the invisible and visible elements of God's mysteries.'"[3] At the core of this explanation of divine signs and actions is the Pauline paradigm of the letter and the spirit, with which the depictions of miracles and miraculous conversions of the medieval stage engage on a number of levels. These scenes present conversions of individuals, constructing them before an audience that it also intends to convert in the sense of bringing the audience to a fuller, deeper, renewed belief in Christian truths.[4] These conversions are brought to life in the physical world on the stage, but these scenes are also clearly constructed dramatizations meant to reveal the spirit that animates them—the Christian truth that they represent.

Dramatic reenactments of Christian mysteries engage participant and audience in ways that allow them to explore critical elements in Christian theology and also to delve into the most complex and controversial elements of that theology by reenacting critical moments of transition and truth, doubt and belief.[5] These fundamental tensions within Christian sacramental theology, those weighted dichotomies between inner and outer meaning, between signifier and signified, are also, as we have seen, core animating tensions within both the hermeneutical Woman and the hermeneutical Jew. Recent important work on medieval drama has emphasized that key figures presented, such as Christ and the Virgin, are sites of cultural negotiations for the communities from which audience and players are comprised.[6] The same is true for the hermeneutical Woman and the hermeneutical Jew as they are manifested on the medieval stage.

In the rich corpus of East Anglian drama, the hermeneutical Woman and hermeneutical Jew are linked in the physicality of their representation through what we might call the topos of the stricken hand.[7] The stricken hand is a typical punishment for lack of faith and reliance on carnal evidence, evidence that must, according to the analogy of the letter and the spirit, be transcended in order for Christian truth to be revealed. The hand, which can touch, grasp, and interact with the world, concretely symbolizes carnality. In the N-Town "Nativity" the skeptical midwife, Salomé, disbelieves that Mary can be both mother and virgin and insists on physically examining her in an attempt to prove that she is no longer a maid. As Salomé probes, her hand is stricken, shriveled, and rendered useless until she touches the swaddling clothes of the infant Jesus, at which time she is converted and her hand subsequently restored. In the Croxton *Play of the Sacrament*, Jonathas the Jew and his men put the host through a series of tortures, and as Jonathas grasps the host to throw it into a cauldron of boiling oil, it becomes attached to his hand. In a frenzied attempt to disengage himself from the host, Jonathas's arm is severed from his body. It is restored upon his subsequent conversion to Christianity, as the healing of his soul is mirrored in his bodily restoration.

These representations are clearly related to the story of doubting Thomas, who disbelieves Christ's Resurrection. Christ invites Thomas to probe his wounds, to "wade," in the words of N-Town, in his "hertblood," after which Thomas famously doubts no more.[8] But the events of the Thomas story, although they resemble the topos of the stricken hand, are not instances of it. Thomas is converted to Christian truth through physical contact with the corporeal suffering of Christ's body, but Thomas's own body is unscathed. "Others" are not so lucky. The doubting midwife and the doubting Jew, like Thomas, do not believe, but they are doubters with a difference—Jewish difference and the difference of gender. Jewish doubt, as we have discussed before, is an example of the origin questioning the end. The Jews' perceived and actual resistance to Christianity's religious truth claims are fundamentally destabilizing to Christianity itself. In this way, Jewish doubt is figured as a special case and a type of spiritual blindness that all other challenges, such as heretical challenges, must reference. Salomé presents another type of challenge. The midwife has a central and controlling role over another crucial type of origin—human reproduction—and is the representative figure of a world of "women on top," as the realm of childbirth, like no other in late medieval English culture, was an emphatically female domain within the male-dominated social order.[9] The midwife, who has authority in this female world, is the mistress of experiential knowledge that is barred to men, experience on which the lives of all born to woman depend.

These "other" doubters symbolically challenge social order by daring to touch and test holy bodies. As a result, their doubt is literally inscribed unto their own bodies as they are deformed or dismembered. Their hands, an emblem of carnal faith, is a sign of how these figures are "hermeneutically handicapped."[10] Only faith, without which one can never achieve

true interpretive triumph, can restore them to wholeness. Their restoration is tied to the transitional moment of conversion, when bodily fragmentation is cured through miraculous touch as the doubter becomes a
whole, believing Christian. The spiritual transition of conversion is represented then as a shift from division to unity. The drama embodies these
figures, and as Douglas's theory of the body as symbol would suggest, it
is the margins of these symbolic bodies that are the focus of theological
and cultural meaning.[11] As in the *Prioress's Tale*, we find the distinct binary
oppositions of the hermeneutical Jew carved into Jewish bodies, although
here, these Jews are given opportunity for conversion and healing.

Through these depictions of "fragmentation and redemption," the
movement of supersession is inscribed upon the bodies of these figures as
well as into the shape of the overall play.[12] The action in *Croxton* hinges
upon the miraculous conversion of doubting Jews, and the overall structure of the N-Town cycle is also shaped by supersession, as enactments
of events from the "Old Testament" are presented as types of the New
Testament, and biblical Jews actively proclaim Christian prophecy, voicing
justification of the supersessionary trajectory of Christian salvation history.
The cycle drama enacts typological understanding of the Old and New
Testaments, bringing to life that harmonization of the two testaments so
central to Christian hermeneutics.[13] The movement of supersession or of
conversion can be seen as a movement from disorder to order, from fragmentation to wholeness, and this is enacted in the larger organization of
the dramas we will be examining but also on the bodies that are represented on the stage, as doubters are brought from a spiritual disorder that
is reflected on their fragmented bodies to a spiritual harmony reflected in
their physical restoration. The conversions of the doubting Jew and the
doubting woman represent a shift of alignment of these figures from the
set of traits with which they are traditionally associated in Christian exegetical paradigms—carnality and the letter and the spiritual death of the letter—to the chain of associations that links the Christian, the spiritual, and
the masculine.

Through these staged conversions, the constructed nature of the
Christian is foregrounded. As they are presented in dramatic form, however, these representations of believers and doubters differ for the audience
in that the dramatic enactment, the embodiment on the stage of the carnal
and the spiritual, offers a very powerful invitation to assume not only the
attitude of the believer but also the place of the doubter.[14] This is perhaps
especially true for the actor who performs the role of the doubter, but also

for the audience member, who may experience reactions ranging from terror and outrage at the depicted assaults on holy bodies to a level of identification with the doubting tester. Doctrines such as the Incarnation and transubstantiation, at the center of the N-Town "Nativity" and *Croxton*, are fundamental tenets of the faith for pious late medieval English Christians, but they are also complex, Christian mysteries debated since their inception not only between Christians and non-Christians, but also among Christians themselves. They are beliefs that make the Christian, but they are not monolithic truths accepted identically by all Christians at all times.

Christian belief and Christian identity can, indeed, be understood as individualized and performative. Even miraculous conversion to Christianity must be accompanied by the performative rituals of confession, penance, and communion, which came increasingly to shape the lives of orthodox Christians in late medieval England.[15] These Christian rituals perform the hermeneutical paradigms that shape the category of the Christian in the exegetical tradition. Christian identity is therefore under construction, a fragile edifice that existed alongside, and yet in contrast to, Christian ideals of wholeness such as the eucharist and the intact virginal body of Mary. In the face of these Christian mysteries and in keeping with the performative nature of Christian ritual, *Croxton* and the N-Town "Nativity" invite audience members themselves to participate in the construction of Christian identity, to assume temporarily the place of the doubter and to negotiate the difficult models of the hermeneutical Jew and the hermeneutical Woman, whose presences stubbornly challenge the transformative Christian paradigm. It is through this experience that the audience is invited to embrace more fully Christian belief and to partake in a universal Christian community.

This dramatic construction of Christian identity before the audience offers great potential for spiritual growth, but it is also potentially disruptive. We have evidence of this explosive potential in one of the most tantalizing missing texts in the medieval English corpus, the York "Funeral of the Virgin" or "Transitus," in which an improbably named Jew, Fergus, attempts to defile the Virgin as she is borne on her funeral bier.[16] As Fergus reaches out to attack her, his arm is stricken and withered. In revelatory terror he cries for healing and, upon his conversion to Christian belief, his arm is restored. In the context of the Assumption story, this conversion also enacts supersession, because the Jew's turn to Christian truth is not only significant to him but has the larger impact of asserting the truth of

Mary's status as the mother of God, thereby also proving the truth of the supersession of Christianity over Judaism. In the York "Transitus," the Jew's body, fragmented through doubt and restored through faith as an emblem of Christian truth, becomes a site through which Christian doubt and truth is enacted. The Jew's hand becomes the ultimate emblem of carnality. He will lay his hands upon Mary to defile her, but these hands are finally overwhelmed by the truth of her body. Before the eyes of all, this truth is proved as the Jew converts and his body is restored.

This scene of disintegration and subsequent reintegration, like those in *Croxton* and the N-Town "Nativity," is not simply an easy expression of harmony, or of stability. These scenes each present destabilizing moments with the potential for creating disorder even as they seem to promote an ordered view of the Christian self. What we know of the York's "Transitus" play, in fact, comes from evidence that it led to provocation and disorder among members of the audience.[17] As both Anna Mill and Ruth Evans have discussed, the York "Transitus" was performed by both the linenmakers and the masons, and, in 1431, as part of a petition that tried to relieve them of their own pageant duties, the goldsmiths pointed to the precedent of the masons, who "have been grumbling (*murmurabant*) about their pageant 'ubi Fergus flagellatus est.'"[18]

In addition to complaining that the play came so late in the cycle that it could not often be performed in daylight, the masons charged that the Fergus play was "not in accordance with Holy Writ" and that it generated laughter and occasional fighting: "'[M]agis risum et clamorem causabat quam devocionem, et quandoque lites, contenciones, et pugne inde proveniebant in populo.'"[19] The moment of Fergus's bodily disintegration, which was probably enacted through "special effects," may have provoked unrest for any variety of reasons. I read this unrest and its accompanying laughter as associated with the scene not only as a moment that presents an act of defilement, but also as itself a representation of a moment of transition, a depiction of the struggle between faith and doubt. One cannot state definitively any kind of uniform "audience reaction" to such stagings of doubt. What is clear, however, is that the moment of bodily disintegration not only presents a symbolic representation of spiritual disruption but can create actual disruption among the spectators. At such a moment, the doubter, whose disbelief is manifest on his or her dismembered body, can be the object of scorn, revulsion, and dis-identification, but also the site of identification for the potential doubter in the audience.

In enacting scenes of miracles, or of critical events in the faith, the audience is invited to believe but also to participate vicariously in moments of violence to the faith and in moments of doubt. Claire Sponsler discusses the violence in medieval drama in relation to the social, economic, and political contexts of late medieval towns. Within late medieval urban communities, Sponsler argues, a premium was placed on "whole, intact bodies," which were literally the form of able-bodied workers needed for the economic life of the community and also served to represent symbolically a divinely ordained social order. The representation of the Crucifixion, which presents Christ's suffering, vulnerable, and mutilated body, can be read as a site or "gesture of resistance" against the symbolism of the whole body, a display that can be experienced in a variety of ways, including, significantly, "vicariously in acts of torture, dismemberment, and death."[20] As critics Jody Enders and Richard Homan have noted, dramatic moments such as the scenes surrounding the torture and crucifixion of Christ are too powerful to provoke any one uniform response.[21] Whether they serve to bring an audience member to a stronger adherence to faith or social order or to strengthen a sense of resistance, these are volatile moments that invite disruption and even laughter, as the records indicate that the York "Transitus" did.[22]

The disruption and the laughter that are potential in these scenes signal the difficulty of the transition they represent. At the very moment that the boundaries of the "zone of uninhabitability" are breached, as Christian and Jewish identities are blurred, the play not only invites a crossing of the abject over into the realm of the self but also raises the possibility of the self assuming the role of the abject, laughing at acts of defilement, as the Jews allegedly did.[23] It is in these moments, when potential splits in the Christian self are revealed and when the boundaries between Christian and Jewish are the most difficult to discern, that we can find both terror and laughter. The terror and laughter derive from the instability of Christian identity and indeed, considering this reaction through the theory of performativity, from the inherently constructed nature of identity itself.

I will argue that representations of the stricken hand as an emblem of carnality and stunted carnal belief in *Croxton* and N-Town are symbolic explorations of the breaching of the zone of uninhabitability and the boundaries between self and abject Other. These narratives of bodily dismemberment and healing are simultaneously narratives of supersession writ small. The body of the doubter is crippled or even torn apart, only to be healed and brought to wholeness through Christianity.[24] This can be seen as the movement of what one might call "Christian comedy" or comedy of the divine sort—a turning from sorrow to joy.[25] But these same scenes are also sites of potential riot and laughter, elements of disruption that could be seen as extraneous or out of keeping with the overall redemptive message of *Croxton* and N-Town. These comic, disruptive moments are exactly in keeping with the overall movement of supersession. Within them, the Christian is invited to assume the place of the doubter, a moment that highlights the constructed nature of Christian identity and stresses that Christians are, in Jerome's words, "made not born"—that Christianity is an identity that requires continual belief and continual action. The moments of disruption occur as the limits of this identity are tested, and indeed, the limits and nature of Christian identity are the very subject of the Croxton *Play of the Sacrament*.

Croxton

The Croxton *Play of the Sacrament* is a mid-fifteenth-century East Anglian drama that Gail McMurray Gibson has convincingly linked to Bury St. Edmunds.[26] Scholars have made compelling arguments that *Croxton* was directed at the Lollard heresy and that the play's Jews are meant to represent Lollards.[27] This argumentation has sometimes unfortunately been pressed to the point where the Jews represented in the play become "Jews," mere referents for Lollards or for "generic" doubters to the exclusion of also acting as referents to actual Jews, expelled from England in 1290. I have argued elsewhere that *Croxton* alludes to the very specific history of the Bury Jews, including the ritual murder accusation lodged against them in 1181.[28] And, as Chapter 3 makes clear, representations of Jews and Lollards shape each other in late medieval English discourse. Both terms are referents in contemporary debates about the nature of Christianity and Christian identity, debates that revolve around the way in which the signifier and the signified are supposed to interact in scriptural exegesis, religious images, and the sacrament of the eucharist. Here, however, I want to focus not on the Lollard context for this play but on an important yet overlooked context, the play's Spanish setting, which is crucial to an understanding of the centrality of conversion in the play and the play's exploration of the construction of Christian identity.[29]

The Banns of the Croxton *Play of the Sacrament* announce the origins of the host desecration story that will be performed:

Vexillator 2: S[o]uereyns, and yt lyke yow to here þe purpoos of þis
    play
  That [ys] representyd now in yower syght,
Whych in Aragon was doon, þe sothe to saye,
  In Eraclea, that famous cyté, aryght—
  Therin wonneth a merchaunte off mekyll myght,
Syr Arystorye was called hys name,
  Kend full fere with mani a wyght,
Full ⌐fer⌐ in þe worlde sprong hys fame.[30]

Stephen Spector has asserted that "the localized setting of the *Play of the Sacrament* is only superficial."[31] I believe, however, that the play's setting in Aragon in 1461, a divergence from continental sources, is important, irrespective of how we might read that date in relation to the creation or performance of the play itself. To regard the Spanish location as "superficial" or arbitrary doesn't give credit to the play's creator(s), nor does it recognize the magnitude and importance of questions of Jewish and Christian identity in Spain in the late fourteenth and early fifteenth centuries.[32]

Occurrences in Spain were indeed at the center of questions of Jewish conversion to Christianity in Western Europe and at the center of controversy over how Jewish and Christian identities could be determined.[33] B. Netanyahu asserts that "parallel to the Spanish tradition of Jew hatred there ran a tradition of hatred for Jewish converts."[34] The issue of the Jews and of Jewish converts to Christianity in Spain had been a point of contention since as early as the Visigothic period and had always been tied to political and economic contexts. Monarchic struggle and power struggles within and between urban centers helped to fuel the violence that led to the mass conversions of Spanish Jews to Christianity in 1391 and in 1412. After these two waves of conversions, the number of converts in Spain and their growing political and economic power has made the status and beliefs of Jews and converts in fifteenth-century Spain no less complicated for modern scholars to discern than it was for contemporary authorities, Christian and Jewish alike. There were not only many Jews who converted under threat of death, some of whom later returned to Judaism or became crypto-Jews, known as *conversos* or *marranos*, but also many who converted voluntarily and some who remained Jewish. For those who underwent the very common occurrence of forced conversion, the rabbis had a specific term, *anusim*.[35] The number of conversions, their circumstances, and the category of "New Christian," or recent convert, created difficulties for both Christian and Jewish authorities, making the question of "which is the Christian here? and which is the Jew?" one that raged in Spain in the 1460s, with works such as Alfonso de Espina's *Fortalitium Fidei* propagating crude and vicious attacks against the Jews, including multiple tales of ritual murder and the charge of host desecration emerging from the Paris account of 1290 that is at the root of the host desecration charge.[36]

Attacks on the *conversos* and on the Jews only became increasingly more heated as the Inquisition gained in momentum. One way of understanding the expulsion of the Jews in 1492 is to argue that, ultimately, the unity and uniformity demanded by an idealized view of Christendom, a view that concurred with the economic and political aims of those who wished to expel the *conversos* from Spain, could not sustain the ambiguity and paradox of having both *conversos* and/or actual Jews in its midst. And, indeed, it was the ambiguous status of the New Christians and the danger of the converts lapsing back into Judaism that can be seen, at least in part, as the reason for Spain's eventual mass expulsion of the Jews in 1492. The magnitude of the Spanish situation and its particular focus not only on Jews but on Jews who converted to Christianity, make it a significant setting for *Croxton*, a play that delves into the very question of the determination of Christian identity. The motives for the persecution of the Spanish Jews and *conversos* are complex; it does seem clear, however, that to write of Jews and conversion in Spain in the fifteenth century was to draw upon a context of contested and ambiguous identities. The Spanish situation tested the boundaries between Christian and Jew. Without recognizing how this central conundrum of Jewish-Christian relations manifests itself in specific historical contexts, such as that of fifteenth-century Spain or fifteenth-century East Anglia, it becomes easy to lose track of what "Jewish conversion" signifies both in the abstract and in the particular.

The idea that the religious turmoil in Spain might be known to the author and/or audience of the *Play of the Sacrament* is a realistic possibility. In the fifteenth century, English trade with Spain was a significant part of an international "network" in which the Low Countries were also integrally involved.[37] Writing of historical accounts of trade with Spain, Wendy Childs has noted that it was "arguably as important and certainly as old as many others in England's economy, and one which formed a constant underlying contact between the people of the two countries, above which the better-studied military and political turbulence eddied."[38] *The Libelle of Englyshe Polycye*, a poem that first appeared in the mid-to-late 1430s, provides a list of the important merchandise imported from Spain:

> Knowe welle all men that profites in certayne
> Commodytes called commynge oute of Spayne
> And marchandy, who so wyll wete what that is,
> Bene fygues, raysyns, wyne, bastarde and dates,
> And lycorys, Syvyle oyle and also grayne,
> Whyte Castell sope and wax is not in vayne,
> Iren, wolle, wadmole, gotefel, kydefel also,
> (For poyntmakers full nedefull be the ij.)
> Saffron, quiksilver; wheche Spaynes marchandy
> Is into Flaundres shypped full craftylye
> Unto Bruges as to here staple fayre.[39]

The author, who is encouraging a policy of increased English mastery of the "narowe see" (l. 7) speaks of the crafty trade relations between Spain and Flanders, who are "as yche othere brothere" (l. 86) and who are as interwoven in their trading relations with each other and with England as the superior English wool that is woven in with Spanish wool to improve the latter's value (ll. 98–101). Trade with Spain is also mentioned by John Fortescue (1394–1476), who provides a list of Spanish imports in "The Commodytes of England," including "1 Oyle, 2 Wyne, 2 Salte, 4 Honye, 5 Wexe, 6 Conysell, 7 geane, Cordewayne."[40] In terms of English exports to Spain, the wool trade, in which Bury was very much engaged, was central, with wool and later finished cloth as well being the English mainstay.[41] Bury merchants marketed both "raw wool and finished cloth" to Iberia and maintained business and official contacts with their foreign trading partners.[42]

When the Spanish context is considered, the actions in the Croxton play appear in a new light. We have understood the hermeneutical Jew as a figure crafted in the interest of Christian self-definition, and the question of Christian self-definition is precisely what *Croxton* explores. Although the *Croxton* Jews convert, the questions of what conversion is and what constitutes a Christian are not easily resolved. In its two main characters,

Aristorius the Christian merchant and Jonathas the Jew, *Croxton* presents figures that, despite their different religious affiliations, are remarkably similar.[43] The striking similarities between Aristorius and Jonathas are built into the very structure of the Croxton play, extending not only to what these characters say but also to how they say it. Aristorius presents himself in the boasting fashion employed by the familiar dramatic characters of Herod and Pilate. He is a merchant renowned throughout the world for his riches and his trading prowess. Aristorius's self-definition is framed with mentions of Christ, but these framing references seem a kind of lip service, especially because the audience already knows from the Banns of the betrayal that will occur. Aristorius's nominal Christianity therefore appears in an inevitably ironic light even before he speaks:

> Now Cryst, þat ys our Creatour, from shame he cure vs;
>   He maynteyn vs with myrth þat meve vpon þe mold;
> Vnto hys en[d]elesse joye myghtly he restore vs,
>   All tho þat in hys name in peas well them hold;
>   For of a merchante most myght therof my tale ys told,
> In Eraclea ys non suche, woso wyll vnderstond,
>   For off all Aragon I am most myghty of syluer and of gold—
> For and yt wer a countré to by, now wold I nat wond. (ll. 81–88)

Aristorius's speech opens with a verbal gesture that suggests a kind of conversion from "shame" to "endelesse joye" but ends with lines that reveal a focus on earthly powers. In the next stanza Aristorius then lists, in a kind of alphabetical order, some forty foreign locales in which he trades with many peoples, including the "Jewes jentle" (l. 105). Subsequent perfunctory thanks to God for his riches and success are followed by a boast of how Aristorius's curate, Isoder, lives to serve him. Aristorius mentions that he will worship Christ and not speak against him, but, as the audience already knows, he will betray Christ readily if the price is right. Aristorius's vices are contagious. Isoder concerns himself more with luxuries than with duties. Aristorius's corrupt clerk's symbolic name, Peter Paul, recalls two founders of the Church, implying an instability in the contemporary ecclesiastical hierarchy that perverts the work begun by these early saints.

Jonathas the Jew's first appearance on stage structurally echoes that of Aristorius. Instead of the long, rhyming, and alliterative lists of trade locations, the audience hears a stylistically similar list of all the marvelous material goods—thirty-six different kinds of jewels, materials, and spices—

that the Jew Jonathas possesses. Jonathas also begins his lines to the audience with a mention of his "god"—in this case, the prophet Mohammed:[44]

> Now, almyghty Machomet, marke in þi magesté,
>   Whose lawes tendrely I have to fulfyll,
> After my dethe bryng me to thy hyhe see,
>   My sowle for to save yff yt be thy wyll;
>   For myn entent ys for to fulfyll,
> As my gloryus God the to honer,
>   To do agen thy entent yt shuld grue me yll,
> Or agen thyn lawe for to reporte. (ll. 149–56)

Jonathas acts against a Christian God, attempting to prove false the sacrament of the eucharist. His exact motivations for the desecration are blurry, but although his attack is, from a Christian perspective, a perverse blasphemy, it is at least more consistent than Aristorius's cheap sell-out. The similarities in the style, tone, and contents of Aristorius's and Jonathas's speeches are, however, striking.

After their introductions and the unfolding of the plot to test and torture the eucharist, Jonathas and Aristorius are paired on the stage. They greet cordially, equally glad to do business with one another. Absent is any show of antagonism. One only need think briefly of Antonio and Shylock's first barbed encounter on the Rialto to imagine what this scene could have been.[45] Instead, Jews and Christians seem to intermingle freely for purposes of profit, and here lies the potential for the erosion of Christian identity. And when so paired, Aristorius and Jonathas do not actually seem very different; both have betrayed and sinned against the host, blurring the lines between definitive Christian and Jewish identities. Both are corrupted by wealth and linked to the very places and goods they have alliteratively itemized before the audience.

By the play's end, however, an important difference between the two merchants does emerge in the consequences of their conversions. Sarah Beckwith observes that "[i]n *Croxton* the figure of the Jew, the archetypal outsider, is brought inside, where he is not executed but not converted."[46] When the oven into which the Jews have thrust the host bursts and Jesus appears, the Jews are immediately converted, kneeling before the "image" of Christ (l. 716b). As one of them, Jason, exclaims, they are baptized in their own tears: "Lacrimis nostris conscienciam nostram baptizemus!" (l.

749). Jesus then commands, "Ite et ostendite vos sacerdotibus meis," [Go and present yourselves to my priests] (l. 765), and the Jews go and then "knele styll" (l. 797b) before the bishop. The bishop enters the Jews' house and changes the image of Jesus back into bread in a kind of inversion of the mass accompanied by the hymn, "O sacrum convivium."[47] Then the Jews, together with Isoder and Aristorius, all accompany the bishop into the church. Aristorius is "converted" in the sense of deepening and truly embracing his Christianity, confessing that he sold the host out of "lucre of mony" and asking to do penance (l. 902). The bishop replies;

> Now for thys offence that þou hast donne
>   Aȝens the Kyng of Hevyn and Emperowr of Hell,
> Ever whyll þou lyuest good dedys for to done
>   And neuermore for to bye nor sell:
>   Chastys thy body as I shall the tell,
> With fastyng and prayng and other good wyrk,
>   To withstond the temtacyon of fendys of hell. (ll. 912–18)

The bishop here admonishes Aristorius not to buy or sell, referring not only to his selling of the host but to the very mercantile activities that put him into contact with the Jews in the first place, and that have defined his identity up to this point. Aristorius converts to a new way of living:

> Into my contré now wyll I fare
>   For to amende myn wyckyd lyfe,
> And to kep þe people owt of care
>   I wyll teache thys lesson to man and wyfe.
>
> Now take I my leave in thys place,
>   I wyll go walke my penaunce to fullfyll. (ll. 972–78)

His life will now revolve around teaching. He will go among his people to amend his ways and to keep his people from harm, teaching one and all about what has occurred, a way of life that will also keep him from the trading activities that first led him into spiritual peril.

For his part, Jonathas begs for "generall absolucion" (l. 930). All the Jews kneel and each confesses a part in the host desecration, verbally repeating their actions for the audience. The stage directions then indicate that the bishop is to "crysten" officially the Jews with "gret solempnyté" (l. 952b). After this christening, which also involves a separation from the powers of Hell, Jonathas is referred to as "Ser Jonathas," indicating a new identity. But neither this newly minted Christian nor the other Jewish converts will remain long among their new coreligionists. Ser Jonathas announces,

> Now owr father and byshoppe þat we well knaw,
>   We thank yow interly, both lest and most.
> Now ar we bownd to kepe Crystys lawe
>   And to serue þe Father, þe Son and þe Holy Gost.
>   Now wyll we walke by contré and cost,
> Owr wyckyd lyuyng for to restore:
>   And trust in God, of myghtys most,
> Neuer to offend as we haue don befor.
>
> Now we take owr lea[v]e at lesse and mare—
>   Forward on owr vyage we wyll vs dresse;
> God send yow all as good welfare
>   As hart can thynke or towng expresse. (ll. 960–71)

Like Aristorius, Jonathas and the Jews will walk out their penance, traveling and spreading the message of their new belief. I find the play's final depiction of the fates of the Jews and Aristorius somewhat ambiguous, but there is a distinction in their fates in that the Jews pledge what sounds like a wandering exile. Aristorius's penance is figured as a homecoming, the same type of return that the conversion of a Christian within Christianity, a stronger embrace of the faith, entails. Despite future wanderings and the continual repetition of what has transpired through his planned retellings, Aristorius will dwell in "his" country. The Jews are converted, but they will remain perpetual foreigners on a penitential "vyage," leaving a community to which they did not belong in the first place. Ambiguous Jewish presence threatens the final stability and unity upon which the resolution of the play's action depends. The play ends with a feeling of unity, but it is a unity specific to a particular vision of the Christian, one that finally cannot acknowledge Christianity's Jewish origin or contain Christians with Jewish origins, a situation that reflects the play's Spanish setting. And, indeed, losing track of the Jewish may be precisely one of the critical moves that shape *Croxton*.

In his analysis of the Jew as a "figure of conversion" in modern English literature, Michael Ragussis shows how Christian comedic form, understood through the very kind of reversal from sorrow to joy that undergirds the movement of supersession, ultimately excises the Jewish as a kind of potentially threatening growth, even as Jewish conversion to "benignity" is portrayed.[48] The most famous example of this, as we will see in the following chapter, is Shylock in Shakespeare's *The Merchant of Venice*. Forcibly converted in the fourth act of this comedy, Shylock disappears and is absent entirely from the obligatory conjugal resolutions of Act V. The text cannot sustain his presence. Shylock's expulsion becomes a key part of a long tradition of representations of Jewish conversion.

Writing of Maria Edgeworth's *Harrington*, a nineteenth-century contribution to this tradition, Ragussis argues, "The sudden departure of the Jewish characters . . . is not solely, or even primarily, a solution to the formal problem of closure. . . . These departures are important political markers; they locate the position that the Jewish minority occupies in relation to the hegemonic or Christian community. In the tradition of comedy, in which the regeneration of the community is represented through a festive wedding at the end, the departure of the Jew signals that he or she has no place in the reconstituted community."[49] The Croxton play ends not with conjugal rites but with another sacrament of union, the eucharist, which can be read as a type of ritual closure. The play's conclusion in fact represents two rituals that are the center of Christian identity: baptism and communion. Like the sacrament of marriage, that one speech-act that creates union, baptism, is, by definition, a one-time event, a radical turning, an embrace of Christian identity marking entrance into the universal Christian community promised in Galatians 3:28, itself a baptismal formula.

Communion is also a ritual of identity. Miri Rubin argues persuasively for the eucharist as the locus of the creation of Christian identity: "So we can observe from the late twelfth century the creation of a systematic and necessary Other to that which was emerging increasingly clearly as the normative. And this is a process fundamental to the creation of any identity, in a confrontation of what is and what ought to be, through the construction of what is not and ought not to be. As the eucharist emerged in its central symbolic role, it was the inevitable locus for this construction."[50] At the center of the attempt to create clear boundaries for Christian identity is the eucharist, which, through the iterative ritual of the mass, acts as the center through which an idealized Christian identity is meant to be constructed—an identity that should be able to create clear boundaries between figures such as Aristorius and Jonathas. The echoes of the celebration of the mass that conclude the play and the transformation of the host also enact iteratively Christ's identity and the identity of the Christian community who partake ritually in his body. But, as the representation of Jewish conversion in the play shows, Jewish participation in the miracle of the host, the mass-like ceremony at the end of the play, or even in baptism does not result in a complete absorption into the body of the Christian. The Croxton play's closure is ultimately predicated on Jewish absence. Finally, there seems to be no place for the Jews in the Croxton play, despite, or perhaps because of, the strong similarities between the Jews and corrupt Christians. The Christian community, despite a basis in universal inclusion through conversion, seems unable to completely absorb Jewish particularity, which functions to represent doubt in the play.

Bodily imagery is central to *Croxton's* exploration of Christian identity and potential threats to it.[51] The play shows how an obsession with the mercantile and the pursuit of wealth can damage and harm all types of bodies—actual human bodies, the holy body of the eucharist, and the corporate Christian body politic that the host both represents and protects. Just as the body of Chaucer's little clergeon presents an image of Christian wholeness, so too is the host represented as unified and whole in the face of attack, in contrast to the bodies of the Jewish attackers, which are permeable and ripped apart.[52] The centerpiece of this symbolism in *Croxton* is the scene in which Jonathas the Jew attacks the host and loses his hand. The eucharist is stolen from the boundaries of the Church and then its physical borders are pierced and defiled. This threatening moment is followed by the exaggerated breakdown of the threatener's body, that of Jonathas the Jew. After the Jews have initially stabbed the host and witnessed it bleeding, they plan to throw it into a pot of boiling oil, but Jonathas is unable to release the host in order to fling it into the cauldron:

> And I shall bryng þat ylke cak
> And throwe yt in, I undertake.
> Out! Out! yt werketh me wrake!
>   I may not awoyd yt owt of my hond.
> I wylle goo drenche me in a lake.
> And in woodnesse I gynne to wake!
>   I renne, I lepe ouer þis lond. (ll. 497–503)

The stage directions indicate that Jonathas "renneth wood, with þe Ost in hys hond" (l. 503b). His short, frantic lines, their comic rhythms emphasized through emphatic end rhyme, create a farcical mood that highlights the host's assault on the boundaries of Jonathas's body. This focus on corporeal boundaries climaxes in the topos of the stricken hand as the Jews, reenacting the Crucifixion, nail the eucharist to a post. The result is the severing of Jonathas's hand from his body in a break as radical and dramatic as conversion itself.

Jonathas's body metaphorically represents the state of his faith. Before conversion he needs empirical proof to believe, a desire that leads him to the wicked torture of the host. But, after he sees and physically experiences incontrovertible evidence of the power of the host, his body, once riven by doubt, is brought to wholeness. The comic potential in this scene, underscored by the play's slapstick portrayal of Jonathas, invites the audience to laugh at him, but their position vis-à-vis Jonathas is also potentially more complex. Perhaps an audience member has also doubted: such an individual is invited to witness the test the Jew performs and to vicariously experience the moment of doubt. The scene resembles the disruptive attack of Fergus the Jew because it could also potentially make the audience feel somehow connected to the torturing Jew, identifying with the doubter rather than with the tortured body of Christ.[53]

The scene tests the limits of the "zone of uninhabitability," symbolically representing those boundaries through depiction of Jonathas the Jew. When the audience members laugh at the depictions on stage, they are like the Jews who tortured Christ, begging these questions: If one could observe this host desecration and laugh, what subject position would one be in? And even if one does not laugh, what does it mean to observe this event? How close is one to the subject position of the torturer by witnessing the torture? Is spectatorship a type of complicity?[54] These questions are central to *Croxton*, which foregrounds the constructed nature of the Christian. Because it is possible for one who is at least nominally a Christian to step outside the bounds of Christian behavior, as Aristorius certainly does and as one who laughs at the host scene seems to do, a more fragile, constructed Christian emerges, a Christian created through acts, made, not born. This fragility seems to necessitate the ejection even of "converted" Jews. For if one who believes that he is a Christian may assume the position of the torturing Jew, how much more so one born a Jew? One might even see this potential laughter as evoking the Jew, only then to exorcise this figure through a closure that demands that the Jewish remain occluded.

Critics are divided on the humor inherent in the Jonathas scenes, but all find intentional humor in the scenes that immediately follow—the appearance of the quack Doctor Brundyche and his smart-aleck servant boy, Colle.[55] Some read this scene as a comic "interpolation," a type of comic relief following the tension of the desecration scenes. The Colle and Brundyche scenes echo the rest of the play through an emphasis on blindness and the threat this blindness can hold for the community, both literally and figuratively.[56] Colle appears onstage in search of his master, informing all in a series of comic speeches that Brundyche is a drunken frequenter of taverns, who kills more patients than he cures. Brundyche, whose lines end in comical triple rhyme, appears and orders Colle to make this "proclamacionem" advertising his services (l. 607b):

All manar off men þat haue any syknes,
    To Master Brentberecly loke þat yow redresse.
    What dysease or syknesse þat euer ye haue,
    He wyll neuer leue yow tyll ye be in yow[r] graue.
    Who hat þe canker, þe collyke, or þe laxe,
    The tercyan, þe quartan, or þe brynny[n]g axs—
    For wormys, for gnawyng, g⌈r⌉yndy[n]g in þe wombe or in þe
        boldyro—
    All maner red eyn, bleryd eyn, and þe myegrym also,
    For hedache, bonache, and therto þe tothache—
    The colt-euyll, and þe brostyn men he wyll undertak,
    All tho þat [haue] þe posse, þe sneke, or þe tyseke—
    Thowh a man w[e]re ryght heyle, he cowd soone make hym sek.
    Inquyre to þe colkote, for ther ys hys loggyng,
    A lyttle besyde Babwell Myll, yf ye wyll haue und[er]stondyn[g].
        (ll. 608–21)

Colle's rhythmic list, which stylistically echoes the opening speeches of Aristorius and Jonathas, describes the numerous possible ailments that can afflict the human body, compounding the play's focus on the physical dismemberment of Jonathas the Jew and the attack on the holy body of Christ. Brundyche, in contrast to Christ, the true physician, won't be able to cure Jonathas.[57] Tavern-frequenter that he is, he is spiritually sick, unable to heal bodies, much less spirits.

Colle's comic speeches deflate and challenge not just any master, but a foreign one from Brabant, a locale with specific meaning for an East Anglian audience.[58] We can see in this quack doctor the comic assertion of a normative English or local identity that complements an ideal Christian identity and that exists in contrast to foreign identity.[59] Quack foreign physicians are stock in what E. K. Chambers calls "English folk drama," but medical traditions were also part of local Bury St. Edmunds culture.[60] Robert Gottfried notes that Bury had a medical tradition that preexisted its numerous hospitals; the abbey's main shrine had always been thought to have curative power. The play makes reference to the hospital at Saint Saviours, located near Babwell Mill, and Bury itself was something of a medical center, boasting six hospitals; however, it seems rather unlikely that Bury had a physician from Brabant; the majority of immigrants from the Low Countries seemed most involved in the trades. But these immigrants were notable in Bury, settling "in increasing numbers in East Anglia in the fifteenth century" to such an extent that, in 1477, the weavers' and linendrapers' guilds created bylaws that restricted the newcomers, measures designed at least in part to keep out competition from highly qualified workers from the Lowlands.[61]

This foreign presence was related to Bury's role as a trading center. At a time when many other towns were in decline, centrally situated Bury, with its Great Market, drew merchants from all over England and Italy and the Low Countries.[62] Robert Gottfried describes a struggle for power between an increasingly prosperous population of wealthy burgesses and the once prosperous Abbey, which slipped continually deeper into economic and political decline throughout the fifteenth century. This tension may be expressed in the play through its linking of spiritual corruption to the pursuit of gain. Commerce brings Christians into contact with Jews, and once they are together, the play shows, it is sometimes difficult to tell them apart. The opening boasting speeches of Aristorius and Jonathas point to this type of corruption, which also infects Brundyche. Colle says of his master: "Men that be masters of scyens be profytable" (647), stressing that the doctor's true work is not healing, but gain.[63] The corruption fostered by greed threatens the body of the Christian community just as the Jews threaten the body of Christ and Colle's litany of illnesses threatens human bodies. As Mervyn James has shown, the human body served as an important medieval metaphor for the body of the community; Colle's detailed litany of bodily ills parallels the social ills threatening his community and, through stylistic echo, ties these ills to mercantile ambition.[64]

The play further underscores the similarities between the Jews, the corrupt merchant, and the corrupt doctor through Colle's emphasis on a specific human ailment, the doctor's blindness. For the doctor, as Colle tells us, day, night, and candlelight are indistinguishable: "He seeth as wele at noone as at nyght, / And sumtyme by a candelleyt / Can gyff a judgyment aryght— / As he þat hathe noon eyn" (ll. 537–40). The good physician from Brabant is so blind, seemingly from drink, that he is quite literally unable to see, just as the Jews are spiritually blind doubters, who need to see with their literal eyes in order to believe in Christ, a state linked to the corruption of Aristorius, blinded by gold. Just as the representation of pagans in the *Second Nun's Tale*, by echoing the *Prioress's Tale*, builds upon the prevalent accusation of Jewish blindness, so too does *Croxton* build upon that same accusation to create a model of spiritual corruption that encompasses sinners beyond the Jews at the same time that it makes the Jews paradigmatic sinners.

The Colle episode is not then a scathing attack on foreigners, but a way of connecting foreigners and "bad Christians," obsessed with trade and profit, to the figure of the Jew, an instance of the connection between Jews and other particular identities that adds another layer of meaning to the already established readings of this play as an anti-Lollard critique. It is in opposition to these figures of difference that a normative idea of Christian identity is created.[65] It is not, then, simply whimsy or slap-stick that brings comic potential to the host desecration and Colle scenes. These scenes establish the normative and comic potential that emerges through playing with oppositions to this norm. The comic scenes challenge the boundaries of "what is and what ought to be" and "what is not and what ought not to be," and in this way, their performance of the boundaries of identity demonstrates both what Christian identity should be and the fragility of this identity.[66] It is not simply that the Jew is recalcitrant, but that the Christian is something under construction, an edifice raised against imagined assaults from demonized Jews and internal corruption. In opposition to this Jewish intransigence is a kind of Christian impermanence, fragility, and constructedness. This view of the individual Christian may have existed alongside, and yet in contrast to, a Christian ideal such as the eucharist and a body of Christ and a body of the Church that is whole and incorruptible. The Christian individual is more like the human body attacked by the litany of diseases that Colle recites—it is subject to a physical corruption that mirrors spiritual corruption—both can only be healed through faith.

It is in moments of crossing between these two poles, represented by the eucharist and the Jew and scenes of conversion, of transubstantiation, and of disintegrating bodies, that the play's comic potential and its goal, the exploration of Christian identity, are most fully expressed. It is finally, however, a model of wholeness that the overall Christian comedic form of the play embraces. The play's need for closure, for the representation of a whole and stable Christian community, cannot long sustain the ambiguity of the risible, and because of this the Jews, converted or not, cannot remain in the midst of Christians. As scholars have often noted, there were almost certainly no actual Jews who saw this play, much less participated in it. The Jews were expelled from Bury St. Edmunds in 1190 and from all of England a century later, but the figure of the Jew was still present and its relationship to the Christian community continually examined. In addition, the play is set in a locale, fifteenth-century Spain, where actual Jewish presence as outsiders and as insiders did test the limits of Christian identity.[67] The historical setting is therefore charged with contemporary political, as well as spiritual, meaning.

The Jew, that abjected Other at the origin of Christian identity, thus becomes the fundamental model for signifying difference in this play, just as the figure of the Jew is the occluded yet essential center at the base of Christian divine comedy.[68] The universalist closure of Christian comedy cannot fully accommodate Jewish particularity, which is never fully subsumed and must be excised or remain uneasily, and perhaps painfully, a nagging thorn in the theological side. The centrality of the figure of the Jew stems from the originary relationship between Judaism and Christianity—the Jew is that uncanny threat, the ultimate model of the outsider within. *Croxton* does not, however, simply act as the vehicle for the expression of a simplistic orthodoxy.[69] Rather, the play takes the risk of showing not only abjected and demonized others who attack Christian unity, but ostensible Christians, such as Aristorius, whose inner corruption is equally destabilizing to the Christian community as they join forces with the Jews. The normative ideal of the Christian in this play is not simply stated but created around an original model of the Jew, who lurks, simultaneously present and absent at the center of Christian identity.

The N-Town "Nativity"

The Jews leave the scene at the end of *Croxton*, entering into their wandering penance, but one can also note that women are strikingly absent throughout the play.[70] The named Jewish characters are all male, in keeping with Rubin's assertion that the host desecration narrative, which Rubin demonstrates to be its own particular genre, requires a Jewish male as perpetrator, because only men were seen as fully moral agents.[71] In the next chapter, we will further explore the figure of the Jewess through the character of Jessica in Shakespeare's *The Merchant of Venice*. There is one born Jewess, however, who is dominant on the medieval stage and whose portrayal as the epitome of moral dignity is central to the meaning and impact of a cycle drama such as N-Town.[72] Lesley Johnson and Jocelyn Wogan-Browne, writing of the role of the life of the Virgin Mary in *Cursor Mundi*, argue that this text "organizes its compilation around the life of the Virgin Mary. She is both divine dedicatee and the fulcrum around which its redemptive history pivots." They stress her purity as a "foundational" component that structures the *Cursor Mundi* narrative, a component that exists in opposition to Jewish exclusion.[73]

I argue that Mary shares a similar structural importance in N-Town, where she is also a fulcrum, her purity making possible the play's structure, which is both redemptive and supersessionist. The N-Town play's unusual focus on Mary is in keeping with Gail McMurray Gibson's assertion that "the incarnational preoccupation of the late Middle Ages tended to make the Virgin Mary—perhaps even more than Christ himself—the very emblem of Christian mystery."[74] The Virgin came to be not only a medieval English preoccupation but one specifically powerful in late medieval East Anglia, the likely origin of the N-Town plays.[75] The purity of Mary's body, explored through pageants such as the Nativity and the Assumption, is as of central importance in the fulfillment of Christian religious claims as is the body of Christ in the depiction of the events surrounding the Crucifixion and Resurrection and has the same shaping pattern in the structure of the drama. Reference to Mary's purity is a steady pulse throughout N-Town, and it is continually tested in dramatic moments that contain the same disruptive potential as those involving the desecration of the host in *Croxton*. And, indeed, these attacks are also of a piece because, as Pamela Sheingorn has noted, "[I]n N-Town there is a repeated insistence that Mary and Jesus share the same flesh."[76]

Denise Despres's research into the connections between Mary and the Jews powerfully demonstrates the connections between "Mary's bodily purity" and the body of Christ in a wide range of nondramatic media, including visual representations and Books of Hours.[77] This continuity makes depicted assaults to both the body of Mary and the body of the eucharist attacks, in a sense, on the same body, as well as on the Christian community, itself a Christian "body." Finally, and importantly, the contradictions and paradoxes explored in dramatic representations of the infancy narratives explore not only theological questions, but as Theresa Coletti has convincingly shown, these dramatizations "transform the biblical story of Christ's conception, birth, and early life into a prominent site of domestic struggle and social critique in the mystery cycles."[78] This struggle is particularly focused around the Woman question, as Marian representations "serve not simply or mainly to reinforce dominant ideologies but rather to expose contradictions and instabilities within the sex and gender system."[79] Just as the bodily imagery in *Croxton* not only illuminates the theological dynamics of transubstantiation but impacts the play's exploration of the negative impact of commercialism and greed on the body of the community, so too is Mary's body a locus for debate.

Recent scholarship has noted N-Town's striking focus not only upon Mary but upon the specifics of her purity, the very types of issues explored in earlier Christian-Jewish debates. Focusing on N-Town's depiction of Mary's mother, Saint Anne, Kathleen Ashley argues for the centrality of Mary in N-Town's "'cosmology' of purity."[80] Other critics have noted N-Town's unique focus on Mary's conception[81] and repeated emphasis on her "theological gynecology."[82] The N-Town "Joseph's Doubt," for example, explores the ticklish human situation resulting from the divine act of the Incarnation. The pageant delicately balances the comic Joseph, the foolish cuckolded old husband, with the devoted and devout earthly husband to the mother of God.[83] N-Town's "Trial of Mary and Joseph," unique among both English and Continental medieval drama, also plays with the issue of the divine Incarnation in a graphic and colloquial way through the trial of the draught.[84]

It is finally the Nativity pageant that explores the mystery of the Incarnation in the most physically graphic way through Salomé's exam of the Virgin's womb. The symbolism of the episode parallels the topos of the stricken hand in *Croxton*. Salomé the midwife's examination of Mary is an assault on a whole, intact body, emphasizing the inviolate nature of Mary's womb in a way in keeping with Gibson's analysis of its depictions in late medieval East Anglia. As I argued earlier, Mary's womb can be seen as a bodily image symbolizing contact between two religions—Christianity and Judaism. She is herself Christian and Jew, and her womb houses the miraculous transition from Judaism to Christianity, the birth of God as man. The representation of this womb as whole and intact is a representa-

tion of the stability and truth of Christian claims to supersession over Judaism. Its absolute boundaries represent absolute difference between
Christian and Jew, without any of the blurriness or potential confusion of
a representation of Christians and Jews such as that we find in *Croxton*,
and, as we shall see, in *The Merchant of Venice*.

The Navitity pageant opens with a lighthearted enactment of the
apocryphal story of the cherry tree. Mary is portrayed as a stereotypical
pregnant woman in the tradition of satirical works such as the *Fifteen Joys
of Marriage*, in which the husband must cope with the needs and whims
not only of his expecting spouse but also of all of her "gossips" and midwives.[85] Joseph stresses that he, as a man, is excluded from the scene of
childbearing:

> It is not conuenyent a man to be
>   Þer women gon in travalynge.
> Wherfore sum mydwyff fayn wold I se,
>   My wyff to helpe þat is so ȝenge. (ll. 134–37)

As he speaks of his worries, the two midwives appear. They are kind and
solicitous to him. The interaction shows that these two women are in a
position to help a man in need, because the realm of childbirth belongs to
them, a fact of which they are confidently aware. Salomé declares,

> Be of good chere and of glad mood,
>   We ij mydwyuys with þe wyll go.
> Þer was nevyr woman in such plyght stood
>   But we were redy here help to do.

> My name is Salomee, all men me knowe
>   For a mydwyff of wurthy fame.
> Whan women travayl, grace doth growe;
>   Þeras I come I had nevyr shame. (ll. 146–53)

The midwives enjoy a kind of fame, as they are known and appreciated in
the community for their skills. When the three arrive at Mary's lodgings,
they are faced with a blinding light such as that featured in the pageant of
the Incarnation; it is so bright that they do not think that they can enter,
but they do, finding to their surprise that Mary already has given birth
unaided.[86] The midwives express their wonder and disbelief that Mary

could still be, as Joseph declares, "a mayd" (l. 200). Zelome offers to examine Mary to determine if she has "nede of medycyn" (l. 219). Mary declares she suffered no pain in birth but offers herself to inspection: "Tast with ȝoure hand ȝoureself alon" (225). Zelome tests—"Hic palpat Zelomye Beatam Virginem"—and declares that Mary is indeed a maid and that she is utterly without pollution, the very type of foulness and taint of mortality found in the polemical debates over the Incarnation:

> A fayr chylde of a maydon is born,
>
> And nedyth no waschynge as other don:
>> Ful clene and pure forsoth is he,
> Withoutyn spott or ony polucyon,
>> His modyr nott hurte of virgynité!
>
> Coom nere, gode systyr Salomé.
>> Beholde þe brestys of þis clene mayd,
> Ful of fayr mylke how þat þei be,
>> And hyre chylde clene, as I fyrst sayd.
>> As other ben nowth fowle arayd,
>>> But clene and pure bothe modyr and chylde.
>> Of þis matyr I am dysmayd,
>>> To se them both thus vndefyled! (ll. 229–41)

Salomé hears Zelome's appraisal and is even more "dismayd" than her colleague at the notion that Mary could give birth and remain a maid and, without being invited as Zelome was, she determines herself to test:

> I xal nevyr trowe it but I it preve!
>> With hand towchynge but I assay,
> In my conscience it may nevyr cleue
> Þat sche hath chylde and is a may. (ll. 246–49)

Here Salomé reveals her carnality. She cannot accept through faith but must use her hand not only to see but to touch the truth. Mary again replies that she will willingly be "ransaked" to have the truth of her virginity tested. Salomé does test and for her "grett dowth and fals beleve" her hand becomes as "ded and drye as claye" (ll. 255–56). Salomé laments her state and particularly that her hand, a key instrument of her skills as a midwife, is now "lorn" of power, "styff as a stykke, and may nowth plyght" (l. 260). The hands of a midwife were particularly important, because as David Cressy reports in a discussion of early modern midwives, only midwives were permitted to touch the genitals of the mother in labor.[87] The life of mother and child were literally in the midwife's hands, and now those very skills that are Salomé's fame are rendered useless. She laments specifically the loss of her skills and calls on God to recognize the good that she once did as a healer:

> Bothe wyff and wedowe þat askyght, for the,
>   And frendles chylderyn þat haddyn grett nede,
> I dude them cure, and all for the,
>   And toke no rewarde of them, nor mede. (ll. 270–74)

An angel then appears, announcing that the midwife will be healed if she touches Christ's swaddling garments. Salomé does so and she is healed.

The scene with the midwives is charged not only because it involves the portrayal of the intimate probing of the body of the mother of God. As Gibson argues, the scene also portrays the intimate space of the birthing chamber, allowing the men in the audience a kind of entry into it, even as it is portrayed by men. The N-Town play stages the birth in an open space, "[i]n an hous þat is desolat, withowty[n] any wall," a contrast to the usually dim and close birthing chamber.[88] This space becomes a symbolic opening of a typically closed female space, into which both Joseph and the audience are granted entry. The power of Christ's Nativity opens that world and destabilizes the power of any human force. The woman who holds so much control in the critical moment of labor is shown humbled, the instrument of her skills, her hand, afflicted due to her disbelief.

The documents surrounding the York Fergus play indicate that stage depiction of the episode of the stricken hand had the potential for disruption and laughter, and I have suggested that the same is true for the incident with the hand of Jonathas the Jew in *Croxton*. But what of the Nativity play? In the chapter entitled "Religious Laughter" in his magisterial *Play Called Corpus Christi*, V. A. Kolve discusses audience reaction to this moment in the context of the problem of risible laughter in the Cycle plays. He argues that there were some moments of comedy or holy laughter in the Cycle dramas but that this probing by the midwives is "terrifying":

But Mary knows she is pure, and so do we—she is untouched by our laughter. The gynecological probing of the midwife is a terrifying action and so the audience would understand it; indeed, it is precisely (and intentionally) parallel to the action of Thomas when he thrusts his fingers into the wounds of Christ. (The two central mysteries of Christianity, the Incarnation and the Resurrection, are thereby formally "doubted.") And it has a terrible end: the midwife withdraws her hand to find it paralyzed, and a miracle of Jesus is needed to make it sound again.[89]

The parallels between Thomas and Salomé are, as previously noted, clear, but the main difference between these episodes—the paralysis of Salomé's hand, is a crucial one, indicative of the potentially raucous "gender trouble" that Gibson finds in the scene. Kolve doesn't disallow the possibility of audience laughter; it is not, he asserts, directed at Mary, who stands amid this coarseness "like a green island in a turbulent and dirty sea." Gibson reads the scene as more volatile and inviting of spiritual questioning and the destabilization of social and gender categories:[90]

But the truth of the midwife's probing hand seems undermined by the very gender roles it both invokes and violates. "Mary" has no womb, clean or unclean, and the female inquisitor who insistently claims the grace and healing of a midwife's touch is no woman either. Willing suspension of disbelief is subverted in this play in ways that seem less to resolve doubt than to invite the continued groping of Mary's —and God's—privy secrets. It might well be argued that the Mary of the N-Town Nativity is less a still island than the furiously contested body where divine miracle and human rule meet.[91]

Gibson uses the fact that this scene is enacted by cross-dressed men to point to the ways in which it actively constructs this scene of belief. If we think about this in terms of the insights into gender construction revealed by Judith Butler's analysis of drag, we can easily see Gibson's point. On one level, Mary is the island so beautifully described by Kolve, but the portrayal before the audience is clearly "performing" Mary in a way that can foster both spiritual exploration and exploration of social roles.

The severed hand episodes of Jonathas and Fergus invite the audience to view and/or to assume the role of the doubter, to see doubt enacted, and, I would argue, this same situation applies with the figure of Salomé, who, like Mary, is also a site of social contestation, even if, of course, a much lesser one. The midwife and Mary are performed by men, but they are meant to represent women, both in their ways "women on top," who have, albeit in quite different ways and to different degrees, control over the man in the scene, Joseph. As the exchange between Joseph and the two midwives before they join Mary makes clear, the midwife is a woman to be reckoned with, a female figure with an important, exclusively female role in a male-dominated world. The midwife plays a crucial role in the birth of every human being, and because of this, I would argue, she is not simply any doubter. Like the doubt of the Jew, the midwife's doubt is special and particular, a challenge to the truth of one of the foundational moments in the history of Christianity and a particularly carnal, feminized challenge to its universal message.

Our historical understanding of late medieval English midwives and midwifery is still being developed. As Monica Green points out, even the term "midwife" is contested, and it is not entirely clear if the category indicates only someone who is involved in aiding in pregnancy and birth-related issues, or a female healer more generally.[92] The importance of midwives is, however, undeniable, and historians of varying opinions on midwives' roles share a belief that midwives are liminal figures, operating "at the boundaries of life and death, with skills few men could fathom."[93] Cressy writes eloquently of some of the roles of early modern midwives that also have relevance to discussions of midwifery in fifteenth-century England:

Midwives were summoned as servants but performed as officiants. They crossed social boundaries and entered homes of all sorts. In the crisis of labour they sup-planted husbands as the principal support for their wives, and took temporary command of the intimate core of his household. The midwife's office allowed her to pass thresholds and open doors, to reach day and night to the heart of *materia materna*. . . . Ministers sometimes looked upon midwives with suspicion because alone among women they occasionally performed a priest-like function, adminis-tering the sacrament of baptism *in extremis* to a child who seemed likely to die.[94]

Because midwives often did have to perform emergency baptisms, they were licensed by the church. Their importance was also acknowledged through their roles in religious customs surrounding childbirth. It is be-cause of this particular position at the crossroads of life and death that the Church attempted to train and license them in rite of baptism *in extremis*, because they were responsible not only for the physical "delivery" of the mother from her travail but also perhaps for the spiritual welfare of the infant in their care.

The licensing of midwives, then, was not concerned with their medi-cal skills, so much as their spiritual competency. Scholars of the history of midwifery point to John Mirk's handbook for parish priests, which in-structs them how to teach midwives in infant baptism. The priests are not to concern themselves with the women's "Sory laten," which will not alter the effect of the sacrament, but they are to instruct them not to recite any extraneous "wymmenes lore."[95] Gibson, writing of the ceremony of churching, argues for a "quasi-clerical" status for midwives, who were, after all, required by canon law to be instructed in the rite of the sacrament of baptism, in order to save the soul of the child. She points to the early modern reformers' strong objections to this power for midwives, which serves as evidence of the importance of their role.[96] It was the midwife who carried the child to the baptismal font, and she was also present at the churching of the mother. As the analyses of churching ritual by Gibson, Becky Lee, and Paula Rieder have shown, purification was not simply about taboos concerning a woman's body and its polluting elements, but also undeniably a "woman's rite," a celebration of birth and maternity in which women seemed to take pleasure and pride, and, indeed, a rite for which some women struggled to ensure their own participation.[97] Rieder shows these occasions were ones in which women held central importance, part of a whole series of customs surrounding childbirth in which women played equal or even dominant roles in relation to the men in their families and communities.[98]

N-Town's Joseph then, the beleaguered husband, is not simply Joseph, husband of Mary, but also a type of comic Every-Husband, facing a female-dominated mystery from which all men are barred. The Nativity pageant is centrally concerned with the truth of the Incarnation and Virgin Birth of Christ, but it explores this central Christian truth through the charged figure of the midwife, at the center of a woman-dominated rite of passage. Myriam Greilsammer argues that "[m]idwives represent the world of empirical knowledge, transmitted from generation to generation, nourished by the consensus and solidarity of women: bonds built on a shared life experience of childbirth and suffering, but also of conviviality and emotion."[99] It is precisely this kind of knowledge upon which Salomé the midwife draws when she insists on her postpartum examination of Mary. Her experience tells her that Mary cannot still be a virgin. All of her experiences as midwife are what make Salomé a figure to be reckoned with and these very experiences are those that lead her to doubt the truth of the Virgin birth, and if the audience laughs at her, they are not simply laughing at any doubter, but deflating the power of a "woman on top."

In this way the midwife symbolizes the power of women in and through reproductive capacity. All humans are born of women, and even those who chose not to participate in the sexuality and reproduction of adult life likely once passed through a midwife's hands. The midwife, this liminal figure who brings a child into the world and who may be responsible for a child's spiritual passage into the next, is a figure for the process of human birth and for woman as origin, as well as for the type of "carnal knowledge" that is the basis of the midwife's craft. This type of understanding is squarely on the side of the carnal, the literal, and the feminine, as is figured through the hermeneutical Woman. The knowledge possessed by the midwife who officiates in this world is transmitted to her through oral tradition and through the experiences of her hands and eyes. It is this knowledge that is trumped, conquered by the spiritual knowledge represented by Mary, who is above this world of women, and by Christ.

The role of the midwife as a figure of reproduction and feminine sexuality is further reinforced through her evocative name, Salomé, a name which, to the best of my knowledge, has gone unremarked upon by critics. The story of the midwives at the nativity goes back to the Evangelium of Pseudo-Matthew and was transmitted through sources such as the *Legenda Aurea*.[100] Various names are given to the "good" midwife who only wishes to test Mary for the sake of her health. In the Pseudo-Matthew, she has the N-Town name, Zelomi, but she is sometimes called Zebel or Tebel, or even Rachel. Lydgate, in his *Life of Our Lady*, calls her Scephora. The incredulous midwife, however, is always called Salomé.[101] The Salomé actually named in the Bible is Mary Salomé, one of the women present at the Crucifixion, who also visited Christ's tomb on the morning of the Resurrection. The other biblical Salomé is the daughter of Herodias, wife of Herod. As reward for a crowd-pleasing dance, Herod promised Salomé anything she desired, including up to half his kingdom. Salomé consulted with Herodias, who instructed her to ask for the head of the imprisoned John the Baptist, who had disapproved of Herod's marriage. Salomé made her mother's request, adding the infamous detail of the "charger" or platter on her own. This dancing girl is not named in the Bible; the name Salomé for this figure enters the tradition through Josephus.[102]

The Salomé figure reached the height of its literary symbolic power in the nineteenth century, but it also had definite resonance in the Middle Ages.[103] As Linda Seidel argues, the Gospel account in Matthew of the martyrdom of John the Baptist followed upon the parables, which are "for those who receive messages through their physical senses but do not comprehend them, 'because seeing they do not see, and hearing they do not hear, nor do they understand' (Mark 13:13)"; Herod, and with him Herodius and Salomé, are likened as well to such folk, limited to understanding by their senses.[104] So is the midwife Salomé limited by her need to rely on what she can touch until her conversion.

Salomé the dancer was also, of course, well known as a figure of female sexuality and eroticism. There are a number of extant medieval illustrations of her lithe gymnastics before Herod, representations that present her as the embodiment of feminine carnality.[105] A dancer communicates through her body, her movements acting as a corporealization of meaning and language, and Salomé's dance, as represented in the Middle Ages, was a sensuous, erotic one. By sharing the name of this infamous dancer, Salomé the midwife becomes associated with a dangerous feminine sexuality, the side of the hermeneutical Woman connected with Eve.[106] She challenges Mary, the embodiment of all that is good in woman, and is punished for her misdeed, conquered by Mary and by Christian truth.

The midwife's role, if not the "witch" role that some have sensationalized it to be, is still an emblem of female power over reproduction, a power further connected to feminine sexuality through the sexualized connotations of the name Salomé.[107] I argue that any laughter directed against this liminal figure in the N-Town "Nativity" is of a similar type to that directed at Jonathas the Jew in the Croxton play. The audience is invited to laugh at the midwife, who through her role as the mistress of the birthing chamber holds power both over men who are excluded from its confines and over women and infants who must submit to and trust in her skills for their very lives when in its confines. She is the butt of laughter, but the audience is potentially invited not only to laugh at her but to stand with her. The Incarnation, although a sacred Christian truth, is, as we have seen, a continual source of doubt and debate. There may well have been members of the audience who were also incredulous, and this scene invites them to witness the ultimate enactment of the problem and to see it in its horror, its power, and its comedy.[108] As Coletti has shown, the infancy narratives are an important site through which to explore social issues, a view that encourages an understanding of the importance of the midwives and the laughter directed at Salomé, not only as a response to the "woman on top" represented by the figure of the midwife, but as a response to all of the challenges to normative social order implicit in the role of Mary in the Incarnation and in the infancy narratives.

Conclusion

After these considerations of parallel dramatic instances of the hermeneutical Woman and the hermeneutical Jew, I turn very briefly to an instance where the two come together—the alleged Jewish attack on the Virgin at the Assumption, which appeared in many forms, including the missing York version and an extant N-Town one.[109] Central to the Assumption narrative in all of its forms is the recognition by both Jews and Christians that the body of Mary, which bore Christ and gave him flesh, serves as corporeal evidence of the Incarnation and all that it entails for belief in Christian truth.[110] Within these narratives, the Jews' motivation for attacking Mary is tied directly to the Incarnation and to the Crucifixion. The attack reaffirms the Jews' treachery against Christ and the truth of the Resurrection, which the Jews' very attack seems to confirm, as their efforts are an attempt to prevent yet another event that reinforces the supersession of Jewish law. In the *Blickling Homilies*, the offending Jew converts and blesses Mary in the Hebrew tongue and then blesses her again on the witness of the books of Moses. These details emphasize the triumph of Christianity over Judaism as represented through Hebrew and the Pentateuch. The converted Jewish priest is then able to cure other offending Jews, stricken with emblematic blindness, by converting them as well.[111]

In N-Town, the antagonism of the Jews toward the Virgin is figured in terms of Jewish law, as Matthew Kinservik argues, as the Jews appear to believe that they can protect "the law" by doing away with her.[112] N-Town, as Sheingorn's perceptive analysis of the Assumption episode shows, emphasizes a Mary who "lived *among* the Jews" but who was not herself one of them.[113] The Assumption episode begins with a "doctor" recounting for the audience the events in Mary's life, emphasizing her purity and her devotion. Immediately following is a "Miles" who cries, "Pes now youre blaberyng, in the develis name!" (l. 27), injecting a stream of profanity into the scene as he bemoans the loss of order that Christ has meant for Jewry and, presumably, for Rome.[114] Next the Episcopus Legis arrives, asserting that the events at hand threaten the Law: "We may not won /To sweche harlotis settyn reddure / That geynseyn oure lawe and oure Scripture. / Now let sere pryncis in purpure, / In savynge of owre lawys now telle on" (ll. 48–52).[115] Then three additional Jews appear, declaring that Mary is about to die and hatching a plot to burn her body and hide the ashes (l. 84). The Episcopus Legis urges them to do so, goading them by stressing that Mary is only a woman. "Art thou ferd of a wenche?" he taunts (l. 66). The Jews determine that they should not slay the Apostles, who are preaching Christ's Resurrection, because this might cause "the comownys to ryse" (l. 81). By burning Mary's body instead, the Jews hope to stave off any damage that she may cause, and in attacking her body, they will attack Christ once more. As Sheingorn notes, the Jews begin their attack on Mary through swearing, their language differing markedly from the reverent and gracious speech used by Mary and the Apostles.[116] Upon her death, Mary is greeted by an Angel, mirroring the Annunciation, and the Apostles also announce her Assumption into heaven, which is accompanied by heavenly music. The Episcopus and Jews, however, hear this heavenly music as "noyse" (l. 371), failing to understand its true significance. They proceed with their plot as the first Jew throws himself at Mary in what he deems a "manly" fashion (l. 421). This attack, however, is immediately foiled as the hands of the "insanus" are ripped from his body.

> Allas, my body is ful of peyne!
>   I am fastened sore to this bere!
> Myn handys are ser bothe tweyne.
>   O, Peter, now prey thy God for me here. (ll. 423–26)

He is converted and restored, after which Peter converts the second Jew as well, asking him to touch a holy palm. Using metaphors of health and sickness that recall *Croxton*, the first Jew encourages others to convert: "Ye Jewys that langour in this gret infyrmyté, / Belevyth in Crist Jesu and ye schal haue helthe" (ll. 464–65). These words connect the sealing of his severed hand to the possibility of spiritual healing held out to all, particularly the unbelieving Jews. The second declares his belief in Crist, "Goddis sone in vnyté," and forsakes his "mavmentryes" (ll. 467–68). After grasping the palm, he declares himself and the other Jew "hol of oure seknesse" (l. 471). The remaining Jews, however, refuse to convert. They are condemned to the devil, and two demons carry them off to hell at the very point when the Lord appears and Mary ascends to him.[117]

As we saw in the twelfth-century debates over the Incarnation, Mary's corporeal intactness is central to Christianity's religious claim as the inheritor of Jewish prophecy. The graphic polemics over Mary's body may seem far removed from the abstraction of hermeneutical supersession, but it is the Incarnation, that moment when the Word becomes flesh in Mary's womb, which marks the movement of supersession, that shift from Judaism to Christianity. Mary's body, not unlike the body of Archisynagogus in the Benediktbeuern play, acts as a symbol for the relationships between Jews and Christians within the framework of Christian theology. Indeed, the Assumption is not only a "logical" end for N-Town, but an essential one, because N-Town could not, as Kinservik asserts, "achieve dramatic or theological closure without assuring the bodily integrity of the Blessed Virgin."[118] The Virgin's body is furthermore not simply symbolic; it is instrumental. In the Assumption narratives, the singularity of Mary's body is emphasized through its transcendence of the corruption of death and the decay of flesh, which parallels Mary's transcendence of the corruption of sexuality and childbirth. *Mirk's Festial* stresses that Mary is taken bodily into heaven because Christ is loathe to allow his own mother, in whose womb he was borne and from whose breasts he fed, to decay into the "corupcyon" of "stynkyng wormys" and "styngkyng careyne" that is mortality.[119]

This emphasis on the corporeal is part of a system of oppositions between believer and nonbeliever, Christian and Jew, that is represented through contrasting images of intact, incorruptible bodies, like that of Virgin and the permeable bodies of the doubting, defiling Jews, which are torn apart and can only be restored through conversion. In the context of the Assumption story, this conversion is supersession writ small, because the Jew's turn to Christian truth is not only significant to him but has the larger impact of asserting Mary's status as the mother of God and Christian supersession over Judaism. The Jew's body, fragmented through doubt and restored through faith as an emblem of Christian truth, becomes a site through which Christian doubt and truth is enacted. The Jew's hand becomes the ultimate emblem of carnality, just as Mary's body is an emblem of the power of spiritual purity to transform the body, to make the corporeal pure. The Jew will lay his hands upon Mary to defile her, but ultimately these hands are overwhelmed by the truth of her body, and before the eyes of all the audience this truth is proved. The attack on Mary is yet another instance of the proof of supersession, inscribed once again on the body of the newly converted Jew, proving not only his conversion but the truth of the nature of Mary's body, that corporeal link between Judaism and Christianity.

The hermeneutical Woman and the hermeneutical Jew function in these dramas in relation not only to sacred bodies but to a range of identities that include Christian and non-Christian, local and foreign. If we can understand Christian hermeneutics as a type of anthropology, then an ability to perceive the spiritual world, to see it based not on facts but on faith is that which differentiates the Christian figures in these dramas from a range of "others." These figures of difference include not only the doubting Jew and midwife, but also those Christians who present chal-

lenges to a unified Christian community, including heretics, a reading in
keeping with the anti-Lollard interpretations of *Croxton*.[120] Also included
is difference of geographical origin, encompassing the play's anti-alien
strands. Ruth Evans writes that Fergus may come to signify "not only the
Jew that is Christianity's excluded other but more specifically the non-
English foreigner that is the excluded other of urban artisanal identity,
perhaps also signalled by his mutilated, and hence imperfect or disabled,
body."[121] The topos of the stricken hand may indeed not only resonate
with Christian conversion but also may be associated, in the case of *Croxton*, with a regional East Anglian identity and even a sense perhaps of
English identity, which we will see in the next chapter is of critical importance in relation to the figures of the hermeneutical Woman and the hermeneutical Jew in Shakespeare's *The Merchant of Venice*. In *Croxton* the
Jew is certainly, as in *Merchant*, associated with a rampant mercantilism
that seems a commentary on the fundamental incompatibility of the pursuit of wealth and the demands of Christian faith.

The doubter on the stage is a figure of difference but also may be a
site of identification. In these dramatized moments of doubt, the links
between the Jewish, the feminine, the literal, and the carnal, which we
have seen as so crucial in the creation of Christian identity, are both embodied on the stage through dramatization and simultaneously destabi-
lized. In the parallel depictions of these incidences of the stricken carnal
hand in *Croxton* and in the N-Town "Nativity," we find the tension between origin and margin that animates the figures of the hermeneutical
Woman and the hermeneutical Jew enacted upon the bodies of nonbelievers. The doubting Jew and midwife each represent a reliance on literal
understanding that is part of the Pauline chain of associations between the
literal, the carnal, the Jewish, and the feminine. The hand becomes a symbol of this carnality, as the believers lose that very instrument of empirical
knowledge upon which they rely, and their bodies are only made whole
again when they no longer rely on their senses, but on faith alone. The
conversions are inscribed on these bodies as they are fragmented by doubt
and then made whole through faith. But, as I have also attempted to argue
here, because these are dramatic representations, their effect is not uniform, but volatile. The boundaries and nature of the Christian community
are explored in these plays, and the audience is invited to assume the perspective of particular identities who embody doubt. Through these liminal
figures, the doubting Jew and the skeptical midwife, the audience can vicariously explore doubts that they may harbor about thorny doctrinal is-

sues that involve crossings from one state to another: transubstantiation, the Incarnation, the Assumption, conversion.

The laughter and disruption these scenes of dismemberment may well have produced is an indication of the crossing of these boundaries and of the difficulties in determining the boundaries between the abject self that does not believe and the true Christian self that does. The audience is invited to see the entire narrative of doubt and conversion unfold, to test for him- or herself the truth of the Virgin's womb or the eucharist along with the doubter portrayed. In this way, he or she can also achieve a conversion to greater faith, but the process is not a stable one and can result in a laughter that may indicate doubt, terror, humor, or a combination thereof. Because the actors involved are not actual women or Jews and therefore not actual figures of doubt, the performative nature of the enactment is emphasized, but this may be precisely the point. The Christian is not meant to always be understood as a stable identity: it is a performative identity. Christians are made, not born, and late medieval East Anglian drama invites them to remake themselves, vicariously experiencing a crisis of faith and its resulting conversion through identification with and in opposition to the figures of woman and Jew.

"O what a goodly outside falsehood hath!" Exegesis and Identity in *The Merchant of Venice*

JAMES SHAPIRO'S *Shakespeare and the Jews* is a landmark book for scholars both of English literature and of Jewish Studies. Among the work's numerous contributions, perhaps the most important is Shapiro's exploration of how "between 1290 and 1656 the English came to see their country defined in part by the fact that Jews had been banished from it."[1] In the fourteenth century, as we have seen, representations of Jews and Judaism were implicated in the central analogy of the letter and the spirit and were an important ontological element not only in formulations about the nature of Christian identity, but also, for example, in ideas of youth, age, and sin. Nevertheless, this Jewish presence was more implicit than explicit. By the late sixteenth and early seventeenth centuries, Shapiro demonstrates, the interrelated questions of who was a Jew, who was a Christian, and who was English had taken on new urgency and immediacy. This can to some degree be accounted for by actual Jewish presence in early modern England. As Shapiro and others have argued, there was a small, but nonetheless visible, Jewish presence in England's *converso* community, which included the Queen's physician Roderigo Lopez, executed for alleged involvement in a plot against her life in 1594.[2]

The presence of actual Jews or other "aliens" does not, however, fully explain English preoccupation with Jewish difference. As Shapiro argues, English thinkers also focused on the nature of Jewish identity as part of their struggles with the conflicted nature of English Christianity, torn as it was between Catholic and Protestant belief systems.[3] And English understandings of Jewishness were also related to responses to other types of Others, notably the Turk.[4] Through Shapiro's cultural history we have come to understand that English anxiety about Jews and counterfeit

Christians was proportional to social, political, and religious upheaval and that emergent English national identity was related in complicated ways to emergent notions of "racial" identity, including Jewish "racial" identity.[5]

But although this early modern understanding of the Jew is culturally and historically specific and therefore unique, it should not be understood as yet another marker of or justification for the traditional periodization boundary between medieval and "Renaissance." Early modern formulations of difference instead need to be scrutinized more carefully in relation to preceding conceptions. Although Shapiro for the most part eschews the traditional medieval-Renaissance divide, even he asserts that "[o]ne of the things that most distinguishes medieval from early modern conceptions of Jews is that Jewish identity had been unquestioned in medieval Europe—on biological, social, and religious grounds—by both Jews and Christians. The early modern Jew, in contrast, confounded those who sought more precise definitions in terms suited to emerging notions of nationhood and race."[6] Research by scholars such as Jonathan Elukin and Steven Kruger has shown, however, that Jewish identity was never without controversy.[7] Furthermore, fourteenth- and fifteenth-century Middle English texts indicate that the representations of the Jew existed in complex relationships to understandings of both local and "proto-national" English identities at least as early as the fifteenth century.[8] We saw this most clearly in *Croxton*, whose Spanish locale and preoccupation with conversion has resonance with similar concerns in *Merchant*. One of the central goals of this chapter is to encourage further bridging of the medieval-Renaissance divide by reading the touchstone literary text of early modern Jewish difference, William Shakespeare's *The Merchant of Venice*, in the context of the Christian exegetical tradition in which the paradigms of the hermeneutical Jew and the hermeneutical Woman took shape. I hope to ground current readings of *Merchant* in a broader understanding of the patristic and medieval Christian hermeneutics that shape the play, focusing particularly on the analogy of the letter and the spirit, which is integral to the play's action and meaning.

My analysis brings together and extends three important but primarily separate strands of criticism that together show the ways in which the patristic and medieval exegetical traditions figure in representations of "racial," ethnic, religious, and gender differences in *Merchant*. The first of these critical strands is exemplified by Barbara Lewalski's "Biblical Allusion and Allegory in *The Merchant of Venice*," in which she reads *Merchant* as an allegory of the triumph of the New Dispensation over the Old.[9] In addition to Lewalski's work, there has been a range of studies examining the biblical and exegetical elements of *Merchant*, particularly in the scene between Launcelot Gobbo and his father (II.ii) and in the trial scene of Act IV.[10] Although they have done much to excavate the biblical and allegorical elements in the play, these analyses have tended to do so without reference to gender, "racial," or often even religious difference, resembling in their Christian-centered focus the Robertsonian approach in medieval studies. The second strand of criticism is Shapiro's historical and theoretical investigations of the relationship between Jewish and English identities. Shapiro's reading of the pound of flesh through the "uncircumcision" and "circumcision of the heart" of Romans engages directly with Christian exegetical elements in the text, but as Mary Janell Metzger has noted, Shapiro's analysis does not take gender into account in any extended way.[11] Using the insights of feminist and postcolonial theory, as well as theoretical analysis of the category of race, feminist scholars such as Metzger, Ania Loomba, and Kim Hall have developed a third strand of *Merchant* criticism, exploring the intersecting categories of gender, "racial," and religious differences.[12] Like Shapiro, these critics use a wide variety of sources to reveal historical, political, and economic discourses that influence *Merchant,* providing critical and convincing analyses of the intersectionality of these categories in the play and in early modern England. What is still missing from both of these recent critical strands, however, is close consideration of the ways in which patristic and medieval Christian exegetical traditions inform not only *Merchant* but early modern formulations of difference in general. Recent work by Julia Reinhard Lupton and Lisa Freinkel has addressed the crucial importance of exegetical background in *Merchant* to questions of Jewish difference. My reading has close affinities with their approaches but differs through emphasis on bringing this type of reading into more explicit engagement with feminist and postcolonial interpretations of the play.[13]

As we have seen, one of the central assumptions of Christian hermeneutics is an opposition between external and internal realities, the division between which is the "hermeneutical divide." My reading of *Merchant* takes this tension between external and internal realities as one of the play's central concerns and the one that most clearly connects the discourse of exegesis with those of "race," gender, and religious difference. Within the framework of Christian hermeneutics, to understand and interpret as a Christian is to be able to see beneath the external in order to grasp internal spiritual meaning. This way of seeing the world is an essential component of Christian identity and, in this way, Christian exegetics becomes both a hermeneutics and an anthropology.[14] In *Merchant* these principles also apply. The Venetians are exegetes who face a potentially hostile, alien world, a world to which, as a center of the trade that sustains them, they must remain open. In order to maintain dominance and to ensure a line of controlled patrimony, the Venetians must outwit the Others, those outside the Christian order who threaten to infiltrate or even destroy it, as in the case not only of Shylock, but also of Jessica and of Portia's foreign suitors. In order to face these threats, the Christian characters in *Merchant* must continually interpret the world around them by seeing beneath exteriors to discern inner meaning and intrinsic worth.

These scenes of exegetical prowess are firmly linked to the hermeneutical tradition of Christian supersession through the scene between Launcelot Gobbo and his father, which alludes to the biblical stories of Esau and Jacob and of the prodigal son so central to Christian understandings of the supersessionary relationship between Judaism and Christianity since Paul.[15] Through these allusions the play reinforces the alignment between Christianity and youth that we saw at work in the *Canterbury Tales*. Shylock represents the old order, the Old Testament, and the thwarted father, conquered by the stronger force of Christian youth, exemplified by the lovers Portia and Bassanio, who accomplish their desires through masterful interpretation. Bassanio must be able to divine the true, inner meanings hidden in the caskets to win Portia, and Portia must interpret the law to thwart Shylock.

The triumph of the Christians is not, however, a simply unalloyed one. Just as the Croxton play is concerned with the ways in which the focus on material gain of characters such as Aristorius can distort and pervert Christian beliefs and ethics, in *Merchant*, the discourses of commerce and exploration can be seen corroding religious discourse throughout the play.[16] To read like a Christian is to see beneath the surface, as the casket riddle demands, but Portia's dismissals of Morocco based on his skin color make clear that surface appearance does, in fact, matter. In the trial scene, the Christians triumph not through Christian mercy but through literalistic mastery of a law they must protect in order to maintain a social order in which commerce rules and all human beings have a price. Such actions make it truly difficult to answer Portia's question "Which is the Merchant here? and which the Jew?" It is through such moments that the play projects the admiration for the powerful Venetian order at the same time that it reveals its risks and costs.

One of the costs of this mercenary order from the standpoint of the Venetian elite is the destabilization of hierarchies of gender, religion, class, and "race" through "miscegenation."[17] In the crucible of Venice, Venetians and aliens, women and men mix together freely, with erotic and material desires acting as catalysts. In this world, governed first and foremost not by Christian theological principles but by a commitment to maintain the "profit of trade," identities are formed and destroyed, joined and separated, with some, like Jessica's, becoming indeterminate. As a center of trade, Venice experiences a ceaseless ebb and flow of aliens within its borders, a state reminiscent of the permeable borders of the Asian city of Chaucer's *Prioress's Tale. The Merchant of Venice* opens with Antonio's ships circling the globe. Likewise, Portia is at the center of brisk international attention, with suitors from Germany, France, England, Spain, and Morocco. All of these encounters between Christians and non-Christians occur because of exploration and commercial traffic, a situation mirroring sixteenth-century English encounters with non-Christians.[18]

Like Venice, London had a significant alien population: "By the end of Elizabeth's reign the number of aliens in London had swelled to upwards of ten thousand, in a population that has been estimated at somewhere between one hundred and fifty and two hundred thousand."[19] As Shapiro shows, there was strong anti-alien sentiment and interclass strife in London in the 1590s. In 1595, "the poor tradesmen made a riot upon the strangers in Southwark, and other parts of the City of London . . . [and] the like tumults began at the same time within the Liberties (as they are called) where such strangers commonly harboured."[20] This riot involved more than a thousand participants who violently resisted the city's efforts to quell them.[21] Both London and Venice opened themselves up for trade and in this way risked "intercourse" with "aliens" on an unprecedented scale. To accommodate an influx necessary to the commonwealth's economic lifeblood, but threatening to its self-definition as Christian and white, Christians must learn to reinterpret their identities and their world, which "intercourse" with aliens has called into question. Venice's openness compromises the ease with which Venetians can define their own identity and the ways in which they can guard their patrimonies against incursion from outside. Venetians must define themselves against the Other who is so very much in their midst. In *Merchant*, this Other has varied forms who are represented through actual characters such as Morocco, Shylock, and Jessica, through shadowy figures such as Launcelot's Moorish mistress, and through figures of speech such as Bassanio's Indian beauty.

The figure who most embodies the threat of indeterminate identity is Jessica, who is both Christian and Jew and whose beautiful exterior may belie an intractable Jewish essence, which she, through her marriage to Lorenzo, threatens to spread into the commonwealth. Jessica's gender makes her position in the commonwealth even more volatile. As a woman, Jessica is property to both her father and her husband, but in her decision to convert and to abandon her father's house, she displays an agency that is as least as much of a threat to Venetian order as Shylock's bond. The figures of the hermeneutical Woman and the hermeneutical Jew have relied on oppositions between Christian and Jew and between good woman and bad in order to generate a vision of the idealized Christian. In Jessica, however, these oppositions collapse along with the breakdown in the opposition between interior and exterior realities. Although seemingly a Christian fantasy of Jewish conversion, Jessica's situation actually calls this very fantasy into question. In Jessica's uneasiness and her continual doubts that she can escape a Jewish essence, the play most clearly reveals its concerns about the fragility of Christian and Venetian identity. Exotic females such as Jessica, made available to the Christian male through commercial "intercourse," threaten the commonwealth with miscegenation that will further complicate any attempt to distinguish between Christian Venetian and Other. The play explores the question of whether trade, which brought on contact with all sorts of "aliens," would ultimately destabilize a Christian England.

Jessica is an important figure with which to conclude this book, throughout which we have examined the intersections of representations of Jews and women and the ways in which the hermeneutical Woman and the hermeneutical Jew both parallel one another and intersect within Christian discourses. Strikingly absent from English vernacular representations of Jews has been the true intersection of the Jewish and the feminine in depictions of post-Crucifixion Jewesses. In comparison to representations of male Jews, there is a relative paucity of both literary and artistic representation of contemporary Jewesses in the medieval period in England.[22] In a discussion of one of the few instances of medieval representation of contemporary female Jews, host desecration narrative, Miri Rubin has proposed that the host desecration narrative requires a male Jew as perpetrator, because the male Jew could be seen as a fully moral agent, unlike a woman: "Female Jews were, like other women, seen as pliant and impressionable, lacking in reasoning and moral faculties."[23] In the far more fully realized and secularized character of Jessica, however, the very question of her character and her ability to convert are explored through intersecting discourses of exegesis, gender, commerce, and "race."

Within the exegetical context we've established, Jessica is aligned with the prodigal offspring evoked in the scene between Launcelot Gobbo and his father. In the logic of supersession, the category of the Christian is aligned with the triumph of youth over the outmoded age of the Old Law. Jessica's abandonment of her father represents precisely such a realignment of herself with the youthful, triumphant Christian Venetians. Jessica is clearly a direct theatrical descendent of Abigail, from Marlowe's *Jew of Malta*, but the exegetical contexts in *Merchant* sharpen her role as the embodiment of the "younger having precedence over the elder," making her conversion a triumph of all Christians over all Jews.[24] This assimilation is accomplished because Jessica is female. She is uncircumcised, unmarked as a Jew, and as a woman, she becomes subject to her Christian husband, her body and goods easily taken into his household and his community. But this transition is not without difficulties. As Peter Berek's analysis of the figure of the male *marrano* shows, in sixteenth-century England, the figure of the converted Jew is linked to "anxiety about change."[25] Jessica's fair beauty and wealth make it easy for her to "pass" into the world of Belmont, but her true assimilation is more questionable.[26] In this Jessica exhibits not only the problematics of Jewish difference and Jewish conversion but the dangerous effects of willful female sexuality that all of the play's females represent. If one could see golden Portia and Launcelot's Moorish mistress as worlds apart, it is Jessica the infidel who stands between them, seemingly able to pass into the world of Belmont through her fair looks and outward actions, but ultimately marked by a difference of blood that is not visually manifested upon her, as difference is upon Launcelot's Moorish mistress, but that still courses through her veins.

I will begin with a reexamination of the exegetical elements in *Merchant* through a focus on the importance of the skills of Christian exegesis, particularly an ability to discern between internal and external realities, with emphasis on the scene between Launcelot Gobbo and his father, the trial scene, and the scenes involving the casket plot. In these readings, particularly that of the casket plot, I will attempt to show the ways in which the discourses of "race," gender, and religion inflect the interrelationships between interpretation and patrimony in the play. I do not offer my own allegorical reading of the play. There are perhaps as many permutations of allegorical readings as there are readers, and I find that reading the play allegorically in any kind of programmatic way is ultimately reductive.[27] My examination of the exegetical elements in the play will instead attempt to illuminate the ways in which theological discourse intersects with the discourses of "race" and gender through the theme of patrimony. This theme has a center in the figure of the "prodigal daughter," Jessica. In Jessica, Shakespeare portrays the greatest threat to the important ability to discern relationships between outer appearance and inner worth, one of the defining techniques of Christian hermeneutics. I will examine Jessica in relation to the other female characters in the play, demonstrating the ways in which this secular representation of a Jewish woman brings together elements of the hermeneutical Woman and the hermeneutical Jew into the evolving literary figure, the "beautiful Jewess."

* * *

Concern with interpreting the surrounding world begins as early in *Merchant* as its more celebrated concern with mercantile venture and the risks of "hazarding all." In the play's opening scene, Salerio, perplexed about Antonio's melancholy, conjectures that Antonio's mind is overcome with concern for his commercial ventures. Were he in Antonio's situation, says Salerio, he too would be distracted:

> . . . should I go to church
> And see the holy edifice of stone
> And not bethink me straight of dangerous rocks,
> Which touching but my gentle vessel's side
> Would scatter all her spices on the stream,
> Enrobe the roaring waters with my silks,
> And in a word, but even now worth this,
> And now worth nothing?[28]

Through an image of a wrecked vessel that suggests both violence and eroticism, Salerio reasons that a man with so much at stake would surely be obsessed with the fate of his ships, so intent upon them that he would be unable to focus on anything else, even to pray. This focus on gain is so distorting that it renders the merchant venturer unable to understand the very things before his eyes.[29] Salerio would look at a Church's "holy edifice" and, instead of seeing a house of God, would envision his ship and her cargo in vivid detail. Although Salerio realizes the transience of such things ("even now worth this / And now worth nothing?") he believes that such thoughts are more than enough to drive a man to sorrow—a belief completely foreign to a Christian disdain for things of the world. A focus on gain becomes in the play a subtle threat from within to Christian identity, altering the Christian's ability to perceive correctly even the holiest of objects connected to his faith.

And even if Antonio's desire to help his friend is the ultimate cause of his worries, it is an earthly bond between men, not a bond between man and God that leads Antonio to Shylock, who is linked to the devil specifically through his monetary practices and his exegetical justifications of them:

> The devil can cite Scripture for his purpose,—
> An evil soul producing holy witness
> Is like a villain with a smiling cheek,
> A goodly apple rotten at the heart.
> O what a goodly outside falsehood hath! (I.iii.93–97)[30]

Antonio employs the polarizing strategies common to Christian hermeneutics to demonize Shylock. Shylock's exegesis may, according to Antonio, have the veneer of scriptural authority, but it is internally corrupt. Antonio charges that Shylock's reading of an "Old Testament" story falsely conflates "natural" reproduction of livestock with what Christians deemed the "unnatural" duplications of usury.[31] Contrasting the "evil" with the "holy," Antonio draws upon the fundamental Christian hermeneutical distinction between inner and outer realities to separate animal husbandry from usury and to condemn Shylock's method of reading the Bible.[32] Through this dichotomy, Antonio both demonizes the Jewish and aligns it with a mode of interpretation that values the exterior and the superficial. This Jewish way of reading, Antonio charges, stands opposed to a holy, Christian way of reading, which values the inner and spiritual meaning.

To justify his usury, Shylock has used the story of Jacob and Laban's sheep.[33] Shylock's identification with Jacob's clever ploy is ironic, because it is later Shylock who will be like Laban, who loses his daughters and much of his property to Jacob, identified in Christian exegetical tradition with Christians. This exegetical connection is alluded to in the interlude between Launcelot Gobbo and his father.[34] The scene draws upon biblical

references to paternity and birthright at the basis of Christianity's configuration of its relationship to Judaism, making explicit the connection between exegesis and questions of patrimony by alluding to the story of Esau
and Jacob. Esau, already cheated out of his birthright by Jacob, comes to
receive his father's blessing. With the help of Rachel, Jacob disguises himself with animal skins so that Isaac, too blind to recognize him, will give
him Esau's rightful blessing.

This story of treacherously stolen patrimony is one of the central stories of Jewish identity, because it is the descendants of Isaac through Jacob
who become the house of Israel. The Jacob and Esau story was also
known, through Paul, as a justification of Christian supersession. In Romans 9:12, Paul declares that the elder (Esau) will serve the younger
(Jacob) just as Christianity supersedes Judaism's spiritual role.[35] Both
Catholic and Protestant early modern English interpretations of the Jacob
and Esau story emphasize the story of the brothers as a prefiguration of
the relationship between Judaism and Christianity, even if commentators
differed on their assessments of the morality of Jacob's various decep-
tions.[36] As John Colley argues, in the allusions to Esau and Jacob in the
Launcelot Gobbo scene, Shakespeare provides "a comic version of the
symbolic core of his drama," bringing together issues of patrimony and
identity and, through the allusion to the Jacob and Esau story, framing
the conflict in the story within Biblical narrative.[37] The resonances of this
story in the comic interlude between Launcelot and his father are part of
the play's focus on proper patrimony and its subversion. Launcelot's
father, Gobbo, is "sand-blind" and, like Isaac, cannot recognize his own
son, who, like Jacob, asks for his blessing. This blindness associates Old
Gobbo with Jewishness through the critical motif of Jewish spiritual blindness, but ultimately, Gobbo is redeemed from this association through his
recognition of and willingness to aid Launcelot, symbolized by his giving
his offering of a dish of doves, traditionally associated with the presentation of the young Christ at the temple (Luke 2:22–24) not to the old
Jewish master, Shylock, but the new Christian one, Bassanio.

As René Fortin points out, the relationship between Shylock and Jessica is yet another version of the father-child relationship that highlights
the importance of filial piety, and, I would add, patrimony, in the play.[38]
Gobbo will not accept Launcelot until Launcelot names his mother, then
claiming him as his "own flesh and blood." Shylock refers to Jessica as his
"flesh and blood," creating verbal echoes between Launcelot's and Jessica's situations and sharpening the play's focus on patrimony. But unlike

Jacob, Launcelot teases his father but does not betray his trust. Instead, Gobbo and son work together to free Launcelot from Shylock's house; were he to remain there he would risk "turning Jew" himself: "I am a Jew if I serve the Jew any longer" (II.ii.106–7), as though association with the Jew can taint identity itself. Launcelot is transferred from the Jew's house to service in a Christian home, where he, a type of Jacob, reinforces the Pauline interpretation of the Esau-Jacob story by serving Christians. So poor that he has no patrimony of his own, Launcelot instead diverts the patrimony of Shylock's house by aiding Jessica in her elopement. The Christian father may be literally blind, but it is the Jewish father who is utterly alienated from his daughter and cannot prevent her escape.

In her elopement, Jessica herself becomes a type of "prodigal daughter," linking her story to another famous biblical story (Luke 15:11–32) read in the Christian tradition as a narrative of supersession.[39] Her actions invert the parable, making the child, aligned here with Christian youth, wiser than the father, who here is Jewish and unforgiving, aligned with the very Pharisees to whom the parable was once addressed.[40] And like Jacob, whose acquisition of patrimony through deception was viewed with ambivalence by biblical commentators, Jessica's actions can be read as both a brave embrace of redemption and a cruel betrayal. The figure of the prodigal runs throughout the play: Launcelot, Antonio, and Bassanio, as well as Jessica, each display prodigal traits. It is in Jessica, though, that the supersessionist readings of the parable become literalized. Ducats and daughter are transferred as the father, Shylock, loses his wealth, his daughter, and his bloodline, his "very flesh and blood," to the Christians. As Salerio's joking mention of "two stones, two rich and precious stones, / Stol'n by my daughter!"(II.viii.20–21) implies through its punning reference to testicles, Jessica's elopement emasculates Shylock and spells the end of his line.[41] Christian inheritance becomes not simply spiritual, but literal.

The play's framing of questions of genealogy and patrimony in biblical terms creates a sense that the quarrel between Shylock and Antonio is equivalent to the struggle between two peoples. Shylock refers frequently to his own Jewish identity through allusion to the stories of the origin of the Jews in Genesis, creating a simultaneity of biblical history and current events. Shylock uses the story of Jacob's sheep to make a point about money lending: when he swears, he swears by "Jacob's staff" (II.v.36). For Shylock, Abraham, Isaac, and Jacob seem to be not ancient ancestors but distant blood relations, as close to him as his coreligionist Tubal

(I.iii.52). Non-Jews are, to Shylock, spurned outsiders. As Launcelot slyly aids Jessica in plotting her elopement, Shylock questions, "What says that fool of Hagar's offspring?" (II.v.43). Shylock here seems not only to refer to Launcelot's low servant status and but also to confuse him with Muslims, because Islam claims a genealogy back to Ishmael, Hagar's son. The story of Hagar and Ishmael is another of the stories about identity and paternity at the root of the Jewish, Christian, and Islamic traditions, once again framing the relationships between the play's characters in terms of religious origin.[42] In Galatians 4:24, Sara, the free woman, allegorically represents the Gospels or New Testament, whereas Hagar, the bond woman, is the Law, but Shylock reads, or in Christian terms, mis-reads, these associations.[43] Ironically, while Shylock is berating Launcelot as an outsider to the tribe of Israel, Launcelot is helping to steal Jessica and considerable wealth from that tribe. Shylock is continually concerned with the fate of his people and his daughter, the rightful recipient of his wealth. For him, this patrimony is connected to the stories of the Hebrew Bible, whereas for the Venetians, who rarely refer to the Bible, patrimony is determined through their own style of exegesis. This exegesis is based on a hierarchy that allegedly places inner over outer meaning in the tradition of neo-Platonic and patristic and medieval Christian exegesis, although as Portia's rejection of Morocco makes clear, surface details, such as a suitor's complexion, can make all the difference.

This discourse of Christian exegesis in *The Merchant of Venice* is nowhere clearer than in the famous courtroom scene, which polarizes letter and spirit, Justice and Mercy, and Jews and Christians. Before Shylock even enters the courtroom, the Venetians' discussion sets up a dichotomy between him and Antonio.[44] Shylock is "a stony adversary, an inhuman wretch," (IV.i.4), his "fury" opposed to Antonio's "quietness of spirit" (IV.i.11–12). Shylock is tied explicitly to the language of Pauline hermeneutics through references to his hardened "Jewish heart" (IV.i.80) and his own vigorous insistence on the word *law*, which continually resonates with the traditional opposition between law and grace. Shylock's defeat in court and his subsequent conversion enact the triumphant supersession of the New Dispensation over the Old. Portia's famous speech about Mercy stresses the necessity of the New Dispensation:

. . . therefore Jew,
Though justice be thy plea, consider this,
That in the course of justice, none of us
Should see salvation. (IV.i.193–96)

The division between justice and mercy and Portia's insistence on the necessity of their cooperation is framed in terms of Christian supersession. Justice runs a course but falls short of the final goal of salvation, a figuration that parallels a Christian view of salvation history, in which the reign of Grace supersedes the reign of Law. Shylock is admonished that he will not be saved unless he accepts this supersessionary Christian version of justice tempered with mercy. Addressed as "Jew," Shylock stands as a representative of all Jews, and Portia's warning sounds as an address from one people to another.[45]

Along these lines, Lewalski and other critics have shown the possibilities for reading the trial scene allegorically, with Shylock representing Old Testament Law and Antonio representing the Grace of the New Dispensation. Lewalski links the scene to medieval representations of the Parliament of Heaven, in which two of God's four daughters, Justice and Mercy, argue for precedence.[46] This backdrop provides a powerful dramatic context, anchoring the play in the tradition of medieval drama and elevating the scene into conflict on a cosmic scale. The trial scene contains other elements of medieval drama as well. Shylock was traditionally played with a red beard like that of Judas in the medieval dramatic tradition, a costuming choice that links Shylock with the archetypal betrayer of Christ.[47] In the Towneley and York cycles, all Jews, not just Judas, were portrayed as those responsible for the torture and death of Jesus; Shylock's bodily threat to Antonio reenacts this view of the Jewish role, pitting Christians against demonized and villainous Jews around the central dividing moment of the Crucifixion.[48] The threat of the bloody bond resembles the bodily peril of crucifixion, and the bond's emphasis on flesh and blood also echoes the elements of the eucharist. Ritual murder and host desecration accusation resonate with the fundamental charge against the Jews as Christ-killers; so too does Shylock's threat to the flesh and blood of a self-sacrificing Christian resonate with these earlier charges, dragging them into a centuries-old vortex of anti-Semitic accusation.[49] A demonized Shylock, representing all Jews, "stands for law" and demands his bond in its name. Antonio stands poised to sacrifice all for his friend's past profligacies and future happiness: in this, Antonio resembles Christ, who stands between two peoples and two interpretations of the law.[50] These allusive references reinforce a sense that a consummation of the bond would reenact the Crucifixion.

The trial is also portrayed as a turning point in Venetian history, paralleling the Crucifixion's pivotal role: at stake in the courtroom battle is

Venice itself, as the threat to Antonio's body echoes the threat to the commonwealth of Venice posed by the aliens who penetrate its borders, paralleling the traditional analogy between the body of Christ and the community of Christian believers. Both sides of the courtroom battle are in rare agreement over the necessity of maintaining Venetian law. Shylock charges, "If you deny it [the bond], let the danger light / Upon your charter and your city's freedom!" (IV.i.38–39), and Portia concurs that "there is no power in Venice / Can alter a decree established: / 'Twill be recorded for a precedent, / And many an error by the same example / Will rush into the state" (IV.i.214–18).[51] The laws of exchange in Venice prevent an influx of error, much akin to the influx of aliens within its bounds. Antonio argues similarly that if Shylock's bond were simply refused that the laws of Venice would be weakened:

> The duke cannot deny the course of law:
> For the commodity that strangers have
> With us in Venice, if it be denied,
> Will much impeach the justice of the state,
> Since that the trade and profit of the city
> Consisteth of all nations. (III.iii.26–31)

Antonio's statement contains a kind of universalizing pull; Venice is the center of trade of "all nations," as all manner of men are bound together by a commitment to justice for the sake of the "trade and profit." I read Antonio's universalizing as a perversion of the universalism we find in Galatians 3:28. Here we find a justice that "consisteth of all nations" joined not in faith but in the mutual pursuit of profit; a commitment in which the demands of the market seem more important than those of Christianity. Only Portia speaks of mercy, and ultimately, the Venetian application of mercy is thin and self-serving. Although Portia and the other Venetians call for mercy, they are not ready to give up the stability and profit linked to justice and must acknowledge the "commodity" belonging to aliens in order to preserve it. Paradoxically, it is this universal commitment to profit that makes Venice vulnerable to the very strangers who help to maintain its wealth.

Just as Launcelot claims that he risked becoming a Jew by remaining in the Jew's house, contact with the alien Shylock through the bond could be seen as influencing, or even corrupting, Christian interpretive practice. Although the Venetians rely upon an opposition to all things Jewish as an indication of their Christian natures, in the course of the trial, Portia's winning decision is based on a reading of the law so close and literal that it "out-Jews" Shylock himself:

> This bond doth give thee here no jot of blood,
> The words expressly are "a pound of flesh":
> Take then thy bond, take thou thy pound of flesh,
> But in the cutting it, if thou dost shed
> One drop of Christian blood, thy lands and goods
> Are (by the laws of Venice) confiscate
> Unto the state of Venice. (IV.i.302–8)

Here, Portia turns to the "express" words of Venetian law, interpreting them to the letter to ensure that Shylock cannot actually collect his bond and leading him to risk his life and goods should he do so. When Shylock asks, "Is that the law?" Portia insists that he himself must see the true nature of the law and the justice he demands and refuses him anything but his original demand. In doing so, Portia seems to be attempting to reveal the true nature of the law in all its awful exactitude, but in her insistence that Shylock take his bond or gain nothing, Portia moves closer and closer to a parody of the very literalness of which Christians accused Jews:

> Therefore prepare thee to cut off the flesh,—
> Shed thou no blood, nor cut thou less nor more
> But just a pound of flesh: if thou tak'st more
> Or less than a just pound, be it but so much
> As makes it light or heavy in the substance,
> Or the division of the twentieth part
> Of one poor scruple, nay if the scale do turn
> But in the estimation of a hair,
> Thou diest, and all thy goods are confiscate. (IV.i.320–28)

Eventually, it is not Portia, but Antonio and the Duke, who pardon Shylock's life and take only part of his goods, which Shylock insists is still tantamount to destroying him. Gone in any case is the fulsome mercy that the Duke explicitly associates with Christians in the opening lines of the scene and the overflowing mercy that Portia describes: "It droppeth as the gentle rain from heaven / Upon the place beneath" (IV.i.181–82). Although Portia has taught Shylock a lesson, in doing so she has redefined her own Christian identity. She shows that the quality of mercy can be withheld so that it "seasons justice" to suit Venetian tastes (IV.i.193). In their devotion to the "profit of trade" and their less-than-liberal bestowing of mercy, the Venetians, staying close to the surface and letter of the law in their judgment, undermine their identity as Christians even as they seem to defend themselves against Jewish onslaught. As in *Croxton*, the boundaries between Christian and Jew blur and, in reaction, the resulting punishment for the Jew is severe, and his ejection from the midst of Christians is demanded. Shylock is completely absent from Act V, even if Jessica's presence keeps Jewish essence ambiguously in play.

The trial scene finally also demonstrates the ways in which exegesis is linked to patrimony in the play. As part of his merciful concessions to Shylock, Antonio takes over the role of Jessica's father, with the ability to bestow patrimony and to determine the contents of Shylock's will. Antonio becomes the administrator of the half of Shylock's estate not ceded to Venice, which he will hold in "use" and "render it / Upon his death unto the gentleman / That lately stole his daughter" (IV.i.379–81). The trial's outcome ensures that Shylock's wealth is turned over to the very man who has stolen the daughter Shylock had intended to produce descendants. Now this money will go to Christian inheritors, and Antonio further demands that Shylock "presently become a Christian" (IV.1.383) and bestow any goods he may later accumulate to his son-in-law and newly baptized daughter. In this way, Antonio ensures the diversion of all of Shylock's wealth and bloodline from Jewish hands into those of Christians. Neither future wealth nor future heirs can be Jewish; Portia's interpretation and Antonio's dealings with it ensure the flow of Jewish wealth into Venetian coffers. In this way, interpretation controls patrimony as all wealth is transferred from the older Jew to the younger Christians.

In *The Merchant of Venice*, we further find not simply a world in which the pursuit of trade causes a man to mistake one thing for another, but a world in which everything seems reducible to a commodity, bearing not an intrinsic worth, but a cash value: Antonio pledges a pound of his flesh for 3,000 ducats, Gratiano and Bassanio wager 1,000 ducats on their first male heir, and Shylock bemoans, in the same breath, the loss of daughter and ducats. Shylock reveals the extent of this commodification most clearly when he claims that his bond must be honored in order to maintain social order in Venice:

What judgment shall I dread doing no wrong?
You have among you many a purchas'd slave,

Which (like your asses, and your dogs and mules)
You use in abject and in slavish parts,
Because you bought them,—shall I say to you,
Let them be free, marry them to your heirs? (IV.i.89–94)

Shylock cites Venetian ownership of slaves to support his right to his bond.
For what else is the bond of a pound of flesh if not the institution of
slavery drawn out to its logical extreme—the commodification of human
flesh down to individual pounds? Crucial here as well is Shylock's reminder
to the Venetians of the separation between slaves and freemen, who are
suitable to be heirs. After all, both love plots in *Merchant* hinge upon a
father attempting to control bloodline and patrimony, with the commodification of Antonio's flesh acting as one link between the two plots and
Jessica, the play's other "flesh and blood," acting as the other. The casket
plot shows a daughter "curb'd by her father's will" from beyond the grave
and Shylock, in losing Jessica, loses both daughter and fortune.

Although Venice and Belmont are sometimes read as diametrically
opposed, the principle of exegesis controlling patrimony is the governing
law willed by Portia's late father. In order to win Portia and her inherited
wealth, the suitors must divine the contents of the caskets, whose written
contents draw heavily on exegetical language, reinforcing the sense that
the suitors must draw upon hermeneutic discourse. Morocco's scroll informs him plainly that he has failed in his quest because he chose outer
luster over inner worth:

All that glisters is not gold,
Often have you heard that told,—
Many a man his life hath sold
But my outside to behold,—
Gilded tombs do worms infold. (II.vii.65–69)

Stressing a division between inner and outer realities, the scroll links the
hermeneutical endeavors of Morocco to those of Shylock, who also con-
fuses gleaming exterior and a rotten core whose association with tombs
could be said to evoke the death of the letter. Because he has failed to
determine inner worth, Morocco not only does not win Portia's patrimony but forfeits the right to create his own—he is forbidden to marry.
Like Shylock, whose insistence on a certain interpretation of the bond

loses daughter, wealth, and religious identity, Morocco, who fails in his interpretation, sees the end of his lineage.

It is in the character of Morocco that the discourse of exegesis combines explicitly with that of "race" through specific emphasis on color, as Morocco's choice of the casket with the most alluring exterior ironically opposes his own self-introduction to Portia.[52] As he is introduced, Morocco has specifically declared that he should be evaluated on his inner worth, not his black appearance, inviting Portia to make an "incision for your love," so that he can prove the "redness" of his blood. Portia tells Morocco that she is not led "solely" by her own eyes, but by her father's decree, but even before Morocco's arrival, Portia has declared "if he have the condition of a saint, and the complexion of a devil, I had rather he should shrive me than wive me" (I.ii.123–25). After Morocco's loss, she further comments, "Let all of his complexion choose me so" (II.vii.79). Here "race" and the exegetical opposition between inner and outer worth combine, because the threat that Morocco poses is clearly one of miscegenation, a dark-skinned suitor winning the fair Portia. Morocco's suit is the most pointed instance of the threat of "intercourse with the Other" in the play, as a black man steps up to court a white Venetian woman who possesses great beauty and vast wealth. One can read Morocco as foiled by his ultimate inability to read like a Christian, to discern inner worth, although Morocco's own plea to be evaluated as a man, which resonates with Shylock's famous assertion of Jewish humanity, inserts an element of uncertainty into any easy correlation between inner and outer worth, once again destabilizing an easy distinction between Christian and Other. And, ironically, Morocco fails when he judges by exteriors, exactly as Portia has judged him.

The appearance of Arragon, the Spanish suitor, although sometimes overlooked by critics, is also marked by the discourse of "racial" difference. If, as Eric Griffin argues, *Othello*, also set in Venice, makes reference to Spanish obsession with purity of blood, then not only Morocco but Arragon advances the theme of "racial" difference in the casket plot.[53] The Spanish situation was one in which faith was linked to a kind of internal essence, which might be cleverly concealed, but which could not be erased. A frequently cited passage from early modern Spanish author Fray Prudencio de Sandoval describes the spiritual intractability of Jews as a type of essence that is similar to blackness of skin color, asserting that both are traits passed on through generations, even if mixed with white or Christian ancestry: "Who can deny that in the descendants of the Jews there persists and endures the evil inclination of their ancient ingratitude and lack of understanding, just as in Negroes [there persists] the inseparability of their blackness: For if the latter should unite themselves a thousand times with white women, the children are born with the dark color of the father. Similarly, it is not enough for the Jew to be three parts aristocrat or Old Christian for one family line [. . .] alone defiles and corrupts him."[54] Such writings suggest that no matter what one's outer appearance is, essential difference may lurk in the blood, beneath the skin. A Jew may have eyes and may bleed when pricked, but that blood itself may be essentially different from Christian blood. The Spanish figure of Arragon not only represents the Spanish focus on pure blood, but poses the threat of miscegenation. Spain was depicted not only as a land obsessed with "purity of blood," but as one lacking in it. In Edmund Spenser's *A View of the Present State of Ireland*, as he laments a potential mixing of Irish and English stock, his character Irenius declares of the Spanish, from whom the Irish claim descent, "of all nations under heaven (I suppose) the Spaniard is the most mingled, and most uncertain."[55] The self-obsessed Arragon is unsuitable not only for his questionable morality but for his questionable genealogy, of which his failure at the casket challenge also spells the end.

In contrast to Morocco and Arragon, the Venetian Bassanio chooses according to inner worth, as the scroll he finds makes explicit: "You that choose not by the view / Chance as fair, and choose as true" (III.ii.131–32). The song Portia commands be played before Bassanio makes his choice hints that he should choose according to the inner nature of things:

> Tell me where is Fancy bred,
> Or in the heart, or in the head?
> How begot, how nourished?
>
> . . . .
> It is engend'red in the eyes,
> With gazing fed, and Fancy dies
> In the cradle where it lies:
> Let us all ring Fancy's knell.
> I'll begin it. Ding, dong, bell. (III.ii.63–71)

Fancy, focused upon the surface of things and driven by visual desire, quickly dies.[56] The ditty's linking of death and decay with improper interpretation echoes the Carrion death in the golden casket and resonates with the Pauline linkage between death and the letter. Erotic desire, according to the casket mottos, should conform to Christian hermeneutic practice and will then lead to a proper end in successful marriage.

Bassanio heeds the ditty's advice, basing his casket choice upon a faith in the superiority of inner content:

> So may the outward shows be least themselves,—
> The world is still deceiv'd with ornament—
> In law, what plea so tainted and corrupt,
> But being season'd with a gracious voice,
> Obscures the show of evil? In religion,
> What damned error but some sober brow
> Will bless it, and approve it with a text,
> Hiding the grossness with fair ornament?
>
> . . . .
>
> Thus ornament is but the guiled shore
> To a most dangerous sea: the beauteous scarf
> Veiling an Indian beauty; in a word,
> The seeming truth which cunning times put on
> To entrap the wisest. (III.ii.73–80, 98–101)

Bassanio's speech draws upon the Christian exegetical principles of the lure of the ornamental, referring first to the more typical descriptions of exegesis and how ornament can deceive men to accept corruption and danger both in a court of law and on the pulpit. These assertions are connected specifically to textual exegesis of both secular law and Scripture. The tension between inner and outer reality seems clear; pleasing but deceptive exterior traits, a "gracious voice" or "sober brow," can mask the internal corruption of a reader of the text and his interpretation—a "damned error" or a plea "tainted and corrupt."

In the metaphor of the Indian woman, however, the stability of the opposition between exterior ornament and interior corruption breaks down in a way even more dramatic than in the case of Morocco. A beautiful scarf may allure the viewer, but underneath hides an "Indian beauty." If this woman is indeed a beauty, then what is the deception proposed here? Is it her darkness, inferior to Elizabethan ideals of fair coloring? By referring to the veil and its "seeming truth," Bassanio's metaphor borrows from traditional treatments of the exegetical veil but shifts them dramatically. As we have seen, in these figurations, the male exegete either lifts a feminized veil to reveal a core of truth, or truth itself is feminized, hidden beneath the ornamental veil of the text's surface. In Bassanio's formulation, however, neither layer, the veil nor the woman shrouded beneath, represents any kind of idealized or sought-after beauty or truth. Instead both exterior and interior are beguiling and potentially dangerous: the Indian beauty's veil is like a "guiled shore" that leads to "a most dangerous sea." Both parts of this metaphor imply threat, as the shore actively seems to conspire with the sea to lure the sailor to his death, a danger heavily weighted in this play in which great portions of the plot hinge upon the tides, as Salerio's opening evocation of a shipwreck shows.

The implied connection between the Indian beauty and the "most dangerous sea" leads to a breakdown in the traditional exegetical tension between inner and outer reality. The beauty that should be contained beneath the veil turns out to be its own kind of paradox—an Indian beauty—not in itself ugly like "damned error" or a tainted plea, but dangerous nonetheless. The threat the Indian woman poses is more than simply disappointment. The lifting of the veil can imply the revelation of a spiritual mystery, but in Bassanio's speech, this mystery leads to yet another cipher and to potential disaster. As Carolyn Dinshaw has shown, the gendered language of Christian exegesis is linked to erotic desire. Once the male viewer is close enough to the Indian beauty to see beneath her veil, it may be too late for him to resist the eroticized scenario initiated by the unveiling. Here is the figure of the captured alien bride, but without the confidence of Deuteronomy's Hebrew warrior by which her exotic allure can be stripped away and thereby controlled, making her a proper wife who can bear legitimate and acceptable offspring. Through her erotic allure, the Indian beauty's ultimate threat therefore seems potential miscegenation, a diversion of bloodline and pure identity through "mixed-race" children who inherit an essence from their alien parent that cannot be stripped away. This possibility is underscored in the play through the courtships of both Morocco and Portia and Lorenzo and Jessica and through Launcelot's liaison with the Moor. In Bassanio's speech, this dilution of identity and bloodline are as threatening as death in an engulfing sea. The catastrophe results from an inability to read signs properly—a skill analogized to the navigation skills necessary to the exploration that facilitates trade and contact with the Other. A failure to read signs and to discern a difference that cannot be eradicated, that is not hidden beneath a veil, but beneath the skin, can lead to disaster, a sexual comingling with alien essence that will produce tainted offspring.

Bassanio's initial discussion of outer perfection and inner corruption maintain their oppositions, but once outside the realm of the familiar, the church and the courtroom, the European explorer finds himself in more ambiguous and indeterminate situations. Led by his desire for the bounty of the land and the body of the woman, the male adventurer must rely upon the shore and the veil as signs by which to determine his course, but these very signs seem to conspire against him and to signify in ways that he cannot understand.[57] As the casket plot itself shows, exegetical enterprises are not without risk. The Venetian man seems to define himself by his willingness to take risks, to explore the seas and "hazard all," but it is through these very quests that he risks both patrimony and identity. The price for his inabilities is high—the loss of pure lineage or even death.

The system of trade in Venice is such that everyone is a potential buyer or seller dealing on the market. This includes women, whose desires are portrayed as active and potentially dangerous. In helping to arrange her rendezvous with Lorenzo, Launcelot tells Jessica that "There will come a Christian by / Will be worth a Jewes eye" (II.v.41–42). Rather than simply being the object of Lorenzo's gaze, Jessica will elope based on her own desire, engendered through the eye, the seat of erotic Fancy and measured for "worth."[58] Jessica's escape from her father's house is open, active, and rebellious; it even involves temporarily disguising herself as a young man.[59] Launcelot makes explicit the active sexuality of his Moorish mistress: "It is much that the Moor should be more than reason: but if she be less than an honest woman, she is indeed more than I took her for" (III.v.37–40). The multiple puns on "more" in these lines indicate a kind of comic and erotic excess, as the desires of the Moor and their consequences seemed poised to disrupt social order.[60] The play depicts female desires—Portia's, Nerissa's, Jessica's, and the Moor's—as having direct effect on both patrimony and its dispersal; the women contrive to marry according to their own desires.

In contrast to the other women in the play, however, Portia's desire, along with her maid Nerissa's, ultimately conforms to the will of the men of Venice; they are part of the same power structure. Portia's role as a powerful woman who ultimately brings about the wishes of deserving worshipers against dangerous Jews resembles that of the Virgin in the Miracles of the Virgin genre.[61] In these narratives, Mary is often extremely powerful but, as in the *Prioress's Tale*, operates within the bounds of Christian society, ultimately under masculine control. But Jessica, an alien woman, reveals the potential dangers to the Venetian male and the commonwealth of unchecked female desires, particularly the danger of miscegenation bringing strange and potentially indeterminate products onto the human market. The play ultimately shows, I argue, that the desire for gain and the pursuit of commerce threaten the foundations of the society as they allow the presence and desire of aliens to crack Venice's once-stable foundation. Portia is won by Bassanio, and her desire is "correct" in that she shuns all alien suitors, choosing a Venetian. But her active nature shows the possibility for the loss of Venetian patrimony and genealogy created by the destabilizing effects of Venice's focus on commerce. The play's last lines make a bawdy pun that sums up the potential dangers of the free exchange of signs made possible by Venice's focus on trade. Gratiano declares, "Well, while I live, I'll fear no thing / So sore, as keeping safe Nerissa's ring" (V.i.306–7). This pun, which conflates Nerissa's gift and her vagina, implies that in order to secure the purity of paternity, genealogy, and patrimony, womens' bodies must be closely monitored and not allowed to circulate freely.[62] A society that allows patriarchal control to be compromised by market demands is one that may allow female desire to circulate too freely, risking bastardy and the secured exchange of patrimony.

The problematic of the alien woman, desiring and desirable, and ultimately indecipherable, finds its fullest characterization in Jessica. Although Jessica's fair appearance and gentle manners make her seem the perfect convert, the play also raises doubts about the efficacy of her conversion. Jessica passes between communities, her marriage forming a link between Jews and Christians, but the moment she is introduced into the play's action, Jessica's identity and true nature are at issue. Even Jessica herself seems unsure of her identity, particularly of her connections to Shylock: "But though I am a daughter to his blood / I am not to his manners" (II.iii.18–19). Jessica poses a question that also splits her self into two aspects—genealogy and character—and she is unsure which determines her identity. In defending Jessica against Shylock's claims to her kinship, Salerio declares, "There is more difference between thy flesh and hers, than between jet and ivory, more between your bloods, than there is between red wine and Rhenish" (III.i.34–36). Salerio polarizes Jessica's relationship to Shylock through binaries that place the exotic Jewess in the same categories as the valuable and foreign goods that fill the stores of Venetian ships. The play, however, continually questions whether Jessica is really the commodity she seems to be. Even if her blood seems finer than Shylock's, a difference as great as the contrast between black jet and white ivory, the fact remains that she is, as he insists, "his flesh and blood."

Launcelot seems to disbelieve that Jessica is actually Jewish, speculating instead that she is the product of an illicit union: "Adieu! tears exhibit my tongue, most beautiful pagan, most sweet Jew!—if a Christian do not play the knave and get thee, I am much deceived" (II.iii.10–12). Because he cannot fit Jessica into the traditional binarisms that link the Jewish with the evil and the ugly in opposition to the Christian, good and beautiful, Launcelot is at a loss to define Jessica—is she Jewish, Christian, or even pagan? Even after she has converted and married Lorenzo, Launcelot still goads Jessica with her past. Teasing her that she is damned because she is a Jew's daughter, Launcelot tells Jessica that her only hope of salvation is the hope of bastardy, that her mother cuckolded Shylock with a Christian: "for truly I think you are damn'd,—there is but one hope in it that can do you any good, and that is but a kind of bastard hope neither" (III.v.5–7). Launcelot argues that Jessica's only hope in transcending a Jewish parentage is to be the bastard child of a Christian father, an accident of blood. Despite her conversion and marriage to a Christian, Launcelot continues to focus on Jessica's birth, implying that, whatever her intentions, there is something essentially Jewish about her. For Launcelot, Jessica's blood takes precedence over her manner, even those very manners that so endeared her to him when he lived under her father's roof. Jessica, who seems to believe in the importance of intention and action over birth, replies that she does not want to be rescued from one sin by another, to which Launcelot responds, "Truly then I fear you are damn'd both by father and mother: thus when I shun Scylla (your father), I fall into Charybdis (your mother); well, you are gone both ways" (III.v.13–16). Launcelot characterizes Jessica's Jewish parentage as monstrous. His reference to her mother as Charybdis, an engulfing whirlpool, recalls the treacherous seas always in the background of the play's action, including the dangerous waters of Bassanio's "guiled" shore and Salerio's wreck. Like Bassanio, Launcelot is placed in the position of interpreter, divining the fate of Jessica's soul through the history of her blood. But, in the case of Jessica, the riddle of interiority remains unsolved.

Jessica responds to Launcelot's charges by claiming that she is saved through her marriage, stressing the efficacy of her conversion. The ensuing dialogue, into which Lorenzo enters, rewrites the question of Jewish and Christian identity in terms of miscegenation and commerce:

> Jes: I shall be sav'd by my husband,—he hath made me a Christian!
> Laun: Truly the more to blame he, we were Christians enow before, e'en as many as could well live one by another: this making of Christians will raise the price of hogs,—if we grow all to be pork-eaters, we shall not shortly have a rasher on the coals for money.
>   . . .
> Lor: I shall grow jealous of you shortly Launcelot, if you thus get my wife into corners!
> Jes: Nay, you need not fear us Lorenzo, Launcelot and I are out,—he tells me flatly there's no mercy for me in heaven, because I am a Jew's daughter: and he says you are no good member of the commonwealth, for in converting Jews to Christians, you raise the price of pork.
> Lor: I shall answer that better to the commonwealth than you can the getting up of the negro's belly: the Moor is with child by you Launcelot!
> Laun: It is much that the Moor should be more than reason: but if she be less than an honest woman, she is indeed more than I took her for. (III.v.17–23, 26–39)

At the core of these jokes lies an anxiety about the Jewish presence within the Christian population and Jessica's role as the link between the two peoples. Launcelot's retort, that Jessica's conversion will raise the price of pork, brings into play once more the inflection of mercantile discourse into the discourses of religion and love, as questions of conversion and paternity become questions of economics. An increase in the number of New Christians will create scarcity for other Christians, a situation that would have had real meaning for an Elizabethan audience that had recently faced devastating food shortages and had rioted against aliens in their midst.[63] And, indeed, the presence of aliens in the English commonwealth had sparked riots among workers and apprentices. For Lorenzo, Jessica's conversion provides wife and wealth, and indeed, the wealth of Jewish converts did often end up in the coffers of the Christian state, benefitting the ruling classes.[64] For members of the lower classes, like Launcelot, the creation of New Christians could mean not an increase in resources but further scarcity.

Rather than commending Lorenzo for bringing another Christian into the fold and creating the potential for more through marriage, Launcelot views this addition as a drain in resources for "legitimate" Christians. I chose "legitimate" deliberately, because Jessica's situation is continually framed by bastardy. Launcelot accuses her of being illegitimate issue, and when Lorenzo appears he comically scolds Launcelot for cornering his wife. Jessica is always thought of in terms of bastardy; as with a bastard it will be difficult to determine the identity of her future children. Such indeterminate children must be accounted for; Lorenzo and Launcelot must "answer to the commonwealth" for the new members they create within it. Will the Venetian community be feeding its own offspring, or those from questionable unions? As was made evident in the courtroom scene, the stability of the commonwealth rests upon the distinctions made between individuals living within it and the regulations governing the relationships between these individuals.[65]

It is easier to answer to the commonwealth for children not notably marked as different. It is precisely this outward appearance that lowers the value of Launcelot's offspring. The children of a Moorish mother and Venetian father would be physically marked as different, displaying to all their mixed origins. The children of Jessica and Lorenzo will presumably not be marked and would have the ability to pass among the Venetian Christians as their own. Lorenzo's reply, however, reveals that Jessica and the Moor are both regarded as potential sources of miscegenation. Lorenzo does not testify to Jessica's exceptional human worth, but rather points to the lesser value of Launcelot's mistress. As Lynda Boose has argued, what is so scandalous in Launcelot's impregnating the Moor is that the offspring of white men and black women confound sixteenth-century patriarchal ideas about paternal dominance, in which the child bears the imprint of the father. This is why, Boose argues, a liaison between a black man and a white woman, such as that between Othello and Desdemona, was imaginable to the Elizabethans, whereas Launcelot's relationship with the Moor is not and remains an unstaged yet disruptive moment in the play: the discussion of miscegenation dead-ends with this remark, and Launcelot's exotic mistress never appears in the play's text.[66] The reference to the pregnant Moor suggests that the threat of miscegenation winds through the casket and elopement plots but that these threads are never fully woven together.

What is being explored in the discussions of Jessica's identity is the nature not only of her difference, but of difference itself. Is identity consti-

tuted through birth or belief? In the Pauline sense expounded in Galatians, Jessica's belief should make her a Christian, but the divisive binaries
that are the foundations of the figures of the hermeneutical Woman and
the hermeneutical Jew cause Christians themselves to have doubts based
on her birth.[67] If Christians and Jews are so diametrically opposed, how
can conversion occur so easily? Jessica should be able to pass among Christians with ease. Even in the most intimate of relationships, marriage, she
remains physically unmarked, because unlike Jewish men, she is uncircumcised.[68]

It is this lack of physical difference, I argue, that accounts in part for
the fantasy of "the beautiful Jewess." As a Jewish male, Shylock bears the
mark of circumcision, a physical sign that distinguishes him from non-
Jews. This mark is a sign of Jewish genealogy cut into the instrument for
perpetuating that genealogy.[69] This mark of Jewish identity is, in Paul, one
of the most notable vestiges of the Law, and Paul's teachings free Christians from the need to circumsize: "For he is not a real Jew who is one
outwardly, nor is true circumcision something external and physical. He is
a Jew who is one inwardly, and real circumcision is a matter of the heart,
spiritual and not literal." (Romans 2:28–29). Paul's interpretation of the
mark of circumcision connects to one of the core principles in *Merchant*,
the ability to distinguish between inner and outer reality, to interpret the
world through the spirit. In exegetical terms, Jessica would seem to be the
triumphant prodigal, signaling Christian supersession. But the idea of an
internal Jewish essence, a lurking presence in medieval discourse and
clearly delineated in early modern Spanish discourse, renders useless the
Christian hermeneutic practice of reading beneath surface exteriors. Because Jessica bears no physical sign of difference, and indeed because her
exterior is so lovely and so beguiling, like the golden casket or the Indian
beauty, she poses an unsolvable exegetical riddle.

Shapiro convincingly argues that Shylock, by threatening to cut Antonio exactly where Paul has said all true Christians are circumcised, threatens to make a Jew in the Christian manner.[70] Shapiro shows how the threat
of circumcision inherent in Shylock's attempt to collect his bond is ironically reversed as Shylock is forced to accept baptism, with the final effect
of "erasing, rather than preserving, the literal and figurative boundaries
that distinguish merchant from Jew."[71] But this possibility of "making a
Jew" lurks threateningly in the play, as Shapiro argues that it did in six-
teenth- and seventeenth-century English culture. Launcelot fears becoming a Jew by remaining in Shylock's house; Antonio refuses to play the Jew

by lending at interest. This threat is, of course, ironically reversed as Shylock is forced by the court to convert to Christianity.

But, in the case of Jessica, the threat remains—her union with Lorenzo might not create Christian offspring, but Jewish ones.[72] Rather than being welcomed into the Christian fold, Shylock disappears completely after Act IV; the harmonies and humor of Act V take place beyond his presence and at his expense. Jessica is, of course, present in Act V, having been accepted into the heart of Belmont and welcomed specifically by Portia. She should blend into the harmonies of the reunited Belmont in Act V, but Act V opens with an awkward tête-à-tête with Lorenzo, in which they compare the night they experience to that experienced by famous lovers. The dialogue focuses oddly on lovers who experienced tragedy—Troilus, Thisbe, Dido, and Medea—and, of these, only Thisbe does not suffer due to treachery and betrayal. After recounting these woeful lovers, Lorenzo then places Jessica in this dubious pantheon and she him:

> Lor: In such a night
> Did Jessica steal from the wealthy Jew,
> And with an unthrift love did run from Venice,
> As far as Belmont.
> Jes: In such a night
> Did young Lorenzo swear he loved her well,
> Stealing her soul with many vows of faith,
> And ne'er a true one. (V.i.14–19)

Although playful, this banter seems strangely uneasy. After Jessica alludes to Medea, infamous for her violent revenge of Jason's betrayal, Lorenzo brings up the story of Jessica's elopement, casting her in the role of betrayer. Rather than delighting in Jessica's flight to him, Lorenzo places her actions in a catalogue of doom. Jessica then applies religious language to the circumstances of her marriage and conversion for the first time, and we find that it is her feelings for Lorenzo, rather than her religious sentiment to which she refers. Jessica does not seem converted in faith, but rather by her erotic desires. Uneasy among Jews in her father's house, she remains so among Christians at Belmont.

A picture of Jessica's unease and lack of integration into Christian company is the last we have of her. In Act V, we find that she is unable to respond to the music so important to Belmont and its harmonies: "I am never merry when I hear sweet music" (V.i.69). Her sentiments recall Shylock's distaste for revels on the night she flees his house; it seems she still bears some of her father's traits even after abandoning him, another sign of her essential difference from Christians. In Jessica's uneasiness and the continual doubts that she can escape a Jewish essence, the play most clearly reveals its questioning of the nature of Christian and Jewish identities, the efficacy of conversion between the two faiths and the threat of miscegenation that follows upon a conversion such as Jessica's.

*   *   *

Shylock's bond threatens to make a Jew through its echo of the ritual of circumcision. Jessica, however, represents the threat of making actual Jews through her union with Lorenzo, invisibly and perhaps inadvertently destabilizing the Christian identities of the Venetians through dilution of their essence. It is in Jessica, the beautiful Jewess, that we find a new combination and hybrid of the hermeneutical Woman and the hermeneutical Jew. Both figures are commonly presented as "hermeneutically handicapped," with both associated with an inability to read and interpret like Christians, to separate the literal and the carnal from the spiritual. The figure of Jessica, however, through her beauty and allure, is herself unreadable, and the Venetians, particularly the Venetian men, are hindered in their understanding of her. The figure of the beautiful Jewess draws its power from this inscrutability. The hermeneutical Woman and the hermeneutical Jew are "tools of Christian self-definition," the objects of exegesis and themselves failed interpreters. Jessica, through these exegetical constructs, is the new Jewish prodigal. The conversion of the prodigal daughter spells the conversion of the Jew in a triumph of youth over age. And yet, through doubts over her conversion, Jessica also represents a more dangerous figure, one who threatens bloodlines. In Jessica, the beautiful Jewess, the binary opposition at the core of both the hermeneutical Jew and the hermeneutical Woman—the opposition between external and internal realities—breaks down. Jessica is the alien woman whose dangerous qualities are not marked and cannot be stripped away. The nature of her identity remains indeterminate through the very fact of her conversion, because as she converts from Jew to Christian, she becomes both loving wife and treacherous daughter. Unlike Portia, who obeys her father's will and avoids miscegenation through her obedience, Jessica's disobedience of her Jewish father spells not only the end of his line but the potential dissolution of Lorenzo's.

Representation of the capture or seduction of an alien woman, be she daughter, wife, or queen, is a symbol of domination found in a wide range of texts and contexts.[73] Each instance, however, although following a generalized pattern of the "captured queen," the alien convert, or even Leslie Fiedler's archetypal "ogre's daughter," has specific cultural configurations.[74] Because of the specific relationship between Judaism and Christianity and the tension between origin and margin always present in that relationship, the willing conversion of the beautiful Jewess, who becomes an enduring type in English and continental literatures, is related to other literary types of exotic beauties, but her conversion has specific ramifications. Through her exegetical connections, she represents the prophesied, biblical supersession of Christianity over Judaism. But through her connections to "exotic" women, such as Launcelot's Moorish mistress and the Indian beauty, she presents an alluring beauty who is herself seductress and whose disconnection between outer appearance and inner essence threatens the dissolution of Christian identity itself. Contact with Jessica and with the other "exotic" beauties in the play is made through the "commercial intercourse" of exploration, trade, and commerce. Like the Croxton play, *Merchant* shows how the pursuit of the worldly and the material can lead to a breakdown in Christian identity. The Christian, itself a constructed, unstable identity, is threatened by temptation on all sides. With the addition of the element of sexuality, through the figure of the desiring and desirable Jewish woman, *Merchant* creates a situation in which the threat of the Jewish cannot finally be sent away. Shylock is absent from Act V, but Jessica remains, a continual and disruptive Jewish presence. Supersession, it seems, may be hijacked by its own success.

Conclusion

We reject, as you know, the honour of being a relic.
—Emmanuel Levinas[1]

We must ask, not "What is a Jew?" but *"What have you made of the Jews?"*
—Jean-Paul Sartre[2]

IN *PLAYING IN THE DARK: Whiteness and the Literary Imagination*, Toni Morrison recounts her search to understand the role of the "Africanist presence" as a shaping one in American literature. In a brilliant analogy she captures the experience of realizing that seemingly disparate elements have been part of an invisible frame:

It is as if I had been looking at a fishbowl—the glide and flick of the golden scales, the green tip, the bolt of white careening back from the gills; the castles at the bottom, surrounded by pebbles and tiny, intricate fronds of green; the barely disturbed water, the flecks of waste and food, the tranquil bubbles traveling to the surface—and suddenly I saw the bowl, the structure that transparently (and invisibly) permits the ordered life it contains to exist in the larger world. In other words, I began to rely on my knowledge of how books get written, how language arrives; my sense of how and why writers abandon or take on certain aspects of their project. . . . What became transparent were the self-evident ways that Americans choose to talk about themselves through and within a sometimes allegorical, sometimes metaphorical, but always choked representation of an Africanist presence.[3]

Through illuminating the Africanist presence, Morrison exposes the literary construction of "whiteness" and the ways in which white authors used the Africanist presence to construct visions of white America. To understand how the Africanist presence functions in literary texts as an instrument of white American self-definition is to see the fishbowl as a structure of thought and imagination.

The historical situation that Morrison examines obviously differs from that of late medieval England; the Africanist presence is not simply a type of discourse, but an actual and substantial human presence. Jews were also, in different times and different places an actual, historical presence in Europe. But during the period in which the texts we have examined were produced, the Jews were banished from England. Despite this lack of a Jewish population, however, the figure of the Jew also had a type of presence in that it was a fundamental component of Christian ideologies in England and was a shaping component of representations of Christians and Christianity, both explicitly and implicitly.[4] Borrowing again from Morrison's formulations about the Africanist presence in the United States, one can say that the Jewish presence in late medieval and early modern English imagination can also be seen as a "shadow [that] hovers in implication, in sign, in line of demarcation."[5] This shadow figure is the hermeneutical Jew, a tool of Christian self-definition.

The contours of the glass bowl, that structure of thought that orders and shapes, are what Simone de Beauvoir set out to describe in *The Second Sex*, and indeed her repeated references to the particular identities of woman, Black, and Jew point to their intersectionality and the different but intertwined relationships that each of these particular identities has to a normative universal identity, which is by default assumed to be masculine, Christian, and white.[6] As we have seen, what Morrison calls the "long history on the meaning of color" is definitely relevant to early texts.[7] Shakespeare winds into the interlocking strands of the traditions of hermeneutical woman and hermeneutical Jew other figures that had also come to haunt the English imagination, such as the Moor and the Spaniard, weaving into his pattern of representation the mark of color.[8] These representations are created within the context of Shakespeare's historical moment, at the dawn of the Age of Exploration, but we should not regard these representations as signs of a clean boundary line of periodization between medieval and Renaissance, either as a rupture or a starting point. Rather, we find in the play a refraction of a continuous and complex tradition, whose patterns endure, shifting and changing into the current day.

The enduring legacy of medieval representation is readily apparent when we consider the power of the dualized figures of virgin and whore in contemporary Western culture. And, as we have seen, the fortunes of the hermeneutical Jew are part of an equally enduring and often intersecting tradition, one that also, I believe, still has power in ways as obvious as they are shocking and disturbing, but also in more subtle ways as well. These more subtle influences have recently been illuminated in fascinating and influential philosophical explorations of the Jew as figure in contemporary ideologies: for example, Žižek's discussion of the Jew as Lacanian symptom or Lyotard's "jews."[9] When we attempt to engage with these analyses of contemporary uses of the Jew as part of an explicit resistance of anti-Semitic or of supersessionist thought, however, we should do so with an eye to the longer tradition of the figure of the Jew. This study has concerned itself with intertwined representations of religious, gender, and racial difference in Christian thought into the sixteenth century, but I hope it is now also perhaps clearer how these earlier entangled traditions might have relevance for us today. Exploration of this earlier representational tradition suggests that we should be wary of making new interpretive frameworks that may unwittingly resemble or reinscribe the strategic and constricting deployment of the Jew. The Jew has been an inextricable part of the Christian theological tradition for two millennia and remains as well a part of the secular inheritance of this tradition. To be mindful of this is not just an interpretive strategy but a means of attempting to move beyond stereotypes not only in literary representation, but in a range of contexts.

The schematic histories of universalism presented by Laclau and Schor both acknowledge the undeniable importance of Christian theology in Western thought, including its secular traditions. The relevance and power of Christian universalism for contemporary thought is evident in Alain Badiou's recent work on Paul, which shares with Laclau's work on universalism a desire to recuperate the universal for radical political ends.[10] Badiou reads Paul's writings as presenting a complex interplay of Jewish, Greek, Christian, and mystical discourses, which expound the Truth-Event of Christianity—the Resurrection.[11] As part of his appropriation of Paul as exponent of radical universalism, Badiou addresses directly the problems posed by two particular identities, Jew and woman. By choosing these figures as his focus through which to explore the problem of difference, Badiou affirms the fundamental paradoxes that they pose to the Christian tradition.

Badiou argues that Paul does not at all advocate abolishing "la particularité juive."[12] But Jewish particularity is for Badiou equated with "le Livre," the Old Testament, which he notes figures so importantly in the Epistle.[13] Although obviously distinct from the context and intention of the figurations of the Jew as bearer of the text in Augustine or even as the text itself in Bernard of Clairvaux, Badiou's connection between Jewish particularity and the Hebrew Bible as Old Testament is part of a continuous tradition. The dubious Jewish honor of being a relic, it seems, is perhaps impossible to revoke.

Although fully cognizant of the powerful advantages of universalism, this book has sought to remind us of its traditional costs. The battle over these costs can be at times bitter. After addressing the Jewish question, Badiou then turns to feminist critiques of Paul, displaying open scorn for the "tribunal du féminisme contemporain" and charging it with anachronistic judgment of Paul's writings.[14] In his defense of Paul as a man of his times, Badiou avoids treating the fundamental paradox that woman poses to the universal as revealed by Beauvoir, Scott, and others. Badiou concludes his section on difference by arguing, "Les différences nous donnent, comme font les timbres instrumentaux, l'univocité reconnaissable de la mélodie du Vrai."[15] Badiou wishes to consider Paul as neither apostle nor saint, but I find it difficult to ignore the tradition in which Paul is both. Can we so easily distinguish between this "mélodie du Vrai" and the harmonies of supersession? The yearning for the universal is, as we have seen, not new, and neither is the price of universalism. And, as this book has attempted to demonstrate, these questions deserve examination not only in light of Paul's writings, but also in relation to the influential reception of Pauline thought in both Christian and secular traditions. The olive tree of Romans is a unified, organic symbol that can stress negotiation and growth, but the supersessionary drive inherent in this analogy must also be recognized. The dynamics of supersession operating within the Christian tradition have shaped the places of both woman and Jew in Western thought and politics.

Questions posed from the perspective of these particulars should not simply be dismissed as the rant of a politically correct tribunal demanding its pound of flesh. Not all such examinations seek moral reckonings; some seek ethical understandings. As this book has demonstrated, these kinds of questions and the issues at stake when they are raised are certainly not new despite the many permutations they have clearly undergone. In the *Canterbury Tales*, we saw "the Jewish question" and "the woman question" intersecting with each other and resonating through broader questions of authority, interpretation, and meaning, as well as shaping representations of heresy, belief, sin, youth, and age. The empty space of the universal was as vigorously contested, negotiated, and debated then as it is now, and the hermeneutical Jew and the hermeneutical Woman were and continue to be tools in these debates. In N-Town and *Croxton* we find negotiations of Christian identity and the never completed task of Christian universalism enacted by and for Christian communities. Supersession is writ large in the structures of these plays, as they move from sorrow to joy, from doubt to belief, from division to unity. It is also inscribed onto the very bodies of specific doubters, as the stubborn Jew and the doubting midwife are corporeally struck by doubt, only to be restored to wholeness through the sacred bodies of the host and the Virgin. In *Merchant*, the question of how to determine meaning, to see beyond the beguiling veil of the exterior to the truth that lies hidden beneath is explored once again, in a different way, through the figures of woman and Jew. The exegetical underpinnings of the hermeneutical Jew and the hermeneutical Woman become complicated by the struggle to define the relationship between contested Christian and English identities and between these identities and a range of Others.

Michael Ragussis calls *Merchant* the "ur-text of the representation of Jewish identity in England."[16] What this book has attempted to suggest is that "ur-texts" are made, not born. *Merchant* weaves together in powerful ways central strands in the much longer Christian traditions of the figures of woman and Jew. We can perhaps begin to explain the ur-text status of *Merchant* not simply through recourse to what so many, myself included, regard as its aesthetic and emotional power. The preeminent influence of *Merchant*, and I suggest, its beauty and power as well, have to do with the way it refracts an image. It has helped to shape subsequent representations of the Jew because it simultaneously reveals and conceals the elements of the exegetical tradition that it engages.

Abbreviations

AHR	*American Historical Review*
CCCM	*Corpus christianorum: Continuatio medievalis* (Turnhout, Belgium: Brepols, 1966–)
CCSL	*Corpus christianorum: Series latina* (Turnhout, Belgium: Brepols, 1953–)
CSEL	*Corpus scriptorum ecclesiasticorum latinorum* (Vienna: F. Tempsky, 1866–)
EETS	Early English Text Society
e.s.	extra series
HTR	*Harvard Theological Review*
JEGP	*Journal of English and Germanic Philology*
MLQ	*Modern Language Quarterly*
NM	*Neuphilologische Mitteilungen*
o.s.	original series
PL	J.-P. Migne, *Patriologiae cursus completus: Series latina* (Paris: Migne, 1841–)

Notes

Chapter 1

1. Simone de Beauvoir, *The Second Sex*, trans. H. M. Parshley (New York: Vintage, 1974), 301.

2. Cited in Karl Morrison, *Understanding Conversion* (Charlottesville: University of Virginia Press, 1992), 62.

3. In the introduction to *The Second Sex*, Beauvoir also several times alludes to the situation of the Jews, pointing out the ways in which the Jews and Blacks, like women, occupy the place of the particular in relation to a normative universal that is not only masculine but Christian and white.

4. As Valerie Smith notes in the introduction to *Not Just Race, Not Just Gender: Black Feminist Readings* (New York: Routledge, 1998), the assumption that gender and race are "mutually dependent, interlocking cultural constructions and projections" is not a recent development, but can be found, for example, in the nineteenth-century work of thinkers and activists such as Sojourner Truth and Harriet Jacobs (xiii).

5. The literature here is extensive. Among the works that have been important to my thinking are Gloria Anzaldúa and Cherríe Moraga, *This Bridge Called My Back: Writings by Radical Women of Color* (Watertown, Mass.: Persephone Press, 1981); bell hooks, *Feminist Theory from Margin to Center* (Boston: South End Press, 1984); Chela Sandoval, "U.S. Third World Feminism: The Theory and Method of Oppositional Consciousness in the Postmodern World," *Genders* 10 (1991): 1–24; Trinh T. Minh-ha, *Woman, Native, Other: Writing Postcoloniality and Feminism* (Bloomington: Indiana University Press, 1989); Barbara Smith, "Toward a Black Feminist Criticism," *Conditions: Two*, no. 2 (October 1977), reprinted in *All the Women Are White, and All the Blacks Are Men, But Some of Us Are Brave: Black Women's Studies*, ed. Gloria T. Hull, Patricia Bell Scott, and Barbara Smith (Old Westbury, N.Y.: Feminist Press, 1982), 157–75. See also Marianne Hirsch and Evelyn Fox Keller, *Conflicts in Feminism* (New York: Routledge, 1990).

6. Recognition of intersectionality is not limited to these theoretical schools. Hans Mayer, *Aussenseiter* (Frankfurt am Main: Suhrkampf, 1981), has had an important impact among German academics and intellectuals, for example.

7. Anne McClintock, *Imperial Leather: Race, Gender and Sexuality in the Colonial Contest* (New York: Routledge, 1995), 5.

8. Kimberlé Crenshaw, "Mapping the Margins: Intersectionality, Identity Politics, and Violence Against Women of Color," in *Critical Race Theory: The Key*

Writings That Formed the Movement, ed. Kimberlé Crenshaw, Neil Gotanda, Gary Peller, and Kendall Thomas (New York: New Press, 1995), 357–83, and "Demarginalizing the Intersection of Race and Sex: A Black Feminist Critique of Antidiscrimination Doctrine, Feminist Theory and Antiracist Politics," *The University of Chicago Legal Forum,* 1989: 139–67.

9. Ania Loomba, *Gender, Race, Renaissance Drama* (Manchester, U.K.: Manchester University Press, 1989), and Kim Hall, *Things of Darkness: Economies of Race and Gender in Early Modern England* (Ithaca, N.Y.: Cornell University Press, 1995). See also Margo Hendricks and Patricia Parker, eds., *Women, "Race," and Writing in the Early Modern Period* (New York: Routledge, 1994).

10. In scholarship on the modern period, studies of "Jews and gender" are extensive. See, for example, Sander Gilman, *Difference and Pathology: Stereotypes of Sexuality, Race and Madness* (Ithaca, N.Y.: Cornell University Press, 1985), and *The Jew's Body* (New York: Routledge, 1991); Nancy Harrowitz and Barbara Hyams, eds., *Jews and Gender: Responses to Otto Weininger* (Philadelphia: Temple University Press, 1995); Andrea Freud Loewenstein, *Loathsome Jews and Engulfing Women: Metaphors of Projection in the Works of Wyndham Lewis, Charles Williams, and Graham Greene* (New York: New York University Press, 1993), and Inge Stephan, Sabine Schilling, and Sigrid Weigel, eds., *Jüdische Kultur und Weiblichkeit in der Moderne* (Köln: Böhlau Verlag, 1994). See also bibliographic references in my "'O My Daughter!': 'Die schöne Jüdin' and 'Der neue Jude' in Hermann Sinsheimer's *Maria Nunnez,*" *The German Quarterly* 71 (1998): 254–70.

11. Important representative articles include Geraldine Heng, "Cannibalism, the First Crusade and the Genesis of Medieval Romance," *differences* 10 (1998): 98–174, and "The Romance of England: *Richard Coeur de Lion,* Saracens, Jews, and the Politics of Race and Nation," in *The Postcolonial Middle Ages,* ed. J. J. Cohen (New York: St. Martin's, 2000), 135–72; Steven F. Kruger, "Becoming Christian, Becoming Male?" in *Becoming Male in the Middle Ages,* ed. Jeffrey Jerome Cohen and Bonnie Wheeler (New York: Garland, 1997), 21–41 (bibliography contains additional references); Denise Despres, "Immaculate Flesh and Social Body: Mary and the Jews," *Jewish History* 12 (1998): 47–69 (bibliography contains additional references). Other important examinations of medieval intersectionality that are not specifically focused on Middle English literature are Kathleen Biddick, "Genders, Bodies, Borders: Technologies of the Visible," in *Studying Medieval Women: Sex, Gender, Feminism,* ed. Nancy F. Partner (Cambridge, Mass.: Medieval Academy of America, 1993), 87–116, and Sara Lipton, *Images of Intolerance: The Representation of Jews and Judaism in the Bible moralisée* (Berkeley: University of California Press, 1999). See also the special issue on "race" of the *Journal of Medieval and Early Modern Studies,* 31, no. 1 (2001). There is a recent book-length examination of the intersection of Jewish and gender difference in medieval Spanish literature: see Louise Mirrer, *Women, Jews, and Muslims in the Texts of Reconquest Castile* (Ann Arbor: University of Michigan Press, 1996).

12. For discussions of these debates, see Linda Zerilli, "This Universalism Which Is Not One," *diacritics* 28 (1998): 3–20, and Eric Lott, "After Identity, Politics: The Return of Universalism," *New Literary History* 31 (2000): 665–78. See also *October* 61 (1992), *Critical Inquiry* 18 (summer 1992), reprinted as *Identities,*

ed. Kwame Anthony Appiah and Henry Louis Gates Jr. (Chicago: University of Chicago Press, 1995) and *differences* 7 (spring 1995).

13. The phrase "the return of universalism" is from Naomi Schor, "French Feminism Is a Universalism," *differences* 7 (spring 1995), 28. Ernesto Laclau, *Emancipation(s)* (New York: Verso, 1996).

14. Ernesto Laclau and Chantal Mouffe, *Hegemony and Socialist Strategy: Towards a Radical Democratic Politics*, 2d ed. (New York: Verso, 2001). Original publication date 1985.

15. Laclau, Emancipation(s), 49.

16. Lott, 670.

17. Laclau, *Emancipation(s)*, 52.

18. Laclau, *Emancipation(s)*, 42.

19. Schor, "French Feminism," 22.

20. Zerilli, 10, and Schor, "French Feminism," 22.

21. Judith Butler, "Restaging the Universal: Hegemony and the Limits of Formalism," in *Contingency, Hegemony, Universality: Contemporary Dialogues on the Left*, ed. Judith Butler, Ernesto Laclau, and Slavoj Žižek (New York: Verso, 2000), 14.

22. Laclau, *Emancipation(s)*, 43, italics in text.

23. Zerilli, 11.

24. Laclau, *Emancipation(s)*, 53.

25. Laclau, *Emancipation(s)*,43.

26. Zerilli, 19.

27. *Emancipation(s)*, 15. Cited in Zerilli, 10.

28. For background on these early contexts of Christian self-definition, see Marcel Simon, *Verus Israel: A Study of the Relations between Christians and Jews in the Roman Empire (135–425)*, trans. H. McKeating (Oxford: Oxford University Press, 1986), and Jaroslav Pelikan, *The Emergence of the Catholic Tradition (100–600)* (Chicago: University of Chicago Press, 1971).

29. Christian universalism can, of course, have varied meanings, and the readings of both exegetical and literary texts in this book can be seen as explorations of what this universalism means in relation to the text in question. For a discussion of the history of this term, particularly in relation to questions of the doctrine of universal salvation (*apokastastasis*), see Richard J. Bauckham, "Universalism: a Historical Survey," *Themelios* 4 (1979): 48–54. Medieval theologies of universal salvation were, as Nicholas Watson demonstrates, "heterogeneous." See his "Visions of Inclusion: Universal Salvation and Vernacular Theology in Pre-Reformation England," *Journal of Medieval and Early Modern Studies* 27 (1997): 147–87.

30. Laclau, *Emancipation(s)*, 22.

31. Laclau, *Emancipation(s)*, 22–23.

32. Laclau, *Emancipation(s)*, 23.

33. Naomi Schor, "The Crisis of French Universalism," *Yale French Studies* 100 (2001): 44.

34. Ibid.

35. Kathleen Biddick, "Coming out of Exile: Dante on the Orient Express,"

in *The Postcolonial Middle Ages*, ed. J. J. Cohen (New York: St. Martin's, 2000), 35–52.

36. Biddick, "Coming out of Exile," 138.

37. Beauvoir, xviii. Laclau speaks of the process of hegemony as a process by which "the dichotomy universality/particularity is superseded." See "Identity and Hegemony: The Role of Universality in the Constitution of Political Logics," in Judith Butler, Ernesto Laclau, and Slavoj Žižek, *Contingency, Hegemony, Universality: Contemporary Dialogues on the Left* (New York: Verso, 2000), 56.

38. Schor, "French Feminism," 33–34, in reference to Irigaray's failure to deal with issues of race in her accounts of universalism.

39. Joan W. Scott, "Universalism and the History of Feminism," *differences* 7, no. 1 (1995): 7. See also her *Only Paradoxes to Offer: French Feminists and the Rights of Man* (Cambridge, Mass.: Harvard University Press, 1996).

40. Adam Sutcliffe, *Judaism and Enlightenment* (New York: Cambridge University Press, 2003), 6. See also his "Myth, Origins, Identity: Voltaire, the Jews and the Enlightenment Notion of Toleration," *The Eighteenth Century* 39 (1998): 107–26 and "Hebrew Texts and Protestant Readers: Christian Hebraism and Denominational Self-Definition," *Jewish Studies Quarterly* 7 (2000): 319–37.

41. On the term "Enlightenment" itself, which I must of necessity use in a general way here, see Sutcliffe, *Judaism*, 11–15.

42. Jeremy Cohen, *Living Letters of the Law: Ideas of the Jew in Medieval Christianity* (Berkeley: University of California Press, 1999), 3 and 13. I thank Professor Cohen for generously sending me sections of this book prior to its publication.

43. For the term "protean," see Denise Despres, "The Protean Jew in the Vernon Manuscript," in *Chaucer and the Jews: Sources, Contexts, Meanings*, ed. Sheila Delany (New York: Routledge, 2002), 145–64.

44. Despres, "Protean," 146.

45. Anna Foa argues that although, for example, Jews were associated with magic and the Devil, they were not treated in the same way as witches or heretics during the Inquisition, because this would have disturbed existing "equilibria" that maintained a view of Jews as unique in relation to Christianity. "The Witch and the Jew: Two Alikes that Were Not the Same," in *From Witness to Witchcraft*, ed. Jeremy Cohen (Wiesbaden: Harrassowitz Verlag, 1996), 364.

46. See David Rokéah, "The Church Fathers and the Jews in Writings Designed for Internal and External Use," in *Antisemitism through the Ages*, ed. Shmuel Almog, trans. Nathan H. Reisner (New York: Pergamon Press, 1988), 64. Cited in Cohen, *Living Letters*, 13. Although I am focusing here on the theological nature of the "hermeneutical Woman," I am also aware of the important nontheological elements at play in the figure. For a magisterial discussion of the figure of woman and its classical components, see Prudence Allen, R.S.M., *The Concept of Woman: The Aristotelian Revolution, 750 B.C.–A.D. 1250*, 2d ed. (Grand Rapids, Mich.: William B. Eerdmans Publishing Company, 1997).

47. Cohen, *Living Letters*, 13.

48. Cohen begins an earlier discussion of the figure of the "hermeneutical Jew" with reference to Michel Foucault's *The Order of Things*, which explores the

centrality of categorization to a "culture's fundamental 'experience of order and of its modes of being.'" Michel Foucault, *The Order of Things: An Archaeology of the Human Sciences* (New York: Random House, 1970), xx–xxi, cited in Jeremy Cohen, "The Muslim Connection or On the Changing Role of the Jew in High Medieval Theology," in *From Witness to Witchcraft: Jews and Judaism in Medieval Christian Thought,* ed. Jeremy Cohen (Wiesbaden: Harrassowitz Verlag, 1996), 141.

49. R. Howard Bloch, *Medieval Misogyny and the Invention of Western Romantic Love* (Chicago: University of Chicago Press, 1991), 31. Bloch's discussion of the figure of woman in relation to this paradigm has been of crucial importance to my analysis.

50. See Bloch, 31.

51. This formulation is indebted to work by Julia Reinhard Lupton, specifically to her reading of Marx on this issue. See her "Shakespeare's Other Europe: Jews, Venice, and Civil Society," *Social Identities* 7 (2001): 485, and more generally *Afterlives of the Saints: Hagiography, Typology, and Renaissance Literature* (Stanford, Calif.: Stanford University Press, 1996), "Exegesis, Mimesis, and the Future of Humanism in *The Merchant of Venice,*" *Religion and Literature* 32 (2000): 123–39, and her forthcoming book, *Citizen-Saints: Shakespeare and Political Theology.*

52. Mary Douglas, *Purity and Danger: An Analysis of the Concepts of Pollution and Taboo* (New York: Ark Paperbacks, 1966), 115.

53. See Ann Eljenholm Nichols, "The Hierosphthitic Topos, or the Fate of Fergus: Notes on the N-Town *Assumption,*" *Comparative Drama* 25 (1991): 29–41.

54. Ruth Evans, "When a Body Meets a Body: Fergus and Mary in the York Cycle," *New Medieval Literatures* 1 (1997): 194–212.

55. James Shapiro, *Shakespeare and the Jews* (New York: Columbia University Press, 1996).

56. Jennifer Summit, *Lost Property: The Woman Writer and English Literary History, 1380–1589* (Chicago: University of Chicago Press, 2000), 18, and Joan Kelly, "Did Women Have a Renaissance?" in *Becoming Visible: Women in European History,* ed. Renate Bridenthal and Claudia Koonz (Boston: Houghton Mifflin, 1977), 137–64. For a reading of Burckhardt, see Lupton, *Afterlives of the Saints* 6–14.

57. For a similar observation, see Yosef H. Yerushalmi, *Assimilation and Racial Antisemitism: The Iberian and the German Models* (New York: Leo Baeck Institute, 1982), 20. Yerushalmi points to examples such as that of Anaclet, arguing that the distinction between medieval prejudice against Jews as religious and modern anti-Semitism as secular and anti-Christian does not hold up to historical scrutiny and "must be tempered, at the very least" (20). The comparison between the Iberian and modern German situations is itself perhaps an overdetermined one. This does not, however, alter for me the value of Yerushalmi's observations. On the use of the German-Iberian connection by Jewish writers during the National-Socialist period, see my "'O My Daughter,'" 264–66.

58. On the questions of Jews and race in early modern England, the most important recent book is Shapiro, *Shakespeare and the Jews,* to which I will turn in

greater detail in Chapter 5. For a discussion of the terms "anti-Semitism" and "anti-Judaism" and an overview of scholarship that argues that the terms represent secular and religious views respectively, see Johannes Heil, "'Antijudaismus' und 'Antisemitismus': Begriffe als Bedeutungsträger," *Jahrbuch für Antisemitismusforschung* 6 (1998): 96. There will be further reference to the Spanish blood laws in Chapters 4 and 5.

59. As William C. Jordan points out in "Why Race?" the lack of discussion of prejudice against Jews in the recent *Journal of Medieval and Early Modern Studies* special issue on race is notable (31, no. 1 [2001], 166).

60. On the medieval-modern periodization divide and its impact on scholarship, see Lee Patterson, "On the Margin: Postmodernism, Ironic History, and Medieval Studies," *Speculum* 65 (1990): 92–95; David Aers, "A Whisper in the Ear of Early Modernists; or, Reflections on Literary Critics Writing the 'History of the Subject' in *Culture and History, 1350–1600: Essays on English Communities, Identities and Writing*, ed. David Aers (Detroit: Wayne State University Press, 1992), 177–202, and Judith M. Bennett, "Medieval Women, Modern Women: Across the Great Divide," in *Culture and History, 1350–1600*, ed. David Aers, 147–75.

61. Jerome Friedman, "Jewish Conversion, the Spanish Pure Blood Laws and Reformation: A Revisionist View of Racial and Religious Antisemitism," *The Sixteenth Century Journal* 18 (1987): 3–29. Example of volumes on early modern English literature whose titles feature the term "race" are: Joyce Green MacDonald, ed., *Race, Ethnicity and Power in the Renaissance* (Madison: Fairleigh Dickinson University Press, 1997), Catherine M. S. Alexander and Stanley Wells, eds., *Shakespeare and Race* (Cambridge: Cambridge University Press, 2000), and Imtiaz Habib, *Shakespeare and Race: Postcolonial Praxis in the Early Modern Period* (New York: University Press of America, 2000). See also the "Forum: Race and the Study of Shakespeare" in *Shakespeare Studies* 26 (1998): 19–82.

62. Kwame Anthony Appiah, "Race," in *Critical Terms for Literary Study*, ed. Frank Lentricchia and Thomas McLaughlin, 2d ed. (Chicago: University of Chicago Press, 1995), 275.

63. For discussion of the ways in which the biological and theological inflect each other in relation to the category of race and particularly through the category of gender in early modern texts, see Ania Loomba, "'Delicious Traffick': Racial and Religious Difference on Early Modern Stages," in *Shakespeare and Race*, ed. Catherine M. S. Alexander and Stanley Wells, 203–24.

64. On the impact of biblical paradigms on ideas of "race," ethnicity, and identity, see Benjamin Braude, "The Sons of Noah and the Construction of Ethnic and Geographical Identities in the Medieval and Early Modern Periods," *The William and Mary Quarterly* 54 (1997): 103–42.

65. Anna Abulafia, *Christians and Jews in the Twelfth-Century Renaissance* (New York: Routledge, 1995); Jeremy Cohen, *The Friars and the Jews: The Evolution of Medieval Anti-Judaism* (Ithaca, N.Y.: Cornell University Press, 1982); Amos Funkenstein, *Perceptions of Jewish History* (Berkeley: University of California Press, 1993), 172–201; Lester K. Little, *Religious Poverty and the Profit Economy in Medieval Europe* (Ithaca, N.Y.: Cornell University Press, 1978); R. I. Moore, *The Forma-*

tion of a Persecuting Society: Power and Deviance in Western Europe, 950–1250 (Oxford, U.K.: Basil Blackwell, 1987).

66. Robert Stacey, "The Conversion of the Jews to Christianity in Thirteenth-Century England," *Speculum* 67 (1992): 278. Cited in Jonathan Elukin, "From Jew to Christian? Conversion and Immutability in Medieval Europe" in *Varieties of Religious Conversion in the Middle Ages*, ed. James Muldoon (Gainesville: Florida University Press, 1997), 177–78.

67. On Anaclet, "the Jewish Pope," see Mary Stroll, *The Jewish Pope: Ideology and Politics in the Papal Schism of 1130* (New York: E. J. Brill, 1987), and Emil Mühlbacher, *Die streitige Papstwahl des Jahres 1130* (Aachen: Scientia Verlag, 1966).

68. Peter Biller, "Views of Jews from Paris around 1300: Christian or 'Scientific'?" in *Christianity and Judaism*, ed. Diana Wood (Oxford, U.K.: Blackwell, 1992), 188.

69. Robert Bartlett, "Medieval and Modern Concepts of Race and Ethnicity," *Journal of Medieval and Early Modern Studies* 31, no. 1 (2001): 42. See also Robert Bartlett, *The Making of Europe: Conquest, Colonization, and Cultural Change, 950–1350* (Princeton, N.J.: Princeton University Press, 1993).

70. Bartlett, "Medieval and Modern," 45.

71. Dealing with the size and nature of this shadow poses complex historiographic and ethical problems for scholars. In thinking about how the Holocaust has come to shape American academic politics, and political consciousness more generally, I have learned much from Peter Novick's provocative *The Holocaust in American Life* (New York: Houghton Mifflin, 1999).

72. David Nirenberg, *Communities of Violence: Persecution of Minorities in the Middle Ages* (Princeton, N.J.: Princeton University Press, 1996), 4–5.

73. Nirenberg, 5. Part of this approach in Jewish historiography is an emphasis on the unique duration and nature of prejudice against the Jews. Gavin Langmuir writes that "the Jews have been the oldest and most universal focus of a social and psychological phenomenon that has been characteristic of the rapidly evolving society of the West, prejudice," in *Toward a Definition of Antisemitism* (Berkeley: University of California Press, 1990), 40–41. A similar sentiment is echoed by Robert Wistrich, author of *Antisemitism: The Longest Hatred*, who writes, "There has been no hatred in Western Christian Civilization more persistent and enduring than that directed against the Jews," in "The Devil, the Jews, and Hatred of the 'Other,'" in *Demonizing the Other: Antisemitism, Racism, and Xenophobia*, ed. Robert Wistrich (Amsterdam: Hanwood Academic, 1999), 1. The remarks of both Langmuir and Wistrich stand out to me as emblematic of the lack of attention to questions of gender by scholars examining medieval representations of Jews and Judaism. Through even the limited examples we have discussed, it would seem clear that Jews do not have a unique claim to being the most long-suffering objects of prejudice in the West, nor, for that matter, does it make sense to attempt to claim this "distinction" for women. Ultimately, invoking such superlatives simply creates a hierarchy of oppressions that is inimical to a fuller understanding of the complex interplay of representations of Jews and women, not to mention other instances of intersectionality.

74. "If it is true that mankind has insisted on murdering Jews for more than

two thousand years, then Jew-killing is a normal, and even human, occupation and Jew-hatred is justified beyond the need of argument." Hannah Arendt, *Antisemitism: The Origins of Totalitarianism*, vol. 1 (New York: Harcourt, Brace, Jovanovich, 1951), 7.

75. Langmuir adopts the term "antisemitism" (he eschews the hyphen) as part of an explicitly post-Holocaust positioning that leads him to draw parallels between medieval attitudes and twentieth-century atrocities. He writes that "Jews did indeed become the target of an unusual kind of hostility in northern Europe in the twelfth and thirteenth centuries, and that that hostility was the same in kind as Hitler's hostility" (*Toward*, 17).

76. For an important discussion of this issue see Langmuir, *Toward*, 311–352. For an egregious example of this type of polemic (that also condenses and distorts medieval views), see Daniel Jonah Goldhagen, *A Moral Reckoning: The Role of the Catholic Church in the Holocaust and Its Unfulfilled Duty of Repair* (New York: Knopf, 2002), 35–37.

77. Kathleen Biddick's recent work challenges medievalists and modernists to rethink division of periodicity and has greatly stimulated my thinking on these issues. See, for example, "Coming out of Exile: Dante on the Orient(alism) Express," *AHR* (October 2000): 1234–49.

78. Just as there is no one usage of the terms "race" and "anti-Semitism" that will satisfy all readers, neither is the term "gender" without controversy, nor the sex/gender distinction natural.

79. Bartlett, "Medieval and Modern," 40. My decision not to format "gender" in a similar way is not an indication that I believe that "sex" is a stable, unified, or natural category. The term "gender" is, however, by no means as contested a category within medieval studies as is "race." The "essentialist-constructivist" debates of the 1980s and early 1990s dealt with the constructed nature of gender at length. As a way into these debates, see Judith Butler, *Gender Trouble: Feminism and the Subversion of Identity* (New York: Routledge, 1990) and *Bodies That Matter: On the Discursive Limits of Sex* (New York: Routledge, 1993) and especially Diana Fuss, *Essentially Speaking: Feminism, Nature and Difference* (New York: Routledge, 1989).

80. Alternative terminology is available. Many German-speaking scholars refer to the term *Judenfeindschaft*, and there is additional scholarly terminology such as "allosemitism." For English-language discussions of allosemitism, a concept developed by Polish theorist Artur Sandauer, see Zygmunt Bauman, "Allosemitism: Premodern, Modern, Postmodern" in *Modernity, Culture and "the Jew*," ed. Bryan Cheyette and Laura Marcus (Stanford, Calif.: Stanford University Press, 1998), 143–56, and Bryan Cheyette, *Constructions of "the Jew" in English Literature and Society: Racial Representations, 1875–1945* (New York: Cambridge University Press, 1993). Medievalist Sylvia Tomasch makes illuminating use of this concept in "Postcolonial Chaucer and the Virtual Jew," in *The Postcolonial Middle Ages*, ed. Jeffrey Jerome Cohen (New York: St. Martin's Press, 2000), 250.

81. McClintock, 8.

Chapter 2

1. "Hear, Jew, take note and understand / that the whole history of the old covenant / and all the sayings of the Prophets / are only a figure for the new covenant." Cited in Erich Auerbach, "Figura," in *Scenes from the Drama of European Literature* (Minneapolis: University of Minnesota Press, 1984), 233 n. 38. For fuller citation and analysis, see Edith Wenzel, *"Do worden die Judden alle geschant": Rolle und Funktion der Juden in spätmittelalterlichen Spielen* (Munich: Wilhelm Fink Verlag, 1992), 226. From the play *Kaiser Constantinus* in A. Keller, ed. *Fastnachtspiele aus dem 15. Jahrhundert*, vol 2. (1853–58; reprint Darmstadt, 1965–66), 801, lines 15–18.

2. Gayatri Spivak, cited in Helena Michie, *The Flesh Made Word: Female Figures and Women's Bodies* (New York: Oxford University Press, 1987), 7.

3. This speech is recorded in *Bulletin diocésain de Toulouse* (1933), 311–12 and cited in Henri de Lubac, *Christian Resistance to Anti-Semitism. Memories from 1940–1944*, trans. Sister Elizabeth Englund, O.C.D. (San Francisco: St. Ignatius Press, 1990), 147–48.

4. Saliège's speech is included by the French Jesuit theologian and medievalist Henri de Lubac as part of his recollections of French Catholic resistance to German occupation. These resistance efforts are connected to the abbey at Fourvière, site of work by major scholars of patristic and medieval exegesis such as Lubac and Henri Daniélou, as Lisa Freinkel has noted in her discussion of their exegesis. See her *Reading Shakespeare's Will: The Theology of Figure from Augustine to the Sonnets* (New York: Columbia University Press, 2002), 1–15. Lubac's collected memoirs of the war era present accounts of resistance to National Socialism and must be understood as part of a larger and conflicted Christian response to the events of World War II and the Shoah and to the ways in which the role of Christians and Christian institutions have been evaluated both for resistance to the National-Socialist regime and for passivity toward it or even complicity with it. For an introduction to the issues from a point of view critical of the Catholic Church, see David I. Kertzer, *The Popes against the Jews* (New York: Alfred A. Knopf, 2002).

5. All citations from the Pauline Epistles are from *The Writings of Saint Paul: A Norton Critical Edition*, ed. Wayne A. Meeks (New York: W. W. Norton, 1972). On Colossians and its place in the Pauline canon, see 112–15.

6. See Max Horkheimer and Theodor Adorno, *Dialectic of Enlightenment*, trans. John Cumming (New York: Continuum, 1972).

7. For an understanding of the context of Romans as one of developing Christian self-definition, see James C. Walters, *Ethnic Issues in Paul's Letter to the Romans* (Valley Forge, Pa: Trinity Press International, 1993). On the sociohistorical context for Romans, see Mikael Tellbe, *Paul between Synagogue and State: Christians, Jews, and Civic Authorities in 1 Thessalonians, Romans, and Philippians*, Coniectanea Biblica New Testament Series, vol. 34 (Stockholm: Almqvist and Wiksell International, 2001), 141–209, 289–97.

8. W. D. Davies argues that these two instances are not "inspiration" for

Romans 11. See "Paul and the Gentiles: A Suggestion Concerning Romans 11:13–24," in *Jewish and Pauline Studies* (Philadelphia: Fortress Press, 1984), 153–63.

9. This is identified as the diatribe style; see D. F. Watson, "Diatribe," and W. S. Campbell, "Olive Tree," both in *Dictionary of Paul and His Letters*, ed., Gerald Hawthorne and Ralph P. Martin (Downer's Grove, Ill: Intervarsity Press, 1993), 213–14 and 643.

10. "And in this way, each person, according to the impulses of his own purpose, will be designated [either] a good olive tree, if he travels down the road of virtue, or a wild olive tree, if he follows the opposite [path]. This, after all, is why even the Lord was saying in the Gospel, 'Either make the tree good and its fruit good; or make the tree evil and its fruit evil,'" in order to show that a tree, good or evil, is made, not born.' Origen, *Commentary on the Epistle to the Romans, Books 6–10*, trans. Thomas P. Scheck (Washington, D.C.: Catholic University of America, 2002), 176 (Book 8. 11.4). "Et sic unusquisque secundum propositi sui motus aut bona oliva, si iter virtutis incedat, aut si contraria sectetur, oleaster nominabitur. Inde denique et Dominus in evangelio dicebat: 'Aut facite arborem bonam et fructus eius bonos; aut facite arborem malam et fructus eius malos', ut ostenderet arborem bonam vel malam non nasci, sed fieri." Theresia Heither, OSB, ed. and trans., *Origenes Commentarii in Epistulam ad Romanos: Liber Septimus, Liber Octavus. Römerbriefkommentar Siebtes u. Achtes Buch* (Freiburg: Herder, 1994), 288. Origen writes this first major exegesis on Romans in the third century. It is clear that Origen participated in actual dialogue with Jews and had firsthand familiarity with Hebrew texts. In the estimation of Peter Gorday, Origen's early interpretation is the closest to Paul's inclusive spirit in Romans 9–11. Chrysostom and Augustine, writing in the fourth century, do not take fully enough into account Paul's mitigated desire to "affirm Judaism." See his *Principles of Patristic Exegesis: Romans 9–11 in Origen, John Chrysostom, and Augustine* (New York: Edwin Mellen Press, 1983), 227. See also N. R. M. de Lange, *Origen and the Jews: Studies in Jewish-Christian Relations in Third-Century Palestine* (Cambridge: Cambridge University Press, 1976).

11. See John Chrysostom, Homily 19 on Romans in *Homilies on Acts and Romans*, trans. J. B. Morris and W. H. Simcox, rev. and ed. George B. Stevens (Grand Rapids, Mich.: Wm. B. Eerdmans, 1956), 486–95. See Gorday, 103–35 and 189–242.

12. *Tractatus Adversus Iudaeos*, PL 42: 51–64. See trans. Sister Marie Liguori in *Treatises on Marriage and Other Subjects*, ed. Roy J. Deferrari (Washington, D.C.: Catholic University of American Press, 1955), 391–92, 414.

13. *Contra Faustum* 9.2. CSEL 25: 308–10.

14. *Enarrationes in Psalmos* 72.2. CCSL 39: 987. See also *Contra Faustum* 26.3. CSEL 25: 730–31.

15. Lisa Freinkel, *Reading Shakespeare's Will: The Theology of Figure from Augustine to the Sonnets* (New York: Columbia University Press, 2002), 14.

16. Heikki Räisänen, "Paul, God, and Israel: Romans 9–11 in Recent Research," in *The Social World of Formative Christianity and Judaism*, ed., Jacob Neusner, Ernest S. Frerichs, Peder Borgen, and Richard Horsley (Philadelphia: Fortress Press, 1988), 176–206. For a detailed cataloging of the responses of impor-

tant Greek and Latin Fathers to the olive tree analogy, see Karl Hermann Schelkle, *Paulus Lehrer der Väter die altkirchliche Auslegung von Römer 1–11* (Düsseldorf: Patmos Verlag, 1956), 389–99. Modern scholarship on Romans is extensive and can only be mentioned here. There has been an important shift in the scholarship since World War II as, following the pathbreaking work of E. P. Sanders, scholars began to take into account, among other factors, a more complex understanding of the relationship of the Jesus movement to Jewish thought, itself more varied and complex than it was previously portrayed. In addition to Räisänen and other sources cited in this chapter, I have found useful John G. Gager, *Reinventing Paul* (New York: Oxford University Press, 2000). A useful introduction and bibliography for nonspecialists interested in modern scholarship on the Epistles is S. J. Hafemann, "Paul and His Interpreters," in the *Dictionary of Paul*, ed. Hawthorne and Martin, 666–679.

17. Sermon 79.5 in Killian Walsh and Irene Edmonds, eds. and trans., *The Works of Bernard of Clairvaux*, 4 vols. (Kalamazoo, Mich.: Cistercian Publications, Inc., 1981), vol. 4, 141–42. "Magna Ecclesiae caritas, quae ne aemulae quidem Synagogae suas delicias invidet. Quid benignius, ut quem diligit anima sua, ipsum communicare parata sit et inimicae? Nec mirum tamen, quia salus ex Iudaeis est. Ad locum unde exierat, revertatur Salvator, ut reliquae Israel salvae fiant. Non rami radici, non matri filii ingrati sint: non rami radici invideant quod ex ea sumpsere, non filii matri quod de eius suxere uberibus. Teneat itaque Ecclesia firmiter salutem quam Iudaea perdidit: ipsa apprehendit, donec plenitudo gentium introeat, et sic omnis Israel salvus fiat. Velit in commune communem venire salutem, quae sic ab omnibus capitur, ut singulis non minuatur. Utique hoc facit, et plus. Quid plus? Quod et nomen sponsae illi optat, et gratiam. Prorsus super salutem hoc." In Jean Leclercq, C. H. Talbot, and H. M. Rochais, eds., *S. Bernardi Opera* (Rome: Editiones Cistercienses, 1957). Subsequent references are to these editions.

18. Sermon 23.2.

19. Friedrich Lotter, "The Position of the Jews in Early Cistercian Exegesis and Preaching," in *From Witness to Witchcraft: Jews and Judaism in Medieval Christian Thought*, ed. Jeremy Cohen (Wiesbaden: Harrassowitz Verlag, 1997), 163–86.

20. On the doctrine of Jewish witness, see Cohen, *Living Letters*, 23–65.

21. Daniel Boyarin, *A Radical Jew: Paul and the Politics of Identity* (Berkeley; University of California Press, 1994), 204–5.

22. Ibid., 205.

23. Ibid., 180–81.

24. See Boyarin, *Radical Jew*, 187, and John Gager, *The Origins of Anti-Semitism: Attitudes Toward Judaism in Pagan and Christian Antiquity* (New York: Oxford University Press, 1983), 225–27. For a contrary view, see A. J. Droge, "Discerning the Body: Early Christian Sex and Other Apocryphal Acts," in *Antiquity and Humanity: Essays on Ancient Religion and Philosophy Presented to Hans Dieter Betz on His Seventieth Birthday*, ed. Adela Yarbro Collins and Margaret M. Mitchell (Tübingen: Mohr Siebeck, 2001), 297–308.

25. "Differentia ista vel gentium vel conditionis vel sexus iam quidem ablata est ab unitate fidei, sed manet in conversatione mortali eiusque ordinem in huius

vitae itinere servandum esse et apostoli praecipiunt, qui etiam regulas saluberrimas tradunt, quemadmodum secum vivant pro differentia gentis Iudaei et Graeci et pro differentia conditionis domini et servi et pro differentia sexus viri et uxores, vel si qua talia cetera occurrunt, et ipse prior dominus, qui ait: "Reddite Caesari, quae Caesaris sunt, et deo, quae dei sunt." *Expositio ad Galatas* 28. *CSEL* 84: 92–93. Translation modified from citation in Kari Elisabeth Børresen, "God's Image, Man's Image? Patristic Interpretation of Gen. 1,27 and I Cor. 11,7," in *The Image of God: Gender Models in Judaeo-Christian Tradition*, ed. Kari Elisabeth Børresen, (Minneapolis: Fortress Press, 1995), 202. On Augustine and social hierarchy, see Peter Brown, *The Body and Society: Men, Women, and Sexual Renunciation in Early Christianity* (New York: Columbia University Press, 1988), 387–427.

26. James Samuel Preus, *From Shadow to Promise: Old Testament Interpretation from Augustine to the Young Luther* (Cambridge, Mass.: Harvard University Press, 1969), 18. Cited in Karlfried Froehlich, " 'Always to Keep the Literal Sense in Scripture Means to Kill One's Soul': The State of Biblical Hermeneutics at the Beginning of the Fifteenth Century," in *Literary Uses of Typology*, ed. E. Miner (Princeton, N.J.: Princeton University Press, 1977), 22.

27. Froehlich, 22.

28. Preus, 18.

29. Ibid., 19.

30. On "The Harmony of the Two Testaments," see Henri de Lubac, *Medieval Exegesis*, vol. 1, "The Four Senses of Scripture," trans. Mark Sebanc (Grand Rapids, Mich.: Eerdmans, 1998), 241–51, esp. 244–45. Originally published as *Exégèse médiévale, 1: Les quatre sens de l'écriture* (Paris: Éditions Montaigne, 1959).

31. Boyarin, *Radical Jew*, 17. Boyarin is careful not to label Paul as either anti-Semitic or misogynistic. His argument shows the potential for these prejudices in Paul's mode of thought, rather than finding them in the thought itself.

32. Boyarin, *Radical Jew*, 15.

33. Ibid.

34. Jean Leclercq, *Monks and Love in Twelfth-Century France: Psycho-Historical Essays* (New York: Oxford University Press), 143.

35. Gager refers to this as the "contradictionist" approach, which he links especially, as does Boyarin, to Räisänen's approach. See Gager, *Reinventing*, 8; Boyarin, *Radical Jew*, 183.

36. Boyarin, *Radical Jew*, 180–200.

37. See Wayne A. Meeks, "The Image of the Androgyne: Some Uses of a Symbol in Earliest Christianity," *Journal of the History of Religions* 13 (1973): 165–208. See also Boyarin, *Radical Jew*, 180–200, esp. 199.

38. Butler, *Gender Trouble*, 11–12, cited in Boyarin, *Radical Jew*, 180 and 199.

39. "Quae non credit, mulier est, et adhuc corporei sexus appellatione signatur; nam quae credit, occurrit in virum perfectum, in mensuram aetatis plenitudinis Christi." Ambrose, *Expositio evangeliis secumdum Lucam*, PL 15:1938 (1887 ed.). Translation (with slight modification) from Vern L. Bullough, "Medieval Medical and Scientific Views of Women," *Viator* 4 (1973): 499. Cited in Carolyn Dinshaw, *Chaucer's Sexual Poetics* (Madison: University of Wisconsin Press, 1989), 204–5, n. 65, Rita Copeland, "Why Women Can't Read: Medieval Hermeneutics, Statutory

Law, and the Lollard Heresy Trials," in *Representing Women: Law, Literature, and Feminism*, ed. Susan Sage Heinzelman and Zipporah Batshaw Wiseman (Durham, N.C.: Duke University Press, 1994), 257, and Joan Cadden, *Meanings of Sex Difference in the Middle Ages: Medicine, Science and Culture* (Cambridge: Cambridge University Press, 1993), 206.

40. Philo, as he explains why a male sheep is a superior offering to a female one, argues that a shift from femaleness to maleness represents improvement: "For progress is indeed nothing else than the giving up of the female gender by changing into the male, since the female gender is material, passive, corporeal, and sense-perceptible, while the male is active, rational, incorporeal, and more akin to mind and thought." *Quaestiones et Solutiones in Exodum I:8. Philo: In Ten Volumes and Two Supplementary Volumes*, supplement 2, trans. Ralph Marcus, The Loeb Classical Library (Cambridge, Mass.: Harvard University Press, 1952), 15–16. Cited in Elizabeth Castelli, "'I Will Make Mary Male': Pieties of the Body and Gender Transformation of Christian Women in Late Antiquity," in *Body Guards: The Cultural Politics of Gender Ambiguity*, ed. Julia Epstein and Kristina Straub (New York: Routledge, 1991), 32. On Philo and gender, see also Allen, 189–93.

41. "Quamdiu mulier partui servit et liberis, hanc habet ad virum differentiam, quam corpus ad animam. Sin autem Christo magis voluerit servire quam saeculo, mulier esse cessabit, et dicetur vir." *Commentariorum in Epistolam ad Ephesios libri* 3 (PL 26:533). Cited in Bullough, 499, and Dinshaw, 205, n. 64. The idea of the spiritual woman as masculinized in the Christian tradition has been quite thoroughly explored in recent years. See, for example, Margaret R. Miles, *Carnal Knowing: Female Nakedness and Religious Meaning in the Christian West* (Boston: Beacon Press, 1989), 53–80, and Barbara Newman, *From Virile Woman to WomanChrist: Studies in Medieval Religion and Literature* (Philadelphia: University of Pennsylvania Press, 1995), esp. 1–45. For an important discussion of gender difference from the point of view of medieval medicine and science, as well as theology, see Cadden, esp. 169–227.

42. We find declarations of transcendence of the female body in some narratives of early Christian female martyrs, such as that of *The Martyrdom of Perpetua and Felicitas* in the third-century text *The Acts of Christian Martyrs* and the story of Thecla in the Apocryphal Acts, who, when she renounces the world, cuts her hair and later dons men's clothing in order to travel the world as a teacher. See Herbert Musurillo, ed. and trans., *The Acts of the Christian Martyrs* (Oxford, U.K.: Clarendon Press, 1972), 106–31, and Castelli. See also Stevan L. Davies, *The Revolt of the Widows: The Social World of the Apocryphal Acts* (Carbondale: Southern Illinois University Press, 1980), and Virginia Burrus, *Chastity As Autonomy: Women in the Stories of the Apocryphal Acts* (Lewiston, N.Y.: Edwin Mellen Press, 1987). For additional examples, see Miles, 52–77.

43. Kari Elisabeth Børresen, "Gender and Exegesis in the Latin Fathers," *Augustinianum* 40 (2000): 71.

44. "Quicumque enim in Christo baptizati estis Christum induistis. Non est iudaeus neque graecus, non est seruus neque liber, non est masculus et femina; omnes enim uos unum estis in Christo Jesu? Numquidnam igitur fideles feminae sexum corporis amiserunt? Sed quia ibi renouantur ad imaginem dei ubi sexus

nullus est, ibi factus est homo ad imaginem dei ubi sexus nullus est, hoc est in spiritu mentis suae. Cur ergo uir propterea non debet caput uelare quia imago est et gloria dei, mulier autem debet quia gloria uiri est, quasi mulier non renouetur spiritu mentis suae, qui renouatur in agnitionem dei secundum imaginem eius creauit eum? Sed quia sexu corporis distat a uiro, rite potuit in eius corporali uelamento figurari pars illa rationis quae ad temporalia gubernanda deflectitur ut non maneat imago dei nisi ex qua parte mens hominis aeternis rationibus conspiciendis uel consulendis adhaerescit, quam non solum masculos sed etiam feminas habere manifestum est." *De Trinitate* 12. 7. 12. CCSL 50: 367. Translation (with modification): *The Trinity*, trans. Stephen McKenna (Washington, D.C.: Catholic University of America Press, 1963), 354–55. My reading here draws upon the conclusions of Børresen, "God's Image, Man's Image?" who cites and analyzes sections of this passage, 201. I have also benefited from discussion of these issues in Rosemary Radford Ruether, "Misogynism and Virginal Feminism in the Fathers of the Church," in Ruether, ed. *Religion and Sexism: Images of Woman in the Jewish and Christian Traditions* (New York: Simon and Schuster, 1974), 150–83.

45. T. J. van Bavel, "Augustine's View on Women," *Augustiniana* 39 (1989): 25. For differing views on Augustine's "feminism," see both works of Børresen and the more apologetic approach of van Bavel. Allen provides a very detailed and balanced examination, 218–40, including a chart of Augustine's complex views, 220.

46. Kim Power, *Veiled Desire: Augustine on Women* (New York: Continuum, 1996), 139.

47. *De Trinitate* 12. 8. 13. CCSL 50: 367. Translation: McKenna, 355.

48. Genevieve Lloyd, *The Man of Reason: "Male" and "Female" in Western Philosophy*, 2d ed. (Minneapolis: University of Minnesota Press, 1993), 31.

49. *De Genesi contra Manichaeos* 2. 11. PL 34: 204–5. Translation: *On Genesis. Two Books on Genesis against the Manichees and on the Literal Interpretation of Genesis: An Unfinished Book*, trans. Ronald J. Teske (Washington, D.C.: Catholic University of American Press, 1991), 111.

50. Power, *Veiled Desire*, 137–38. My readings here have benefited much from Power's stimulating discussion of the figure of the veil.

51. "Quomodo ergo per apostolum audiuimus uirum esse imaginem dei unde caput uelare prohibetur, mulierem autem non et ideo ipsa hoc facere iubetur nisi, credo, illud esse quod iam dixi cum de natura humanae mentis agerem, mulierem cum uiro suo esse imaginem dei ut una imago sit tota illa substantia; cum autem ad adiutorium distribuitur, quod ad eam ipsam solam attinet non est imago dei; quod autem ad uirum solum attinet imago dei est tam plena atque integra quam in unum coniuncta muliere? Sicut de natura humanae mentis diximus quia et si tota contempletur ueritatem, imago dei est, et cum ex ea distribuitur aliquid et quadam intentione deriuatur ad actionem rerum temporalium, nihilominus ex qua parte conspectam consulit ueritatem imago dei est; ex qua uero intenditur in agenda inferiora non est imago dei." *De Trinitate* 12. 7. 10. CCSL 50: 364–65. Translation (with slight modification): McKenna, 352. I draw on here as well discussion and translation in Børresen, "God's Image, Man's Image?" 200, and in Power, *Veiled Desire*, 138.

52. As Margaret Miles asserts in her discussion of early Christian writings, "In Christianity women were understood to be capable of religious subjectivity." *Carnal Knowing*, 83.

53. Steven Kruger points out crucial connections between gender, Jewish, Muslim, and heretical difference and the medieval Christian "feminization" of these religious others. His use of a wide variety of medieval Latin and vernacular sources takes a different approach than I do here but provides what I see as a complementary understanding of the relationship between Jewishness and gender in medieval Christian writings. See "Becoming Christian, Becoming Male?"

54. "Quamuis enim uetera priora sint tempore, noua tamen anteponenda sunt dignitate, quoniam illa uetera praeconia sunt nouorum." *De Civitate Dei* 20.4. CCSL 48: 703. *Concerning the City of God against the Pagans*, trans. Henry Bettenson, 2d ed. (New York: Penguin Books, 1984), 899. See discussion in Jill Robbins, *Prodigal Son/Elder Brother: Interpretation and Alterity in Augustine, Petrarch, Kafka, Levinas* (Chicago: University of Chicago Press, 1991), 4. For an extensive list of Christian authors expressing echoing views of the relationship between Old and New Testaments, see Lubac, *Medieval Exegesis*, 245 ff.

55. For these and other images, see Lubac, *Medieval Exegesis*, 246–61.

56. This is analyzed brilliantly by Robbins, 1–48. See also Ruether, "The *Adversus Judaeos* Tradition in the Church Fathers: The Exegesis of Christian Anti-Judaism," in *Essential Papers on Judaism and Christianity in Conflict from Late Antiquity to the Reformation*, ed. Jeremy Cohen (New York: New York University Press, 1991), 179–80.

57. See Cohen, *Living Letters*, esp. 59–62, as well as Robbins, 6–7.

58. In quali ergo opprobrio sunt Iudaei? Codicem portat Iudaeus, unde credat christianus. Librarii nostri facti sunt, quomodo solent serui post dominos codices ferre, ut illi portando deficiant, illi legendo proficiant. In tale opprobrium dati sunt Iudaei; et impletum est quod tanto ante praedictum est: 'Dedit in opprobrium conculcantes me.' Quale autem opprobrium est, fratres, ut hunc uersum legant, et ipsi caeci adtendant ad speculum suum? Sic enim apparent Iudaei de scriptura sancta quam portant, quomodo apparet facies caeci de speculo: ab aliis uidetur, ab ipso non uidetur. 'Dedit in opprobrium conculcantes me.' Augustine, *Enarrationes in Psalmos*, 56, 9. CCSL 39: 700. Translation (with modification) from Robbins, 6. See also Cohen, *Living Letters*, 36.

59. See Cohen, *Living Letters*, as well as Simon and Pelikan on these early contexts.

60. Cohen, *Friars and the Jews*, provides an excellent discussion of this problematic relationship. Cohen notes that early in the history of the Church, Augustine dealt with this double bind, setting the tone for the Church's attitude toward Jews until well into the thirteenth century. See 19–23.

61. "Vivi quidam apices nobis sunt, repraesentantes iugiter Dominicam passionem. Propter hoc et in omnes dispersi sunt regiones, ut dum iustas tanti facinoris poenas luunt ubique, testes sint nostrae redemptionis." Epistola CCCLXIII. *Opera*, ed. Leclercq, Talbot, and Rochais, vol. 8, p. 316. See Cohen, *Living Letters*, 2 and 244.

62. "Non enim una eademque omnibus potest convenire doctrina; sed aliter

sapientes, aliter insipientes; aliter divites, aliter pauperes; aliter sani, aliter infirmi docendi sunt. Aliter tunc rudis populus Judaeorum sub legis umbra manens erudiendus fuit, et aliter nunc Christianus populus in veritate Evangelii, legis mysteria explanata conspiciens, in virum perfectum est nutriendus." Rabanus Maurus, *Enarrationum in Librum Numerorum* PL 108: 631A. Translation modified from Lubac, *Medieval Exegesis*, 426, n. 47.

63. Ephesians models this manhood against an idea of "childhood," spiritual immaturity. The child-adult model, however, does not detract from my argument, I believe, but instead points to the ways in which another dichotomy, that between adult and child, maps upon the dichotomies of Christian-Jewish and masculine-feminine in complicated ways. This will be further explored in relation to the figure of Chaucer's little clergeon in Chapter 3.

64. Heinz Schreckenberg notes a parallel between representations of the Jew and representations of woman in medieval and early modern visual arts in a glossary entry on "Antijudaismus und Antifeminimus: Die in der christlichen Bildkunst des hohen Mittelalters und der frühen Neuzeit allenthalben anzutreffende Judenfeindschaft hat in gewisser Weise eine Parallele in dem Antifeminismus vieler Bilder. Zum Beispiel in den stark didaktisch angelegten Gegenüberstellungen 'Altes Testament: Neues Testament' wird jenes oft zur Negativfolie des Neuen Testaments, und nicht selten erscheinen in diesem ikonographischen Zusammenhang unfreundliche Darstellungen Evas, die zur generalisierenden Einbeziehung aller weiblichen Wesen einladen." *Christliche Adversus-Judaeos-Bilder: Das Alte und Neue Testament im Spiegel der christlichen Kunst* (New York: Peter Lang, 1999), 401.

65. Elisa Narin van Court, "Socially Marginal, Culturally Central: Representing Jews in Late Medieval English Literature," *Exemplaria* 12 (2000): 296.

66. On the distortion created by overemphasis on binaries, see Theresa Tinkle, *Medieval Venuses and Cupids: Sexuality, Hermeneutics and English Poetry* (Stanford, Calif.: Stanford University Press, 1996), esp. 1–43. See also Penny Schine Gold, *The Lady and the Virgin: Image, Attitude, and Experience in Twelfth-Century France* (Chicago: University of Chicago Press, 1985), esp. xv–xxi.

67. Frederick Brittain, ed., *Penguin Book of Latin Verse* (Baltimore: Penguin Books, 1962), 129. Cited in Marina Warner, *Alone of All Her Sex: The Myth and Cult of the Virgin Mary* (New York: Vintage Books, 1976), 385, n. 22, who notes that it dates from the seventh or eighth century (262).

68. Eileen Power, "The Position of Women," in *The Legacy of the Middle Ages*, ed. C. G. Crump and E. F. Jacob (Oxford, U.K.: Clarendon, 1926), 401. The excellent, concise introduction to Alcuin Blamires, ed., *Woman Defamed and Woman Defended: An Anthology of Medieval Texts* (Oxford, U.K.: Clarendon Press, 1992), gives a brief overview of the wide variety of medieval representation of women, although the opposition in the book's very title points to the importance of binarisms in these representations. On the "two archetypes," see also Shulamith Shahar, *The Fourth Estate: A History of Women in the Middle Ages*, trans. Chaya Galai (New York: Metheun, 1983), 22–28.

69. Elizabeth Clark, "Devil's Gateway and Bride of Christ: Women in the Early Christian World," in *Ascetic Piety and Women's Faith: Essays on Late Ancient*

Christianity (Lewiston/Queenston, N.Y.: Edwin Mellen Press, 1986), 25. In the essay, Clark attempts to provide reasons for this split in traditional Greek and Hebrew belief systems on social-historical grounds and in accordance with woman's role as a symbol of sexuality.

70. Elizabeth Clark, "Devil's Gateway," 24–25.

71. Rosemary Radford Ruether, "Misogynism and Virginal Feminism in the Fathers of the Church," in *Religion and Sexism: Images of Woman in the Jewish and Christian Traditions,* ed. Rosemary R. Ruether (New York: Simon and Schuster, 1974), 150.

72. Bloch, *Medieval Misogyny.* Debates about Bloch's thesis began in response to his essay "Medieval Misogyny," *Representations* 20 (1987): 1–24. For the debate and Bloch's responses, see *Medieval Feminist Newsletter* 6 (fall 1988): 2–12; 7 (spring 1989), 6–10.

73. "*Adversus Judaeos,*" 174–92; Rosemary Radford Ruether, *Faith and Fratricide: The Theological Roots of Anti-Semitism* (New York: Seabury Press, 1974), and Harold Fisch, *The Dual Image: A Study of the Figure of the Jew in English Literature* (London: World Jewish Congress, 1959), 9–23. Gilbert Dahan also points to a "bi-polarity" between views of actual Jews and the "theological Jew" in representations of Jews at the conclusion of his *Les intellectuels chrétiens et les juifs au moyen age* (Paris: Éditions du Cerf, 1990); 584–85. Dahan believes that a simple recourse to negative connotations cannot describe the tension between the actual and the "theological" Jew in the minds of Christian authors. See also Cohen, *Living Letters,* 3.

74. See Elisa Narin van Court, "Critical Apertures: Medieval Anti-Judaisms and Middle English Narrative" (Ph.D. diss., University of California, Berkeley, 1994), 26. Narin van Court deploys the terms "revered/reviled" to discuss this phenomenon. See also her essay "Socially Marginal." The idea of revered/reviled is also interestingly echoed in Jonathan Boyarin's discussion of Jews and Native Americans: "In this respect at least, contemporary Jews and Native Americans are in the same situation as contemporary Greeks. They are simultaneously seen as noble cultural ancestors of the groups that dominate them (Christian Europe and white Americans, respectively) and denigrated as marginal and backward relics." *Storm from Paradise: The Politics of Jewish Memory* (Minneapolis: University of Minnesota Press, 1992), 11.

75. See Narin van Court, "Critical Apertures," 26–47, and Cohen, *Living Letters,* 23–65.

76. "Ardorem desiderii patrum suspirantium Christi in carne praesentiam frequentissime cogitans, compungor et confundor in memetipso. Et nunc vix contineo lacrimas, ita pudet teporis torporisque miserabilium temporum horum." Sermon 2.1., trans. Walsh and Edmonds, vol. 1, 8.

77. Sermon 14. Latin ed. 75–81. English translation, Walsh and Edmonds, vol. 1, 97–104. For further analysis of Bernard's *Sermones* in relation to themes examined here, see Cohen, *Living Letters,* 221–45, David Damrosch, "*Non Alia Sed Aliter*: The Hermeneutics of Gender in Bernard of Clairvaux," in *Images of Sainthood in Medieval Europe,* ed. Renate Blumenfeld Kosinski and Timea Szell (Ithaca, N.Y.: Cornell University Press, 1991),181–95 and Lisa Lampert, "After

Eden, Out of Zion: Defining the Christian in Early English Literature" (Ph.D. diss., University of California, Berkeley, 1996), 34–79.

78. David Bevington, *Medieval Drama* (Boston: Houghton Mifflin, 1975), 184, lines 90–94.

79. Ibid., 186, line 167b.

80. "Archisynagogus cum suis Judaeis valde obstrepet auditis prophetiis, et dicat trudendo socium suum, movendo caput suum et totum corpus et percutiendo terram pede, baculo etiam imitando gestus Judaei in omnibus, et sociis suis indignando dicat." Latin and translation from Bevington, 183.

81. Sylvia Tomasch and Peter Travis have commented on the performative nature of the Archisynagogus figure and the way he represents a body that serves as a contrasting model for the Christian at the same time that he represents a mind and body that cannot be completely controlled by Christian culture. "The Twitching Jewish Body" (paper delivered to the International Congress on Medieval Studies, Kalamazoo, Mich., 2000). I thank Professors Tomasch and Travis for sharing the text of this unpublished work with me. David Bachrach suggested to me that perhaps this representation drew on actual observation of Jewish prayer. The practice of swaying during prayer, or "shuckeling" as it is sometimes called, does seem to have existed in the medieval period. In its entry on "Prayer," *Encyclopedia Judaica* states that there is evidence in the Zohar (3:218b-19a) for movement during prayer or study. Gilbert Dahan has shown there is also evidence for a curiosity among medieval Christians concerning the rites of the Jews. See Dahan, "La prière juive au regard des chrétiens au moyen âge," *Revue des Études juives,* 154 (1995): 437–48 and *Les intellectuels,* 530–38. Therefore this possibility seems plausible.

82. This play, as well as the *Ordo Repraesentationis Adae* and the *Ordo Prophetarum,* draws upon the pseudo-Augustinian *Sermo contra Judeos, Paganos, et Arianos.* See Karl Young, *Drama of the Medieval Church,* vol. 2 (Oxford, U.K.: Clarendon Press, 1933), 126–31, for text of the sermon, in which Hebrew prophets, as well as figures from the New Testament and pagan antiquity, "come forward to testify against the obstinacy of the Jews in failing to heed the plain evidence— even among their own authors—of the advent of Christ" (Bevington 113, n. 744). See also Rosemary Woolf, *The English Mystery Plays* (Berkeley: University of California Press, 1972), 12; Wolfgang Seiferth, *Synagogue and Church in the Middle Ages: Two Symbols in Art and Literature,* trans. Lee Chadeayne and Paul Gottwald (New York: Frederick Ungar Publishing, 1970), 77–79; Regula Meyer Evitt, "Undoing the Dramatic History of the Riga *Ludus Prophetarum,*" *Comparative Drama* 25 (1991): 242–56.

83. Colin Kruse, *The Second Epistle to the Corinthians: An Introduction and Commentary* (Grand Rapids, Mich.: Eerdmans, 1987), 92.

84. See E. P. Sanders, *Paul, the Law, and the Jewish People* (Philadelphia: Fortress Press, 1983), 137–42.

85. "Cum enim figurate dictum sic accipitur, tamquam proprie dictum sit, carnaliter sapitur. Neque ulla mors animae congruentius appellatur, quam cum id etiam, quod in ea bestiis antecellit, hoc est, intellegentia carni subicitur sequendo litteram." *De Doctrina Christiana* 3.5.9. CCSL 32: 82–83. Translation in D. W.

Robertson, *On Christian Doctrine* (New York: Macmillan, 1958), 84. In relation to questions of gender, see Copeland, "Why Women Can't Read," 256.

86. The phrase comes from Boyarin, *Radical Jew*, 13.

87. *De Doctrina*, 3.6.10. CCSL 32: 83–84.

88. Brian Stock, *Augustine the Reader: Meditation, Self-Knowledge and the Ethics of Interpretation* (Cambridge, Mass.: Harvard University Press, 1996), 54.

89. Ibid, 53.

90. Dinshaw, 24–25.

91. The agency of captive bride's actions varies between the Hebrew and Septuagint versions of this passage, possibly due to graphic confusion over the difference between verb forms. In the Hebrew version, the bride shaves her own head and pares her own nails. In the Septuagint, the captured woman is rendered passive through the verbal forms. It is possible that the immediacy of the second person used in the Septuagint translation invited Origen to place himself imaginatively in the role of the Hebrew warrior in the first place, a move followed by Jerome. I thank my Hebrew teacher, Angela Y. Kim, and my fellow students in Theology 509 at Notre Dame for their help in examining the Hebrew and Greek versions of this passage.

92. "Quid ergo mirum, si et ego sapientiam saecularem propter eloquii uenustatem et membrorum pulchritudinem de ancilla atque captiua Israhelitin facere cupio, si, quidquid in ea mortuum est idolatriae, uoluptatis, erroris, libidinum, uel praecido uel rado et mixtus purissimo corpori uernaculos ex ea genero domino sabaoth?" Epistle 70, CSEL 54: 702. Translation (with slight modification) from *The Principal Works of St. Jerome, Select Library of Nicene and Post-Nicene Fathers,* 2d ed., vol. 6 (1893; reprint, Grand Rapids, Mich.: Eerdmans, 1954), 383–84. Cited in Dinshaw, 23, and Copeland, "Why Women Can't Read," 257.

93. On the importance of the image of the naked female body in Western Christian thought, see Miles, *Carnal Knowing.*

94. Dinshaw, 23.

95. Angela Kim suggested to me how Jerome or Origen might have made this association. There is a description of a covering for the portable tent of meeting in Num 4:8 that uses the word "himation" or covering, which is the Greek word found in Deut 21:13. What could have happened is that Jerome associated the veil "kalumma" in Exod 27 and 34 with the "covering" (himation/himatia) in Num 4:8 and Deut 21:13, therefore concluding that Paul's text from 2 Cor 3:14–16, which quotes Exod 34:34, applies to Deut 21:13 as well.

96. Dinshaw, 205, n. 67. Lubac, *Medieval Exegesis*, 213. See the section on the beautiful captive, 211–24.

97. "From a Christian perspective Leviticus may be the most 'Jewish' of all the books of the Torah, with its holiness code, as well as being the most carnal, the most concerned with the physicality of the body." Charlotte Elisheva Fonrobert, *Menstrual Purity: Rabbinic and Christian Reconstructions of Biblical Gender* (Stanford, Calif.: Stanford University Press, 2000), 198. See her reading of Origen, 198–209.

98. "Verum tamen et ego frequenter "exivi ad bellum contra inimicos meos et vidi ibi" in praedam "mulierem decora specie." Quaecumque enim bene et

rationabiliter dicta invenimus apud inimicos nostros, si quid apud illos sapienter et scienter dictum legimus, oportet nos mundare id et ab scientia, quae apud illos est, auferre et resecare omne quod emortuum et inane est—hoc enim sunt omnes capilli capitis et ungulae mulieris ex inimicorum spoliis adsumptae—et ita demum facere eam nobis uxorem, cum iam nihil ex illis, quae per infidelitatem mortua dicuntur, habuerit, nihil in capite habeat mortuum, nihil in manibus, ut neque sensibus neque actibus immundum aliquid aut mortuum gerat. Nihil enim mundum habent mulieres hostium nostrorum, quia nulla est apud illos sapientia, cui immunditia aliqua non sit admixta." *Homilien zum Hexateuch in Rufins Übersetzung*, vol. 6, *Origenes Werke*, ed. W. A. Baehrens (Leipzig: J. C. Hinrich, 1920), 390. Translation adapted from *Origen: Homilies on Leviticus 1–16*, trans. Gary Wayne Barkley (Washington, D.C.: Catholic University of America Press, 1990), 150.

99. Translation (with slight modification), Barkley, 150. "Velim tamen dicerent mihi Iudaei, quomodo apud eos ista serventur. Quid causae, quid rationis est 'decalvari' mulierem et 'ungulas eius demi'? Verbi causa, si ponamus quod ita invenerit eam is, qui dicitur invenisse, ut neque capillos neque ungulas habeat: quid habuit quod secundum legem demere videretur?" Baehrens, 391.

100. Translation (with slight modification), Barkley, 150. "Nos vero, quibus militia spiritalis est et 'arma non carnalia, sed potentia Deo ad destruenda consilia', 'decora' mulier si repperta fuerit apud hostes et rationabilis aliqua disciplina, hoc modo purificabimus eam, quo superius diximus. Oportet ergo eum, qui mundus est, non solum 'dividere ungulam' et non solum praesentis et futuri saeculi actus et opera discernere, sed et 'ungulas producere' vel, ut alibi legimus, 'abicere', ut 'purificantes nos ab operibus mortuis' permaneamus in vita. Baehrens, 391.

101. The gendering of spiritual reading has its roots as far back as Philo who saw woman as a symbol of sense and man as a symbol of mind. These ideas are picked up in Augustine; see Dinshaw, 204, n. 63, and Børresen, "Gender and Exegesis" and "Patristic 'Feminism': The Case of Augustine," *Augustinian Studies* 25 (1994): 139–52.

102. Copeland, "Why Women Can't Read," 257.

103. For a discussion of debility in relation to the construction of otherness, see Kruger, "Medieval Christian (Dis)identifications: Muslims and Jews in Guibert of Nogent," *New Literary History* 28 (1997): 199–201.

104. "Aperite tandem oculos, reserate aures et soli caeci in mundo apparere, soli surdi inter mortales remanere erubescite." *Adversus Iudaeorum inveteratam duritiem*. CCCM 58:10. Translation is from Cohen, *Living Letters*, 255.

105. The view of Jewish blindness, despite its prevalence, did not prevent Christians from having contact with Jews and consulting them on the Hebrew text, as did, for example, Andrew of St. Victor. See Beryl Smalley, *The Study of the Bible in the Middle Ages* (Notre Dame, Ind.: Notre Dame University Press, 1964), 112–94. On *Hebraica Veritas* and Jewish-Christian exchange in matters of Biblical scholarship, see also Dahan, *Les intellectuels*; Aryeh Grabois, "The *Hebraica Veritas* and Jewish-Christian Intellectual Relations in the Twelfth Century," *Speculum* 50 (1975): 613–34; Friedrich Lotter, "Das Prinzip der '*Hebraica Veritas*' und die heilgeschichtliche Rolle Israels bei den frühen Zisterziensern," in *Bibel in jüdischer*

und christlicher Tradition, ed. Helmut Merklein, Karlheinz Müller, and Günter Stemberger (Frankfurt am Main: Hain, 1993), 479–517; Michael Signer, "*Peshat, Sensus Litteralis*, and Sequential Narrative: Jewish Exegesis and the School of St. Victor in the Twelfth Century," *Jewish History* 6 (1992–93): 203–16.

106. Patristic and medieval Christian writers declare Jews both blind and deaf so often that Margaret Schlauch writes, "[T]o cite the examples of this obvious metaphor would in itself require a volume." "The Allegory of Church and Synagogue," *Speculum* 13 (1939): 452. Even the thorough and encyclopedic Henri de Lubac truncates a footnote on the Pauline veil with an abrupt and uncharacteristic "etc." See *Medieval Exegesis*, 445, n. 1. For an excellent overview on approaches to the Gospel of John and issues of anti-Judaism, see David Rensberger, "Anti-Judaism and the Gospel of John," in *Anti-Judaism and the Gospels*, ed. William R. Farmer (Harrisburg, Pa: Trinity Press International, 1999), 120–57, and the responses by Mark Goodwin (158–71) and Thomas Lea (172–75) in the same volume.

107. For a complex and important reading of this Pauline passage, see Boyarin, *Radical Jew*, 98–105.

108. For a striking example in the writings of a Jewish convert to Christianity, see Herman-Judah, *Hermannus quondam Judaeus. Opusculum de conversione sua, Monumenta Germaniae Historica*, ed. G. Niemayer, Quellen zur Geistegeschichte des Mittelalters 4 (Weimar: Hermann Bohlaus, 1963), 104–5. Translation in Karl Morrison, *Conversion and Text: The Cases of Augustine of Hippo, Herman-Judah, and Constantine Tsatsos* (Charlottesville: University of Virginia Press), 98–99. See also Kruger's reading of Herman's conversion in, "Spectral Jew."

109. *Contra Faustum*, 22.23 and CSEL 25: 618.

110. Seiferth, 131.

111. For a Roman example, see Schreckenberg, *Christliche Adversus-Judaeos-Bilder*, 37.

112. We must distinguish between the connections between the Jewish and the feminine that I am tracing here in biblical, patristic, and medieval sources and modern stereotypes of the Jewish male as effeminate, stereotypes nineteenth- and twentieth-century Zionist discourse often sought to combat through figures such as the "Muskeljude." Further, the figure of Synagoga is clearly related to the modern figure of the "beautiful Jewess," who is central to modern ideologies of gender and Jewish difference. For more on these issues, including a bibliography, see my "O My Daughter," 254–70. There has been further discussion of the "feminization" of the male Jew in the medieval and early modern periods in regard to the myth of the menstruating male Jew mentioned in the widely read book by Joshua Trachtenberg, *The Devil and the Jews: The Medieval Conception of the Jew and Its Relation to Modern Anti-Semitism* (Philadelphia: Jewish Publication Society of America, 1943), 149. The myth, understood as a sign of Jewish male effeminacy, weakness, and sinfulness, seems to be an early modern twist on a motif that has its origins in at least the twelfth century. On this question, see David S. Katz, "Shylock's Gender: Jewish Male Menstruation in Early Modern England," *The Review of English Studies*, n.s. 50 (1999): 440–62; Willis Johnson, "The Myth of Jewish Male Menses," *Journal of Medieval History* 24 (1998): 273–74; and Irven M. Resnick, "Medieval Roots of the Myth of Jewish Male Menses," *HTR* 93, no. 3

(2000): 241–63; Shapiro, *Shakespeare and the Jews*, 37–38; and Kruger, "Becoming Christian, Becoming Male?" 23–24. Johnson argues against using gender models for reading this myth in its medieval manifestations, linking it to ideas about male Jews suffering from hemorrhoids in the early sources, which then later became linked to menstruation.

113. For a photograph of these statues, see Heinz Schreckenberg, *The Jews in Christian Art: An Illustrated History* (New York: Continuum, 1996), 47. Further examples on pp. 31–74.

114. For a discussion of exegetical readings of Samson as a figure of Christ betrayed by the seductive Delilah, who comes to stand for the Synagogue, see Gilbert Dahan, "Les 'figures' des Juifs et de la Synagogue: L'exemple de Dalila. Fonctions et méthodes de la typologie dans l'exegèse médiévale," *Recherches Augustiniennes* 23 (1988): 125–45. For an extensive list of other related typological correspondences, see p. 132.

115. On the connection between Synagoga and other vices, see Michael Camille, *The Gothic Idol: Ideology and Image-Making in Medieval Art* (Cambridge, U.K.: Cambridge University Press, 1989), 175–79.

116. "Fornicaria est, quae cum pluribus copulatur. Adultera, quae unum virum deserens, alteri jungitur. Quorum utrumque est Synagoga, quae si permanserit in fornicatione et adulterio, auferet ab ea Deus vestem et ornamenta quae dederat." *Commentariorum In Osee.* 1.2. PL 25:830. Cited in Marcel Simon, "Christian Anti-Semitism," in *Essential Papers on Judaism*, ed. Jeremy Cohen 169, n. 76. Translation is mine.

117. "Redemptoris mater juxta carnem Synagoga exstitit ex qua ad nos per corpus uisibilis processit. Sed hunc intra se tegmine litterae adopertum tenuit dum ad spiritalem eius intellegentiam mentis oculos aperire neglexit. Hunc quia in carne humani corporis latentem uidere Deum noluit quasi in diuinitate nudum considerare contempsit. Sed nudus de utero matris exiit quia a Synagogae carne prodiens conspicuus ad gentes uenit." Gregory the Great, *Moralia in Iob.* CCSL 143: 96–97. Gregory the Great, *Morals on the Book of Job*, vol. 1, trans. John Henry Parker (London: n.p., 1844), 108–9 (with modifications). For another example of a connection between Potiphar's wife and the Synagogue, this time in the meditative tradition, see analysis of a selection from Bonaventure in Thomas Bestul, *Texts of the Passion: Latin Devotional Literature and Medieval Society* (Philadelphia: University of Pennsylvania Press, 1996), 96.

118. "Dum enim mulier adultera male illo uti uoluisset relicto pallio fugit foras, quia dum Synagoga Dominum purum hominem credens quasi adulterino complexu constringere uoluit, ipse tegmen litterae eius oculis reliquit et ad cognoscendam diuinitatis suae potentiam conspicuum se gentibus praebuit." Gregory the Great, *Moralia in Iob.* CCSL 143: 96–97. Gregory the Great, *Morals on the Book of Job*, vol. 1, 108–9 (with modifications).

119. "Unde et Paulus dicit: Usque hodie, dum legitur Moyses, uelamen est super cor eorum, quia uidelicet adultera mulier apud semetipsam pallium retinuit et quem male tenebat, nudum amisit. Quia ergo a Synagoga ueniens, fidei gentium conspicuus apparuit ex utero matris nudus exiuit. Sed numquid hanc omnimodo deserit? Et ubi est quod per prophetam dicitur: Si fuerit numerus filiorum Israel

quasi arena maris, reliquiae saluae fient? Ubi quod scriptum est: Donec plenitudo gentium introiret et sic omnis Israel saluus fieret. Erit ergo quando conspicuus etiam Synagogae appareat. Erit in fine mundi procul dubio quando gentis suae reliquiis semetipsum sicut est Deus, innotescat." Gregory the Great, *Moralia in Iob.* CCSL 143: 96–97. Gregory the Great, *Morals on the Book of Job*, vol. 1, 108–9 (with modifications).

120. For the image of Mary wrapping Christ in her flesh, see the Prologue to Chaucer's "Second Nun's Tale," line 42.

121. "Notus in Iudaea Deus, in Israel magnum nomen eius. Populus gentium, qui ambulabat in tenebris, vidit lucem magnam, quae erat in Iudaea et in Israel, voluitque accedere et illuminari, ut qui aliquando non populus, nunc populus esset, lapisque unus angularis ambos in se parietes venientes e diverso reciperet, et esset de cetero in pace locus eius. Porro fiduciam dabat invitantis vox quae iam sonuerat: Laetamini, gentes, cum plebe eius. Ergo accedere voluit; sed vetuit Synagoga, immundam asserens Ecclesiam de Gentibus et indignam, idololatriae faecem et ignorantiae caecitatem improperans, et dicebat: 'Tu enim quo merito? Noli me tangere.' 'Cur?' inquit. 'An Iudaeorum tantum Deus? Nonne et Gentium?'" Sermon 14:1, p. 75. English translation: Walsh and Edmonds, vol. 1, p. 97.

122. Sermon 14.4, Walsh and Edmonds, vol. 1, p. 101. The English translation of this text mistakenly translates *velo* as *evil.* "At vero Ecclesia, scisso velo occidentis litterae in morte Verbi crucifixi, audacter ad eius penetralia praeeunte spiritu libertatis irrumpit, agnoscitur, placet, sortitur aemulae locum, fit sponsa, fruitur praereptis amplexibus, et in calore spiritus Christo Domini, cui confricatur, inhaerens, stillante ac fundente undique sui oleum exsultationis, prae participibus suis excipiens ipsum, ait: oleum effsum nomen tuum." Sermon 14:1 p. 78.

123. "As 'in the Last Days,' the Word of God, which was clothed with the flesh of Mary, proceeded into this world. What was seen in him was one thing; what was understood was something else. For the sight of his flesh was open for all to see, but the knowledge of his divinity was given to the few, even the elect. So also when the Word of God was brought to humans through the Prophets and the Lawgiver, it was not brought without proper clothing. For just as there it was covered with the veil of flesh, so here with the veil of the letter, so that indeed the letter is seen as flesh but the spiritual sense hiding within is perceived as divinity." Barkley, 29.

124. Tale ergo est quod et nunc invenimus librum Levitici revolventes, in quo sacrificiorum ritus et hostiarum diversitas ac sacerdotum ministeria describuntur. Sed haec secundum litteram, quae tamquam caro verbi Dei est et indumentum divinitatis eius, digni fortassis vel adspiciant, vel audiant et indigni. Sed 'beati sunt illi oculi,' qui velamine litterae obtectum intrinsecus divinum Spiritum vident; et beati sunt, qui ad haec audienda mundas aures interioris hominis deferunt. Alioquin aperte in his sermonibus 'occidentem litteram' sentient." *Hom. in Lev.* 1.1 *Homilien zum Hexateuch in Rufins Übersetzung*, 280–81. Translation in Barkley, 29 (with minor modifications). Beryl Smalley also uses this quote to begin her first chapter "The Fathers," in *Study of the Bible*, 1. On this passage, see also Fonrobert, 199–200.

125. Barkley, "Introduction," 15, in translation/paraphrase of Origen, *Hom. in Lev.* 1.1.

126. "adeo autem non omnia imagines sed et veritates, nec omnia umbrae sed et corpora, ut in ipsum quoque dominum insigniora quaeque luce clarius praedicarentur. nam et virgo concepit in utero non figurate, et peperit Emmanuelem, nobiscum deum [Iesum], non oblique." *Q. Septimii Florentis Tertulliani De Resurrectione Carnis Liber/Tertullian's Treatise on the Resurrection: The Text Edited with an Introduction, Translation and Commentary,* ed. and trans. Ernest Evans (London: SPCK, 1960), 54–55 (translation modified). Passage also cited in Auerbach, "Figura," 32.

127. "Primarily, the Christian focus of medieval culture meant that people thought and talked about themselves and what they did in a language which included, as one of its major assumptions, the Incarnation." J. B. Allen, *The Friar As Critic: Literary Attitudes in the Later Middle Ages* (Nashville: Vanderbilt University Press, 1971), 3.

128. See Mirella Levi D'Anacona, *The Iconography of the Immaculate Conception in the Middle Ages and Early Renaissance* (New York: College Art Association of America, 1957); Nancy Mayberry, "The Controversy over the Immaculate Conception in Medieval and Renaissance Art, Literature and Society, " *Journal of Medieval and Renaissance Studies* 21 (1991): 207–24; Edward Dennis O'Connor, *The Dogma of the Immaculate Conception* (Notre Dame, Ind.: Notre Dame University Press, 1958); Warner, 236–54.

129. Charles T. Wood, "The Doctor's Dilemma: Sin, Salvation and the Menstrual Cycle in Medieval Thought," *Speculum* 56 (1981): 710–27.

130. Daniel J. Lasker, *Jewish Philosophical Polemics against Christianity in the Middle Ages* (New York: Ktav Publishing House, 1977), 109–10 and 118–19.

131. Daniel Lasker, "Jewish Philosophical Polemics in Ashkenaz," in *Contra Iudaeos: Ancient and Medieval Polemics between Christians and Jews,* ed. Ora Limor and Guy G. Stroumsa (Tübingen: J. C. B. Mohr, 1996), 204.

132. For discussion and examples of the *Toledot Yeshu* tradition, see Samuel Krauss, ed., *Das Leben Jesu nach jüdischen Quellen* (1902; reprint, New York: George Olms Verlag, 1994). See also Lange, *Origen and the Jews,* 66–73, and further bibliography in Cohen, *Living Letters,* 131 n. 24. On issues of menstruation and ritual purity in the Jewish tradition, see Charlotte Elisheva Fonrobert and Jonathan Klawans, *Impurity and Sin in Ancient Judaism* (Oxford, U.K.: Oxford University Press, 2000), esp. 38–42; 104–8. On medieval Christian views on menstruation, see Cadden, esp. 170–77; Danielle Jacquart and Claude Thomassett, *Sexuality and Medicine in the Middle Ages,* trans. Matthew Adamson (Princeton, N.J.: Princeton University Press, 1985), passim; and the introduction to Helen Rondite Lemay, *Women's Secrets: A Translation of the Pseudo-Albertus Magnus' De Secretis Mulierum with Commentaries* (Albany: State University of New York Press, 1992), 1–58. On the question of references to Mary in the Talmud itself and the role of this question in Jewish-Christian relations, see also Hyam Maccoby, *Judaism on Trial: Jewish-Christian Disputations in the Middle Ages* (London: Littman Library of Jewish Civilization, 1996), 19–38; William Chester Jordan, "Marian Devotion and the Talmud Trial of 1240," in *Religionsgespräche im Mittelalter,* ed. Bernard

Lewis and Friedrich Niewöhner (Wiesbaden: Harrassowitz Verlag, 1992), 61–76, and Simon, *Verus Israel;* 179–201.

133. Joseph Kimḥi, *The Book of the Covenant,* trans. Frank Talmage (Toronto: Pontifical Institute for Medieval Studies, 1972), 36–37. Hebrew text: *Sefer ha-Berit,* ed. Frank Talmage (Jerusalem: Bialik Institute, 1974), 29. Cited also in Kruger, "Medieval Christian (Dis)Identifications," 199, where Kruger explores these debates in relation to both Jewish and Muslim difference through the writings of Guibert de Nogent.

134. The author here is contested. The text is from Frank Talmage, "An Anti-Christian Polemic in Eastern Europe in the Style of Sephardic Polemics—A Unique Manuscript," *Kiryat Sefer* 56 (1980–81): 369–72 [in Hebrew]. Cited in Lasker, who posits that the author is Menachem ben Jacob Shalem, "Jewish Philosophical Polemics in Askenaz," 203–6. The translation is Lasker's, 204.

135. Robert Chazan, *In the Year 1096: The First Crusade and the Jews* (Philadelphia: Jewish Publication Society, 1996), 91.

136. For rabbinic architectural metaphors, see Fonrobert, 40–67. For a reference to menstrual blood as a "virtually fatal poison" in a Hebrew treatise, see Frank Talmage, "An Hebrew Polemical Treatise: Anti-Cathar and Anti-Orthodox," *HTR* 60 (1967): 341.

137. See Abulafia, *Christians and Jews,* esp. 77–93. This work provides an excellent overview of Christian-Jewish relations in this period, including detailed analyses of these debates from which my analysis here has greatly benefitted. There is controversy about the timing and nature of a change in Christian anti-Jewish polemic. Amos Funkenstein proposed that a major shift occurred in the twelfth century. Cohen argues for a shift in the thirteenth century. The debate has also been taken up by a number of historians, including David Berger and Robert Chazan. See Funkenstein, *Perceptions of Jewish History,* 172–201; Cohen, *Friars and the Jews;* David Berger "Mission to the Jews and Jewish-Christian Contacts in the Polemical Literature of the High Middle Ages," *AHR* 91 (1986): 576–91; Robert Chazan, *Daggers of Faith: Thirteenth-Century Christian Missionizing and Jewish Response* (Berkeley: University of California Press, 1989), and Abulafia, *Christians and Jews.* For an overview of the debate and additional discussion of Jewish response, see Daniel J. Lasker, "Jewish-Christian Polemics at the Turning Point: Jewish Evidence from the Twelfth Century," *HTR* 89 (1996): 161–73.

138. Anselm of Canterbury, *Why God Became Man and the Virgin Conception and Original Sin,* trans. Joseph M. Colleran (Albany, N.Y.: Magi Book, Inc., 1969), 67. "Obiciunt nobis deridentes simplicitatem nostram infideles, quia deo facimus iniuriam et contumeliam, cum eum asserimus in uterum mulieris descendisse, natum esse de femina, lacte et alimentis humanis nutritum crevisse, et, ut multa alia taceam, quae deo non videntur convenire, lassitudinem, famem, sitim, verbera et inter latrones crucem mortemque sustinuisse." *Cur Deus Homo,* 1. 3., ed. Schmitt (Bonn: Petri Hanstein, 1929), 7.

139. On Anselm's intended audience and the scholarly debate surrounding its composition, see Abulafia, *Christians and Jews,* 42–46.

140. See Colleran's introduction to his translation of *Cur Deus Homo,* 35–37.

141. Kruger, "Medieval Christian (Dis)identifications."

142. See Abulafia, *Christians and Jews*, and also Caroline Walker Bynum, *Jesus as Mother: Studies in the Spirituality of the High Middle Ages* (Berkeley: University of California Press, 1982).

143. See Anna Abulafia, "Theology and the Commercial Revolution: Guibert of Nogent, St. Anselm and the Jews of Northern France," in *Church and City 1000–1500: Essays in Honour of Christopher Brooke*, ed. David Abulafia, Michael Franklin, and Miri Rubin (Cambridge, U.K.: Cambridge University Press, 1992), 24.

144. "In quodam vos valde ridemus et insanos judicamus. Dicitis enim Deum, in maternis visceribus obceno [*sic*] carcere fetidi ventris clausum, novem mensibus pati, et tandem pudendo exitu (qui intuitum sine confusione non admittit), decimo mense progredi, inferentes Deo tantum dedecus, quantum de nobis, quamvis vere, sine magna tamen verecundia non dicimus." PL 160: 1110. English translation adapted from Odo of Tournai, *On Original Sin and a Disputation with the Jew, Leo, Concerning the Advent of Christ, the Son of God: Two Theological Treatises*, trans. Irven M. Resnick (Philadelphia: University of Pennsylvania Press, 1994), 95. Cited also in Robert Worth Frank Jr., "Miracles of the Virgin, Medieval Anti-Semitism, and the 'Prioress's Tale,'" in *The Wisdom of Poetry: Essays in Early English Literature in Honor of Morton W. Bloomfield*, ed. Larry D. Benson and Siegfried Wenzel (Kalamazoo, Mich.: Medieval Institute Publications, 1982), 183. Resnick makes the argument that this work is not based on *Cur Deus Homo* and that it is based on an actual encounter between Odo and a Jew, 29–33. For a view that raises doubts that the encounter actually occurred, see Abulafia, *Christians and Jews*, 83–85.

145. Resnick, 96. See also Abulafia, *Christians and Jews*, 108–10.

146. Resnick, 97.

147. Resnick, 95.

148. "Etsi Judaica inertia de Filii Dei intra Virginem conceptione submurmurat, nimirum res est inolita genti, et pudendum quiddam sibi aestimat incuti, cum a suis Deum, qui sibi Salvator advenerat, progenitoribus traditum audit cruci." "Although Judaism grumbles about the conception of the son within the Virgin, and she considers herself attacked with a shameful accusation when she hears that God, who came as her Savior, was given up to the cross by her own ancestors, people have evidently grown used to this." PL 156: 489 (1880 edition). My translation.

149. "Nullus, inquiunt, nisi qui desipiat, credit Deum ad uteri feminei sese dimittere voluisse vilitatem, et consuetudinarii incrementi pertulisse moras. Illud potissimum horrori est ut is, qui Deus diceretur, per mulieris virginalia funderetur. Isdem quoque natus, cum non dissimilia humanitati membra haberet, et feminalibus usus est, et edendi ac bibendi necessitati subjacens, his etiam quae consequuntur aerumnis addictus est. Unde prorsus ridiculum est ut is talis Deus habeatur qui in nullo a miseriis discrepare communibus videatur." PL 156: 492. No one but a moron, they say, believes that God wanted to send himself to the vileness of a woman's uterus, and to endure the whole period of the customary gestation. But the thing that is most alarming is that he who was called God should be brought forth through the private parts of a woman; and that once born from these very

same parts, since he had body parts not unlike the rest of humanity, he both made use of the female parts and, being subject to the necessity of eating and drinking he was made subject even to the pains that follow therefrom. So it is utterly ridiculous that such a one as this should be considered God, who seems in no respect to differ from the suffering that we all share." My translation.

150. "Hominis Deus omnia suscepit.—Interroga, putidissime et nequam, de Domino nostro, si spuerit, si nares emunxerit, si pituitas oculorum vel aurium digitis hauserit, et intellige quia qua honestate superiora haec fecerit, et residua peregerit. Aut dic mihi, ille tuus, qui Abrahae apparuit Deus, ea quae comedit in quem alium [f., alvum] deposuit? quomodo etiam, aut si factum est, quod consequens fuit? Contremisco dum de his disputo; sed vos, filii diaboli, me cogitis." PL 156:499. Cited in Kruger, "Medieval Christian (Dis)Identifications," 200. Translation adapted from Kruger.

151. Phrase is from an earlier version of Kruger, "Medieval Christian (Dis)-identifications," www.georgetown.edu/labyrinth/conf/cs95/papers/kruger.html. On Guibert and his obsessions, see Abulafia, Kruger, and also Cohen, *Living Letters*, 192–201.

152. Abulafia, *Christians and Jews*, 113.

153. "Jactitant itaque sordidis rictibus hostes deificae nativitatis verba putentia. Dicam, et astruam certe digniora fuisse illa membra, quae illo tunc partui deservissent, quam sint ora spurcissima, quae se quotidianis fraudibus et luxuriis imbuunt, et vivifica sacramenta derident. Quid, quaeso, displicet in his membris, nisi foedae voluptatis expletio? Aufer libidinis suspicionem, non erit quod horreas, sed quod venereris. Vos qui turpitudines amatis, juste damnabimini, qui ea ipsa quae vos turpes efficiunt membra damnatis. Deus omnipotens, quid gratius, quid bonae menti suavius esse potest quam vera virginitas et illibatus animus?" "Thus the enemies of the holy birth toss about filthy words with dirty laughter (smiles). Let me say and affirm that this body, which served him in good stead as a baby, was more worthy than the foul mouths that continually gorge themselves with deceits and lust and which deride the life-giving sacraments. What, I ask, is displeasing in this if not the fulfillment of foul desire? Put aside suspicion of lust. It will not be what you fear, but what you ought to worship. You who love foulness will rightfully be damned." Col. 497. Translation is mine.

154. Laclau, *Emancipation(s)*, 23.

155. Douglas, 115; 121. Recently Douglas has revised her readings of Leviticus in *Purity and Danger*, but these revisions do not impact her theories of the body as symbol. For a concise discussion of Douglas's revised views on purity in the Jewish biblical tradition, see Klawans, 7–10.

156. See Theresa Coletti, "Purity and Danger: The Paradox of Mary's Body and the En-gendering of the Infancy Narrative in the English Mystery Cycles," in *Feminist Approaches to the Body in Medieval Literature*, ed. Linda Lomperis and Sarah Stanbury (Philadelphia: University of Pennsylvania Press, 1993), 66–67.

157. Julia Kristeva, *Powers of Horror: An Essay on Abjection*, trans. Leon Roudiez (New York: Columbia University Press, 1982).

158. Butler, *Bodies*, 3.

159. Kristeva, 4.

160. Butler, Laclau, and Žižek, *Contingency, Hegemony, Universality; 14*.

Chapter 3

1. The literature here is extensive. Among the book-length studies I have found most useful are Dinshaw; Elaine Tuttle Hansen, *Chaucer and the Fictions of Gender* (Berkeley: University of California Press, 1992); Susan Crane, *Gender and Romance in Chaucer's Canterbury Tales* (Princeton, N.J.: Princeton University Press, 1994); H. Marshall Leicester, *The Disenchanted Self* (Berkeley: University of California Press, 1990) and Jill Mann, *Geoffrey Chaucer* (Atlantic Highlands, N.J.: Humanities Press International, 1991), which appears in a revised edition as *Feminizing Chaucer* (New York: D. S. Brewer, 2002).

2. In addition to the literature cited in the body of this chapter, there are two outstanding review essays on *Prioress's Tale* scholarship. See Florence Ridley, *The Prioress and the Critics*, University of California Publications, English Studies 30 (Berkeley: University of California Press, 1965); Beverly Boyd, ed., *A Variorum Edition of the Works of Geoffrey Chaucer, Part 20: The Prioress's Tale* (Norman: University of Oklahoma Press, 1987), 27–50. A pathbreaking article that does move beyond critical ghettoization on a number of levels and which has greatly influenced how I understand the tale and its criticism is Louise O. Fradenburg, "Criticism, Anti-Semitism and the *Prioress's Tale*," *Exemplaria* 1 (1989): 69–115. For a reading that takes Muslim difference into account in relation to the tale's location in "Asie," see Sheila Delany, "Chaucer's Prioress, the Jews, and the Muslims," in *Medieval Encounters* 5 (1999): 198–213. The essay is reprinted in an important new volume that also provides examination of the figure of the Jew outside the ghetto walls; see Sheila Delany, ed., *Chaucer and the Jews: Sources, Contexts, Meanings* (New York: Routledge, 2002), 43–58. Several additional essays from that volume will be referenced here.

3. For Fradenburg, see note 2 above. On this variation, see Narin van Court, "Socially Marginal." In thinking about traumatic representation and its limits, I have learned much from Michael Rothberg, *Traumatic Realism: The Demands of Holocaust Representation* (Minneapolis: University of Minnesota Press, 2000).

4. As noted earlier, I draw here on Sutcliffe's weaving analogy.

5. I borrow the phrase "analogy of analogies" from Bloch, *Medieval Misogyny*. Bloch briefly comments on exegetical connections between representations of Jews, women, and heretics: see 31 and 217, n.14.

6. This view of the controversy is Ralph Hanna III's from the textual notes to Larry Benson, ed., *The Riverside Chaucer*, 3d ed. (Boston: Houghton Mifflin, 1987), 1121. Subsequent references to this edition will appear in the text. The textual history of the *Man of Law's Prologue, Tale,* and *Endlink* have been the subject of great debate ever since the Bradshaw shift was first proposed. See N. F. Blake, *The Textual Tradition of the Canterbury Tales* (London: Edward Arnold, 1985), 24–43.

Fragment VII consists of the following tales: *Shipman's Tale; Prioress's Prologue and Tale; Prologue and Tale of Sir Thopas; The Tale of Melibee; Monk's Prologue and Tale; Nun's Priest's Prologue, Tale, and Endlink*. For brief overviews on the *Endlink* and its role in the context of general textual concerns, see *The Riverside Chaucer*, 5, 10, 15, 862, 1118–1122. There is considerable literature on the Bradshaw shift controversy; see Donald C. Baker, "The Bradshaw Order of *The Canterbury Tales*: A Dissent," *Neuphilologische Mitteilungen* 4 (1962): 245–61; Lee Sheridan Cox, "A Question of Order in *The Canterbury Tales*," *Chaucer Review* 4 (1967): 228–52; E. Talbot Donaldson, "The Ordering of *The Canterbury Tales*," in *Medieval Literature and Folklore Studies: Essays in Honor of Francis Lee Utley*, ed. Jerome Mandel and Bruce A. Rosenberg (New Brunswick, N.J.: Rutgers University Press, 1970), 193–204; John Gardner, "The Case Against the 'Bradshaw Shift': Of the Mystery of the MS in the Trunk," *Papers on Language and Literature* 2, Supplement (1967): 80–106; George Keiser, "In Defense of the Bradshaw Shift," *Chaucer Review* 12 (1978): 191–201; Charles Owen Jr., "The Alternative Reading of *The Canterbury Tales*: Chaucer's Text and the Early Manuscripts," *PMLA* 97 (1982): 237–50; and Robert A. Pratt, "The Order of *The Canterbury Tales*," *PMLA* 66 (1951): 1141–67.

7. The *Second Nun's Tale* belongs to Fragment VIII, which scholars argue could be preceded by Fragment VI as well as by Fragment VII. I read Fragment VIII as following Fragment VII, but as Larry D. Benson notes in *The Riverside Chaucer*, although the ordering of these three fragments is disputed, they "form a coherent group that recapitulates earlier themes of the whole work" (941–42).

8. *The Riverside Chaucer*, 863.

9. My references to the Lollards tend to make them seem like a more coherent and organized group than they actually were. As W. R. Jones notes, "Lollardy after Wyclif was not a systematic body of belief, but, rather, a loose assortment of opinions and attitudes concerning Christianity and its institutions" (31). "Lollards and Images: The Defense of Religious Art in Later Medieval England," *Journal of the History of Ideas* 24 (1973): 27–50. For an introduction to the subject of Lollardy in relation to the study of medieval English literature, see Steven Justice, "Lollardy" in *The Cambridge History of Medieval English Literature*, ed. David Wallace (Cambridge, U.K.: Cambridge University Press, 1999), 662–89.

10. *Riverside Chaucer*, 863. For another approach to Chaucer and the question of Lollardy, see Ruth M. Ames, "Corn and Shrimps: Chaucer's Mockery of Religious Controversy," in *The Late Middle Ages, Acta*, vol. 8, ed. Peter Cocozzella (Binghamton: State University of New York, 1984), 71–88.

11. The *Man of Law's Endlink*, as recorded in the Selden MS, is the basis for the argument that the *Shipman's Tale* may have originally been assigned to the Wife of Bath, which would account for the Shipman's incongruous references to himself as female (Pratt, 1154). If one understands this as an early vision of the tales, a reading might develop as follows: the Host raises the question of heresy, a splintering of Christian identity through differences of interpretation and doctrine. Then, if the Wife had objected to "glosing" and told the tale eventually assigned to the Shipman at this original juncture, she would have been responding to a question of heresy with a tale of moral leveling. The splintering of Christian iden-

tity created by Lollardy would be reflected through the merchant's usury, which blurs the distinction between Christian and Jew. The Prioress, in turn, counters this moral chaos with a highly orthodox tale that redeems the feminine (a maneuver that is even more appropriate after having a woman tell the *Shipman's Tale*) and that unites and redefines the Christian community in relation to a demonized Jewry.

12. Kantik Ghosh, *The Wycliffite Heresy: Authority and the Interpretation of Texts* (Cambridge, U.K.: Cambridge University Press, 2002), 15.

13. John Ganim, *Chaucerian Theatricality* (Princeton, N.J.: Princeton University Press, 1990), 44. Although my focus differs from Ganim's, I have benefited much from the ways his model of theatricality allows for an understanding of negotiation and multi-vocality within the *Tales*. Peggy Knapp uses a term coined by Raymond Williams, "emergent discourse," to consider Wycliffite ideas in relation to Chaucer's intellectual and religious milieu. *Chaucer and the Social Contest* (New York: Routledge, 1990), 65. On reading the *Canterbury Tales* as the product of a "pre-Arundelian" world, see Nicholas Watson, "Censorship and Cultural Change in Late-Medieval England: Vernacular Theology, the Oxford Translation Debate, and Arundel's Constitutions of 1409," *Speculum* 70 (1995): 857–58. Among other important studies, see Paul Strohm, "Chaucer's Lollard Joke: History and the Textual Unconscious," *Studies in the Age of Chaucer* 17 (1995): 23–42; Sheila Delany, *The Naked Text: Chaucer's Legend of Good Women* (Berkeley: University of California Press, 1994); and David Lyle Jeffrey, "Chaucer and Wyclif: Biblical Hermeneutic and Literary Theory in the Fourteenth Century," in *Chaucer and Scriptural Tradition*, ed. David Lyle Jeffrey (Ottawa, Canada: University of Ottawa Press, 1984), 89–108. A critical resource into issues of the vernacular is Jocelyn Wogan-Browne, Nicholas Watson, Andrew Taylor, and Ruth Evans, *The Idea of the Vernacular: An Anthology of Middle English Literary Theory, 1280–1520* (University Park: Pennsylvania State University Press, 1999).

14. Watson, "Visions," 171.

15. Watson, "Visions," 171.

16. Boyarin, *Radical Jew*, 204–5.

17. Watson, "Visions," 167.

18. Kempe was also threatened with burning as a Lollard. Margery Kempe, *The Book of Margery Kempe*, ed. Sanford Brown Meech and Hope Emily Allen, EETS, vol. 212 (Oxford, U.K.: Oxford University Press, 1940), 124. For a somewhat different reading of this moment in relation to discussion of Kempe's representations of Jews, see Judith Rosenthal, "Margery Kempe and Medieval Anti-Judaic Ideology," *Medieval Encounters* 5 (1999): 409–20, esp. 413–14. See also Despres, "Immaculate Flesh and Social Body;" 62–63, and Ruth Evans, "The Jew, the Host, and the Virgin Martyr: Fantasies of the Sentient Body," in *Medieval Virginities*, ed. Sarah Salih, Anke Bernau, and Ruth Evans (Cardiff: University of Wales Press, forthcoming). I thank Dr. Evans for sharing this work with me prior to publication.

19. My thinking on these connections in the next eight paragraphs owes much to Ruth Nissé, who also coined the title of this chapter. See her "Reversing

Discipline: The *Tretise of Miraclis Pleyinge*, Lollard Exegesis, and the Failure of Representation," *The Yearbook of Langland Studies* 11 (1997): 163–94, and "Prophetic Nations," *New Medieval Literatures* 4 (2001): 95–115.

20. Anne Hudson, ed., *Selections from English Wycliffite Writings* (Cambridge, U.K.: Cambridge University Press, 1978), 127. Cited in Rita Copeland, "Rhetoric and the Politics of the Literal Sense in Medieval Literary Theory: Aquinas, Wyclif, and the Lollards," in *Interpretation: Medieval and Modern*, ed. Piero Boitani and Anna Torti (London: D. S. Brewer, 1992), 17, and in Anne Hudson, "Lollardy: The English Heresy?" in *Lollards and Their Books* (London: Hambledon Press, 1985), 141.

21. On the meaning of "open" in Lollard contexts, see Ralph Hanna III, "The Difficulty of Ricardian Prose Translation: The Case of the Lollards," *Modern Language Quarterly* 51 (1990): 319–40; Copeland, "Rhetoric"; and Nissé, "Reversing Discipline."

22. Hudson, *Selections*, 127–28. Hudson notes that the idea that Paul wrote in different languages was a "common medieval belief" (200).

23. J. Forshall and F. Madden, eds., *The Holy Bible . . . Made from the Latin Vulgate by John Wycliffe and His Followers*, vol. 1 (Oxford, U.K.: Oxford University Press, 1850), 57–59. For discussion see Nissé, "Reversing Discipline," 164.

24. Copeland, "Rhetoric," 14–15.

25. *De veritate sacrae scripturae*, ed. Rudolf Buddensieg (London: Trübner and Co., 1905), 1:2/7–10. Citation and translation (with slight modification) from Copeland, "Rhetoric," 15. For an English translation of the tract (abridged), see *John Wyclif: On the Truth of Holy Scripture*, trans. Ian Christopher Levy (Kalamazoo, Mich.: Medieval Institute, 2001).

26. G. R. Evans, "Wyclif on the Literal and Metaphorical," in *From Ockham to Wyclif*, ed. Anne Hudson and Michael Wilks (Oxford, U.K.: Basil Blackwell), 263–64. On fifteenth-century discussion in orthodox contexts of the idea of "the literal sense" as inherited from Augustine, see Froehlich. See also A. J. Minnis, "'Authorial Intention' and 'Literal Sense' in the Exegetical Theories of Richard Fitzralph and John Wyclif: An Essay in the Medieval History of Biblical Hermeneutics," *Proceedings of the Royal Irish Academy* 75, Section C (1975): 1–30, and Michael Hurley, "'Scriptura Sola': Wyclif and His Critics," *Traditio* 16 (1960): 275–352.

27. Copeland, "Rhetoric," 17, and Hanna, "Difficulty."

28. Mary Dove, "Chaucer and the Translation of Jewish Scriptures," in *Chaucer and the Jews*, ed. Delany, 89.

29. Rita Copeland, *Pedagogy, Intellectuals, and Dissent in the Later Middle Ages* (Cambridge, U.K.: Cambridge University Press, 2001).

30. On this intellectual lineage of reevaluation of the literal, see Copeland, *Pedagogy*, 101 ff. On *Hebraica Veritas* and Jewish-Christian exchange in matters of Biblical scholarship, see Dahan, *Les intellectuels;* Grabois, "*Hebraica Veritas*"; 613–34; Lotter, "Das Prinzip"; Signer, "*Peshat*," 203–16; Smalley, *Study of the Bible*, 149–72.

31. 56–57. Cited in Nissé, "Reversing Discipline," 186. See also "Prophetic," 111.

32. Nissé, "Reversing Discipline," esp. 185–86. See also "Prophetic."

33. Nissé, "Reversing Discipline," 186.

34. Anne Hudson, ed. *English Wycliffite Sermons*, vol. 3, (Oxford, U.K.: Clarendon Press, 1990), 42. See also comments on the sermon, which draws greatly upon Lyre, in *English Wycliffite Sermons*, vol. 5., ed. Anne Hudson and Pamela Gradon (Oxford, U.K.: Clarendon Press, 1996), 294–95.

35. Hudson, *English Wycliffite Sermons*, vol. 3, 42–43.

36. Hudson, *English Wycliffite Sermons*, vol. 3, 42.

37. Nissé, "Reversing Discipline," 181. See also Dove, 94.

38. Churchill Babington, ed. *The Repressor of Over Much Blaming of the Clergy*, vol. 1 (London: Longman, Green, Longman, and Roberts, 1860), 69. On Pecock, see Anne Hudson, *The Premature Reformation: Wycliffite Texts and Lollard History* (Oxford, U.K.: Clarendon Press, 1988), 55–58.

39. Pecock, *The Repressor*, 58–59.

40. Ronald Waldron, "Trevisa's Original Prefaces on Translation: A Critical Edition," in *Medieval English Studies Presented to George Kane*, ed. Edward Donald Kennedy, Ronald Waldron, and Joseph S. Wittig (Bury St. Edmunds, U.K.: St. Edmundsbury Press, 1988), 292 and 293. See Andrew Cole, "Chaucer's English Lesson," *Speculum* 77 (2002): 1150.

41. Prologue to the *Treatise on the Astrolabe*, *Riverside Chaucer*, page 662, line 51. On the sources of the *Treatise*, see Dorothee Metlitzki, *The Matter of Araby in Medieval England* (New Haven, Conn.: Yale University Press, 1977), 75–80.

42. Prologue, lines 28–40.

43. Cole, 1167.

44. Thomas Hahn, "Money, Sexuality, Wordplay, and Context in the *Shipman's Tale*," in *Chaucer in the Eighties*, ed. Julian Wasserman and Robert J. Blanch (Syracuse, N.Y.: Syracuse University Press, 1986), 236.

45. Hahn, "Money," 238.

46. Hahn, "Money," 241–43.

47. See John Noonan, *The Scholastic Analysis of Usury* (Cambridge, Mass.: Harvard University Press, 1957), 39–81. This notion of usury as an "unnatural" act resonates clearly with contemporary ideas about "sodomy" as unnatural. On usury and sodomy, see John Boswell, *Christianity, Social Tolerance, and Homosexuality: Gay People in Western Europe from the Beginning of the Christian Era to the Fourteenth Century* (Chicago: University of Chicago Press, 1980), 330–32. See also the suggestive associations in Moore, *Formation of a Persecuting Society; 66–99*.

48. Cited in Hahn, "Money," 242. "Unde fit quidam partus cum denarius ex denario crescit. Et ideo etiam ista acquisitio pecuniarum est maxime praeter naturam: quia secundum naturam est, ut denarii acquirantur ex rebus naturalibus, non [ne] autem ex denariis." *In octo libros Politicorum Aristotelis Expositio*, ed. R. M. Spiazzi (Turin, Rome: Marietti, 1966), 41. Cited, with slight modification, in Hahn, "Money," 249 n. 21.

49. For a connection between usury and prostitution in the writings of Thomas of Chobham, see Jacques Le Goff, *Your Money or Your Life: Economy and Religion in the Middle Ages*, trans. Patricia Ranum (New York: Zone Books, 1988), 50.

50. Lines 19701–19704 from Guillaume de Lorris and Jean de Meun, *Le Roman de la Rose*, vol. 5, ed. Ernest Langlois (Paris: Librairie Ancienne Édouard Champion, 1914), 12. Charles Dahlberg translates these lines as "Plow, for God's sake, my barons, plow and restore your lineages. Unless you think on plowing vigorously, there is nothing that can restore them." *The Romance of the Rose* (Hanover, N.H.: University of New England Press, 1971), 324–25. The passage continues with an extended metaphor of sexual intercourse.

51. Fourteenth-century moralists deemed masturbation another type of "unnatural" sin, counter to the aims of reproduction. See James A. Brundage, *Law, Sex, and Christian Society in Medieval Europe* (Chicago: University of Chicago Press, 1987), 533–36.

52. We know the merchant can perform sexually from passage VII. 372–81.

53. Hahn, "Money," 243.

54. See, for example, Gerhard Joseph, "Chaucer's Coinage: Foreign Exchange and the Puns of the *Shipman's Tale*," *Chaucer Review* 17 (1983): 345–46.

55. This unnatural proliferation of money and sin is accompanied by what appears to be actual reproductive sterility. Although, of course, one cannot assume a childless marriage simply because no children are mentioned in the tale, I do find suggestive the description of the girl who accompanies the wife, who does not seem to be her own child but is perhaps a ward or a servant. The wife has a "mayde child . . . in hire compaignye, / Which as hir list she may governe and gye, / For yet under the yerde was the mayde" (VII. 95–97). The merchant has been married for some time; his wife greets him "of oold usage" (VII. 374), but one could argue that the taint of the merchant's dealings poisons natural reproduction. The wife's actions could also result in a pregnancy by daun John, seriously subverting paternity and patrimony.

56. Marc Shell, "The Wether and the Ewe: Verbal Usury in *The Merchant of Venice*," *Kenyon Review* 14 (1979): 66.

57. For a detailed discussion of the tale's puns, see Joseph.

58. My thinking about the *Prioress's Tale* as a response to the *Shipman's Tale* owes much to my discussions with Wendy Roth. I am also grateful to her sharing with me " 'Taillynge Ynough' in the *Shipman's Tale* and the *Prioress's Tale*," unpublished essay (University of California, Berkeley, 1992).

59. On the sources and analogues for the *Prioress's Tale*, see Carleton Brown, "The *Prioress's Tale*" in *Sources and Analogues of Chaucer's Canterbury Tales*, ed. W. F. Bryan and Germaine Dempster (New York: Humanities Press, 1958), 447–85.

60. See also Lee Patterson, " 'Living Witnesses of Our Redemption': Martyrdom and Imitation in Chaucer's *Prioress's Tale*," *Journal of Medieval and Early Modern Studies* 31 (2001): 512.

61. Eileen Power, *Medieval English Nunneries* (Cambridge, U.K.: University of Cambridge Press, 1922), 69. Cited in Hardy Long Frank, "Seeing the Prioress Whole," *Chaucer Review* 25 (1991): 230.

62. Frank, 230.

63. Thomas Hahn, "The Performance of Gender in the Prioress," *Chaucer Yearbook* 1 (1992): 111–32.

64. In Arthur T. Broes, "Chaucer's Disgruntled Cleric: The *Nun's Priest's*

Tale," *PMLA* 78 (1963): 156–62. Broes argues that the Nun's Priest satirizes the Prioress in his tale. See also Ridley, 34–35.

65. The Host responds to the Shipman with the incorrect Latin "Wel seyd, by *corpus dominus*"(VII. 435). On one level, however, Harry Bailley is correct; the *Shipman's Tale* does focus on a worship of the material and bodily pleasure, whereas the Prioress attempts to transcend this corporeality with a focus on the birth of God into a corporeal form.

66. According to the *MED* the verb *ravishen* has a wide range of meanings, including "to steal," "to plunder," "to plagiarize," "to compel," "to attract," and "to carry off (a woman) by force, esp. for the purpose of rape." The *MED* places the usage of *ravishen* in the *Prioress's Prologue* under the definition "to compel (sth.) by attraction, draw, attract; draw (Christ, the Holy Ghost to one-self), captivate (someone's heart)," meanings that clearly have both spiritual and worldly impact. The denotations and connotations of *ravishen* reinforce a reading that recognizes the strongly active Virgin in the Prioress's depiction. For other critical discussions of the active nature of this passage, see Stephen Spector, "Empathy and Enmity in the *Prioress's Tale,*" in *The Olde Daunce: Love, Friendship and Marriage in the Medieval World,* ed. Robert R. Edwards and Stephen Spector (Albany: State University of New York Press, 1991), 211; Edward Condren comments on active meaning and sexual overtones in this passage: "The Prioress: A Legend of Spirit, A Life of Flesh," *The Chaucer Review* 23 (1989): 216 n. 28.

67. Jo Ann Hoeppner Moran, *The Growth of English Schooling, 1340–1548: Learning, Literacy, and Laicization in Pre-Reformation York Diocese* (Princeton, N.J.: Princeton University Press, 1985), 69–70. For more on the song schools, see Moran, 21–62, and Katherine Zieman, "Reading and Singing: Liturgy, Literacy, and Literature in Late Medieval England" (Ph.D. diss., University of California, Berkeley, 1997). In referring to medieval English educational institutions, Nicholas Orme himself refers to the schools and universities, as opposed to home education, as part of the "masculine world," because these were "wholly confined to men in the later Middle Ages, except for a few elementary schools for young boys and girls in London and elsewhere." Nicholas Orme, *Education and Society in Medieval and Renaissance England* (London: Hambledon Press, 1989), 231. For a reading with an emphasis on music and music pedagogy, see Bruce Holsinger, "Pedagogy, Violence, and the Subject of Music: Chaucer's *Prioress's Tale* and Ideologies of Song," *New Medieval Literatures* 1 (1997): 157–92.

68. It is interesting that Chaucer's little clergeon, unlike some of the boys in the analogues, is 7 and not 10. Shulamith Shahar notes that the age of 7 is the typical age of the end of the first stage of childhood, where the child is still under complete parental control and responsibility. *Childhood in the Middle Ages*, trans. by Chaya Galai (New York: Routledge, 1992), 23–26.

69. Sister Mary Madeleva interprets the grain as the eucharist; see "Chaucer's Nuns" in *Chaucer's Nuns and Other Essays* (New York: Appleton, 1925), 39–40. For an elegant discussion of the overall importance of the eucharist to the tale, see Denise Despres, "Cultic Anti-Judaism and Chaucer's Litel Clergeon," *Modern Philology* 91 (1994): 413–27. For an overview of other interpretations of the grain, see Boyd, 160–61.

70. Sumner Ferris, "The Mariology of the *Prioress's Tale*," *American Benedictine Review* 32 (1981): 232–54.

71. Alfred David has also detected this link between the punishment and the murder: "The hatred for the Jews and the violence of the murder are in sharp contrast to the school scene but are cut from the same cloth." He argues that the Prioress regards the little clergeon as destined to suffer and that she reacts to his suffering as she would to the mice and lapdogs mentioned in her *General Prologue* portrait, *The Strumpet Muse: Art and Morals in Chaucer's Poetry* (Bloomington: University of Indiana Press, 1976), 211. See also Fradenburg's useful discussion of this violence and its treatment by critics, esp. 100–108.

72. Robert Hanning, "From *Eva* and *Ave* to Eglentyne and Alisoun: Chaucer's Insight into the Roles Women Play," *Signs* 2 (1977): 590.

73. On the triangle of mother, child, and Jew in anti-Semitic discourse, see Fradenburg, 90. She also points to the displacement of blame onto the Jews, 105.

74. Albert Friedman, "The Prioress's Tale and Chaucer's Anti-Semitism," *Chaucer Review* 9 (1974): 118. Gavin Langmuir, who notes that ritual murder accusation was "created and initially most fully developed in England," defines "ritual murder as the killing of a human, not merely from motives of religious hatred, but in such a way that the *form* of the killing is at least partly determined by ideas allegedly or actually important in the religion of the killers or the victims"
(240). Langmuir identifies two types of ritual murder accusation raised by medieval Christians against Jews. The earliest incidents involved accusing the Jews of annually crucifying a Christian boy "to insult Christ and as a sacrifice" (240). Later the accusation grew to include the notion that Jews used the blood of a murdered Christian child for ritual or medicinal purposes (240). Langmuir, *Toward*. See also Joe Hillaby, "The Ritual-Child-Murder Accusation: Its Dissemination and Harold of Gloucester," *Jewish Historical Studies* 34 (1994–96): 69–109; R. Hsia, *The Myth of Ritual Murder: Jews and Magic in Reformation Germany* (New Haven, Conn.: Yale University Press, 1986), and *Trent 1475: Stories of a Ritual Murder Trial* (New Haven, Conn.: Yale University Press, 1992); John McCulloh, "Jewish Ritual Murder: William of Norwich, Thomas of Monmouth, and the Early Dissemination of the Myth," *Speculum* 72 (1997): 698–740; Miri Rubin, *Gentile Tales: The Narrative Assault on Late Medieval Jews* (New Haven Conn.: Yale University Press, 1999).

75. Langmuir, *Toward*, 245.

76. Boyd, 17.

77. See Marie Hamilton, "Echoes of Childermas in the Tale of the Prioress," *Modern Language Review* 34 (1939): 1–8, and John C. Hirsh, "Reopening the *Prioress's Tale*," *Chaucer Review* 10 (1975): 30–45.

78. Hirsh, 33.

79. For another reading of displacement that ultimately links the Prioress to the Jews, see Stephanie Gaynor, "He Says, She says: Subjectivity and the Discourse of the Other in the *Prioress's Portrait and Tale*," *Medieval Encounters* 5 (1999): 375–90.

80. The segregationary regulations of Lateran IV are particularly relevant here. See Jacob Marcus, *The Jew in the Medieval World* (New York: Harper and

Row, 1938), 137–40, and Diane Owen Hughes, "Distinguishing Signs: Ear-Rings, Jews and Franciscan Rhetoric in the Italian Renaissance City," *Past and Present* 112 (1986): 3–59.

81. My thinking on boundary imagery and "permeable boundaries" in the tale was deeply enriched by an unpublished paper by Irene Tucker, "Hosting the Jews: Boundary Permeability in Chaucer's *Prioress's Tale*," (University of California, Berkeley, 1989). I thank her for generously sharing her unpublished work with me. See also Fradenburg, 99.

82. Butler, *Bodies that Matter* 3.

83. To Friedman, the Prioress here seems to be hesitating, suggesting "a gathering of courage before reluctantly uttering the unwonted foulness" (*The Prioress's Tale*, 126). Kelly argues that the Prioress's emphasis here is not on the Jews, but on the privy, which shows her own "childish fascination for excrement" (367). Edward Kelly, "By Mouth of Innocentz: The Prioress Vindicated," *Papers on Language and Literature* 5 (1969): 362–74. I, however, read this emphasis on the privy as very much a part of the rhetorical strategy of the tale. The earlier verses surrounding the murder establish a connection between the Jews and the Devil. The Prioress makes the connection explicit: "Oure firste foo, the serpent Sathanas, / That hath in Jues herte his waspes nest" (VII.558–59). The Jews are connected to the devil, who incites them to murder the boy. The Prioress describes the murder and then focuses on its scatological details, creating a nexus of Jews, violent murder, and filth. The Prioress demonizes, criminalizes, and then soils these Jew figures with emphasis on the privy as the crowning touch to this process. There are, of course, further traditional connections between Jews and excrement. Denise Despres connects the privy to the chamberpot inscribed with Hebrew letters in the Grünewald Altarpiece's Nativity tableau; see "Cultic," 424. Isaiah Shachar in *The Judensau: A Medieval Anti-Jewish Motif and Its History* (London: Warburg Institute, 1974) traces such a tradition in art. Although Shachar makes a point of noting the absence of the *Judensau* image in the English manuscripts he has examined, his discussion of wider sources for the "exclusively German" *Judensau* nevertheless suggests a widespread and common association between Jews and filth. See also Trachtenberg, *Devil and the Jews*, esp. chapter 8.

84. See Steven F. Kruger, "The Bodies of Jews in the Late Middle Ages," in *The Idea of Medieval Literature: New Essays on Chaucer and Medieval Culture in Honor of Donald R. Howard*, ed. James M. Dean and Christian K. Zacher (Cranbury, N.J.: Associated University Presses, 1992), 301–22, esp. 304–8. See also Fradenburg, 99-101.

85. This representation of a dead child is reminiscent of the *Pearl* poem, which also emphasizes the virginity of the dreamer's lost pearl, connecting her as well to the 144,000 virgins. *Pearl* in *The Poems of the Pearl Manuscript*, ed. Malcolm Andrew and Ronald Waldron (Berkeley: University of California Press, 1978), 107, line 1147.

86. Spector, 222.

87. Warner, *Alone of All Her Sex*, 73. See also Coletti, "Purity and Danger," 89 n. 15.

88. The use of the term "privee place" in the *Wife of Bath's Prologue* rein-

forces, I think, my sense that the description of the privy has sexual/reproductive overtones. Alysoun says that "[y]et have I Martes mark upon my face, / And also in another privee place" (III.D.619–20). If we consider the possibility that Chaucer may have intended the *Shipman's Tale* for the Wife, this echo seems even more likely. There are medieval references to the womb as a site of impurity and danger as well. For example, in his influential *Etymologies*, Isidore of Seville attributes to menstrual blood properties that kill plant life, rust iron, and make rabid dogs who eat it. See Lemay, *Women's Secrets*, 37 and 161 n. 110. See also the comparison between a brothel and a "commune gong, where as men purgen hire ordure" in the *Parson's Tale* (X.885).

89. Kruger, "Bodies," 306. In his reading of the *Prioress's Tale*, Kruger shows how the tale creates an opposition between Christian bodies, which are attacked, but ultimately are whole and incorruptible, in contrast to Jewish bodies, which ultimately destroy themselves and can only be made whole through conversion, which is not an option in this tale but is in other texts, such as the Croxton *Play of the Sacrament*, which Kruger also examines. Drawing upon and expanding the insights of historians Bynum and R. I. Moore, Kruger has explored a wide range of Middle English and Latin texts, developing a theory of medieval Christian attitudes toward both their own bodies and those of the Jewish and Muslim Other, as well as the bodies of women, lepers, and homosexuals. His essays have influenced me greatly and I thank him for generously sharing much of this work with me prior to its subsequent publication. For this discussion of the body, see esp. his "Bodies" and "Medieval Christian (Dis)identifications."

90. On Jewish representations of Christian bodies that date to the massacres of 1096 and became part of the liturgy of Tishah B'Av in the medieval period, see Linda Weinhouse, "Faith and Fantasy: The Texts of the Jews," *Medieval Encounters* 5 (1999): 391–408. See also Anna Sapir Abulafia, "Invectives against Christianity in the Hebrew Chronicles of the First Crusade," in *Crusade and Settlement*, ed. Peter W. Edbury (Cardiff, Wales: University College Cardiff Press, 1985), 66–72.

91. She argues that the older boy's inability to explain the *Alma* to the clergeon and the clergeon's desire to learn the song despite not understanding the lyrics "are the heart of the tale and the key to both it and the Prioress. One cannot escape the fundamental parallel between her religious practices and the children's attitude toward the song. To *lerne* the song, the outward, by rote, not to gain a full understanding, but in order to manifest praise and love, is for her, if not for us, an emblem of true, innocent faith." Carolyn Collette, "Sense and Sensibility in *The Prioress's Tale*," *The Chaucer Review* 15 (1981): 143.

92. Katherine Zieman argues that the Prioress "fashions an ideal form of piety which is specifically unlettered and implicitly anti-clerical." Katherine Zieman, "Reading, Singing, and Understanding: Constructions of Women's Literacy in Late Medieval England," in *Literacy and Learning in the Middle Ages*, ed. Sarah Rees-Jones (Turnholt, Belgium: Brepols, 2002), 102–3. I thank her for sharing this work with me prior to its subsequent publication. It is also interesting to note here that the Prioress is presenting a model of piety that can be illuminated by Julia Kristeva's concept of the semiotic. The connection to the maternal figure of the Virgin, a devotion taught to a fatherless boy by his mother, calls to mind the

Kristevan semiotic and the sheer power of the maternal as something prior to and beyond the Law of the Father. See Fradenburg for an extended reading and Corey J. Marvin, " 'I Will Thee Not Forsake': The Kristevan Maternal Space in Chaucer's *Prioress's Tale* and John of Garland's *Stella Maris*," *Exemplaria* 8 (1996): 35–58.

93. Shulamith Shahar discusses the stages of early childhood development as conceived in the late medieval period: "Most authors specify the age of 7 as the commencement of the second stage, since from this age onwards the child can express himself properly, distinguish between good and evil, and choose between them. He has reached 'the years of choice and discretion' (*annis discretionis*). In selecting the ability to express oneself as the distinguishing feature of the second stage of childhood, the medieval scholars were following the Roman approach, according to which the inability to express oneself is one of the characteristic signs of early childhood. In this period the child is denoted *infans*, 'because he is incapable of speech.' . . . A young man who still behaved childishly was sometimes denoted *infans*, and the term was also sometimes applied to an adult who, for whatsoever reason, could not express himself properly." *Childhood in the Middle Ages*, 24.

94. Carleton Brown, who also points to the importance of the clergeon's age in Chaucer's version, notes that the detail of the older child who teaches the younger is Chaucer's own significant emendation to earlier versions (465). The older boy teaches the younger "prively."

95. In other versions it is a Jewish boy who knows Latin who explains the text of the *Alma* to the other Jews. The play on the letter and the spirit here recalls Lollard reformist pleas for access to the vernacular in order to further Christian understanding for all.

96. For a different reading of the connection between the two tales, see Gail Berkeley Sherman, "Saints, Nuns, and Speech in the *Canterbury Tales*," in *Images of Sainthood in Medieval Europe*, ed. Renate Blumenfeld-Kosinski and Timea Szell (Ithaca, N.Y.: Cornell University Press, 1991), 136–60. Kruger, "Bodies," also compares the two tales, 302, 304–5. In addition to the other works about the *Second Nun's Tale* cited in this chapter, I have found the following essays useful: Paul E. Beicher, "Confrontation, Contempt of Court, and Chaucer's Cecelia," *Chaucer Review* 8 (1974): 198–204; Saul Brody, "Chaucer's Rhyme Royal Tales and the Secularization of the Saint," *Chaucer Review* 20 (1985): 113–31; Carolyn P. Collette, "A Closer Look at Seinte Cecile's Special Vision," *Chaucer Review* 10 (1987): 337–49; John Hirsh, "The Politics of Spirituality: The Second Nun and the Manciple," *Chaucer Review* 12 (1977): 121–46; and Sherry L. Reames, "The Cecilia Legend as Chaucer Inherited It and Retold It: The Disappearance of an Augustinian Ideal," *Speculum* 55 (1980): 38–57. (Additional essays by Reames included in bibliography).

97. On the relations between the two prologues, see Robert A. Pratt, "Chaucer's Borrowing from Himself," *Modern Language Quarterly* 7 (1946): 259–64.

98. For a discussion of the terms "legende" and "miracle," see Paul Strohm, "*Passioun, Lyf, Miracle, Legende*: Some Generic Terms in the Middle English Hagiographical Narrative," *Chaucer Review* 10 (1975–76): 154–71. "Miracle" is discussed on 158–61, "Legende" on 161–64.

99. For a characterization of the Second Nun as faceless and anonymous see Sherman, 141–42.

100. Power, *Medieval English Nunneries*, 62–63.

101. Alexandra Barratt points out that the "learning and literacy of nuns in England actually deteriorated during the Middle Ages" from the Anglo-Saxon period when convents had a reputation for scholarship. But she does point to various examples of medieval English nuns who translated from Latin, as Chaucer portrays his Second Nun as doing (3). She also notes that "in the fourteenth and fifteenth centuries it was a commonplace that English nuns did not understand Latin, only French or English, but they wrote hardly anything in either language" (3). But, as she discusses, literacy was not out of the question for a fourteenth-century English nun, and it was possible for one to have been making translations from Latin. As Barratt also mentions, translation was considered an "appropriate" form of literary endeavor for women (13). Eileen Power's discussion of the decline in nuns' literacy and education in *Medieval English Nunneries* is suggestive. Because literacy among nuns had demonstrably and scandalously declined, one could read the Second Nun's learned tale and her active, educated female protagonist as a response to the Prioress's promotion of a devotion that utters religious praise without knowing what the words really mean as specifically directed at this cultural situation.

102. V. A. Kolve, "Chaucer's *Second Nun's Tale* and the Iconography of Saint Cecilia," in *New Perspectives in Chaucer Criticism*, ed. Donald H. Rose (Norman, Okla.: Pilgrim Books, 1981): 151–52.

103. Sherman, 144.

104. Cecelia is interestingly not masculinized, as are so many of the early female virgin martyrs. She is the only one of these early virgin martyrs to marry, and the tale does not thematize her transformation to a masculinized woman, a common occurrence in these early tales.

105. Jocelyn Wogan-Browne, "The Virgin's Tale," in *Feminist Readings in Middle English Literature: The Wife of Bath and All Her Sect*, ed. Ruth Evans and Lesley Johnson (New York: Routledge, 1994), 177–78.

106. Jones, 30.

107. Ibid., 33.

108. Unpublished sermon partially cited in Jones, 34. Full version found in G. Owst, *Literature and Pulpit in Medieval England: A Neglected Chapter in the History of English Letters & of the English People*, 2d rev. ed. (Oxford, U.K.: Blackwell, 1961), 144.

109. Lynn Staley, "Chaucer and the Postures of Sanctity," in *The Powers of the Holy: Religion, Politics, and Gender in Late Medieval English Culture*, by David Aers and Lynn Staley (University Park: Pennsylvania State University Press, 1996), 207.

110. See Boyarin, *Radical Jew*, 13.

111. A line of argumentation that I am not pursuing here is the question of women in the Lollard movement. As Shannon McSheffrey has shown, anti-Lollard polemic seizes on the heresy's alleged appeal to women as a way of "casting aspersions" rather than as an indication of the realities of the movement. See *Gender*

and Heresy: Women and Men in Lollard Communities, 1420–1530 (Philadelphia: University of Pennsylvania Press, 1995), 139.

112. There is, of course, widely ranging modern critical assessment of the tale in terms of stylistics and thematics. Lee Patterson, "'What Man Artow?' Authorial Self-Definition in *The Tale of Sir Thopas* and *The Tale of Melibee*," *Studies in the Age of Chaucer* 11 (1989): 117–75, provides an excellent critical overview.

113. There are multiple readings of the meaning of this line. D. W. Robertson reads "tretys" as referring to the entire *Canterbury Tales; Preface to Chaucer* (Princeton, N.J.: Princeton University Press, 1963), 368–69. Bernard Huppé appears to concur, arguing, "The sentence of the *Tale of Melibeus* is the sentence of the *Canterbury Tales*." *A Reading of the Canterbury Tales*, rev. ed. (Albany: State University of New York Press, 1967), 236. Glending Olson reads this line as saying that although this version of the story will be different from earlier ones, it will have essentially the same meaning. "A Reading of *Thopas-Melibee* Link," *Chaucer Review* 10 (1975–76): 147–53, esp. 150–51. Dominick Grace reads "litel tretys" and "treatise lite" as referring to the *Melibee* and its French source respectively, thereby demonstrating not unity but an ironic multiplicity of meaning. "Chaucer's Little Treatises," *Florilegium* 14 (1995–96): 157–70. On the sources, see Patterson, "'What Man Artow?'" esp. 139–41.

114. Patterson, "'What Man Artow?'" 135.

115. Ibid., 152.

116. Ibid., 164. Jill Mann also focuses on the child, specifically on the important implications of the parent-child relationship as a figure for a larger Chaucerian thematic—the relationship between human beings and the divine forces that control the universe. "Parents and Children in the "Canterbury Tales," in *Literature in Fourteenth-Century England*, ed. Piero Boitani and Anna Torti (Tübingen: Narr Verlag, 1983), 165–83.

117. Patterson, "'What Man Artow?'" 164.

118. Ibid.

119. Ibid., 171. On the Innocents and the Christ child, see Leah Sinanoglou, "The Christ Child As Sacrifice: A Medieval Tradition and the Corpus Christi Plays," *Speculum* 48 (1973): 491–509.

120. On the concept of supersession, see introduction to Boyarin, *Radical Jew*, 1–12. Jill Robbins has shown how Augustine's exegesis of stories of brothers—Cain and Abel, Esau and Jacob, Ishmael and Isaac, and the story of the prodigal son—develops an understanding of the relationship of supersession between the Old Testament and the New, and between Jews and Christians, in which Christians always represent the younger brother who takes precedence over the older one. See her *Prodigal Son*, 1–48. See also Ruether, "*Adversus Judaeos*," 179–80.

121. On Rachel as a type of Mary, see Despres, "Immaculate Flesh," 53. Robert Adams reads the Rachel figure ironically, which inevitably aligns him with the so-called hard readings of the tale and portrait that often try to exculpate Chaucer from charges of anti-Semitism. "Chaucer's 'New Rachel' and the Theological Roots of Medieval Anti-Semitism," *Bulletin of the John Rylands University Library*

of Manchester 77 (autumn 1995): 9–18. For a different reading see also Patterson, "Living Witnesses." For a survey of "hard and soft" critical readings (terms coined by Ridley), see Boyd, 43–50.

122. For examples of these visual images, see Schreckenberg, *Jews in Christian Art*, 273–90.

123. Alan T. Gaylord, "*Sentence* and *Solaas* in Fragment VII of *The Canterbury Tales*: Harry Bailley as Horseback Editor," *PMLA* 82 (1967): 226.

124. Ibid.

125. Lawrence Besserman reads Chaucer as analogizing himself, as author of the *Melibee*, to the evangelists. See "*Glosynge Is a Glorious Thyng*: Chaucer's Biblical Exegesis," in *Chaucer and Scriptural Tradition*, ed. David Lyle Jeffrey (Ottawa, Canada: University of Ottawa Press, 1984), 72.

126. Following John 19, see Jeremy Cohen, "The Jews As the Killers of Christ in the Latin Tradition, From Augustine to the Friars," *Traditio* 39 (1983): 1–27; William Chester Jordan, "The 'Last Tormentor of Christ': An Image of the Jew in Ancient and Medieval Exegesis, Art, and Drama," *The Jewish Quarterly Review* 78 (1987): 21–47, and Bestul, *Texts of the Passion*, 69–110.

127. Siegfried Wenzel links the tale firmly to the penitential tradition. "Notes on the Parson's Tale," *Chaucer Review* 16 (1982): 248–49. Lee Patterson also shows important influences from this tradition. "*The Parson's Tale* and the Quitting of the *Canterbury Tales*," *Traditio* 34 (1978): 331–80. On the sources of the tale, see Patterson, "*Parson's Tale*," 340, n.29 and Siegfried Wenzel's notes in the *Riverside Chaucer*, 956–57.

128. Thomas Bestul, "Chaucer's Parson's Tale and the Late-Medieval Tradition of Religious Meditation," *Speculum* 64 (1989): 607. Patterson also points out this change from the source, "*Parson's Tale*," 353–54.

129. Patterson, "*Parson's Tale*," 341.

130. "And ye shul understonde that in mannes synne is every manere of ordre or ordinaunce turned up-so-doun" (X.259). Cited in Patterson, "*Parson's Tale*," 341, where he also discusses the "unmaking" of the Christian through sin in the tale.

131. See also Bestul, "Parson's Tale" and *Texts of the Passion*, in which he argues that "the way Jews were represented in the Passion narratives not only reflected, but actively contributed to, the anti-Judaism of the later Middle Ages" (110). For an example of a vision of the Jews at the Passion, see Kempe, 347. For a text designed to help create such a meditative vision, see Lydgate's *Merita Missae*, Appendix V in T. F. Simmons, ed., *The Lay Folks Mass Book* (London: EETS, 1879), 151. See also Lisa Lampert, "The Once and Future Jew: The Croxton *Play of the Sacrament*, Little Robert of Bury and Historical Memory," *Jewish History* 15 (2001): 235–55.

132. On this harmony, see Lubac, *Medieval Exegesis*, vol. 1, 241–61.

133. I invoke the title of an important volume edited by Daniel Boyarin and Jonathan Boyarin, *Jews and Other Differences: The New Jewish Cultural Studies* (Minneapolis: University of Minnesota Press, 1999). The reference to "analogy of analogies," is from Bloch, *Medieval Misogyny*, 31.

Chapter 4

1. Robert L. A. Clark and Claire Sponsler have pointed to the ways in which the cross-dressing of the medieval stage exemplifies it as "the site of intense cultural and ideological negotiations involving the testing and contesting of conventional social roles and cultural categories such as race, class, and gender." Robert L. A. Clark and Claire Sponsler, "Queer Play: The Cultural Work of Crossdressing in Medieval Drama," *New Literary History* 28 (1997): 319. Robert L. A. Clark and Claire Sponsler, "Othered Bodies: Racial Crossdressing in the *Mistere de la Sainte Hostie* and the Croxton *Play of the Sacrament*," *Journal of Medieval and Early Modern Studies* 29 (1999): 61–87. I thank Professors Clark and Sponsler for sharing their work with me prior to its publication. On cross-dressing in relation to medieval representations of the bodily embrace, specifically in N-Town, see Pamela Sheingorn, "The Bodily Embrace or Embracing the Body: Gesture and Gender in Late Medieval Culture," in *The Stage as Mirror: Civic Theatre in Late Medieval Europe*, ed. Alan E. Knight (Rochester, N.Y.: D. S. Brewer, 1997), 51–89, esp. 79–89.

2. Evans, "When a Body Meets a Body," 196.

3. Gail McMurray Gibson, "Writing Before the Eye: The N-Town Woman Taken in Adultery and the Medieval Ministry Play," *Comparative Drama* 27 (1993–94): 401.

4. On the multiple meanings of conversion, see Morrison, *Understanding Conversion*, ix–xxii and 1–27.

5. As Sarah Beckwith asserts, "[I]t is surely in theatre that the full sacramental definition of signs as sacred things can be most fully exploited, because in theatre iconic identity can be exploited, as can the very tension between outward form and inner thing, between sign and signified, and between the visible and the invisible at the heart of sacramental theology." Sarah Beckwith, "*Sacrum Signum*: Sacramentality and Dissent in the York Theatre of Corpus Christi," in *Criticism and Dissent in the Middle Ages*, ed. Rita Copeland (Cambridge, U.K.: University of Cambridge Press, 1996), 277.

6. There is an exciting body of recent work on medieval English drama that explores these issues, with critics such as Beckwith, Clark, Coletti, Evans, Gibson, Sheingorn, and Sponsler at its forefront. In addition to the works cited throughout this chapter, my understanding of the dynamics of dramatic embodiment has been much influenced by Sarah Beckwith, *Christ's Body: Identity, Culture and Society in Late Medieval Writings* (New York: Routledge, 1993).

7. Nichols, "Hierosphthitic Topos," 29–41, who discusses many of the same dramatic scenes that I do here, employs "hierosphthitic topos" to refer to the violation of a sacred object. I have chosen not to employ this term, because my focus is on the hand itself, rather than the holy object defiled.

8. "The Appearance to Thomas" in *The N-Town Play Cotton MS Vespasian D.8*, ed. Stephen Spector, vol. 1, EETS (New York: Oxford University Press, 1991), 381, line 370. Subsequent references to this edition will appear in the text. On N-Town's manuscript history, provenance, the linguistic evidence linking the play to

East Anglia, and the various towns proposed as origins for the play, see the introduction to Spector's edition, xiii–xviii. Gail McMurray Gibson locates N-Town in Bury, "Bury St. Edmunds, Lydgate and the N-Town Cycle," *Speculum* 56 (1981): 56–90. See also Peter Meredith, ed., *The Mary Play from the N-Town Manuscript* (Exeter, U.K.: University of Exeter Press, 1997), 1–28.

9. Natalie Zemon Davis, "Women on Top," in *Society and Culture in Early Modern France* (Stanford, Calif.: Stanford University Press, 1965), 124–51. On the lying-in period and "women on top," see page 145.

10. Copeland, "Why Women Can't Read," 257.

11. See Chapter 2 above.

12. This phrase is the title of Caroline Walker Bynum's important collection of essays, *Fragmentation and Redemption: Essays on Gender and the Human Body in Medieval Religion* (New York: Zone Books, 1992). I have learned much from Bynum's work on gender and medieval corporeality. Especially interesting in relation to the themes of this chapter is Bynum's introductory discussion of "history in the comic mode," 24–26.

13. On the typology of the cycle drama, see V. A. Kolve, *The Play Called Corpus Christi* (Stanford, Calif.: Stanford University Press, 1966). See also the introduction to Narin van Court, "Critical Apertures."

14. See Evans's discussion of "the ways in which the styles of the text and of bodies in performance enlist their audiences in the processes of representation, invite them to take up positions and elicit their desires" ("When a Body," 196).

15. On these rituals, see Eamon Duffy, *The Stripping of the Altars: Traditional Religion in England, 1400–1580* (New Haven, Conn.: Yale University Press, 1992).

16. The most important and innovative reading of the York Assumption and its significance is that by Evans ("When a Body"), whose focus on the disruption and laughter in this episode I find particularly insightful and revealing.

17. As Evans notes, records of the York play provide one of the only pieces of evidence of "contemporary audience response" to medieval drama that we possess ("When a Body," 199).

18. On the documents concerning the Fergus play, see Anna J. Mill, "The York Plays of the Dying, Assumption, and Coronation of our Lady," *PMLA* 65 (1950): 868–69. Cited in Evans, "When a Body," 203.

19. Mill, 868–69. See also Evans, "When a Body," 203.

20. Claire Sponsler, *Drama and Resistance: Bodies, Goods and Theatricality in Late Medieval England* (Minneapolis: Minnesota University Press), 138.

21. An important study of violence in medieval drama is Jody Enders, *The Medieval Theater of Cruelty: Rhetoric, Memory, Violence* (Ithaca, N.Y.: Cornell University Press, 1999). Richard Homan has also addressed this issue; see Richard L. Homan, "Mixed Feelings about Violence in the Corpus Christi Plays," in *Violence in Drama*, ed. James Redmond (Cambridge, U.K.: Cambridge University Press, 1991), 93–100. Both critics point to the multiplicity of possible responses. See critique of Homan in Enders, 233.

22. Virginia Schaefer Carroll argues that comic moments in the cycle plays

function as a "noble gyn," a device to trick audiences into greater spiritual awareness. I don't fully agree with the idea of these comic moments as "contrivances"
(17), but Carroll's observations about the participatory lure of these moments is
very relevant here. *The "Noble Gyn" of Comedy in the Middle English Cycle Plays*
(New York: Peter Lang, 1989).

23. See discussion of Butler and the "zone of uninhabitability" in Chapter 2.

24. See Kruger's analysis of the symbolics of the Christian body in "Bodies"
and "Medieval Christian (Dis)identifications" discussed in Chapter 3.

25. The *locus classicus* is Dante's contested "Letter to Congrande." Dante
Alighieri, *Dantis Alagherii Epistolae—The Letters of Dante*, ed. and trans. Paget
Toynbee, 2d ed. (Oxford, U.K.: Clarendon Press, 1966), 160–211. See also Northrop Frye, *Anatomy of Criticism: Four Essays* (Princeton, N.J.: Princeton University Press, 1957), 181; Frances M. Leonard, "The School for Transformation: A
Theory of Middle English Comedy," *Genre* 9 (1976): 179–91; and Howard Schless,
"Dante: Comedy and Conversion," in *Versions of Medieval Comedy*, ed. Paul Ruggiers (Norman: University of Oklahoma Press, 1977), 137–38. On the exclusion of
the Jewish from comedic form, see Ragussis (note 49) and Sylvia Tomasch's discussion of the absent yet present Jew at the heart of the *Commedia*: "Judecca, Dante's
Satan, and the *Dis*-placed Jew," in *Text and Territory: Geographical Imagination
in the European Middle Ages*," ed. Sylvia Tomasch and Sealy Gilles (Philadelphia:
University of Pennsylvania Press, 1998), 247–67. Both of these innovative studies
pave the way for new research on the connections between generic form and religious difference.

26. Gail McMurray Gibson argues convincingly that *The Play of the Sacrament* was performed near Bury St. Edmunds; see *The Theater of Devotion: East
Anglian Drama and Society in the Late Middle Ages* (Chicago: University of Chicago Press, 1989), 34–35.

27. David Bevington characterizes the play's Jews as generic doubters, designed "to be deplored not because of their particular ethnic origin but because
they are heathens lacking faith in Christ's divinity." See his *Medieval Drama*, 754.
Cecelia Cutts pioneered the anti-Lollard reading with her "The English Background of the *Play of the Sacrament*" (Ph.D. diss., University of Washington, 1938)
and "The Croxton Play: An Anti-Lollard Piece," *Modern Language Quarterly* 5
(1944): 45–60. Ann Nichols analyzes the play's use of "Lollard" language in "Lollard Language in the Croxton *Play of the Sacrament*," *Notes and Queries* 36, no. 1
(1989): 23–25. Gail McMurray Gibson also argues that the play is directed at Lollards, seeing Jonathas and his men as "Jews," rather than referents to actual Jews;
Theater of Devotion, 34–41.

28. "Once and Future Jew," 235–55.

29. My attention was first drawn to this Spanish setting by the careful close
reading of Rebecca Brackmann. I thank her and the other students in my fall 1997
"Jews and Gender" graduate seminar for their sharp insights.

30. Lines 9–16. All quotations from the Croxton *Play of the Sacrament* will
be from the standard edition, Norman Davis, ed., *Non-Cycle Plays and Fragments*,
EETS, suppl. ser. 1 (London: Oxford University Press, 1970). A facsimile edition
can be found in Norman Davis, ed., *Non-Cycle Plays and the Winchester Dialogues*

(Leeds, U.K.: School of English, 1979). The text of the play survives in folios 338r-56r of Trinity College, Dublin, M.S. F.4.20 (Catalogue No. 652); this copy of the play appears to have been made in the mid-sixteenth century. For a discussion of the importance of the context of the play's copying and transmission with a very different emphasis than this analysis, see Seth Lerer, " 'Represented Now in Yower Syght': The Culture of Spectatorship in Late Fifteenth-Century England," in *Bodies and Disciplines: Intersections of Literature and History in Fifteenth-Century England*, ed. Barbara Hanawalt and David Wallace (Minneapolis: University of Minnesota Press, 1996), 29–62.

31. Stephen Spector, "Time, Space and Identity in the *Play of the Sacrament*," in *The Stage As Mirror: Civic Theatre in Late Medieval Europe*, ed. Alan E. Knight (Rochester, N.Y.: D. S. Brewer, 1997), 190. Spector, following Bevington, categorizes the play as "fundamentally a story of conversion" (189). I disagree with Spector on the importance of setting, but my reading against the context of the Inquisition draws on his essay's important and early insistence there and elsewhere on reading medieval representations of Jews as Jews. Donnalee Dox has also called attention to the centrality of the conversion in the play; she uses its alternate title, *The Conversion of Ser Jonathas*, to emphasize this important element. See her "Medieval Drama as Documentation: 'Real Presence' in the Croxton *Conversion of Ser Jonathas the Jewe by the Myracle of the Blessed Sacrament*," *Theatre Survey* 38 (1997): 97–115, and "Representation Without Referent: The Jew in Medieval English Drama. An Exploration of Christian Alterity in *The Conversion of Ser Jonathas the Jew by Miracle of the Blessed Sacrament*" (Ph.D. diss., University of Minnesota, 1995). For a discussion of the Spanish locations in relation to a possible presentation of a related play before Leonore of Aragon in 1473, see William Tydeman, *English Medieval Theatre* (Boston: Routledge and Kegan Paul; 1986), 55.

32. In "Othered Bodies," Clark and Sponsler present a provocative discussion of the issue of "race" in relation to the Croxton play, although they do not focus specifically on the Spanish context. For a reading of the specificity of the play's setting as a foregrounding of its own modernity, see Michael Jones, "Theatrical History in the Croxton *Play of the Sacrament*," *ELH* 66 (1999): 223–60.

33. Jerome Friedman, "Jewish Conversion," 3–29.

34. B. Netanyahu, *The Origins of the Inquisition in Fifteenth Century Spain* (New York: Random House, 1995), 266. Sentence is italicized in original. The literature on the Jews of medieval and early modern Spain and Portugal and *conversos/marranos* is vast. I have found useful Friedman, Nirenberg, and Marc Shell, "Marrano (Pigs), or from Coexistence to Toleration," *Critical Inquiry* 17 (1991): 306–35, Yerushalmi, *Assimilation*, Norman Roth, *Conversos, Inquisition and the Expulsion of the Jews from Spain* (Madison: University of Wisconsin Press, 1995), and Elie Kedourie, ed., *Spain and the Jews* (London: Thames and Hudson, 1992). For a brief, insightful discussion of the politics of modern historiography on this topic, see Shapiro, *Shakespeare and the Jews*, 15–16.

35. Friedman, 13.

36. Netanyahu, *Origins*, 830–33.

37. Wendy R. Childs, *Anglo-Castilian Trade in the Later Middle Ages* (Manchester, U.K.: Manchester University Press, 1978), 4.

38. Childs, 2.

39. *The Libelle of Englyshe Polycye: A Poem on the Use of Sea-Power*, ed. George Warner (Oxford, U.K.: Clarendon Press, 1926), ll. 50–60. Subsequent references to this edition cited in the body of the text. An excellent discussion of the text, which includes discussion of dating and manuscripts, is Carol M. Meale, " *The Libelle of Englyshe Polycye* and Mercantile Literary Culture in Late-Medieval London," in *London and Europe in the Later Middle Ages*, ed. Julia Boffey and Pamela King (London: Centre for Medieval and Renaissance Studies, University of London, 1995), 181–227. Trade with Spain is also mentioned as part of an international trade network, specifically trade in wool, in another poem on England's role in trade modeled on the "Libelle." It is dated during the reign of Edward IV. See "On England's Commercial Policy," *Political Poems and Songs Relating to English History Composed during the Period from the Accession of Edw. III to That of Ric. III*, vol. 2, ed. Thomas Wright 1861; Reprint; Wiesbaden: Krauss, 1965), p. 284.

40. *The Commodyties of England . . . Copied from a Very Old Ms. in the Bodleian Library*, ed. T. O. Payne (London: n.p. 1863), 6. I thank Maura Nolan for generously helping me to gain access to this rare tract.

41. On the importance, dynamics, and history of the medieval English wool trade, see Childs as well as Eileen Power, *The Wool Trade in English Medieval History* (Oxford, U.K.: Oxford University Press, 1941), and T. H. Lloyd, *The English Wool Trade in the Middle Ages* (Cambridge, U.K.: Cambridge University Press, 1977).

42. Robert Gottfried, *Bury St. Edmunds and the Urban Crisis: 1290–1539* (Princeton, N.J.: Princeton University Press, 1982), 92.

43. For a somewhat different reading of this scene, see Kruger, "Bodies," 309–10.

44. On the subject of the connections between medieval Christian views of Judaism and Islam, see Cohen, *Living Letters*, 47–166, and Kruger, "Medieval Christian (Dis)identifications."

45. *Merchant of Venice* I.3.

46. Sarah Beckwith, "Ritual, Church and Theatre: Medieval Dramas of the Sacramental Body," in *Culture and History: 1350–1600*, ed. David Aers (Detroit: Wayne State University Press, 1992), 73.

47. Sister Nicholas Maltman, O.P., "Meaning and Art in the Croxton *Play of the Sacrament*," *ELH* 41 (1974): 151.

48. Michael Ragussis, *Figures of Conversion: 'The Jewish Question' and English National Identity* (Durham, N.C.: Duke University Press, 1995), 26–86.

49. Ragussis, 76.

50. Miri Rubin, "The Eucharist and the Construction of Medieval Identities," in *Culture and History: 1350–1600*, ed. David Aers (Detroit: Wayne State University Press. 1992), 57.

51. See Kruger, "Bodies," 308–19.

52. See Chapter 3 and Kruger, "Bodies."

53. Richard L. Homan, "Devotional Themes in the Violence and Humor of the *Play of the Sacrament*," *Comparative Drama* 20 (1986): 327–40, distinguishes the host desecration scene from the Crucifixion sequences that Kolve analyzes in

terms of game in *The Play Called Corpus Christi*, arguing that Jonathas and his men are serious as they torture the host. I see the problem as similar; however, the question is how one deals with the laughter, the complicity in the torture, which links the Christian audience member to the position of the Jews.

54. An important discussion of these issues can be found in Enders.

55. For differing views on the comic in the play, see Homan, "Devotional Themes," and Maltman. In "Representation without Referent," Dox provides a useful critical overview of these issues. See esp. 23–28.

56. On the play's humor as unifying, see Homan, "Devotional Themes" 328–334.

57. For a discussion of Christ as the true physician in the play, see Victor Scherb, "The Earthly and Divine Physicians: *Christus Medicus* in the Croxton *Play of the Sacrament*," in *The Body and the Text*, ed. Bruce Clark and Wendell Aycock (Lubbock: Texas Tech University Press, 1990), 161–71. The references to disease might have relevance to the anti-heretical readings of the play. R. I. Moore discusses twelfth-century metaphoric comparisons between diseases of the body and heresy as a disease of the soul in "Heresy As Disease," in *The Concept of Heresy in the Middle Ages (11th–13th c)*, ed. W. Lourdaux and D. Verhelst (Leuven, Belgium: Leuven University Press, 1976), 1–11. On the relationship between representations of heretics and Jews, see also Lipton, *Images of Intolerance*, 82–111.

58. Just as I would not argue for exact correspondences to the Spanish setting of the drama, I would not suggest that the play pokes fun at a specific physician from Brabant. Gibson suggests that the Colle episode critiques local practices at St. Saviour's hospital, which catered to rich clients, a reading not incompatible with mine (*Theater of Devotion*, 38).

59. Flemish drunkenness was legendary in the Middle Ages. See David Wallace, "In Flaundres," *Studies in the Age of Chaucer* 19 (1997): 80. Exactly how this stereotype might apply to Brabant remains unclear to me.

60. E. K. Chambers, *The English Folk-Play* (Oxford, U.K.: Clarendon Press, 1933), 58.

61. Gottfried, 103–4.

62. Gottfried, 8. Gottfried writes that a "1436 mandate, permitting aliens to reside in England, listed six resident foreigners in Bury St. Edmunds, four merchants, a weaver, and a tailor. They were two Dutchmen, two Brabanters, and two Germans" (93). On the relationship between England and the Low Countries and the subject of immigration, see Wallace and also Sylvia Thrupp, "A Survey of the Alien Population of England in 1440," *Speculum* 32 (1953): 262–73, and "Aliens in and around London in the Fifteenth Century," in *Studies in London History: Presented to Philip Edmund Jones*, ed. A. E. J. Hollaender and William Kellaway (London: Hodder and Stoughton, 1969), 251–72.

63. Other critics have discussed the play's focus on the dangers that come with trade and wealth. Alexandra Reid Schwartz argues that the play expresses "a generalized anxiety about mercantilism and about mercantilism's absorption of the host into its commercial economy." See "Economies of Salvation: Commerce and the Eucharist in the Profanation of the Host and the Croxton *Play of the Sacrament*," *Comitatus* 25 (1994): 2. In "Violence and the Social Body in the Croxton

Play of the Sacrament," in *Violence in Drama*, ed. James Redmond (Cambridge, U.K.: Cambridge University Press, 1991), Victor Scherb argues that the play's violence shows both divisions and the effects of healing in the community, an argument with parallels to my own. See also Theresa Coletti, "*Paupertas est donum Dei*: Hagiography, Lay Religion, and the Economics of Salvation in the Digby *Mary Magdalene*," *Speculum* 76 (2001): 368–69.

64. Mervyn James, "Ritual, Drama and Social Body in the Late Medieval English Town," *Past and Present* 98 (1983): 3–29.

65. This normative identity could also be seen to stand in opposition to a heretical, specifically Lollard identity, associated with a denial of transubstantiation, among other beliefs and practices.

66. Rubin, "Eucharist," 57.

67. On Jewish presence in England between the expulsion and readmission, see the issue of the *Domus Conversorum* in Robin R. Mundill, *England's Jewish Solution: Experiment and Expulsion, 1269–1290* (Cambridge, U.K.: Cambridge University Press, 1998); see also Stacey. For further literature on Jewish presence and the importance of Jews in post-Expulsion England, see Jones, "Theatrical Identity," 257 n. 59.

68. See Tomasch, "Judecca."

69. As Sarah Beckwith notes in "*Sacrum Signum*," "heresy and orthodoxy exist only in relation to each other" (280 n. 4). There is no easy division between these two terms, which continually complicate a normative model of the Christian that is not simply advanced, but actually explored, in this play.

70. On *Croxton* and the Wandering Jew, see my "Once and Future Jew," 248–49.

71. Rubin, *Gentile Tales, 71.* On the treatment of actual Jewish women during ritual murder trials, see Hsia on the treatment of Jewish women in ritual murder trials in his *Trent 1475,* 105–16.

72. For discussion of the variation in Marian portrayals, see Elizabeth A. Witt, *Contrary Marys in Medieval English and French Drama* (New York: Peter Lang, 1995).

73. Lesley Johnson and Jocelyn Wogan-Browne, "National, World and Women's History: Writers and Readers of English in Post-Conquest England," in *The Cambridge History of Medieval English Literature*, ed. David Wallace (Cambridge, U.K.: Cambridge University Press, 1999), 107.

74. Gibson, *Theater of Devotion*, 137. Numerous critics have commented on the centrality of Mary to N-Town. See Theresa Coletti, "Devotional Iconography in the N-Town Marian Plays," *Comparative Drama* 11 (1977): 22, and Woolf, *English Mystery Plays*, 226. See also the preface and introduction to Meredith, vi–viii, 1–28.

75. On the Virgin in late medieval East Anglia, see Gibson's chapter "Mary's Dower: East Anglian Drama and the Cult of the Virgin," *Theater of Devotion*, 137–78.

76. Pamela Sheingorn, "Bodily Embrace," 70. See also Matthew Kinservik, "The Struggle over Mary's Body: Theological and Dramatic Resolution in the N-Town Assumption Play," *JEGP* 95 (1996): 197.

77. Despres, "Immaculate Flesh," 47–69.

78. Coletti, "Purity and Danger," 66. For another important discussion of a dramatic representation of gender inversion, see Theresa Coletti, "Ther Be But Women: Gender Conflict and Gender Identity in the Middle English Innocents Plays," *Mediaevalia* 18 (1995, for 1992): 245–61.

79. Coletti, "Purity and Danger," 66.

80. Kathleen Ashley, "Image and Ideology: Saint Anne in Late Medieval Drama and Narrative," in *Interpreting Cultural Symbols: Saint Anne in Late Medieval Society* (Athens: University of Georgia Press, 1990), 117 .

81. Kinservik, 194.

82. Gail McMurray Gibson, "Scene and Obscene: Seeing and Performing Late Medieval Childbirth," *Journal of Medieval and Early Modern Studies* 29 (1999): 17.

83. See Tom Flanigan, "Everyman or Saint? Doubting Joseph in the Corpus Christi Cycles," *Medieval and Renaissance Drama in England* 8 (1996): 19–48.

84. See Woolf, 174–77.

85. Paula Marie Rieder, "Between the Pure and the Polluted: The Churching of Women in Medieval Northern France, 1100–1500" (Ph.D. diss. University of Illinois, Urbana-Champaign, 2000), 241–42.

86. On sources for this notion of a blinding light, which is like that that blinds Joseph as he approaches Mary after the Annunciation, see Sheingorn, 70. See Gibson, *Theater of Devotion*, 146–52 on visual representations and possible stagings.

87. David Cressy, *Birth, Marriage and Death: Ritual, Religion, and the Life-Cycle in Tudor and Stuart England* (Oxford, U.K.: Oxford University Press, 1997), 61–62.

88. Gibson, "Scene and Obscene," 17. On the birthing chamber, see also Cressy, 82.

89. 139. Woolf does not discuss humor or laughter in this episode, finding it unaesthetic, "random," and "tasteless" (178–80).

90. Kolve, *Corpus Christi*, 139. Gibson, "Scene and Obscene," 20. She refers here, of course, to Butler's *Gender Trouble*.

91. Gibson, "Scene and Obscene," 20.

92. Monica Green, "Documenting Medieval Women's Medical Practice," in *Practical Medicine from Salerno to the Black Death*, ed. Luis García-Ballester, Roger French, Jon Arrizabalaga, and Andrew Cunningham (Cambridge, U.K.: Cambridge University Press, 1994), 336–37.

93. Cressy, 120.

94. Cressy, 61.

95. John Mirk, *Instructions for Parish Priests*, ed. Edward Peacock, 2d rev. ed., EETS o.s. 31 (London: Kegan Paul, Trench, and Trübner, 1902). Cited in Gibson, "Scene and Obscene," 15–16.

96. Gail McMurray Gibson, "Blessing from Sun and Moon: Churching as Women's Theater," in *Bodies and Disciplines: Intersections of Literature and History in Fifteenth-Century England*, ed. Barbara A. Hanawalt and David Wallace (Minneapolis: University of Minnesota Press, 1996), 139–54.

97. See Gibson, "Scene and Obscene," and "Blessing from Sun and Moon." Becky R. Lee, "The Purification of Women after Childbirth: A Window onto Medieval Perceptions of Women," *Florilegium* 14 (1995–96): 43–55, and Rieder, esp. 233–76.

98. Rieder, esp. 203–33.

99. Myriam Greilsammer, "The Midwife, the Priest, and the Physician: The Subjugation of Midwives in the Low Countries at the End of the Middle Ages," *Journal of Medieval and Renaissance Studies* 21 (1991):323. Greilsammer also stresses the midwife's liminal status, although I find her statements about persecution of midwives less convincing in light of research by scholars such as Monica Green. See Green's "Documenting," and "Women's Medical Practice and Health Care in Medieval Europe," *Signs* 14 (1989): 434–72.

100. On these sources, see *A Critical Edition of John Lydgate's Life of Our Lady*, ed., Joseph A. Lauritis, Ralph A. Klinefelter, and Vernon F. Gallagher (Pittsburgh: Duquesne University Press, 1961), 692–93, n. 355.

101. J. Vriend, *The Blessed Virgin Mary in the Medieval Drama of England with additional Studies in Middle English Literature* (Amsterdam: J. Muusses, 1928), 98.

102. Josephus, *Jewish Antiquities*, vol. 9, trans. Louis H. Feldman, Loeb Classical Library (Cambridge, Mass.: Harvard University Press, 1963), 930. On the origins of the story in antiquity, see Helen Grace Zagona, *The Legend of Salome and the Principle of Art for Art's Sake* (Paris: Librarie Minard, 1960), 3–22.

103. On the modern Salomé, see Sander Gilman, "Salome, Syphilis, Sarah Bernhardt, and the Modern Jewess," in *The Jew in the Text: Modernity and the Construction of Identity*, ed. Linda Nochlin and Tamar Garb (London: Thames and Hudson, 1995), 97–120.

104. Linda Seidel, "Salome and the Canons," *Women's Studies* 11 (1984): 41–42.

105. For examples, see Hugo Haffner, *Salome: Ihre Gestalt in Geschichte und Kunst* (Munich: Hugo Schmidt, 1912), 27–76, and Seidel.

106. In early modern Northern Italy there were also portrayals of Salomé as a positive, feminine model of spirituality; see Victoria Reed, "Salome in Renaissance Art" (Undergraduate essay, Sarah Lawrence College, 1996).

107. One finds in some publications on medieval and early modern midwifery an association between midwives and witches. The best case in point is perhaps the provocatively titled *The Midwife and the Witch* by Thomas Rogers Forbes (New Haven, Conn.: Yale University Press, 1966). David Harley argues that this connection is the stuff of novels, not of history. He asserts that midwifery required its practitioners "to be respectable and trustworthy" and that the connection between midwives and witches derives not from historical record but from the writings of demonologists, such as the fifteenth-century texts the *Formicarius*, by Johannes Nider and Sprenger and Kramer's *Malleus Maleficarum* (1487). See "Historians as Demonologists: The Myth of the Midwife-Witch," *The Society for the Social History of Medicine* (1990): 1. In "Documenting," Monica Green points to polemical writings that link old women or *vetulae* with a variety of outsiders, including converted Jews in the work of medical author Henri de Mondeville

(336). It seems important that these connections be followed further without recourse to sensationalizing the connections between the figures of Jew, midwife, and witch. Newall calls for such an examination through folklore; "The Jew as Witch Figure," in *The Witch Figure: Folklore Essays by a Group of Scholars in England Honouring the Seventy-fifth birthday of Katharine M. Briggs*, ed. Venetia Newall (Boston: Routledge and Kegan Paul, 1973), 95–124.

108. Enders's discussions of violence also suggest this varied response to dramatic representation.

109. *N-Town Play*, vol. 1, 387–409.

110. Celebration of the Assumption or Dormition of Mary dates back at least as far as the sixth century. On the Assumption, beliefs surrounding it, and the history of its feast, see Hilda Graef, *Mary: A History of Doctrine and Devotion*, vol. 1 (New York: Sheed and Ward, 1963), 133–38.
The story is not unique to the York cycle; it goes back at least as far as the *Legenda Aurea* and appeared in England in a wide variety of texts, including the *Blickling Homilies*, the *Cursor Mundi*, and the *South English Legendary*. There are also visual representations and dramatic versions, which appear in the N-Town cycle as well as in continental drama. On sources, see also Nichols, "Hierosphthitic."

111. *The Blickling Homilies of the Tenth Century*, ed. and trans. R. Morris (London: EETS), o.s. vols. 58, 63, 73. Reprinted as one volume, 1967.

112. Kinservik, 199.

113. Sheingorn, 78. The N-Town "Assumption" is a textual interpolation, written "in a different hand, on different paper" and is "prosodically, stylistically, and orthographically distinct from the other plays" (Spector, *N-Town*, vol. 2, 527). This does not, however, change the important theological and thematic elements present in the Assumption play, nor the echoes of the Nativity play, whether or not these elements were recognized by the interpolator.

114. The text shows "Mi," which appears to signify "*Miles*." See Spector, *N-Town*, vol. 2, 528, n. 41/27.

115. Kinservik's analysis reveals the importance of "the law" to this play; see esp. 192–96.

116. Sheingorn, 78.

117. On staging, see J. Francas Massip, "The Staging of the Assumption in Europe," *Comparative Drama* 25 (1991–92): 17–28.

118. Kinservik, 190.

119. *Mirk's Festial*, 225.

120. See note 28.

121. Evans, "When a Body," 203–4. See Sponsler on the artisan's body, *Drama and Resistance*, 138, and Nissé, "Reversing Discipline" and "Prophetic," on the relationship between Lollard and nascent English identity, as well as Heng, "Romance of England."

Chapter 5

1. Shapiro, *Shakespeare and the Jews*, 42.

2. On actual Jews in Elizabethan England, see Shapiro, *Shakespeare and the*

Jews, esp. 62–76. See also David S. Katz, *The Jews in the History of England, 1485–1850* (Oxford, U.K.: Clarendon Press, 1994), and Yosef Kaplan, "The Jewish Profile of the Spanish-Portuguese Community of London during the Seventeenth Century," *Judaism* 41 (1992): 229–40.

3. See Shapiro, *Shakespeare and the Jews*, esp. 20–26.

4. See Ania Loomba, *Shakespeare, Race, and Colonialism* (Oxford, U.K.: Oxford University Press, 2002). I thank Professor Loomba for sharing this work with me prior to its subsequent publication. See also Julia Reinhard Lupton, "Othello Circumcised: Shakespeare and the Pauline Discourse of Nations," *Representations* 57 (1997): 73–89, which provides an important reading of Christian exegetical paradigms in *Othello* and in the exploration of early modern discourses of "race."

5. Shapiro, *Shakespeare and the Jews*, 26.

6. Ibid., 5.

7. See Introduction of this book.

8. See Chapters 3 and 4, and Nissé, "Prophetic"; Heng; and Sponsler, *Drama and Resistance*.

9. Barbara Lewalski, "Biblical Allusion and Allegory in *The Merchant of Venice*," in *Shylock*, ed. Harold Bloom (New York: Chelsea House, 1991), 236–51. Originally published in *Shakespeare Quarterly* 13 (1962): 327–43.

10. Readings that treat the biblical-exegetical elements are numerous. For my readings in this chapter I have found most useful: Douglas Anderson, "The Old Testament Presence in *The Merchant of Venice*," *ELH* 52 (1985): 119–32; C. L. Barber, *Shakespeare's Festive Comedy* (Princeton, N.J.: Princeton University Press, 1959); John Scott Colley, "Launcelot, Jacob, and Esau: Old and New Law in *The Merchant of Venice*," *Yearbook of English Studies* 10 (1980): 181–89; Lawrence Danson, *The Harmonies of The Merchant of Venice*" (New Haven, Conn.: Yale University Press, 1978), esp. 56–81; Lars Engle, "'Thrift Is Blessing': Exchange and Explanation in *The Merchant of Venice*," *Shakespeare Quarterly* 37 (1986): 20–37; René Fortin, "Launcelot and the Uses of Allegory in *The Merchant of Venice*," *SEL* 14 (1974): 259–70; Dorothy Hockey, "'The Patch is Kind Enough,'" *Shakespeare Quarterly* 10 (1959): 448–50; Joan Ozark Holmer, *The Merchant of Venice: Choice, Hazard and Consequence* (New York: St. Martin's Press, 1995); Susan McLean, "Prodigal Sons and Daughters: Transgression and Forgiveness in *The Merchant of Venice*," *PLL* 32 (1996): 45–63; Judith Rosenheim, "Allegorical Commentary in *The Merchant of Venice*," *Shakespeare Studies* 24 (1996): 156–210. (Note also errata to Rosenheim article, *Shakespeare Studies* 26 (1998): 425–26).

11. Mary Janell Metzger, "'Now by My Hood, a Gentle and No Jew': Jessica, *The Merchant of Venice*, and the Discourse of Early Modern English Identity," *PMLA* 113 (1998): 52–53. Shapiro focuses on the problem posed by the question of the Jewess on page 132 of *Shakespeare and the Jews*.

12. Ania Loomba, "'Delicious Traffick': Racial and Religious Difference on Early Modern Stages," in *Shakespeare and Race*, ed. Catherine M. S. Alexander and Stanley Wells (Cambridge, U.K.: Cambridge University Press, 2000), 203–24, and Kim Hall, "Guess Who's Coming to Dinner? Colonization and Miscegenation in *The Merchant of Venice*," *Renaissance Drama* n.s. 23 (1992): 87–112.

13. See Lupton, esp. "Exegesis" and "Shakespeare's Other Europe," and Freinkel, *Reading*. For a model of this type of exploration in the field of history, see Braude, "Sons of Noah," 103–42.

14. See Boyarin, *Radical Jew*, 13.

15. See Robbins, 1–48.

16. Daryl W. Palmer explores in depth the importance of commercial discourse in conceptions of the Jew in three sixteenth-century English plays; see "Merchants and Miscegenation: *The Three Ladies of London, The Jew of Malta*, and *The Merchant of Venice*," in *Race, Ethnicity and Power in the Renaissance*, ed. Joyce Green MacDonald (Madison, N.J.: Fairleigh Dickinson University Press, 1997), 36–66.

17. The sexual connotation of "intercourse" and the coinage of the term "miscegenation" both derive from eighteenth-century usage. I follow, however, Kim Hall's use of these terms in "Guess Who's Coming to Dinner?" in order to draw upon the resonance these have for modern and, specifically, American readers and to, as Hall does, "locate an emerging modern dynamic for which there was no adequate language" (106, n. 1).

18. Michele Marrapodi writes that "the alterity of Italy is used ideologically and politically to set off the concept of England and of Englishness from the construction, adaptation and modification of, as well as resistance to, a diverse range of shifting traditions and national identities, including cultural and racial differences alongside of, as well as distinct from, questions of empire and colonialism." "Introduction to Shakespeare and Italy: Past and Present," in *Shakespeare and Italy*, ed. Holger Klein and Michele Marrapodi (Lewiston, N.Y.: Edwin Mellen Press, 1999), 3. See also Avraham Oz, "Dobbin on the Rialto: Venice and the Division of Identity," in *Shakespeare's Italy: Functions of Italian Locations in Renaissance Drama*, ed. Michele Marrapodi, A. J. Hoenselaars, Marcello Cappuzzo, and L. Falzon Santucci (New York: Manchester University Press, 1993), 185–212, and Tony Tanner, "Which is the Merchant here? and which the Jew?: The Venice of Shakespeare's *Merchant of Venice*," in *Venetian Views, Venetian Blinds: English Fantasies of Venice*, ed. Manfred Pfister and Barbara Schaff (Atlanta: Rodopi, 1999), 45–62. Walter Cohen understands the Venetian setting as a way of dealing with the play's representation of concerns about the emerging dominance of capitalism; see "*The Merchant of Venice* and the Possibilities of Historical Criticism," *ELH* 49 (1982): 765–89.

19. Shapiro, *Shakespeare and the Jews*, 75.

20. John Strype, *A Survey of the Cities of London and Westminster . . . Written by John Stow . . . Corrected, Improved, and Very Much Enlarged by John Strype*, 2 vols. (1720), vol. 2, page 303. Cited in Shapiro, *Shakespeare and the Jews*, 187.

21. Shapiro, *Shakespeare and the Jews*, 187.

22. In contrast, see Spanish tradition discussed in Mirrer. In addition to the figure of Synagoga and the host desecration narratives discussed by Miri Rubin in *Gentile Tales*, there is, for example, the narrative of the Jewish girl impregnated by a sly Christian clerk who tells her parents she is a virgin. The Jewish community expects the messiah, a hope dashed when the child is a girl. See "Der Falsche Messias," in *Die Reimpaarsprüche*, ed. Hans Fischer (Munich: 1961), 92–96. Lio-

nel Trilling, "The Changing Myth of the Jew," in *Speaking of Literature and Society*, ed. Diana Trilling (Oxford, U.K.: Oxford University Press, 1982) 50–77, discusses the "Jew's Daughter" ballad tradition. See also Steven Kruger's discussion of Caesarius of Heisterbach's depictions of Jewesses, who are beautiful "like many of [their] race" in "Becoming Christian," 25.

23. Rubin, *Gentile Tales*, 71.

24. On Jessica's conversion in relation to Abigail's in Marlowe's *The Jew of Malta*, see Shapiro, *Shakespeare and the Jews*, 157. On the relationship between the two plays, see also Maurice Charney, "Jessica's Turquoise Ring and Abigail's Poisoned Porridge: Shakespeare and Marlowe as Rivals and Imitators," *Renaissance Drama* n.s. 10 (1979): 33–45. James Shapiro focuses specifically on the rivalry between the two professional dramatists in "'Which Is *The Merchant* Here, and Which *The Jew?*': Shakespeare and the Economics of Influence," *Shakespeare Studies* 20 (1988): 269–82.

25. Peter Berek, "The Jew as Renaissance Man," *Renaissance Quarterly* 51 (1998): 158.

26. Metzger's reading of *Merchant* specifically addresses the issue of Jessica's "whiteness"; my reading here has benefited much from hers.

27. On this problem, see Fortin, esp. 260 and 268–70.

28. I.i.29–36. William Shakespeare, *The Merchant of Venice*, The Arden Shakespeare, ed. John Russell Brown (New York: Routledge, 1964). Subsequent citations to this play are in the text and refer to this edition.

29. Douglas Bruster reads this scene in light of the "inescapable anxiety" increasingly attached to the "business of commerce" in the late sixteenth century (56). His richly historicized readings of a wide variety of texts from this period support the contention that *Merchant* is deeply concerned with the effects of the markets. See Douglas Bruster, *Drama and Market in the Age of Shakespeare* (Cambridge, U.K.: Cambridge University Press, 1992). Karen Newman focuses on the gendering of Salerio's imagery, arguing that "the feminine personification of merchant ship as woman wounded figures both the commodification of woman and her violation" ("Portia's Ring," 19). Newman's feminist analysis, informed by anthropology, makes an important contribution to the understanding of the "traffic in women" in the text, but her acknowledged omission of questions of racial and religious difference leaves much room for further discussion. See Karen Newman, "Directing Traffic: Subjects, Objects, and the Politics of Exchange in *The Merchant of Venice*," *differences* 2 (1990): 41–54, "Portia's Ring: Unruly Women and Structures of Exchange in *The Merchant of Venice*," *Shakespeare Quarterly* 38 (1987): 19–33, and "Reprise: Gender, Sexuality and Theories of Exchange in *The Merchant of Venice*," in *The Merchant of Venice*, ed. Nigel Wood (Bury St. Edmunds, U.K.: St. Edmundsbury Press, 1996), 102–33.

30. For a discussion of this passage in terms of sixteenth-century Protestant discourses of thrift and husbandry in relation to usury and race, see Lorna Hutson, *The Usurer's Daughter: Male Friendship and Fictions of Women in Sixteenth-Century England* (New York: Routledge, 1994) 224–38. The question of the homoerotics raised by the relationship between Antonio and Bassanio bears further discussion, particularly in relation to the connections made between usury and

sodomy in the medieval period. For a perspective on queer readings of the text, see Alan Sinfield, "How to Read *The Merchant of Venice* without Being Heterosexist," in Martin Coyle, ed., *The Merchant of Venice, William Shakespeare*, New Casebooks (New York: St. Martin's Press, 1998): 161–79. On usury and "unnatural" sexuality, see Chapter 3.

31. For more on Antonio as Christ, see Lewalski, 343.

32. On inner and outer realities, see Boyarin, *Radical Jew*, 14–15.

33. For an interesting discussion of this biblical usage in relation to the economic currents in the play, see Engel, esp. 28–32. For an important reading of "Shylock's hermeneutics" in this passage in a Pauline frame, see Lupton, "Exegesis," 134–35.

34. Hockey points this out but denies thematic relevance.

35. Robbins, 4. The allegorical significance of Esau and Jacob was the subject of Christian-Jewish polemic since the early days of Christianity. For a detailed discussion of Jewish and Christian exegesis on the Esau-Jacob story and its implications for Jewish concerns about usury, see Gerson D. Cohen, "Esau as Symbol in Early Medieval Thought," in *Jewish Medieval and Renaissance Studies*, ed. Alexander Altman (Cambridge, Mass.: Harvard University Press, 1967), 19–48.

36. On early modern receptions of the Jacob and Esau story, see Arnold Williams, *The Common Expositor: An Account of the Commentaries on Genesis, 1527–1633* (Chapel Hill: University of North Carolina Press, 1948), 169–73.

37. Colley, 186.

38. Fortin, 262.

39. The Geneva Bible glosses the parable with reference to Christ's equal importance to Gentile and Jew. *The Geneva Bible: A Facsimile of the 1560 Edition*, ed. Lloyd E. Berry (Madison: University of Wisconsin Press, 1969).

40. McLean, 52.

41. See Charney, 36.

42. See Galatians 4:22–30. See also Robbins, 4–6.

43. The Geneva Bible makes very specific associations in its gloss. Hagar and Sinai are "the Law," Sara and Jerusalem "The Gospel." Ishmael is the "Jewish synagogue" and Isaac is "the Church of Christ."

44. Shylock has himself played upon these polarities in his first appearance in the play declaring an bitter enmity between two polarized communities: "I hate him for he is a Christian" (I.iii.37).

45. Colley, 184.

46. Lewalsky, 339.

47. According to Lelyveld, Edmund Kean's use of a black beard for Shylock in 1814 caused a tremendous "stir": "Some writers believe that dressing Shylock in this manner was an attempt to make the character mirror Judas Iscariot, whose beard was traditionally red." Toby Lelyveld, *Shylock on the Stage* (Cleveland: Press of the Western Reserve University, 1960), 8.

48. For further discussion of the use of the Jew figure from medieval drama by both Shakespeare and Marlowe, see Bernard Glassman, *Anti-Semitic Stereotypes without Jews: Images of the Jews in England, 1290–1700* (Detroit: Wayne State Uni-

versity Press, 1975), 67–68. See also Stephen Spector, "Anti-Semitism and the English Mystery Plays," *Comparative Drama* 13.1 (1979): 3–16.

49. The play here, however, presents an ironic twist to the gravity of these anti-Semitic charges. Antonio, through a bond that will support Bassanio's quest for the wealthy Portia, has commodified his own flesh in a way that betrays the spirit of Christ's self-sacrificing payment for human sin. The barter literally commodifies Antonio's body down to its weight and, furthermore, links him to the slave trade that Shylock throws into the faces of the Venetians during his trial.

50. The comedic progression between this trial scene and Belmont mirrors the tensions between the universal salvific goal of Christian exegetical thought and the hierarchical differentiation underlying this universalism. Belmont is a location where difference has been soundly rejected; all inhabitants are Christian and Belmont's lady has extended this process of conversion beyond its borders. Act IV demonstrates the hierarchical rift between Christians and Jews only to bring them together.

51. On related boundary imagery, see chapter 3.

52. There is a growing literature on the question of skin color in relation to questions of "racial" and religious difference in early modern English literature. I have found especially useful the writings of Loomba, Boose, and Lupton as well as the important recent book by Kim Hall, *Things of Darkness*.

53. Eric Griffin, "Un-sainting James: Or, *Othello* and the "Spanish Spirits" of Shakespeare's Globe," *Representations* 62 (1998): 58–99.

54. ¿Mas quién podrá negar que en los descendientes de judíos permanece y dura la mala inclinación de su antigua ingratitud y mal conocimiento, como en los negros el accidente inseparable du su negrura? Que si bien mil veces se juntan con mujeres blancas, los hijos nacen con el color moreno de sus padres. Así al judio no le basta [ser] por tres partes hidalgo, o cristiano viejo, que sola una raza lo inficiona y daña, para ser en sus hechos, de todas maneras, judíos dañosos por extremo en las comunidades." Fray Prudencio de Sandoval, *Historia de la vida y hechoes del emperador Carlos V*, vol. 82, *Biblioteca de autores españoles* (Madrid: Editiones Atlas, 1956), 319. English translation from Friedman, "Jewish Conversion," 17, who translates "raza" as "bloodline," although, as Dara Goldman noted to me, this word is interesting for its connections to the emerging conceptions of "race" that we are examining. Also cited in Loomba, "'Delicious Traffick,'" 208, and Metzger, 55. Loomba links essence to interiority, 208.

55. Edmund Spenser, *A View of the Present State of Ireland: From the First Printed Edition (1633)*, ed. Andrew Hadfield and Willy Maleyn (London: Blackwell, 1997), 50. Cited in Loomba, *Shakespeare, Race and Colonialism*, 137.

56. Fancy can also be reached through the ear. In Book IV of *Paradise Lost*, Satan is discovered "Squat like a Toad, close at the ear of *Eve*; / Assaying by his Devilish art to reach / The Organs of her Fancy, and with them forge / Illusions as he list" (800–803). In Book V, Adam describes Fancy in terms of early modern "faculty psychology," associating her with "external things" and wild, misguiding imaginings:

But know that in the Soul
Are many lesser Faculties that serve

Reason as chief; among these Fancy next
Her office holds; of all external things,
Which the five watchful Senses represent,
She forms Imaginations, Aery shapes,
Which Reason joining or disjoining, frames
All what we affirm or what deny, and call
Our knowledge or opinion; then retires
Into her private Cell when Nature rests.
Oft in her absence mimic Fancy wakes
To imitate her; but misjoining shapes,
Wild work produces oft, and most in dreams,
Ill matching words and deeds long past or late. (ll. 100–113)

57. Her dangerous allure recalls the poisonous treachery of Duessa in Spenser's *Fairie Queene*. Readers familiar with Klaus Theweleit's analysis of fascism will see the suggestive possibilities for his analysis of the fascist depiction of the female as an engulfing threat to explicate this passage. Klaus Theweleit, *Male Fantasies*, vol. 1, trans. Stephen Conway, Erica Carter, and Chris Turner (Minneapolis: University of Minnesota Press, 1987), esp. 229–408.

58. See Marc Shell, "The Wether and the Ewe: Verbal Usury in *The Merchant of Venice*," *Kenyon Review* 14 (1979): 79.

59. This is in contrast to Abigail, the erotic object in Marlowe's *Jew of Malta*, who, at least initially, acts at her father's request.

60. Lynda E. Boose, "'The Getting of a Lawful Race': Racial Discourse in Early Modern England and the Unrepresentable Black Woman," in *Women, "Race," and Writing in the Early Modern Period*, ed. Margo Hendricks and Patricia Parker (New York: Routledge, 1994), 46, and Hall, "Guess Who's Coming to Dinner?" 92.

61. This brilliant connection between Portia and the Virgin is found in Hyam Maccoby, "The Delectable Daughter," *Midstream* 24 (1970): 52.

62. The free circulation of female desire within Venice threatens the stability of Venetian male identity. Because paternity itself must be taken on faith, female desire and female bodies must be controlled in order to ensure their purity. There are no mothers appearing on the stage in *The Merchant of Venice*; they exist only as potentials or memories. But they are an important shadowy background to the play, since it is they who produce heirs and who, by giving birth, determine patrimony. And indeed, mothers burst onto the scene in *Merchant* in some pointed moments. Old Gobbo only recognizes Launcelot as his son when Launcelot can name his mother "Margery," and indeed the names of mothers in this play, notably absent in Portia's case, seem to highlight the importance of the woman as the bearer of children, patrimony, and identity. In that moment that most critics point to as one of Shylock's most humanizing, he weeps for the loss of a ring his wife Leah had given him, which he "would not have given . . . for a wilderness of monkeys" (III.i.113). And, finally, the figure of the Moor, shadowy and unseen,

threatens to act as the origin of new, mixed identities when she gives birth to Launcelot's child.

63. Shapiro, *Shakespeare and the Jews*, 184. On this scene, see also 131–32.

64. Ibid., 146–51.

65. Shylock argues that denying him his bonds will lead to the collapse of such hierarchies:

> What judgment shall I dread doing no wrong?
> You have among you many a purchas'd slave,
> Which (like your asses, and your dogs and mules)
> You use in abject and in slavish parts,
> Because you bought them,—shall I say to you,
> Let them be free, marry them to your heirs? (IV.i.89–94)

Denying the validity of a purchase or agreement under law will, Shylock threatens, lead to unthinkable unions, creating a mixing of humans of different classes that is, as he describes it, bestial, tantamount to marrying one's child to an ass or dog and acknowledging the issue. Bastardy and miscegenation become associated with a complete collapse of social order and the union of human and beast.

66. Boose, 46–47.

67. In *Acts and Monuments*, John Foxe refers to a Jewish convert as a "Christian Jew," implying that Jewish difference can never be completely erased. Cited in Shapiro, *Shakespeare and the Jews*, 146.

68. See Shapiro, *Shakespeare and the Jews*, 120.

69. In addition to discussions of circumcision by Shapiro, Metzger, and Lupton, I am indebted to Daniel Boyarin's analysis in Chapter 5 of *Radical Jew*, 106–35.

70. Shapiro, *Shakespeare and the Jews*, 127.

71. Ibid., 130.

72. Shapiro's reading lays the groundwork for these implications; see *Shakespeare and the Jews*, 172–73.

73. See Loomba, "Delicious Traffick." For an analysis of the figure of the Queen, see Louise O. Fradenburg, *City, Marriage, Tournament: Arts of Rule in Late Medieval Scotland* (Madison: University of Wisconsin Press, 1991).

74. Leslie Fiedler, *The Stranger in Shakespeare* (New York: Stein and Day, 1973), 111–12.

Conclusion

1. Emmanuel Levinas, "Israel and Universalism," in *Difficult Freedom: Essays on Judaism*, trans. Seán Hand (Baltimore: Johns Hopkins University Press, 1990), 175. Originally appeared in *Le Journal des Communeautés* (1958) as a response to a lecture by Daniélou on the three religions of the Book.

2. Jean-Paul Sartre, *Anti-Semite and Jew*, trans. George J. Becker (New York: Schocken Books, 1965), 69.

3. Toni Morrison, *Playing in the Dark: Whiteness and the Literary Imagination* (New York: Random House, 1993), 17.

4. See Tomasch, "Postcolonial Chaucer," Despres, "Cultic Anti-Judaism," and Glassman.

5. Morrison, 47.

6. See the introduction, xv–xxxiv.

7. Morrison, 49. Morrison references possible intersections between her work and investigations of anti-Semitism; see 90.

8. Although I have had to limit the scope of this book in a way that has not allowed me to treat questions of normative "whiteness" at any length, the issue of color is clearly important to the questions of universalism and normative identity treated in this book and relevant to discussions of medieval as well as early modern texts. For important readings, see the *Journal of Medieval and Early Modern Studies* special issue on race (31, vol. 1; 2001), ed. Thomas Hahn, as well as Bruce Holsinger, "The Color of Salvation: Desire, Death, and the Second Crusade in Bernard of Clairvaux's *Sermons on the Song of Songs*," in *The Tongue of the Fathers: Gender and Ideology in Twelfth-Century Latin*, ed. David Townsend and Andrew Taylor (Philadelphia: University of Pennsylvania Press, 1998), 156–86.

9. Slavoj Žižek, *The Sublime Object of Ideology* (New York: Verso, 1989), and Jean François Lyotard, *Heidegger and "the jews,"* trans. Andreas Michel and Mark Roberts (Minneapolis: University of Minnesota Press, 1990).

10. Alain Badiou, *Saint Paul: La fondation de l'universalisme* (Paris: Presses Universitaires de France, 1997).

11. See the discussion in Slavoj Žižek, *The Ticklish Subject: The Absent Centre of Political Ontology* (New York: Verso, 1999), 127–69.

12. Badiou, 110.

13. Ibid.

14. Ibid., 111.

15. Ibid., 113.

16. Ragussis, *Figures of Conversion*, 11.

Bibliography

Abulafia, Anna Sapir. *Christians and Jews in the Twelfth-Century Renaissance*. New York: Routledge, 1995.

————. "Invectives against Christianity in the Hebrew Chronicles of the First Crusade." In *Crusade and Settlement*, ed. Peter W. Edbury, 66–72. Cardiff, Wales: University College Cardiff Press, 1985.

————. "Theology and the Commercial Revolution: Guibert of Nogent, St Anselm and the Jews of Northern France." In *Church and City, 1000–1500: Essays in Honour of Christopher Brooke*, ed. David Abulafia, Michael Franklin, and Miri Rubin, 23–40. Cambridge, U.K.: Cambridge University Press, 1992.

Adams, Robert. "Chaucer's 'New Rachel' and the Theological Roots of Medieval Anti-Semitism." *Bulletin of the John Rylands University Library of Manchester* 77 (autumn 1995): 9–18.

Aers, David. "A Whisper in the Ear of Early Modernists; or, Reflections on Literary Critics Writing the 'History of the Subject.'" In *Culture and History, 1350–1600: Essays on English Communities, Identities and Writing*, ed. David Aers, 177–202. Detroit: Wayne State University Press, 1992.

Aers, David, ed. *Culture and History, 1350–1600*. Detroit: Wayne State University Press, 1992.

Aers, David, and Lynn Staley. *The Powers of the Holy: Religion, Politics, and Gender in Late Medieval English Culture*. University Park: Pennsylvania State University Press, 1996.

Akbari, Suzanne Conklin. "Imagining Islam: The Role of Images in Medieval Depictions of Muslims." *Scripta Mediterranea* 19–20 (1998–99): 9–27.

————."Rhetoric of Antichrist in Western Lives of Muhammed." *Islam and Christian-Muslim Relations* 8 (1997): 297–307.

Alexander, Catherine M. S., and Stanley Wells , eds. *Shakespeare and Race*. Cambridge, U.K.: Cambridge University Press, 2000.

Alighieri, Dante. *Dantis Alagherii Epistolae—The Letters of Dante*. Ed. and trans. Paget Toynbee. 2d ed. Oxford, U.K.: Clarendon Press, 1966.

Allen, J. B. *The Friar As Critic: Literary Attitudes in the Later Middle Ages*. Nashville: Vanderbilt University Press, 1971.

Allen, Prudence, R.S.M. *The Concept of Woman: The Aristotelian Revolution, 750 B.C.–A.D. 1250*. 2d ed. Grand Rapids, Mich.: William B. Eerdmans, 1997.

Ambrose. *Expositio evangeliis secundum Lucam. PL* 15: 1525–850.

Ames, Ruth M. "Corn and Shrimps: Chaucer's Mockery of Religious Controversy." In *The Late Middle Ages*, ed. Peter Cocozzella, 71–88. Binghamton: State University of New York Press, 1984.

Anderson, Douglas. "The Old Testament Presence in *The Merchant of Venice*." *ELH* 52 (1985): 119–32.

Anselm of Canterbury. *Liber Cur Deus Homo*. Ed. Schmitt. Bonn: Petri Hanstein, 1929.

———. *Why God Became Man and the Virgin Conception and Original Sin*. Trans. Joseph Colleran. Albany, N.Y.: Magi Books, 1969.

Anzaldúa, Gloria, ed. *Making Face, Making Soul: Creative and Critical Perspectives by Women of Color*. San Francisco: Aunt Lute Foundation, 1990.

Anzaldúa, Gloria, and Cherríe Moraga. *This Bridge Called My Back: Writings by Radical Women of Color*. Watertown, Mass.: Persephone Press, 1981.

Appiah, Kwame Anthony. "Race." In *Critical Terms for Literary Study*, ed. Frank Lentricchia and Thomas McLaughlin, 274–87. 2d ed. Chicago: University of Chicago Press, 1995.

Appiah, Kwame Anthony, and Henry Louis Gates Jr., eds. *Identities*. Chicago: University of Chicago Press, 1995.

Aquinas, Thomas. *In octo libros Politicorum Aristotelis Expositio*. Ed. R. M. Spiazzi. Rome: Marietti, 1966.

Arendt, Hannah. *Antisemitism*. New York: Harcourt, Brace and Jovanovich, 1951.

Ashley, Kathleen. "Image and Ideology: Saint Anne in Late Medieval Drama and Narrative." In *Interpreting Cultural Symbols: Saint Anne in Late Medieval Society*, ed. Kathleen Ashley and Pamela Sheingorn, 111–30. Athens: University of Georgia Press, 1990.

Auerbach, Erich. "Figura." In *Scenes from the Drama of European Literature*. Minneapolis: University of Minnesota Press, 1984.

Augustine. *Basic Writings of St. Augustine*. Ed. Whitney J. Oates. New York: Random House, 1948.

———. *Concerning the City of God against the Pagans*. Trans. Henry Bettenson. 2d ed. New York: Penguin Books, 1984.

———. *Contra Faustum. CSEL* 25. Vienna: F. Tempsky, 1891.

———. *De civitate Dei*. Ed. Bernardus Dombart and Alphonus Kalb. CCSL 47–48. Turnhout, Belgium: Brepols, 1955.

———. *De doctrina christiana*. Ed. J. Martin. CCSL 32. Turnhout, Belgium: Brepols, 1962.

———. *De Genesi contra Manichaeos*. PL 34: 171–220.

———. *De Trinitate*. Ed. W. J. Mountain and Fr. Glorie. CCSL 50–50A. Turnhout, Belgium: Brepols, 1967.

———. *Enarrationes in Psalmos*. Eds. D. Eligius Dekkers and Iohannes Fraipont. CCSL 38–40. Turnhout, Belgium: Brepols, 1956.

———. *Expositio ad Galatas*. CSEL 84. Vienna: F. Tempsky, 1871.

———. *De Genesi Contra Manichaeos* PL 34: 171–220.

———. *Expositions on the Book of Psalms*. Ed. A. Cleveland Coxe. Nicene and Post-Nicene Fathers. Vol. 8. Grand Rapids, Mich.: Eerdmans, 1961.

———. *On Christian Doctrine*. Trans. D. W. Robertson Jr. Indianapolis: Bobbs-Merrill, 1958.

———. *On Genesis. Two Books on Genesis Against the Manichees and on the Literal Interpretation of Genesis: An Unfinished Book*. Trans. Ronald. J. Teske.

Fathers of the Church. Vol. 84. Washington, D.C.: Catholic University of American Press, 1991.

———. *Reply to Faustus the Manichaean*. Trans. Richard Stothert, 152–345. In *St. Augustin: The Writings Against the Manichaeans and Against the Donatists*. Nicene and Post-Nicene Fathers. Vol. 4. Grand Rapids, Mich.: Wm. B. Eerdmans, 1956.

———. *Tractatus Adversus Iudaeos*. PL 42: 51–64.

———. *Tractatus Adversus Iudaeos*. Trans. Sister Marie Liguori, I.H.M. In *Treatises on Marriage and Other Subjects*, ed. Roy J. Deferrari. Fathers of the Church. Vol. 27. Washington, D.C.: Catholic University of American Press, 1955.

———. *The Trinity*. Trans. Stephen McKenna. Fathers of the Church. Vol. 18. Washington, D.C.: Catholic University of America Press, 1963.

Badiou, Alain. *Saint Paul: La fondation de l'universalisme*. Paris: Presses Universitaires de France, 1997.

Baker, Donald C. "The Bradshaw Order of *The Canterbury Tales*: A Dissent." *NM* 4 (1962): 245–61.

Barber, C. L. *Shakespeare's Festive Comedy*. Princeton, N.J.: Princeton University Press, 1959.

Barratt, Alexandra, ed. *Women's Writing in Middle English*. New York: Longman, 1992.

Bartlett, Robert. *The Making of Europe: Conquest, Colonization, and Cultural Change: 950–1350*. Princeton, N.J.: Princeton University Press, 1993.

———. "Medieval and Modern Concepts of Race and Ethnicity." *Journal of Medieval and Early Modern Studies* 31, no. 1 (2001).

Bauckham, Richard J. "Universalism: A Historical Survey." *Themelios* 4 (1979): 48–54.

Bauman, Zygmunt. "Allosemitism: Premodern, Modern, Postmodern." In *Modernity, Culture and "the Jew,"* ed. Bryan Cheyette and Laura Marcus, 143–56. Stanford, Calif.: Stanford University Press, 1998.

Bavel, T. J. van. "Augustine's View on Women." *Augustinana* 39 (1989): 5–53.

Beauvoir, Simone de. *The Second Sex*. Trans. H. M. Parshley. New York: Vintage, 1974.

Beckwith, Sarah. *Christ's Body: Identity, Culture and Society in Late Medieval Writings*. New York: Routledge, 1993.

———. "Ritual, Church and Theatre: Medieval Dramas of the Sacramental Body." In *Culture and History, 1350–1600*, ed. David Aers, 65–89. Detroit: Wayne State University Press, 1992.

———. "Sacrum Signum: Sacramentality and Dissent in the York Theatre of Corpus Christi." In *Criticism and Dissent in the Middle Ages*, ed. Rita Copeland, 264–88. Cambridge, U.K.: University of Cambridge Press, 1996.

Beichner, Paul E. "Confrontation, Contempt of Court, and Chaucer's Cecelia." *Chaucer Review* 8 (1974): 198–204.

Bennett, Judith M. "Medieval Women, Modern Women: Across the Great Divide." In *Culture and History, 1350–1600*, ed. David Aers, 147–75. Detroit: Wayne State University Press, 1992.

Berek, Peter. "The Jew as Renaissance Man." *Renaissance Quarterly* 51 (1998): 128–62.

Berger, David. "Mission to the Jews and Jewish-Christian Contacts in the Polemical Literature of the High Middle Ages." *AHR* 91 (1986): 576–91.

Bernard of Clairvaux. *S. Bernardi Opera.* Ed. Jean Leclercq, C. H. Talbot, and H. M. Rochais. Rome: Editiones Cistercienses, 1957.

———. *The Works of Bernard of Clairvaux.* Ed. Killian Walsh and Irene Edmonds. 4 vols. Kalamazoo, Mich.: Cistercian Publications, Inc., 1981.

Besserman, Lawrence. "*Glosynge Is a Glorious Thyng*: Chaucer's Biblical Exegesis." In *Chaucer and Scriptural Tradition*, ed. David Lyle Jeffrey, 65–73. Ottawa: University of Ottawa Press, 1984.

Bestul, Thomas. "Chaucer's Parson's Tale and the Late-Medieval Tradition of Religious Meditation." *Speculum* 64 (1989): 607.

———. *Texts of the Passion: Latin Devotional Literature and Medieval Society.* Philadelphia: University of Pennsylvania Press, 1996.

Bevington, David, ed. *Medieval Drama.* Boston: Houghton Mifflin Company, 1975.

Biddick, Kathleen. "Coming out of Exile: Dante on the Orient(alism) Express," *AHR* (October 2000): 1234–49.

———. "Coming out of Exile: Dante on the Orient Express." In *The Postcolonial Middle Ages*, ed. Jeffrey Jerome Cohen, 35–52. New York: St. Martin's, 2000.

———. "Genders, Bodies, Borders: Technologies of the Visible." In *Studying Medieval Women: Sex, Gender, Feminism*, ed. Nancy F. Partner, 87–116. Cambridge, Mass.: Medieval Academy of America, 1993.

Biller, Peter. "Views of Jews from Paris around 1300: Christian or 'Scientific'?" In *Christianity and Judaism: Papers Read at the 1991 Summer Meeting and the 1992 Winter Meeting of the Ecclesiastical History Society*, ed. Diana Wood, 187–207. Oxford, U.K.: Blackwell, 1992.

Blake, N. F. *The Textual Tradition of the Canterbury Tales.* London: Edward Arnold, 1985.

Blamires, Alcuin, ed. *Woman Defamed and Woman Defended: An Anthology of Medieval Texts.* Oxford, U.K.: Clarendon Press, 1992.

The Blickling Homilies of the Tenth Century. Ed. and trans. R. Morris. London: EETS. o.s. vols. 58, 63, 73. Reprinted as one volume, 1967.

Bloch, R. Howard. *Etymologies and Genealogies: A Literary Anthropology of the French Middle Ages.* Chicago: University of Chicago Press, 1983.

———. "Medieval Misogyny." *Representations* 20 (1987): 1–24.

———. *Medieval Misogyny and the Invention of Western Romantic Love.* Chicago: University of Chicago Press, 1991.

Bloom, Harold, ed. *Major Literary Characters: Shylock.* Philadelphia: Chelsea House, 1991.

Boose, Lynda E. " 'The Getting of a Lawful Race': Racial Discourse in Early Modern England and the Unrepresentable Black Woman." In *Women, "Race," and Writing in the Early Modern Period*, ed. Margo Hendricks and Patricia Parker, 35–54. New York: Routledge, 1994.

Børresen, Kari Elisabeth. "Gender and Exegesis in the Latin Fathers." *Augustinianum* XXXX (2000): 65–76.

———. "God's Image, Man's Image? Patristic Interpretation of Gen. 1,27 and I Cor. 11,7." In *The Image of God: Gender Models in Judaeo-Christian Tradition*, ed. Kari Elisabeth Børresen, 188–208. Minneapolis: Fortress Press, 1995.

———."Imago Dei, privilêge masculin? Interprétation augustinienne et pseudo-augustinienne de Gen 1,27 et 1 Cor 11,7." *Augustinianum* 25 (1985): 213–34.

———. "Patristic 'Feminism': The Case of Augustine." *Augustinian Studies* 25 (1994): 139–52.

Boswell, John. *Christianity, Social Tolerance, and Homosexuality: Gay People in Western Europe from the Beginning of the Christian Era to the Fourteenth Century*. Chicago: University of Chicago Press, 1980.

Boyarin, Daniel. *A Radical Jew: Paul and the Politics of Identity*. Berkeley: University of California Press, 1994.

Boyarin, Daniel, and Jonathan Boyarin. "Diaspora: Generation and the Ground of Jewish Identity." In *Identities*, ed. Kwame Anthony Appiah and Henry Louis Gates Jr., 305–37. Chicago: University of Chicago Press, 1995.

Boyarin, Daniel, and Jonathan Boyarin, eds. *Jews and Other Differences: The New Jewish Cultural Studies*. Minneapolis: University of Minnesota Press, 1997.

Boyarin, Jonathan. *Storm from Paradise: The Politics of Jewish Memory*. Minneapolis: University of Minnesota Press, 1992.

Boyd, Beverly, ed. *The Prioress's Tale: A Variorum Edition of the Works of Geoffrey Chaucer*. Norman: University of Oklahoma Press, 1987.

Braude, Benjamin. "The Sons of Noah and the Construction of Ethnic and Geographical Identities in the Medieval and Early Modern Periods." *The William and Mary Quarterly* 54 (1997): 103–42.

Brittain, Frederick, ed. *Penguin Book of Latin Verse*. Baltimore: Penguin Books, 1962.

Brody, Saul Nathaniel. "Chaucer's Rhyme Royal Tales and the Secularization of the Saint." *Chaucer Review* 20 (1985): 113–31.

Broes, Arthur T. "Chaucer's Disgruntled Cleric: The Nun's Priest's Tale." *PMLA* 78 (1963): 156–62.

Brown, Carleton. "The *Prioress's Tale*." In *Sources and Analogues of Chaucer's Canterbury Tales*, ed. W. F. Bryan and Germaine Dempster, 447–85. New York: Humanities Press, 1958.

Brown, Peter. *The Body and Society: Men, Women, and Sexual Renunciation in Early Christianity*. New York: Columbia University Press, 1988.

Brundage, James A. *Law, Sex, and Christian Society in Medieval Europe*. Chicago: University of Chicago Press, 1987.

Bruster, Douglas. *Drama and Market in the Age of Shakespeare*. Cambridge, U.K.: Cambridge University Press, 1992.

Bryan, W. F., and Germaine Dempster, eds. *Sources and Analogues of Chaucer's Canterbury Tales*. Boston: Humanities Press, 1958.

Bullough, Vern. "Medieval Medical and Scientific Views of Women." *Viator* 4 (1973): 485–520.

Burrus, Virginia. *Chastity As Autonomy: Women in the Stories of the Apocryphal Acts*. Lewiston, N.Y.: Edwin Mellen Press, 1987.

Butler, Judith. *Bodies That Matter: On the Discursive Limits of Sex*. New York: Routledge, 1993.

———. *Gender Trouble: Feminism and the Subversion of Identity*. New York: Routledge, 1990.

Butler, Judith, Ernesto Laclau, and Slavoj Žižek. *Contingency, Hegemony, Universality: Contemporary Dialogues on the Left*. New York: Verso, 2000.

Bynum, Caroline Walker. *Fragmentation and Redemption: Essays on Gender and the Human Body in Medieval Religion*. New York: Zone Books, 1992.

———. *Jesus as Mother: Studies in the Spirituality of the High Middle Ages*. Berkeley: University of California Press, 1982.

Cadden, Joan. *Meanings of Sex Difference in the Middle Ages: Medicine, Science and Culture*. Cambridge, U.K.: Cambridge University Press, 1993.

Camille, Michael. *The Gothic Idol: Ideology and Image-Making in Medieval Art*. Cambridge, U.K.: Cambridge University Press, 1989.

Carroll, Virginia Schaefer. *The "Noble Gyn" of Comedy in the Middle English Cycle Plays*. New York: Peter Lang, 1989.

Castelli, Elizabeth. "'I Will Make Mary Male': Pieties of the Body and Gender Transformation of Christian Women in Late Antiquity." In *Body Guards: The Cultural Politics of Gender Ambiguity*, ed. Julia Epstein and Kristina Straub, 29–49. New York: Routledge, 1991.

Chambers, E. K. *The English Folk-Play*. Oxford, U.K.: Clarendon Press, 1933.

Charney, Maurice. "Jessica's Turquoise Ring and Abigail's Poisoned Porridge: Shakespeare and Marlowe as Rivals and Imitators." *Renaissance Drama* n.s. 10 (1979): 33–45.

Chaucer, Geoffrey. *The Riverside Chaucer*. Ed. Larry Benson. 3d ed. Boston: Houghton Mifflin Co., 1987.

Chazan, Robert. *Daggers of Faith: Thirteenth-Century Christian Missionizing and Jewish Response*. Berkeley: University of California Press, 1989.

———. *In the Year 1096: The First Crusade and the Jews*. Philadelphia: Jewish Publication Society, 1996.

Cheyette, Bryan. *Constructions of "The Jew" in English Literature and Society: Racial Representations, 1875–1945*. Cambridge, U.K.: Cambridge University Press, 1993.

Childs, Wendy R. *Anglo-Castilian Trade in the Later Middle Ages*. Manchester, U.K.: Manchester University Press, 1978.

Chrysostom, John. *Homilies on Romans*. In *Homilies on Acts and Romans*. Trans. J. B. Morris and W. H. Simcox. Rev. and ed. George B. Stevens. 335–564. Library of Nicene and Post-Nicene Fathers. Vol. 11. Grand Rapids, Mich.: WM. B. Eerdmans, 1956.

Clark, Elizabeth A. *Ascetic Piety and Women's Faith: Essays on Late Ancient Christianity*. Studies in Women and Religion. Vol. 20, Lewiston, N.Y.: Edwin Mellen Press, 1986.

———. "Response to R. Howard Bloch." *Medieval Feminist Newsletter* 6 (1988): 2–3.

Clark, Elizabeth A., Wendy Clein, Elaine Hansen, Peggy Knapp, Marshall Leicester, Linda Lomperis, Carol Neel, and Helen Solterer. "Commentary" on
Bloch, "Medieval Misogyny." Bloch's response and "Editor's Note." *Medieval Feminist Newsletter* 6 (fall 1988): 2–12; 7 (spring 1989), 6–10.

Clark, Robert L. A., and Claire Sponsler. "Othered Bodies: Racial Crossdressing
in the *Mistere de la Sainte Hostie* and the Croxton *Play of the Sacrament.*"
Journal of Medieval and Early Modern Studies 29 (1999): 61–87.

———. "Queer Play: The Cultural Work of Crossdressing in Medieval Drama."
New Literary History 28 (1997): 319–44.

Cohen, Gerson D. "Esau as Symbol in Early Medieval Thought." In *Jewish Medieval and Renaissance Studies*, ed. Alexander Altman, 19–48. Cambridge,
Mass.: Harvard University Press, 1967.

Cohen, Jeremy. *The Friars and the Jews: The Evolution of Medieval Anti-Judaism.*
Ithaca, N.Y.: Cornell University Press, 1982.

———. "The Jews As Killers of Christ in the Latin Tradition, from Augustine to
the Friars." *Traditio* 39 (1985): 1–27.

———. *Living Letters of the Law: Ideas of the Jew in Medieval Christianity.* Berkeley: University of California Press, 1999.

———. "The Muslim Connection or On the Changing Role of the Jew in High
Medieval Theology." In *From Witness to Witchcraft: Jews and Judaism in
Medieval Christian Thought*, ed. Jeremy Cohen, 141–62. Wiesbaden, Ger-
many: Harrassowitz Verlag, 1997.

Cohen, Jeremy, ed. *Essential Papers on Judaism and Christianity in Conflict from
Late Antiquity to the Reformation.* New York: New York University Press,
1991.

———. *From Witness to Witchcraft: Jews and Judaism in Medieval Christian
Thought.* Wiesbaden, Germany: Harrassowitz Verlag, 1997.

Cole, Andrew. "Chaucer's English Lesson." *Speculum* 77 (2002): 1128–67.

Coletti, Theresa. "Devotional Iconography in the N-Town Marian Plays." *Comparative Drama* 11 (1977): 22–44.

———. "*Paupertas est donum Dei*: Hagiography, Lay Religion, and the Economics of Salvation in the Digby *Mary Magdalene.*" *Speculum* 76 (2001):
337–78.

———. "Purity and Danger: The Paradox of Mary's Body and the En-gendering
of the Infancy Narrative in the English Mystery Cycles." In *Feminist Approaches to the Body in Medieval Literature*, ed., Linda Lomperis and Sarah
Stanbury, 65–95. Philadelphia: University of Pennsylvania Press, 1993.

———. "Ther Be But Women: Gender Conflict and Gender Identity in the Middle English Innocents Plays." *Mediaevalia* 18 (1995, for 1992): 245–61.

Collette, Carolyn P. "A Closer Look at Seinte Cecile's Special Vision." *Chaucer
Review* 10 (1987): 337–49.

———. "Sense and Sensibility in *The Prioress's Tale.*" *Chaucer Review* 15 (1981):
138–50.

Colley, John Scott. "Launcelot, Jacob, and Esau: Old and New Law in *The Merchant of Venice.*" *Yearbook of English Studies* 10 (1980): 181–89.

Condren, Edward I. "The Prioress: A Legend of Spirit, A Life of Flesh." *Chaucer Review* 23 (1989): 192–218.

Copeland, Rita. "Childhood, Pedagogy, and the Literal Sense: From Late Antiquity to the Lollard Heretical Classroom." *New Medieval Literatures* 1 (1997): 125–56.

———. *Pedagogy, Intellectuals, and Dissent in the Later Middle Ages*. Cambridge, U.K.: Cambridge University Press, 2001.

———. "Rhetoric and the Politics of the Literal Sense in Medieval Literary Theory: Aquinas, Wyclif, and the Lollards." In *Interpretation: Medieval and Modern*, ed. Piero Boitani and Anna Torti, 1–23. London: D. S. Brewer, 1992.

———. "Why Women Can't Read: Medieval Hermeneutics, Statutory Law, and the Lollard Heresy Trials." In *Representing Women: Law, Literature and Feminism*, ed. Susan Sage Heinzelman and Zipporah Batshaw Wiseman, 253–86. Durham, N.C.: Duke University Press, 1994.

Cox, Lee Sheridan. "A Question of Order in *The Canterbury Tales*." *Chaucer Review* 4 (1967): 228–52.

Crane, Susan. *Gender and Romance in Chaucer's Canterbury Tales*. Princeton, N.J.: Princeton University Press, 1994.

Crenshaw, Kimberlé. "Demarginalizing the Intersection of Race and Sex: A Black Feminist Critique of Antidiscrimination Doctrine, Feminist Theory and Antiracist Politics." *The University of Chicago Legal Forum* (1989): 139–67.

———. "Mapping the Margins: Intersectionality, Identity Politics, and Violence against Women of Color." In *Critical Race Theory: The Key Writings That Formed the Movement*. New York: New Press, 1995.

Cressy, David. *Birth, Marriage and Death: Ritual, Religion, and the Life-Cycle in Tudor and Stuart England*. Oxford, U.K.: Oxford University Press, 1997.

Cutts, Cecilia. "The Croxton Play: An Anti-Lollard Piece." *Modern Language Quarterly* 5 (1944): 45–60.

Daffner, Hugo. *Salome: Ihre Gestalt in Geschichte und Kunst*. Munich: Hugo Schmidt, 1912.

Dahan, Gilbert. "La prière juive au regard des chrétiens au moyen âge." *Revue des Études Juives* 154 (1995): 437–48

———. "Les 'figures' des Juifs et de la Synagogue: L'exemple de Dalila. Fonctions et méthodes de la typologie dans l'exégèse médiévale." *Recherches Augustiniennes* 23 (1988): 125–45.

———. *Les intellectuels chrétiens et les juifs au moyen âge*. Paris: Éditions du Cerf, 1990.

Damrosch, David. "*Non Alia Sed Aliter*: The Hermeneutics of Gender in Bernard of Clairvaux." In *Images of Sainthood in Medieval Europe*, ed. Renate Blumenfeld-Kosinski and Timea Szell, 181–95. Ithaca, N.Y.: Cornell University Press, 1991.

D'Anacona, Mirella Levi. *The Iconography of the Immaculate Conception in the Middle Ages and Early Renaissance*. New York: College Art Association of America, 1957.

Danson, Lawrence. *The Harmonies of* The Merchant of Venice. New Haven, Conn.: Yale University Press, 1978.

David, Alfred. *The Strumpet Muse: Art and Morals in Chaucer's Poetry*. Bloomington: University of Indiana Press, 1976.

Davidson, Clifford, ed. *A Tretise of Miraclis Pleyinge*. Kalamazoo, Mich: Medieval
Institute Publications, 1993.

Davies, Stevan. *The Revolt of the Widows: The Social World of the Apocryphal Acts*.
Carbondale: Southern Illinois University Press, 1980.

Davies, W. D. "Paul and the Gentiles: A Suggestion Concerning Romans 11:13–
24." In *Jewish and Pauline Studies*, 153–63. Philadelphia: Fortress Press, 1984.

Davis, Natalie Zemon. *Society and Culture in Early Modern France*. Stanford,
Calif.: Stanford University Press, 1965.

Davis, Norman, ed. *Non-Cycle Plays and Fragments*. Early English Text Society,
ss. 1. Oxford, U.K.: Oxford University Press, 1970.

———. *Non-Cycle Plays and the Winchester Dialogues*. Leeds, U.K.: School of
English, 1979.

Deansley, Margaret. *The Lollard Bible and Other Medieval Biblical Versions*. Cambridge, U.K.: Cambridge University Press, 1920.

Delany, Sheila. *Chaucer and the Jews: Sources, Contexts, Meanings*. New York:
Routledge, 2002.

———. "Chaucer's Prioress, the Jews, and the Muslims." *Medieval Encounters* 5
(1999): 198–213.

———. *The Naked Text: Chaucer's Legend of Good Women*. Berkeley: University
of California Press, 1994.

de Lorris, Guillaume, and Jean de Meun. *Le Roman de la Rose*. Ed. Ernest Langlois. Paris: Librairie Ancienne Édouard Champion, 1914.

———. *The Romance of the Rose*. Trans. Charles Dahlberg. Hanover, N.H.: University of New England Press, 1971.

Despres, Denise. "Cultic Anti-Judaism and Chaucer's Litel Clergeon." *Modern
Philology* 91 (1994): 413–27.

———. "Immaculate Flesh and Social Body: Mary and the Jews." *Jewish History*
12 (1998): 47–69.

———. "Mary of the Eucharist: Cultic Anti-Judaism in Some Fourteenth-Century
English Devotional Manuscripts." In *From Witness to Witchcraft: Jews and
Judaism in Medieval Christian Thought*, ed. Jeremy Cohen, 375–401. Wiesba-
den, Germany: Harrassowitz Verlag, 1997.

———. "The Protean Jew in the Vernon Manuscript." In *Chaucer and the Jews:
Sources, Contexts, Meanings*, ed. Sheila Delany, 145–64. New York:
Routledge, 2002.

Dinshaw, Carolyn. *Chaucer's Sexual Poetics*. Madison: University of Wisconsin
Press, 1989.

Douglas, Mary. *Purity and Danger: An Analysis of Concepts of Pollution and
Taboo*. New York: Ark Paperbacks, 1966.

Dove, Mary. "Chaucer and the Translation of Jewish Scriptures." In *Chaucer and
the Jews: Sources, Contexts, Meanings*, ed. Sheila Delany, 89–107. New York:
Routledge, 2002.

Elukin, Jonathan. "From Jew to Christian? Conversion and Immutability in

Medieval Europe." In *Varieties of Religious Conversion in the Middle Ages*, ed. James Muldoon, 171–89. Gainesville: University of Florida Press, 1997.

Enders, Jody. *The Medieval Theater of Cruelty: Rhetoric, Memory, Violence*. Ithaca, N.Y.: Cornell University Press, 1999.

Evans, Ruth. "The Jew, the Host, and the Virgin Martyr: Fantasies of the Sentient Body." In *Medieval Virginities*. Ed. Sarah Salih, Anke Bernau, and Ruth Evans. Cardiff, Wales: University of Wales Press, 2003.

———. "When a Body Meets a Body: Fergus and Mary in the York Cycle." *New Medieval Literatures* 1 (1997): 193–212.

Farmer, William R. *Anti-Judaism and the Gospels*. Harrisburg, Pa: Trinity Press International, 1999.

Fiedler, Leslie. *The Stranger in Shakespeare*. New York: Stein and Day, 1973.

Fisch, Harold. *The Dual Image: A Study of the Figure of the Jew in English Literature*. London: World Jewish Congress, 1959.

Foa, Anna. "The Witch and the Jew: Two Alikes That Were Not the Same." In *From Witness to Witchcraft: Jews and Judaism in Medieval Christian Thought*, ed. Jeremy Cohen, 361–74. Wiesbaden, Germany: Harrassowitz Verlag, 1997.

Fonrobert, Charlotte Elisheva. *Menstrual Purity: Rabbinic and Christian Reconstructions of Biblical Gender*. Stanford, Calif.: Stanford University Press, 2000.

Forbes, Thomas Rogers. *The Midwife and the Witch*. New Haven, Conn.: Yale University Press, 1966.

Forshall, J., and F. Madden, eds. *The Holy Bible . . . Made from the Latin Vulgate by John Wycliffe and His Followers*. 4 vols. Oxford, U.K.: Oxford University Press, 1850.

Fortescue, John. *The Commodyties of England . . . Copied from a Very Old Ms. in the Bodleian Library*. Ed. T. O. Payne. London, 1863.

Fortin, René. "Launcelot and the Uses of Allegory in *The Merchant of Venice*." *SEL* 14 (1974): 259–70.

Foucault, Michel. *The Order of Things: An Archaeology of the Human Sciences*. New York: Random House, 1970.

Fradenburg, Louise O. *City, Marriage, Tournament: Arts of Rule in Late Medieval Scotland*. Madison: University of Wisconsin Press, 1991.

———. "Criticism, Anti-Semitism and the Prioress's Tale." *Exemplaria* 1 (1989): 69–115.

Frank, Hardy Long. "Seeing the Prioress Whole." *Chaucer Review* 25 (1991): 229–37.

Frank, Robert Worth, Jr. "Miracles of the Virgin, Medieval Anti-Semitism, and the 'Prioress's Tale.'" In *The Wisdom of Poetry: Essays in Early English Literature in Honor of Morton W. Bloomfield*, ed. Larry D. Benson and Siegfried Wenzel, 177–88. Kalamazoo, Mich.: Medieval Institute Publications, 1982.

Freinkel, Lisa. *Reading Shakespeare's Will: The Theology of Figure from Augustine to the Sonnets*. New York: Columbia University Press, 2002.

Friedman, Albert B. "The Prioress's Tale and Chaucer's Antisemitism." *Chaucer Review* 9 (1974): 118–29.

Friedman, Jerome. "Jewish Conversion, the Spanish Pure Blood Laws and Reformation: A Revisionist View of Racial and Religious Antisemitism." *The Six-teenth Century Journal* 18 (1987): 3–29.

Froehlich, Karlfried. "'Always to Keep the Literal Sense in Scripture Means to Kill One's Soul': The State of Biblical Hermeneutics at the Beginning of the Fifteenth Century." In *Literary Uses of Typology*, ed. E. Miner, 20–48. Princeton, N.J.: Princeton University Press, 1977.

Frye, Northrop. *Anatomy of Criticism: Four Essays*. Princeton, N.J.: Princeton University Press, 1957.

Funkenstein, Amos. "Changes in the Patterns of Christian Anti-Jewish Polemics in the Twelfth Century." *Zion* 33 (1968): 125–144 [Hebrew]. English translation in Funkenstein, *Perceptions of Jewish History* (Berkeley: University of California Press, 1993).

Fuss, Diana. *Essentially Speaking: Feminism, Nature and Difference*. New York: Routledge, 1989.

Gager, John. *The Origins of Anti-Semitism: Attitudes toward Judaism in Pagan and Christian Antiquity*. New York: Oxford University Press, 1983.

———. *Reinventing Paul*. New York: Oxford University Press, 2000.

Ganim, John. *Chaucerian Theatricality*. Princeton, N.J.: Princeton University Press, 1990.

Gardner, John. "The Case against the 'Bradshaw Shift': Or the Mystery of the MS in the Trunk." *PLL* 2 Supplement (1967): 80–106.

Gash, Anthony. "Carnival against Lent: The Ambivalence of Medieval Drama." In *Medieval Literature: Criticism, Ideology and History*, ed. David Aers, 74–98. Sussex, U.K.: Harvester, 1986.

Gaylord, Alan T. "*Sentence* and *Solaas* in Fragment VII of *The Canterbury Tales*: Harry Bailly as Horseback Editor." *PMLA* 82 (1967): 226–35.

Gaynor, Stephanie. "He Says, She Says: Subjectivity and the Discourse of the Other in the *Prioress's Portrait and Tale*." *Medieval Encounters* 5 (1999): 375–90.

Genet, J. P., ed. *Four English Political Tracts of the Later Middle Ages*. Camden Society, 4th Series. Vol. 18. London: Royal Historical Society, 1977.

The Geneva Bible: A Facsimile of the 1560 Edition. Ed. Lloyd E. Berry. Madison: University of Wisconsin Press, 1969.

Gerould, Gordon H. "The Second Nun's Prologue and Tale." In *Sources and Analogues of Chaucer's Canterbury Tales*, ed. W. F. Bryan and Germaine Dempster. New York: Humanities Press, 1958.

Ghosh, Kantik. *The Wycliffite Heresy: Authority and the Interpretation of Texts*. Cambridge, U.K.: Cambridge University Press, 2002.

Gibson, Gail McMurray. "Blessing from Sun and Moon: Churching as Women's Theater." In *Bodies and Disciplines: Intersections of Literature and History in Fifteenth-Century England*, ed. Barbara A. Hanawalt and David Wallace, 139–54. Minneapolis: University of Minnesota Press, 1996.

———. "Bury St. Edmunds, Lydgate and the N-Town Cycle." *Speculum* 56 (1981): 56–90.

———. "Scene and Obscene: Seeing and Performing Late Medieval Childbirth." *Journal of Medieval and Early Modern Studies* 29 (1999): 7–24.

————. *The Theater of Devotion: East Anglian Drama and Society in the Late Middle Ages*. Chicago: University of Chicago Press, 1989.

————. "Writing Before the Eye: The N-Town Woman Taken in Adultery and the Medieval Ministry Play." *Comparative Drama* 27 (1993–94): 399–407.

Gilman, Sander, *Difference and Pathology: Stereotypes of Sexuality, Race and Madness*. Ithaca, N.Y.: Cornell University Press, 1985.

————. *The Jew's Body*. New York: Routledge, 1991.

————. "Salome, Syphilis, Sarah Bernhardt, and the Modern Jewess." In *The Jew in the Text: Modernity and the Construction of Identity*, ed. Linda Nochlin and Tamar Garb, 97–120. London: Thames and Hudson, 1995.

Gilman, Sander, and Steven T. Katz, eds. *Anti-Semitism in Times of Crisis*. New York: New York University Press, 1991.

Gilson, Étienne. *The Mystical Theology of Saint Bernard*. New York: Sheed and Ward, 1940.

Girard, René. "To Entrap the Wisest." In *Major Literary Characters: Shylock*, ed. Harold Bloom, 291–304. Philadelphia: Chelsea House, 1991.

Glassman, Bernard. *Anti-Semitic Stereotypes without Jews: Images of the Jews in England, 1290–1700*. Detroit: Wayne State University Press, 1975.

Gold, Penny Schine. *The Lady and the Virgin: Image, Attitude, and Experience in Twelfth-Century France*. Chicago: University of Chicago Press, 1985.

Goldhagen, Daniel Jonah. *A Moral Reckoning: The Role of the Catholic Church in the Holocaust and Its Unfulfilled Duty of Repair*. New York: Knopf, 2002.

Gorday, Peter. *Principles of Patristic Exegesis: Romans 9–11 in Origen, John Chrysostom, and Augustine*. New York: Edwin Mellen Press, 1983.

Gottfried, Robert. *Bury St. Edmunds and the Urban Crisis: 1290–1539*. Princeton, N.J.: Princeton University Press, 1982.

Grabois, Aryeh. "The *Hebraica Veritas* and Jewish-Christian Intellectual Relations in the Twelfth Century." *Speculum* 50 (1975): 613–34.

Grace, Dominick. "Chaucer's Little Treatises." *Florilegium* 14 (1995–96): 157–70.

Graef, Hilda. *Mary: A History of Doctrine and Devotion*. 2 vols. New York: Sheed and Ward, 1963.

Green, Monica. "Documenting Medieval Women's Medical Practice." In *Practical Medicine from Salerno to the Black Death*, ed. Luis García-Ballester, Roger French, Jon Arrizabalaga, and Andrew Cunningham, 322–52. Cambridge, U.K.: Cambridge University Press, 1994.

————. "Women's Medical Practice and Health Care in Medieval Europe." *Signs* 14 (1989): 434–72.

Gregory the Great. *Moralia in Iob*. Ed. M. Adriaen. CCSL 143; 143A; 143B. Turnhout, Belgium: Brepols, 1979.

————. *Morals on the Book of Job*. Trans. John Henry Parker. London, 1844.

Greilsammer, Myriam. "The Midwife, the Priest, and the Physician: The Subjugation of Midwives in the Low Countries at the End of the Middle Ages." *Journal of Medieval and Renaissance Studies* 21 (1991): 285–329.

Griffin, Eric. "Un-sainting James: Or, *Othello* and the 'Spanish Spirits' of Shakespeare's Globe." *Representations* 62 (1998): 58–99.

Guibert of Nogent. *Tractatus de Incarnatione contra Judeos*. PL 156, cols. 489–528.

Gussenhoven, Sister Frances. "Corpus Christi Drama as Medieval Comedy." Ph.D. diss., Stanford University, 1977.

Habib, Imtiaz. *Shakespeare and Race: Postcolonial Praxis in the Early Modern Period*. New York: University Press of America, 2000.

Haffner, Hugo. *Salome: Ihre Gestalt in Geschichte und Kunst*. Munich: Hugo Schmidt, 1912.

Hahn, Thomas. "Money, Sexuality, Wordplay, and Context in the *Shipman's Tale*." In *Chaucer in the Eighties*, ed. Julian Wasserman and Robert J. Blanch, 235–49. Syracuse, N.Y.: Syracuse University Press, 1986.

———. "The Performance of Gender in the Prioress." *Chaucer Yearbook* 1 (1992): 111–32.

Hall, Kim. "Guess Who's Coming to Dinner? Colonization and Miscegenation in *The Merchant of Venice*." *Renaissance Drama* n.s. 23 (1992): 87–112.

———. *Things of Darkness: Economies of Race and Gender in Early Modern England*. Ithaca, N.Y.: Cornell University Press, 1995.

Hamilton, Marie. "Echoes of Childermas in the Tale of the Prioress." *MLR* 34 (1939): 1–8.

Hanna, Ralph, III. "The Difficulty of Ricardian Prose Translation: The Case of the Lollards." *MLQ* 51 (1990): 319–40.

Hansen, Elaine Tuttle. *Chaucer and the Fictions of Gender*. Berkeley: University of California Press, 1992.

Harley, David. "Historians as Demonologists: The Myth of the Midwife-Witch." *The Society for the Social History of Medicine* (1990): 1–26.

Hanning, Robert. "From *Eva* and *Ave* to Eglentyne and Alisoun: Chaucer's Insight into the Roles Women Play." *Signs* 2 (1977): 580–99.

Harrowitz, Nancy. *Antisemitism, Misogyny, and the Logic of Cultural Difference*. Lincoln: University of Nebraska Press, 1994.

Harrowitz, Nancy, and Barbara Hyams. *Jews and Gender: Responses to Otto Weininger*. Philadelphia: Temple University Press, 1995.

Hawthorne, Gerald, and Ralph P. Martin, eds. *Dictionary of Paul and His Letters*. Downer's Grove, Ill: Intervarsity Press, 1993.

Heil, Johannes. " 'Antijudaismus' und 'Antisemitismus': Begriffe als Bedeutungsträger." *Jahrbuch für Antisemitismusforschung* 6 (1999): 92–114.

Hendricks, Margo, and Patricia Parker. *Women, "Race," and Writing in the Early Modern Period*. New York: Routledge, 1994.

Heng, Geraldine. "The Romance of England: *Richard Coeur de Lion*, Saracens, Jews, and the Politics of Race and Nation." In *The Postcolonial Middle Ages*, ed. J. J. Cohen, 135–72. New York: St. Martin's, 2000.

———. "Cannibalism, the First Crusade and the Genesis of Medieval Romance." *differences* 10 (1998): 98–174.

Hillaby, Joe. "The Ritual-Child-Murder Accusation: Its Dissemination and Harold of Gloucester." *Jewish Historical Studies* 34 (1994–96): 69–109.

Hirsch, Marianne, and Evelyn Fox Keller. *Conflicts in Feminism*. New York: Routledge, 1990.

Hirsh, John C. "The Politics of Spirituality: The Second Nun and the Manciple." *Chaucer Review* 12 (1977): 121–46.

———. "Reopening the Prioress's Tale." *Chaucer Review* 10 (1975): 30–45.

Hockey, Dorothy. "'The Patch is Kind Enough.'" *Shakespeare Quarterly* 10 (1959): 448–50.

Holmer, Joan Ozark. *The Merchant of Venice: Choice, Hazard and Consequence.* New York: St. Martin's Press, 1995.

Holsinger, Bruce. "The Color of Salvation: Desire, Death, and the Second Crusade in Bernard of Clairvaux's *Sermons on the Song of Songs.*" In *The Tongue of the Fathers: Gender and Ideology in Twelfth-Century Latin,* ed. David Townsend and Andrew Taylor, 156–86. Philadelphia: University of Pennsylvania Press, 1998.

———. "Pedagogy, Violence, and the Subject of Music: Chaucer's *Prioress's Tale* and Ideologies of Song." *New Medieval Literatures* 1 (1997): 157–92.

Homan, Richard L. "Devotional Themes in the Violence and Humor of the *Play of the Sacrament.*" *Comparative Drama* 20 (1986): 327–40.

———. "Mixed Feelings about Violence in the Corpus Christi Plays." In *Violence in Drama,* ed. James Redmond, 93–100. Cambridge, U.K.: Cambridge University Press, 1991.

hooks, bell. *Feminist Theory: From Margin to Center.* Boston: South End Press, 1984.

Horkheimer, Max, and Theodor Adorno. *Dialectic of Enlightenment.* Trans. John Cumming. New York: Continuum, 1972.

Hsia, R. Po-Chia. *The Myth of Ritual Murder: Jews and Magic in Reformation Germany.* New Haven, Conn.: Yale University Press, 1988.

———. *Trent 1475: Stories of a Ritual Murder Trial.* New Haven, Conn.: Yale University Press, 1992.

Hudson, Anne. *Lollards and Their Books.* London: Hambledon Press, 1985.

———. *The Premature Reformation: Wycliffite Texts and Lollard History.* Oxford, U.K.: Clarendon Press, 1988.

Hudson, Anne, ed., *Selections from English Wycliffite Writings.* Cambridge: Cambridge University Press, 1978.

Hudson, Anne, and Pamela Gradon, eds. *English Wycliffite Sermons.* 5 vols. Oxford, U.K.: Clarendon Press, 1983–96.

Hughes, Diane Owen. "Distinguishing Signs: Ear-Rings, Jews and Franciscan Rhetoric in the Italian Renaissance City." *Past and Present* 112 (1986): 3–59.

Hull, Gloria T. , Patricia Bell Scott, and Barbara Smith, eds. *All the Women are White, and All the Blacks Are Men, But Some of Us Are Brave: Black Women's Studies.* Old Westbury, N.Y.: Feminist Press, 1982.

Huppé, Bernard. *A Reading of the Canterbury Tales.* Rev. ed. Albany: State University of New York Press, 1967.

Hurley, Michael. "'Scriptura Sola': Wyclif and his Critics." *Traditio* 16 (1960): 275–352.

Hutson, Lorna. *The Usurer's Daughter: Male Friendship and Fictions of Women in Sixteenth-Century England.* New York: Routledge, 1994.

Jacquart, Danielle, and Claude Thomassett. *Sexuality and Medicine in the Middle Ages.* Trans. Matthew Adamson. Princeton, N.J.: Princeton University Press, 1985.

James, Mervyn. "Ritual, Drama and Social Body in the Late Medieval English Town." *Past and Present* 98 (1983): 3–29.

Jerome. *Commentariorum in Epistolam ad Ephesios.* PL 26: 439–554.

———. *Commentariorum in Osee.* PL 25: 815–946.

———. *Epistulae.* Ed. Isidorus Hilberg. CSEL 54–56. 3 vols. Vienna: F. Tempsky, 1912.

———. *The Principal Works of Saint Jerome.* Trans. W. H. Fremantle. Vol. 6 of *A Select Library of Nicene and Post-Nicene Fathers of the Christian Church,* 1892. Rpt. Grand Rapids, Mich.: Eerdmans, 1954.

Johnson, Lesley, and Jocelyn Wogan-Browne. "National, World and Women's History: Writers and Readers in Post-Conquest England." In *The Cambridge History of Medieval English Literature,* ed. David Wallace, 92–121. Cambridge, U.K.: Cambridge University Press, 1999.

Johnson, Willis. "The Myth of Jewish Male Menses." *Journal of Medieval History* 24 (1998): 273–74.

Jones, Michael. "Theatrical History in the Croxton *Play of the Sacrament.*" *ELH* 66 (1999): 223–60.

Jones, W. R. "Lollards and Images: The Defense of Religious Art in Later Medieval England." *Journal of the History of Ideas* 24 (1973): 27–50.

Jordan, William Chester. "The Last Tormentor of Christ: An Image of the Jew in Ancient and Medieval Exegesis, Art and Drama." *The Jewish Quarterly Review* 78 (1987): 21–47.

———. "Marian Devotion and the Talmud Trial of 1240." In *Religionsgespräche im Mittelalter,* ed. Bernard Lewis and Friedrich Niewöhner, 61–76. Wiesbaden: Harrassowitz Verlag, 1992.

———. "Why Race?" *Journal of Medieval and Early Modern Studies* 31 (2001): 165–73.

Joseph, Gerhard. "Chaucer's Coinage: Foreign Exchange and the Puns of the *Shipman's Tale.*" *Chaucer Review* 17 (1983): 341–57.

Josephus. *Jewish Antiquities.* Trans. Louis H. Feldman. Loeb Classical Library. Cambridge, Mass.: Harvard University Press, 1963.

Justice, Steven. "Lollardy." In *The Cambridge History of Medieval English Literature,* ed. David Wallace, 662–89. Cambridge, U.K. Cambridge University Press, 1999.

Kaplan, Yosef. "The Jewish Profile of the Spanish-Portuguese Community of London during the Seventeenth Century." *Judaism* 41 (1992): 229–40.

Katz, David S. *The Jews in the History of England, 1485–1850.* Oxford, U.K.: Clarendon Press, 1994.

———."Shylock's Gender: Jewish Male Menstruation in Early Modern England." *The Review of English Studies* n.s. 50 (1999): 440–62.

Kaye-Kantorowitz, Melanie. *The Issue Is Power: Essays on Women, Jews, Violence and Resistance.* San Francisco: Aunt Lute Books, 1992.

Kedourie, Elie, ed. *Spain and the Jews.* London: Thames and Hudson, 1992.

Keiser, George. "In Defense of the Bradshaw Shift." *Chaucer Review* 12 (1978): 191–201.

Kelly, Edward. "By Mouth of Innocentz: The Prioress Vindicated." *Papers on Language and Literature* 5 (1969): 362–74.

Kelly, Joan. "Did Women Have a Renaissance?" In *Becoming Visible: Women in European History*, ed. Renate Bridenthal and Claudia Koonz, 137–64. Boston: Houghton Mifflin, 1977.

Kempe, Margery. *The Book of Margery Kempe*. Ed. Sanford Brown Meech and Hope Emily Allen. EETS. Vol. 212. Oxford, U.K.: Oxford University Press, 1940.

Kertzer, David I. *The Popes Against the Jews*. New York: Alfred A. Knopf, 2002.

Kimḥi, Joseph. *The Book of the Covenant*. Trans. Frank Talmage. Toronto: Pontifical Institute for Medieval Studies, 1972.

———. *Sefer Ha-Berit*. Ed. Frank Talmage. Jerusalem, Bialik Institute: 1974. [In Hebrew].

Kinservik, Matthew J. "The Struggle over Mary's Body: Theological and Dramatic Resolution in the N-Town Assumption Play." *JEGP* 95 (1996): 190–203.

Klawans, Jonathan. *Impurity and Sin in Ancient Judaism*. Oxford, U.K.: Oxford University Press, 2000.

Klein, Holger, and Michele Marrapodi, eds. *Shakespeare and Italy*. Lewiston, N.Y.: Edwin Mellen Press, 1999.

Knapp, Peggy. *Chaucer and the Social Contest*. New York: Routledge, 1990.

Kolve, V. A. "Chaucer's *Second Nun's Tale* and the Iconography of Saint Cecilia." In *New Perspectives in Chaucer Criticism*, ed. Donald H. Rose, 137–74. Norman, Okla.: Pilgrim Books, 1981.

———. *The Play Called Corpus Christi*. Stanford, Calif.: Stanford University Press, 1966.

Krauss, Samuel, ed. *Das Leben Jesu nach jüdischen Quellen*. 1902. Reprint. New York: George Olms Verlag; 1994.

Kristeva, Julia. *Powers of Horror: An Essay on Abjection*. Trans. Leon Roudiez. New York: Columbia University Press, 1982.

Kruger, Steven. "Becoming Christian, Becoming Male?" In *Becoming Male in the Middle Ages*, ed. Jeffrey Jerome Cohen and Bonnie Wheeler, 21–41. New York: Garland, 1997.

———. "The Bodies of Jews in the Late Middle Ages." In *The Idea of Medieval Literature: New Essays on Chaucer and Medieval Culture in Honor of Donald R. Howard*, ed. James M. Dean and Christian K. Zacher, 301–22. Cranbury, N.J.: Associated University Presses, 1992.

———. "Medieval Christian (Dis)identifications: Muslims and Jews in Guibert of Nogent." *New Literary History* 28 (1997): 185–203.

———. "The Spectral Jew." *New Medieval Literatures* 2 (1998): 9–35.

Kruse, Colin. *The Second Epistle to the Corinthians: An Introduction and Commentary*. Grand Rapids, Mich.: Eerdmans, 1987.

Laclau, Ernesto. *Emancipation(s)*. New York: Verso, 1996.

Laclau, Ernesto, and Chantal Mouffe. *Hegemony and Socialist Strategy: Towards a Radical Democratic Politics*. 2d ed. New York: Verso, 2001.

Lampert, Lisa. "'O My Daughter!': 'Die schöne Jüdin' and 'Der neue Jude' in

Hermann Sinsheimer's *Maria Nunnez.*" *The German Quarterly* 71 (1998): 254–70.

———. "The Once and Future Jew: The Croxton *Play of the Sacrament*, Little Robert of Bury and Historical Memory." *Jewish History* 15 (2001): 235–55.

Lange, N. R. M. de. *Origen and the Jews: Studies in Jewish-Christian Relations in Third-Century Palestine*. Cambridge, U.K.: Cambridge University Press, 1976.

Langmuir, Gavin. *History, Religion and Antisemitism*. Berkeley: University of California Press, 1990.

———. *Toward a Definition of Antisemitism*. Berkeley: University of California Press, 1990.

Lasker, Daniel J. "Jewish-Christian Polemics at the Turning Point: Jewish Evidence from the Twelfth Century." *Harvard Theological Review* 89 (1996): 161–73.

———. *Jewish Philosophical Polemics against Christianity in the Middle Ages*. New York: Ktav Publishing House Inc., Anti Defamation League of B'nai B'rith, 1977.

———. "Jewish Philosophical Polemics in Ashkenaz." In *Contra Iudaeos: Ancient and Medieval Polemics between Christians and Jews*, ed. Ora Limor and Guy G. Stroumsa, 195–214. Tübingen, Germany: J. C. B. Mohr; 1996.

Leclercq, Jean. *Monks and Love in Twelfth-Century France: Psycho-historical Essays*. New York: Oxford University Press, 1979.

Lee, Becky R. "The Purification of Women after Childbirth: A Window onto Medieval Perceptions of Women." *Florilegium* 14 (1995–96): 43–55.

Le Goff, Jacques. *Your Money or Your Life: Economy and Religion in the Middle Ages*. Trans. Patricia Ranum. New York: Zone Books, 1988.

Leicester, H. Marshall. *The Disenchanted Self*. Berkeley: University of California Press, 1990.

Lelyveld, Toby. *Shylock on the Stage*. Cleveland, Ohio: Press of the Western Reserve University, 1960.

Lemay, Helen Rondite. *Women's Secrets: A Translation of the Pseudo-Albertus Magnus' De Secretis Mulierum with Commentaries*. Albany: State University of New York Press, 1992.

Leonard, Frances M. "The School for Transformation: A Theory of Middle English Comedy." *Genre* 9 (1976): 179–91.

Lerer, Seth. "'Represented Now in Yower Syght': The Culture of Spectatorship in Late Fifteenth-Century England." *Bodies and Disciplines; Intersections of Literature and History in Fifteenth-Century England*, ed. Barbara Hanawalt and David Wallace, 29–62. Minneapolis: University of Minnesota Press, 1996.

Levinas, Emmanuel. *Difficult Freedom: Essays on Judaism*. Trans. by Seán Hand. Baltimore: Johns Hopkins University Press, 1990.

Lewalski, Barbara. "Biblical Allusion and Allegory in *The Merchant of Venice*." In *Shylock*, ed. Harold Bloom, 236–51. New York: Chelsea House, 1991. Originally published in *Shakespeare Quarterly* 13 (1962): 327–43.

Lipton, Sara. *Images of Intolerance: The Representation of Jews and Judaism in the Bible moralisée*. Berkeley: University of California Press, 1999.

Little, Lester K. *Religious Poverty and the Profit Economy in Medieval Europe*. Ithaca, N.Y.: Cornell University Press, 1978.

Lloyd, Genevieve. *The Man of Reason: "Male" and "Female" in Western Philosophy*. 2d ed. Minneapolis: University of Minnesota Press, 1993.

Lloyd, T. H. *The English Wool Trade in the Middle Ages*. Cambridge, U.K.: Cambridge University Press, 1977.

Loewenstein, Andrea Freud. *Loathsome Jews and Engulfing Women: Metaphors of Projection in the Works of Wyndham Lewis, Charles Williams, and Graham Greene*. New York: New York University Press, 1993.

Loomba, Ania. " 'Delicious Traffick': Racial and Religious Difference on Early Modern Stages." In *Shakespeare and Race*, ed. Catherine M. S. Alexander and Stanley Wells, 203–24. Cambridge, U.K.: Cambridge University Press, 2000.

———. *Gender, Race, Renaissance Drama*. Manchester, U.K.: Manchester University Press, 1989.

———. *Shakespeare, Race, and Colonialism*. Oxford, U.K.: Oxford University Press, 2002.

Lott, Eric. "After Identity, Politics: The Return of Universalism." *New Literary History* 31 (2000): 665–78.

Lotter, Friedrich. "Das Prinzip der *"Hebraica Veritas"* und die heilgeschichtliche Rolle Israels bei den frühen Zisterziensern." In *Bibel in jüdischer und christlicher Tradition*, ed. Helmut Merklein, Karlheinz Müller and Günter Stemberger, 479–517. Frankfurt am Main: Hain, 1993.

———. "The Position of the Jews in Early Cistercian Exegesis and Preaching." In *From Witness to Witchcraft: Jews and Judaism in Medieval Christian Thought*, ed. Jeremy Cohen, 163–86. Wiesbaden, Germany: Harrassowitz Verlag, 1997.

Lubac, Henri de. *Christian Resistance to Anti-Semitism. Memories from 1940–1944*. Trans. Sister Elizabeth Englund, O.C.D. San Francisco: St. Ignatius Press, 1990.

———. *Medieval Exegesis*. Vol. 1, "The Four Senses of Scripture." Trans. Mark Sebanc. Grand Rapids, Mich.: Eerdmans, 1998. Originally published as *Exégèse médiévale, 1: Les quatre sens de l'écriture* (Paris: Éditions Montaigne, 1959).

Lupton, Julia Reinhard. *Afterlives of the Saints: Hagiography, Typology, and Renaissance Literature*. Stanford, Calif.: Stanford University Press, 1996.

———. "Citizen-Saints: Shakespeare and Political Theology." Forthcoming.

———. "Exegesis, Mimesis, and the Future of Humanism in *The Merchant of Venice*." *Religion and Literature* 32 (2000): 123–39.

———. "Othello Circumcised: Shakespeare and the Pauline Discourse of Nations." *Representations* 57 (1997): 73–89.

———. "Shakespeare's Other Europe: Jews, Venice, and Civil Society. " *Social Identities* 7 (2001): 479–91.

Lydgate, John. *A Critical Edition of John Lydgate's Life of Our Lady*. Ed. Joseph A. Lauritis, Ralph A. Klinefelter, and Vernon F. Gallagher. Pittsburgh, Pa.: Duquesne University Press, 1961.

Lyotard, Jean François. *Heidegger and "the jews."* Trans. Andreas Michel and Mark Roberts. Minneapolis: University of Minnesota Press, 1990.

Maccoby, Hyam. "The Delectable Daughter." *Midstream* 24 (1970): 50–60.

———. *Judaism on Trial: Jewish-Christian Disputations in the Middle Ages.* London: Littman Library of Jewish Civilization, 1996.

MacDonald, Joyce Green, ed. *Race, Ethnicity and Power in the Renaissance.* Madison, Wis.: Fairleigh Dickinson University Press, 1997.

Madeleva, Mary. *Chaucer's Nuns and Other Essays.* New York: Appleton, 1925.

Maltman, Sister Nicholas, O.P. "Meaning and Art in the Croxton *Play of the Sacrament*." *ELH* 41 (1974): 149–64.

Mann, Jill. *Geoffrey Chaucer.* Atlantic Highlands, N.J. Humanities Press International, 1991.

———. "Parents and Children in the 'Canterbury Tales.'" In *Literature in Fourteenth-Century England*, ed. Piero Boitani and Anna Torti, 165–83. Tübingen, Germany: Narr Verlag, 1983.

Marcus, Jacob. *The Jew in the Medieval World.* New York: Harper and Row, 1938.

Marks, Elaine. *Marrano As Metaphor: The Jewish Presence in French Writing.* New York: Columbia University Press, 1996.

Marlowe, Christopher. *The Jew of Malta.* In *Drama of the English Renaissance. Vol. 1, The Tudor Period*, ed. Russell A. Fraser and Norman Rabkin, 263–94. New York: Macmillan, 1976.

Marvin, Corey, J. "'I Will Thee Not Forsake': The Kristevan Maternal Space in Chaucer's Prioress's Tale and John of Garland's Stella Maris." *Exemplaria* 8.1 (1996): 35–58.

Massip, J. Francesc. "The Staging of the Assumption in Europe." *Comparative Drama* 25 (1991–92): 17–28.

Mayberry, Nancy. "The Controversy over the Immaculate Conception in Medieval and Renaissance Art, Literature and Society." *Journal of Medieval and Renaissance Studies* 21 (1991): 207–24.

Mayer, Hans. *Aussenseiter.* Frankfurt am Main: Suhrkampf, 1981.

McClintock, Anne. *Imperial Leather: Race, Gender and Sexuality in the Colonial Contest.* New York: Routledge, 1995.

McCulloh, John. "Jewish Ritual Murder: William of Norwich, Thomas of Monmouth, and the Early Dissemination of the Myth." *Speculum* 72 (1997): 698–740.

McLean, Susan. "Prodigal Sons and Daughters: Transgression and Forgiveness in *The Merchant of Venice*." *Papers in Language and Literature* 32 (1996): 45–62.

Meale, Carol M. "*The Libelle of Englyshe Polycye* and Mercantile Literary Culture in Late Medieval London." In *London and Europe in the Later Middle Ages*, ed. Julia Boffey and Pamela King, 181–227. London: Centre for Medieval and Renaissance Studies, University of London, 1995.

Meeks, Wayne A. "The Image of the Androgyne: Some Uses of a Symbol in Earliest Christianity." *Journal of the History of Religions* 13 (1973): 165–208.

Meredith, Peter, ed. *The Mary Play from the N. Town Manuscript.* Exeter, U.K.: University of Exeter Press, 1997.

Merkel, Kerstin. *Salome: Ikonographie im Wandel*. Frankfurt am Main: Peter Lang, 1990.

Metlitzki, Dorothee. *The Matter of Araby in Medieval England*. New Haven, Conn.: Yale University Press, 1977.

Metzger, Mary Janell. "'Now by My Hood, a Gentle and No Jew': Jessica, *The Merchant of Venice*, and the Discourse of Early Modern English Identity." *PMLA* 113 (1998): 52–63.

Miles, Margaret R. *Carnal Knowing: Female Nakedness and Religious Meaning in the Christian West*. Boston: Beacon Press, 1989.

Mill, Anna J. "The York Plays of the Dying, Assumption, and Coronation of Our Lady." *PMLA* 65 (1950): 866–76.

Milton, John. *Complete Poems and Major Prose*. Ed. Merritt Y. Hughes. New York: Macmillan Publishing Company, 1957.

Minh-ha, Trinh T. *Woman, Native, Other: Writing Postcoloniality and Feminism*. Bloomington: Indiana University Press, 1989.

Minnis, A. J. "'Authorial Intention' and 'Literal Sense' in the Exegetical Theories of Richard Fitzralph and John Wyclif: An Essay in the Medieval History of Biblical Hermeneutics." *Proceedings of the Royal Irish Academy* 75, Section C (1975): 1–30.

Mirk, John. *Instructions for Parish Priests*. Ed. Edward Peacock. 2d rev. ed., EETS o.s. 31. London: Kegan Paul, Trench, and Trübner, 1902.

———. *Mirk's Festial*. Ed. Theodor Erbe. EETS e.s. 96. London: Kegan Paul, Trench, and Trübner, 1905.

Mirrer, Louise. *Women, Jews, and Muslims in the Texts of Reconquest Castile*. Ann Arbor: University of Michigan Press, 1996.

Moore, R. I. *The Formation of a Persecuting Society: Power and Deviance in Western Europe, 950–1250*. Oxford, U.K.: Basil Blackwell, 1987.

———. "Heresy as Disease." In *The Concept of Heresy in the Middle Ages (11th–13th c).*, ed. W. Lourdaux and D. Verhelst, 1–11. Leuven, Belgium: Leuven University Press, 1976.

Moran, Jo Ann Hoeppner. *The Growth of English Schooling, 1340–1548. Learning, Literacy, and Laicization in Pre-Reformation York Diocese*. Princeton, N.J.: Princeton University Press, 1985.

Morrison, Karl. *Conversion and Text: The Cases of Augustine of Hippo, Herman-Judah, and Constantine Tsatsos*. Charlottesville: University of Virginia Press, 1992.

———. *Understanding Conversion*. Charlottesville: University of Virginia Press, 1992.

Morrison, Toni. *Playing in the Dark: Whiteness and the Literary Imagination*. New York: Random House, 1993.

Mühlbacher, Emil. *Die streitige Papstwahl des Jahres 1130*. Aachen, Germany: Scientia Verlag, 1966.

Mundill, Robin. *England's Jewish Solution: Experiment and Expulsion, 1269–1290*. Cambridge, U.K.: Cambridge University Press, 1998.

Musurillo, Herbert, ed. and trans. *The Acts of the Christian Martyrs*. Oxford, U.K.: Clarendon Press, 1972.

Narin van Court, Elisa. "Critical Apertures: Medieval Anti-Judaisms and Middle English Narrative." Ph.D. diss., University of California, Berkeley, 1994.

———. "Socially Marginal, Culturally Central: Representing Jews in Late Medieval English Literature." *Exemplaria* 12 (2000): 293–326.

Netanyahu, B. *The Origins of the Inquisition in Fifteenth Century Spain.* New York: Random House, 1995.

Newall, Venetia. "The Jew as Witch Figure." In *The Witch Figure: Folklore Essays by a Group of Scholars in England Honouring the Seventy-fifth Birthday of Katharine M. Briggs,* ed. Venetia Newall, 95–124. Boston: Routledge and Kegan Paul, 1973.

Newman, Barbara. *From Virile Woman to WomanChrist: Studies in Medieval Religion and Literature.* Philadelphia: University of Pennsylvania Press, 1995.

Newman, Karen. "Directing Traffic: Subjects, Objects, and the Politics of Exchange in *The Merchant of Venice.*" *differences* 2 (1990): 41–54.

———. "Portia's Ring: Unruly Women and Structures of Exchange in *The Merchant of Venice.*" *Shakespeare Quarterly* 38 (1987): 19–33.

———. "Reprise: Gender, Sexuality and Theories of Exchange in *The Merchant of Venice.*" In *The Merchant of Venice,* ed. Nigel Wood, 102–33. Bury St. Edmunds, U.K.: St. Edmundsbury Press, 1996.

Nichols, Ann Eljenholm. "The Hierosphthitic Topos, or the Fate of Fergus: Notes on the N-Town *Assumption.*" *Comparative Drama* 25 (1991): 29–41.

Nirenberg, David. *Communities of Violence: Persecution of Minorities in the Middle Ages.* Princeton, N.J.: Princeton University Press, 1996.

Nissé, Ruth. "Prophetic Nations." *New Medieval Literatures* 4 (2001): 95–115.

———."Reversing Discipline: The *Tretise of Miraclis Pleyinge,* Lollard Exegesis, and the Failure of Representation." *The Yearbook of Langland Studies* 11 (1997): 163–94.

Noonan, John. *The Scholastic Analysis of Usury.* Cambridge, Mass.: Harvard University Press, 1957.

Novick, Peter. *The Holocaust in American Life.* New York: Houghton Mifflin, 1999.

O'Connor, Edward Dennis. *The Dogma of the Immaculate Conception.* Notre Dame, Ind.: Notre Dame University Press, 1958.

Odo of Tournai. *On Original Sin and a Disputation with the Jew, Leo, Concerning the Advent of Christ, the Son of God: Two Theological Treatises.* Trans. Irven M. Resnick. Philadelphia: University of Pennsylvania Press, 1994.

———. *Opera omnia.* PL 160.

Olson, Glending. "A Reading of *Thopas-Melibee* Link." *Chaucer Review* 10 (1975–76): 147–53.

Olson, Paul A. *The Canterbury Tales and the Good Society.* Princeton, N.J.: Princeton University Press, 1986.

"On England's Commercial Policy." In *Political Poems and Songs relating to English History Composed during the Period from the Accession of Edw. III to That of Ric. III,* vol. 2, ed. Thomas Wright, 282–87. 1861. Reprint, Wiesbaden, Germany: Krauss, 1965.

Origen. *Commentary on the Epistle to the Romans Books 6–10.* Trans. Thomas P.

Scheck. The Fathers of the Church. Vol. 104. Washington, D.C.: Catholic University of America, 2002.

———. *Homilien zum Hexateuch in Rufins Übersetzung. Origenes Werke*. Vol. 6. Ed. W. A. Baehrens. Leipzig, Germany: J. C. Hinrich, 1920.

———. *Origen: Homilies on Leviticus 1–16*. Trans. Gary Wayne Barkley. The Fathers of the Church. Vol. 83. Washington, D.C.: Catholic University of America Press, 1990.

———. *Origenes Commentarii in Epistulam ad Romanos: Liber Septimus, Liber Octavus Römerbriefkommentar Siebtes u. Achtes Buch*. Ed. and trans., Theresia Heither. Freiburg, Germany: Herder, 1994.

Orme, Nicholas. *Education and Society in Medieval and Renaissance England*. London: Hambledon Press, 1989.

Owen, Charles, Jr. "The Alternative Reading of *The Canterbury Tales*: Chaucer's Text and the Early Manuscripts." *PMLA* 97 (1982): 237–50.

Owst, G. *Literature and Pulpit in Medieval England; A Neglected Chapter in the History of English Letters & of the English People*. 2d rev. ed. Oxford, U.K.: Blackwell, 1961.

Oz, Avraham. "Dobbin on the Rialto: Venice and the Division of Identity." In *Shakespeare's Italy: Functions of Italian Locations in Renaissance Drama*, ed. Michele Marrapodi, A. J. Hoenselaars, Marcello Cappuzzo, and L. Falzon Santucci, 185–212. New York: Manchester University Press, 1993.

Palmer, Daryl W. "Merchants and Miscegenation: *The Three Ladies of London, The Jew of Malta*, and *The Merchant of Venice*." In *Race, Ethnicity and Power in the Renaissance*, ed. Joyce Green MacDonald, 36–66. Madison, N.J.: Fairleigh Dickinson University Press, 1997.

Patterson, Lee. "'Living Witnesses of Our Redemption': Martyrdom and Imitation in Chaucer's *Prioress's Tale*." *Journal of Medieval and Early Modern Studies* 31 (2001): 507–60.

———. "On the Margin: Postmodernism, Ironic History, and Medieval Studies." *Speculum* 65 (1990): 92–95.

———. *Negotiating the Past: The Historical Understanding of Medieval Literature*. Madison: University of Wisconsin Press, 1987.

———. "*The Parson's Tale* and the Quitting of the *Canterbury Tales*." *Traditio* 34 (1978): 331–80.

———. "'What Man Artow?' Authorial Self-Definition in *The Tale of Sir Thopas* and *The Tale of Melibee*." *Studies in the Age of Chaucer* 11 (1989): 117–75.

Paul. *The Writings of St. Paul*. Ed. Wayne A. Meeks. New York: Norton, 1972.

Pecock, Reginald. *The Repressor of Over Much Blaming of the Clergy*. 2 vols. Ed. Churchill Babington. London: Longman, Green, Longman, and Roberts, 1860.

Pelikan, Jaroslav. *The Emergence of the Catholic Tradition (100–600)*. Chicago: University of Chicago Press, 1971.

Peter the Venerable. *Adversus Iudeorum inveteratam duritiem*. Ed. Y. Friedman. CCCM 58. Turnhout, Belgium: Brepols, 1985.

Philo of Alexandria. *Questions and Answers on Exodus*. Trans. Ralph Marcus. The Loeb Classical Library. Cambridge, Mass.: Harvard University Press, 1952.

Power, Eileen. *Medieval English Nunneries.* Cambridge, U.K.: University of Cambridge Press, 1922.

———. "The Position of Women." In *The Legacy of the Middle Ages,* ed. C. G. Crump and E. F. Jacob, 401–33. Oxford, U.K.: Clarendon, 1926.

———. *The Wool Trade in English Medieval History.* Oxford, U.K.: Oxford University Press, 1941.

Power, Kim. *Veiled Desire: Augustine on Women.* New York: Continuum, 1996.

Pratt, Robert A. "Chaucer's Borrowing from Himself." *MLQ* 7 (1946): 259–64.

———. "The Order of *The Canterbury Tales.*" *PMLA* 66 (1951): 1141–67.

Preus, James Samuel. *From Shadow to Promise: Old Testament Interpretation from Augustine to the Young Luther.* Cambridge, Mass.: Harvard University Press, 1969.

Rabanus Maurus. *Enarrationum in Librum Numerorum.* PL 108: 587–858.

Ragussis, Michael. *Figures of Conversion: "The Jewish Question" and English National Identity.* Durham, N.C.: Duke University Press, 1995.

Räisänen, Heikki. "Paul, God, and Israel: Romans 9–11 in Recent Research." In *The Social World of Formative Christianity and Judaism.* Ed. Jacob Neusner, Ernest S. Frerichs, Peder Borgen, and Richard Horsley, 178–206. Philadelphia: Fortress Press, 1988.

Reames, Sherry L. "The Cecilia Legend as Chaucer Inherited It and Retold It: The Disappearance of an Augustinian Ideal." *Speculum* 55 (1980): 38–57.

———. "A Recent Discovery Concerning the Sources of Chaucer's 'Second Nun's Tale.'" *Modern Philology* (1990): 337–61.

———. "The Sources of Chaucer's 'Second Nun's Tale.'" *Modern Philology* (1978): 111–35.

Reed, Victoria. "Salome in Renaissance Art." Essay, Sarah Lawrence College, 1996.

Reid Schwartz, Alexandra. "Economies of Salvation: Commerce and the Eucharist in the Profanation of the Host and the Croxton *Play of the Sacrament.*" *Comitatus* 25 (1994): 1–20.

Resnick, Irven M. "Medieval Roots of the Myth of Jewish Male Menses." *Harvard Theological Review* 93 (2000): 241–63.

Ridley, Florence. *The Prioress and the Critics.* University of California Publications, English Studies, vol. 30. Berkeley: University of California Press, 1965.

Rieder, Paula Marie. "Between the Pure and the Polluted: The Churching of Women in Medieval Northern France, 1100–1500." Ph.D. diss, University of Illinois, Urbana-Champaign, 2000.

Robbins, Jill. *Prodigal Son/Elder Brother: Interpretation and Alterity in Augustine, Petrarch, Kafka, Levinas.* Chicago: University of Chicago Press, 1991.

Robertson, D. W., Jr. *A Preface to Chaucer: Studies in Medieval Perspectives.* Princeton, N.J.: Princeton University Press, 1962.

Rokéah, David. "The Church Fathers and the Jews in Writings Designed for Internal and External Use." In *Antisemitism through the Ages,* ed. Shmuel Almog and trans. Nathan H. Reisner, 39–70. New York: Pergamon Press, 1988.

Rosenheim, Judith. "Allegorical Commentary in *The Merchant of Venice.*" *Shake-*

speare Studies 24 (1996): 156–210. Errata: *Shakespeare Studies* 26 (1998): 425–26.

Rosenthal, Judith. "Margery Kempe and Medieval Anti-Judaic Ideology." *Medieval Encounters* 5 (1999): 409–20.

Roth, Norman. *Conversos, Inquisition and the Expulsion of the Jews from Spain.* Madison: University of Wisconsin Press, 1995.

Roth, Wendy. " 'Taillynge Ynough' in the *Shipman's Tale* and the *Prioress's Tale.*" Unpublished paper, University of California, Berkeley, 1992.

Rothberg, Michael. *Traumatic Realism: The Demands of Holocaust Representation.* Minneapolis: University of Minnesota Press, 2000.

Rubin, Miri. *Corpus Christi: The Eucharist in Late Medieval Culture.* Cambridge, U.K.: Cambridge University Press, 1991.

——. "The Eucharist and the Construction of Medieval Identities." In *Culture and History, 1350–1600*, ed. David Aers, 43–63. Detroit: Wayne State University Press, 1992.

——. *Gentile Tales: The Narrative Assault on Late Medieval Jews.* New Haven, Conn.: Yale University Press, 1999.

Ruether, Rosemary. "The *Adversus Judaeos* Tradition in the Church Fathers: The Exegesis of Christian Anti-Judaism." In *Essential Papers on Judaism and Christianity in Conflict from Late Antiquity to the Reformation*, ed. Jeremy Cohen, 174–192. New York: New York University Press, 1991.

——. *Faith and Fratricide: The Theological Roots of Anti-Semitism.* New York: Seabury Press, 1974.

——. "Misogynism and Virginal Feminism in the Fathers of the Church." In *Religion and Sexism: Images of Woman in the Jewish and Christian Traditions.* New York: Simon and Schuster, 1974.

Ruggiers, Paul. *The Art of the Canterbury Tales.* Madison: University of Wisconsin Press, 1965.

Sandoval, Chela. "U.S. Third World Feminism: The Theory and Method of Oppositional Consciousness in the Postmodern World." *Genders* 10 (1991): 1–24.

Sartre, Jean-Paul. *Anti-Semite and Jew.* Trans. George J. Becker. New York: Schocken Books, 1948.

Schelkle, Karl Hermann. *Paulus Lehrer der Väter. Die altkirchliche Auslegung von Römer 1–11.* Düsseldorf, Germany: Patmos Verlag, 1956.

Scherb, Victor I. "The Earthly and Divine Physicians: *Christus Medicus* in the Croxton *Play of the Sacrament.*" In *The Body and the Text*, ed. Bruce Clark and Wendell Aycock, 161–71. Studies in Comparative Literature 22. Lubbock: Texas Tech University Press, 1990.

——. "Violence and the Social Body in the Croxton *Play of the Sacrament.*" In *Violence in Drama*, ed. James Redmond. Cambridge, U.K.: Cambridge University Press, 1991.

Schlauch, Margaret. "The Allegory of Church and Synagogue." *Speculum* 13 (1939): 448–64.

Schless, Howard. "Dante: Comedy and Conversion." In *Versions of Medieval Comedy*, ed. Paul Ruggiers, 135–49. Norman: University of Oklahoma Press, 1977.

Schreckenberg, Heinz. *Christliche Adversus-Judaeos-Bilder: Das Alte und Neue Testament im Spiegel der christlichen Kunst*. New York: Peter Lang, 1999.

———. *The Jews in Christian Art: An Illustrated History*. New York: Continuum, 1996.

Schor, Naomi. "The Crisis of French Universalism." *Yale French Studies* 100 (2001): 43–64.

———. "French Feminism Is a Universalism." *differences* 7 (spring 1995): 15–47.

Scott, Joan Wallach. *Only Paradoxes to Offer: French Feminists and the Rights of Man*. Cambridge, Mass.: Harvard University Press, 1996.

———. "Universalism and the History of Feminism." *differences* 7, no. 1 (1995): 1–14.

Seidel, Linda. "Salome and the Canons." *Women's Studies* 11 (1984): 29–66.

Seiferth, Wolfgang. *Synagogue and Church in the Middle Ages: Two Symbols in Art and Literature*. Trans. Lee Chadeayne and Paul Gottwald. New York: Frederick Ungar Publishing, 1970.

Shachar, Isaiah. *The Judensau: A Medieval Anti-Jewish Motif and Its History*. London: Warburg Institute, 1974.

Shahar, Shulamith. *Childhood in the Middle Ages*. Trans. Chaya Galai. New York: Routledge, 1992.

———. *The Fourth Estate: A History of Women in the Middle Ages*. Trans. Chaya Galai. New York: Metheun, 1983.

Shakespeare, William. *The Merchant of Venice*. Ed. John Russell Brown. *The Arden Shakespeare*. New York: Routledge, 1964.

Shapiro, James. *Shakespeare and the Jews*. New York: Columbia University Press, 1996.

———. "'Which is *The Merchant* here, and Which *The Jew?*': Shakespeare and the Economics of Influence." *Shakespeare Studies* 20 (1988): 269–82.

Sheingorn, Pamela. "The Bodily Embrace or Embracing the Body: Gesture and Gender in Late Medieval Culture." In *The Stage As Mirror: Civic Theatre in Late Medieval Europe*, ed. Alan E. Knight, 51–89. Rochester, N.Y.: D. S. Brewer, 1997.

Shell, Marc. "Marranos (Pigs), or From Coexistence to Toleration." *Critical Inquiry* 17 (1991): 306–35.

———. "The Wether and the Ewe: Verbal Usury in *The Merchant of Venice*." *Kenyon Review* 14 (1979): 65–92.

Sherman, Gail Berkeley. "Saints, Nuns, and Speech in the *Canterbury Tales*." In *Images of Sainthood in Medieval Europe*, ed. Renate Blumenfeld-Kosinski and Timea Szell, 136–60. Ithaca, N.Y.: Cornell University Press, 1991.

Signer, Michael. "*Peshat, Sensus Litteralis*, and Sequential Narrative: Jewish Exegesis and the School of St. Victor in the Twelfth Century." *Jewish History* 6 (1992–93): 203–16.

Simmons, T. F., ed. *The Lay Folks Mass Book*. London: EETS, 1879.

Simon, Marcel. "Christian Anti-Semitism." In *Essential Papers on Judaism and Christianity in Conflict from Late Antiquity to the Reformation*, ed. Jeremy Cohen, 174–192. New York: New York University Press, 1991.

———. *Verus Israel: A Study of the Relations between Christians and Jews in the*

Roman Empire (135–425). Trans. H. McKeating. New York: Oxford University Press, 1986.

Sinanoglou, Leah. "The Christ Child As Sacrifice: A Medieval Tradition and the Corpus Christi Plays." *Speculum* 48 (1973): 491–509.

Sinfield, Alan. "How to Read *The Merchant of Venice* without Being Heterosexist." In *The Merchant of Venice, William Shakespeare*, ed. Martin Coyle, 161–80. New Casebooks. New York: St. Martin's Press, 1998.

Smalley, Beryl. *The Study of the Bible in the Middle Ages*. Notre Dame, Ind.: Notre Dame University Press, 1964.

Smith, Barbara. "Toward a Black Feminist Criticism." In *All the Women Are White, and All the Blacks Are Men, But Some of Us Are Brave: Black Women's Studies*, ed. Gloria T. Hull, Patricia Bell Scott, and Barbara Smith, 157–75. Old Westbury, N.Y.: Feminist Press, 1982.

Smith, Valerie. *Not Just Race, Not Just Gender: Black Feminist Readings*. New York: Routledge, 1998.

Southern, Richard. "The English Origins of the 'Miracles of the Virgin.'" *Mediaeval and Renaissance Studies* 4 (1958): 176–216.

Spector, Stephen. "Empathy and Enmity in the *Prioress's Tale*." In *The Olde Daunce: Love, Friendship and Marriage in the Medieval World*, ed. Robert R. Edwards and Stephen Spector, 211–28. Albany: State University of New York Press, 1991.

———. "Time, Space and Identity in the *Play of the Sacrament*." In *The Stage As Mirror: Civic Theatre in Late Medieval Europe*, ed. Alan E. Knight. Rochester, N.Y.: D. S. Brewer, 1997.

Spector, Stephen, ed. *The N-Town Play Cotton MS Vespasian D.8*. 2 vols. EETS. Oxford, U.K.: Oxford University Press, 1991.

Spenser, Edmund. *The Faerie Queene*. Ed. A. C. Hamilton. New York: Longman, 1977.

———. *A View of the Present State of Ireland: From the First Printed Edition (1633)*. Ed. Andrew Hadfield and Willy Maleyn. London: Blackwell, 1997.

Sponsler, Claire. *Drama and Resistance: Bodies, Goods and Theatricality in Late Medieval England*. Minneapolis: University of Minnesota Press, 1997.

Stacey, Robert. "The Conversion of the Jews to Christianity in Thirteenth-Century England." *Speculum* 67 (1992): 263–83.

Stephan, Inge, Sabine Schilling, and Sigrid Weigel, eds. *Jüdische Kultur und Weiblichkeit in der Moderne*. Cologne, Germany: Böhlau Verlag, 1994.

Stock, Brian. *Augustine the Reader: Meditation, Self-Knowledge and the Ethics of Interpretation*. Cambridge, Mass.: Harvard University Press, 1996.

Strohm, Paul. "Chaucer's Lollard Joke: History and the Textual Unconscious." *Studies in the Age of Chaucer* 17 (1995): 23–42.

———. "*Passioun, Lyf, Miracle, Legende*: Some Generic Terms in Middle English Hagiographical Narrative." *Chaucer Review* 10 (1975): 62–75, 154–71.

Stroll, Mary. *The Jewish Pope: Ideology and Politics in the Papal Schism of 1130*. New York: E. J. Brill, 1987.

Summit, Jennifer. *Lost Property: The Woman Writer and English Literary History, 1380–1589*. Chicago: University of Chicago Press, 2000.

Sutcliffe, Adam. "Hebrew Texts and Protestant Readers: Christian Hebraism and Denominational Self-Definition." *Jewish Studies Quarterly* 7 (2000): 319–37.

———. *Judaism and Enlightenment.* New York: Cambridge University Press, 2003.

———. "Myth, Origins, Identity: Voltaire, the Jews and the Enlightenment Notion of Toleration." *The Eighteenth Century* 39 (1998): 107–26.

Talmage, Frank. "An Anti-Christian Polemic in Eastern Europe in the Style of Sephardic Polemics—A Unique Manuscript." *Kiryat Sefer* 56 (1980–81): 369–72. [in Hebrew.]

———. "A Hebrew Polemical Treatise: Anti-Cathar and Anti-Orthodox." *Harvard Theological Review* 60 (1967): 212–37.

Tanner, Tony. "Which Is the Merchant Here? and Which the Jew? The Venice of Shakespeare's *Merchant of Venice.*" In *Venetian Views, Venetian Blinds: English Fantasies of Venice,* ed. Manfred Pfister and Barbara Schaff, 45–62. Atlanta: Rodopi, 1999.

Tellbe, Mikael. *Paul between Synagogue and State: Christians, Jews, and Civic Authorities in 1 Thessalonians, Romans, and Philippians.* Coniectanea Biblica New Testament Series, vol. 34. Stockholm: Almqvist and Wiksell International, 2001.

Tertullian. *Q. Septimii Florentis Tertulliani De Resurrectione Carnis Liber / Tertullian's Treatise on the Resurrection: The Text Edited with an Introduction, Translation and Commentary.* Ed. and trans. Ernest Evans. London: SPCK, 1960.

Theweleit, Klaus. *Male Fantasies.* Trans. Stephen Conway, Erica Carter, and Chris Turner. Minneapolis: University of Minnesota Press, 1987.

Tomasch, Sylvia. "Judecca, Dante's Satan, and the *Dis*-placed Jew." In *Text and Territory: Geographical Imagination in the European Middle Ages,* ed. Sylvia Tomasch and Sealy Gilles, 247–67. Philadelphia: University of Pennsylvania Press, 1998.

———. "Postcolonial Chaucer and the Virtual Jew." In *The Postcolonial Middle Ages,* ed. Jeffrey Jerome Cohen, 243–60. New York: St. Martin's, 2000.

Thrupp, Sylvia. "Aliens in and around London in the Fifteenth Century." In *Studies in London History: Presented to Philip Edmund Jones,* ed. A. E. J. Hollaender and William Kellaway, 251–72. London: Hodder and Stoughton, 1969.

———. "A Survey of the Alien Population of England in 1440." *Speculum* 32 (1953): 262–73.

Tinkle, Theresa. *Medieval Venuses and Cupids: Sexuality, Hermeneutics and English Poetry.* Stanford, Calif.: Stanford University Press, 1996.

Trachtenberg, Joshua. *The Devil and the Jews: The Medieval Conception of the Jew and Its Relation to Modern Anti-Semitism.* Philadelphia: Jewish Publication Society of America, 1943.

Travis, Peter. "The Social Body of the Dramatic Christ in Medieval England." *Early Drama to 1600 Acta,* 13 (1985): 17–36.

Trilling, Lionel. "The Changing Myth of the Jew." In *Speaking of Literature and Society,* ed. Diana Trilling. Oxford, U.K.: Oxford University Press, 1982.

Tucker, Irene. "Hosting the Jews: Boundary Permeability in Chaucer's 'Prioress's Tale.'" Unpublished essay, University of California, Berkeley, 1989.

Tydeman, William. *English Medieval Theatre*. Boston: Routledge and Kegan Paul; 1986.

Vriend, J. *The Blessed Virgin Mary in the Medieval Drama of England with Additional Studies in Middle English Literature*. Amsterdam: J. Muusses, 1928.

Waldron, Ronald, ed. "Trevisa's Original Prefaces on Translation: A Critical Edition." In *Medieval English Studies Presented to George Kane*, ed. Edward Donald Kennedy, Ronald Waldron, and Joseph S. Wittig, 285–99. Bury St. Edmunds, U.K.: St. Edmundsbury Press, 1988.

Wallace, David, ed. *The Cambridge History of Medieval English Literature*. Cambridge, U.K.: Cambridge University Press, 1999.

———. "In Flaundres." *Studies in the Age of Chaucer* 19 (1997): 63–91.

Walters, James C. *Ethnic Issues in Paul's Letter to the Romans*. Valley Forge, Pa: Trinity Press International, 1993.

Ward, Benedicta. *Miracles and the Medieval Mind: Theory, Record, and Event, 1000–1215*. Philadelphia: University of Pennsylvania Press, 1982.

Warner, Marina. *Alone of All Her Sex: The Myth and Cult of the Virgin Mary*. New York: Vintage Books, 1976.

Watson, Nicholas. "Censorship and Cultural Change in Late-Medieval England: Vernacular Theology, the Oxford Translation Debate, and Arundel's Constitutions of 1409." *Speculum* 70 (1995): 822–64.

———. "Visions of Inclusion: Universal Salvation and Vernacular Theology in Pre-Reformation England." *Journal of Medieval and Early Modern Studies* 27 (1997): 147–87.

Weinhouse, Linda. "Faith and Fantasy: The Texts of the Jews." *Medieval Encounters* 5 (1999): 400–408.

Wenzel, Edith. *"Do worden die Judden alle geschant": Rolle und Funktion der Juden in spätmittelalterlichen Spielen*. Munich: Wilhelm Fink Verlag, 1992.

Wenzel, Siegfried. "Notes on the Parson's Tale." *Chaucer Review* 16 (1982): 237–56.

Williams, Arnold. *The Common Expositor: An Account of the Commentaries on Genesis, 1527–1633*. Chapel Hill: University of North Carolina Press, 1948.

Wistrich, Robert, ed. *Demonizing the Other: Antisemitism, Racism, and Xenophobia*. Amsterdam: Hanwood Academic, 1999.

Witt, Elizabeth A. *Contrary Marys in Medieval English and French Drama*. New York: Peter Lang, 1995.

Wogan-Browne, Jocelyn. "The Virgin's Tale." In *Feminist Readings in Middle English Literature: The Wife of Bath and All Her Sect*, ed. Ruth Evans and Lesley Johnson, 165–94. New York: Routledge, 1994.

Wogan-Browne, Jocelyn, Nicholas Watson, Andrew Taylor, and Ruth Evans, eds. *The Idea of the Vernacular: An Anthology of Middle English Literary Theory, 1280–1520*. University Park, Pa.: Pennsylvania State University Press, 1999.

Wood, Charles T. "The Doctor's Dilemma: Sin, Salvation and the Menstrual Cycle in Medieval Thought." *Speculum* 56 (1981): 710–27.

Woolf, Rosemary. *The English Mystery Plays.* Berkeley: University of California Press, 1972.

Wyclif, John. *De veritate sacrae scripturae.* Ed. Rudolf Buddensieg. 3 vols. London: Trübner and Co., Wycliff Society, 1905.

———. *John Wyclif: On the Truth of Holy Scripture.* Trans. Ian Christopher Levy. Kalamazoo, Mich.: Medieval Institute, 2001.

Yerushalmi, Yosef. *Assimilation and Racial Anti-Semitism: The Iberian and the German Models.* Leo Baeck Memorial Lecture 26. New York: Leo Baeck Institute, 1982.

Young, Karl. *Drama of the Medieval Church.* Oxford: Clarendon Press, 1933.

Zagona, Helen Grace. *The Legend of Salome and the Principle of Art for Art's Sake.* Paris: Librarie Minard, 1960.

Zerilli, Linda. "This Universalism Which Is Not One." *diacritics* 28 (1998): 3–20.

Zieman, Katherine. "Reading and Singing: Liturgy, Literacy, and Literature in Late Medieval England." Ph.D. diss., University of California, Berkeley, 1997.

———. "Reading, Singing, and Understanding: Constructions of Women's Literacy in Late Medieval England." In *Literacy and Learning in the Middle Ages,* ed. Sarah Rees-Jones, 93–117. Turnholt, Belgium: Brepols, 2002.

Žižek, Slavoj. *The Sublime Object of Ideology.* New York: Verso, 1989.

———. *The Ticklish Subject: The Absent Centre of Political Ontology.* New York: Verso, 1999.

Index

abjection, 55–56, 77
"absent fullness," 4
Abulafia, Anna, 17, 51–52
Adversus Iudaeorum inveteratam duritiem
 (Peter the Venerable), 43
Africanist presence, in American literature,
 168–69
Albertanus of Brescia, 93
aliens: antagonism toward, 142–43, 162;
 commerce and, 151, 159–60; conversion of,
 155–67; foreign bride (Deut. 21:10–13),
 40–42, 55, 158, 193*n*.91; miscegenation,
 141–42, 155–66; women, 160–66
allosemitism, 182*n*.80
Alma Redemptoris Mater, 74, 81–82, 83, 88,
 211*n*.91
Ambrose, 30
Anaclet II, pope, 17
"analogy of analogies," 10, 59
Anne, Saint, 124
Anselm of Canterbury, 51, 53
anti-Judaism, 18, 215*n*.131; use of term,
 180*n*.58
anti-Semitism: Christian response to, 183*n*.4;
 Christian universalism and, 10–11; defined,
 18–19; medieval context, 16, 179*n*.57; use
 of term, 180*n*.58, 182*n*.75
anusim, 110
Anzaldúa, Gloria, 2
Appiah, Kwame Anthony, 16
Aquinas, 69
Archisynagogus, 37–38, 43, 53–55, 192*n*.81
Arendt, Hannah, 18
Ashley, Kathleen, 124
audience reaction, to medieval drama,
 106–7, 118–19, 127–28, 136–37
Augustine, 5, 23, 24, 27–28, 31–34, 37, 43, 48;
 as a Christian reader, 39; doctrine of relative toleration, 36–37; letter and spirit,
 38–39

Augustine the Reader (Stock), 39
Ave Maris Stella, 35

Badiou, Alain, 170–71
baptism, 114, 116, 164; by midwives, 129–30
Bartlett, Robert, 17, 19
bastardy, 232*n*.65
Beauvoir, Simone de, 1, 2, 7, 30, 169, 175*n*.3
Beckwith, Sarah, 113–14, 216*n*.5
Berek, Peter, 144
Bernard of Clairvaux, 17, 24–25, 37, 46–47,
 171
Bestul, Thomas, 98–99
"Biblical Allusion and Allegory in *The Merchant of Venice*" (Lewalski), 139–40
Biddick, Kathleen, 7
Biller, Peter, 17
birthing chamber, 127
Blickling Homilies, 133–37
Bloch, R. Howard, 36
body imagery: bodily boundaries, 54–55, 118;
 Cecelia, Saint, 88; Christian identity and,
 117–18, 211*n*.89; conversion through faith,
 136–37; in Croxton *Play of the Sacrament,*
 117–19; doubters and, 103–4, 107–8; Incarnation and, 11, 51–52; Jesus Christ, 53, 55,
 123–24; Jews, 78–80, 211*n*.89; Mary, 49–55,
 80, 123–25, 133–37; pursuit of wealth and,
 117; restoration of, 103–4; as societal symbol, 11, 78–80, 120–21; symbolic disintegration of, 103–8; topos of the stricken
 hand, 102–4, 107–8, 126–28, 136; virginal,
 78–79; wholeness of, 105, 107; women and,
 30
Boose, Lynda, 163
Boyarin, Daniel, 26, 28–30, 38, 62
Bradshaw shift, 59–60, 61
Bury Jews, 108
Bury St. Edmunds, 108, 111, 120
Butler, Judith, 5, 30, 55, 56, 128

Caesarius of Heisterbach, 17
Canterbury Tales (Chaucer), 3, 19, 58–100, 141, 171–72; anti-Semitism in, 58–59; Bradshaw shift, 59–60, 61; idealized Christian identity in, 12–13, 83, 88–87; Jews in, 11–13, 58–59; Lollards in, 60–61; pilgrimage symbolism, 61; "sentence" in, 59; supersession and, 33; textual ordering, 59–60; universality in, 61–62; women in, 58
captive foreign bride (Deut. 21:10–13), 40–42, 55, 158, 193*n*.91
carnality: Incarnation and, 52; Jews and, 29, 34, 52–53, 106, 126–27, 132; of Mary, 29; women and, 29–32, 44–45
Cecelia, Saint, 12, 83–88, 213*n*.104
Chambers, E. K., 120
chapeleyne, 84
Chaucer, Geoffrey, 3, 11–12, 19, 58–100; self-presentation of, 13, 92–94, 96
Chaucer, Lewis, 68
Chaucerian Theatricality (Ganim), 61
Chaucer's Sexual Poetics (Dinshaw), 28
Chazan, Robert, 50, 51
Childermas, 76–77
children: baptism by midwives, 129–30; Chaucer's use of, 94–96; in Fragment VII, 94; murdered by Jews, in the *Prioress's Tale*, 74–82, 94–96; parent-child relationship, 214*n*.116; piety of, 81–82; reenactment of Crucifixion with, 96; stages of childhood, 208*n*.68, 212*n*.93; supersession and, 95; understanding of "sentence" by, 95; virginal, 78–79. *See also* youth
Childs, Wendy, 110–11
Christian comedy, 108, 116, 121–22, 127–28
Christian identity: belief and, 108; body and, 117–18; children, 95–96; commerce and, 162, 167; development of, 22–23; drama and, 105–6; eucharist and, 116; fragility of, 5–6, 15, 107, 121, 137; gender and, 29–32; heretics and, 97–98; idealized, in *Canterbury Tales*, 12–13, 83, 86–87; Jewish identity blurred with, 107, 110, 124–25, 153; Jewish particularity and, 1–2, 60, 111–12, 122, 169–72; Mary's body symbolizing, 80; in medieval drama, 101; miscegenation and, 162; mothers, 95–96; the Other and, 97–98, 116–17; Pauline definition of, 13; reading and, 39, 47; in relation to the Other,

1, 56–57; rituals and, 14, 105; in Spain, 109–12; spiritual understanding and, 140–41, 211*n*.91; supersession and, 10–11, 24–26; symbolic boundaries, 11; universalism/particularity model and, 4–7; wholeness, 105, 107; women and, 2, 169–72; youth and, 96
Christians and Christianity: body imagery, 211*n*.89; decentering from normative position, 1; living near Jews, 77–78; Old Testament and, 28–29; reading by, 39–43, 49, 97, 141; renewed belief through conversion, 102, 114–15; rituals, 105, 116; separating Jews from, 77–78
Christian universalism. *See* universalism
Chrysostom, John, 23
circumcision, 164, 166
Cistercians, 25
Clark, Elizabeth, 36
Cohen, Jeremy, 9, 17, 34, 189*n*.60
Cole, Andrew, 68
Coletti, Theresa, 55, 124, 132
Collette, Carolyn, 81, 211*n*.91
Colley, John, 147
Colossians, 22
commerce: aliens and, 151, 159–60; Christian identity and, 162; concerns about, 227*n*.29; corruption through, 136, 141, 145–47, 151–53, 167; female personification of, 227*n*.29; women and, 158–62. *See also* trade; wealth
communion, 116
Communities of Violence: Persecution of Minorities in the Middle Ages (Nirenberg), 18
Contra Faustum (Augustine), 23
conversion: of doubters, 14, 107–8; of Jews, to Christianity, 12–13, 34, 99, 109–14, 143–44, 160–67; New Christians, 110, 162; renewed belief by Christians, 102, 114–15; restoration of stricken hand through, 103–4
conversos, 109–10, 138
Copeland, Rita, 43, 65
Corinthians, 10, 29, 32, 38, 43–47, 65
corruption: commerce and, 141, 151–53; by wealth, 113–14
Crenshaw, Kimberlé, 3
Cressy, David, 129
Crispin, Gilbert, 51
cross-dressing, in medieval drama, 101, 128, 216*n*.1

Croxton *Play of the Sacrament*, 3, 13, 38, 108–22, 153, 172; bodily imagery in, 117–19; Christian universality and, 101; humor in, 108, 118–19, 121–22, 127–29, 132; setting for, 108–12, 139; supersession in, 104; topos of the stricken hand in, 103

Crucifixion, 93, 130; murder of children and, 76, 77; reenacted with children, 96; as transition between Judaism and Christianity, 47; wholeness and, 107

crypto-Jews, 109–10

Cur Deus Homo (Anselm), 51

currency traders, 69

Cursor Mundi (Wogan-Browne), 123

De Civitate Dei (Augustine), 33

De mandatis divinis (Wyclif), 89–90

Despres, Denise, 3, 9, 123

De Trinitate (Augustine), 31

Deuteronomy, 40–42

Dinshaw, Carolyn, 10, 28, 39–40, 43, 158

Disputatio contra Judaeum Leonem nomine de adventu Christi filii Dei (Odo of Tournai), 52

divine comedy, 108, 116

double supersession, 67

doubters: converted through faith, 14, 101, 103–4, 107–8, 136–37; Jews, in Croxton *Play of the Sacrament*, 13–14, 101, 103, 104, 121, 136, 218n.27; Jews, in N-Town "Nativity," 123–32, 136; Lollards as, 108; midwife, in N-Town "Nativity," 13–14, 103–4, 123–32, 136

doubting Thomas, 103

Douglas, Mary, 11, 54–55, 80, 104

Dove, Mary, 65, 68

East Anglian drama, 101–37

Eberle, Patricia J., 60

Ecclesia, 44–45

Edgeworth, Maria, 116

education: male-dominated, 74, 76, 208n.67; of nuns, 213n.101; of women, 84–85

Elukin, Jonathan, 139

Emancipation(s) (Laclau), 4

Enarrationes in Psalmos (Augustine), 24

Enders, Jody, 107

England: foreigners in, 142–43; Jewish identity in, 138–40, 172; Jews expelled from, 11, 62, 122, 138, 169; trade with Spain, 110–11, 220n.40

English vernacular, 62, 93–94, 212n.95

Enlightenment, 7–9

Ephesians, 34, 190n.63

erotic desire, 158–59, 165, 231n.62

Esau, 147

Espina, Alfonso de, 110

ethnicity: defined, 19; medieval context of, 16–20. *See also* race

eucharist, 113, 117–18; attacks on, 124; Christian identity and, 116

Eva/Ave anagram, 35

Evans, Ruth, 101–2, 106, 136

Eve, 35–36

fascism, 231n.57

Feast of the Holy Innocents, 77

feminism, 7

Ferris, Sumner, 75

Fiedler, Leslie, 167

filial piety, 147

filth, Jews and, 210n.83

Folz, Hans, 21

foreign bride (Deut. 21:10–13), 40–42, 55, 158, 193n.91; purification of, 40–42. *See also* aliens

Fortalitium Fidei (Alfonso de Espina), 110

Fortescue, John, 111

Fortin, René, 147

Fradenburg, L. O. Aranye, 58

Fragment VI, *Canterbury Tales*, 203n.7

Fragment VII, *Canterbury Tales*, 13, 59, 60, 203n.7; role of child figure in, 94–96; "sentence" in, 96–97

Fragment VIII, *Canterbury Tales*, 13, 59, 203n.7

Frank, Hardy Long, 73

Freinkel, Lisa, 24, 140

French universalism, 6

Friars and the Jews (Cohen), 189n.60

Friedman, Jerome, 16

Fonrobert, Charlotte, 41

"Funeral of the Virgin" or "Transitus" (York), 105–7

Funkenstein, Amos, 17

Galatians, 27, 29, 116, 149, 151, 164

Ganim, John, 61

Gaylord, Alan, 96

gender: characteristics of, 187n.40; Christian identity and, 29–32; education and, 74, 76; Jesus Christ and, 31; Jewishness and, 189n.53; piety and, 12–13, 75–76, 80, 91; race and, 2–3; reading and, 39–40; spirituality and, 30–32; supersession and, 30–31; use of term, 182n.79. *See also* women

Gentiles, 22–23

Germany, persecution of Jews in, 21–22, 183n.4

Ghosh, Kantik, 61, 65

Gibson, Gail McMurray, 102, 108, 123, 124, 127, 128, 218n.27

Gottfried, Robert, 120

Green, Monica, 129

Gregory the Great, 45

Greilsammer, Myriam, 130

Griffin, Eric, 155

Guibert of Nogent, 51–53, 55

Hahn, Thomas, 69

Hall, Kim, 3, 140

Hanning, Robert, 76

Harrington (Edgeworth), 116

Hegemony and Socialist Strategy (Laclau and Mouffe), 4, 7

hegemony theory, 5, 56

Heng, Geraldine, 3

heretics: Christian identity and, 97–98; classification of, 41. *See also* Lollardy; Wycliffite movement

"hermeneutical divide," 140

Herod, 95, 131

Herodias, 131

"hierosphthitic topos," 216n.7

Hilton, Walter, 62

Holocaust, 18

Homan, Richard, 107

Homilies on Leviticus (Origen), 41, 48

homoerotics, 227n.30

hooks, bell, 2

host desecration, 108, 110, 114–15, 117–18, 123, 150, 227n.22; "zone of uninhabitability" and, 118–19

Hugh of Lincoln, 76

humor: in Croxton *Play of the Sacrament,* 108, 118–19, 121–22; functions of, 116, 137, 217n.22; in *Merchant of Venice,* 230n.50; in N-Town "Nativity," 127–29, 132

Huppé, Bernard, 97

identity politics, 3–4

idol worship, 87–88, 90

imago Dei, gender and, 31

Immaculate Conception, 49, 50

Incarnation: Christian defense of, 51; in Croxton *Play of the Sacrament,* 105; doubt/debate over, 49–55, 124–26, 132; *infideles* (unbelievers) and, 51; Jewish objection to, 50–54; mystery of, 102; in N-Town "Nativity," 105, 124, 128; as reproduction, 73–74; supersession and, 53–54, 134–35; symbolism of, 11; as transition between Judaism and Christianity, 48–49

infideles (unbelievers), 51

inner worth, 155–59

Inquisition, 110, 219n.32

"intercourse": with the Other, 155; sexual connotation of, 227n.17. *See also* commerce

"intersectionality," 3

Ireland, 156

Isaac, 147

Isaiah, 43

Israel, 95; olive tree symbolism, 22–24, 26

Jacob, 147

Jacob Shalem, Menachem ben, 50

James, Mervyn, 120

Jeremiah, 22–23, 95

Jerome, 1, 30, 40–41, 108

"Jerusalem celestial," 99

Jesus Christ: blindness (depicted) of Jews to, 45–46; body of, 53, 55, 123–24; conception of, 49–50; conversion of Jews and, 113–14; gender and, 31; Jews as depicted killers of, 98–99, 150; in medieval drama, 102; in the *Prioress's Tale,* 75; suffering of (Passion), 98; unity in, 22

Jew of Malta (Marlowe), 144

Jews and Judaism: assaults on Mary, 123–24, 133–37; bifurcated views of, 2, 35, 36–38; bodies of, 78–80, 211n.89; in *Canterbury Tales* (Chaucer), 11–13, 58–59; captive foreign bride (Deut. 21:10–13), 40–42, 55, 158, 193n.91; carnality and, 29, 34, 52–53, 106, 126–27, 132; as child murderers, 74–83, 91; Christian identity blurred with, 107, 110, 124–25, 153; Christian universalism and, 1–2, 7, 35–38, 54–55, 62–63, 111–12, 122, 169–72; contemporary attitudes toward,

191*n*.74; conversion of, 12–13, 34, 99, 103–4, 109–14, 143–44, 160–67; in Croxton *Play of the Sacrament,* 108–22; depicted in Passion, 215*n*.131; as doubters, 13–14, 103, 121, 123–32, 218*n*.27; English concerns about, 138–40; Enlightenment attitudes toward, 7–8, 9–10; expelled from England, 11, 62, 122, 138, 169; expelled from Spain, 110; expulsion of, 115, 116; fallen women and, 44–45, 47; feminization of male, 195*n*.112; filth and, 210*n*.83; idealized, before Christ, 38, 66; Incarnation and, 50–54; incompleteness of, 34; as killers of Christ, 98–99, 150; as letter, 48; living near Christians, 77–78; as marginalized and central, 56; in *Merchant of Venice,* 14–15; murder of, 181–82*n*.74; Old Testament and, 28–29, 33–34, 170–71; paradoxical roles of, 55–56; in *Parson's Tale,* 98–100; patrimony and, 147–50, 154–55; persecution of, 10–11, 21–22, 110; portrayal of, in medieval drama, 101; prejudice against, 17–18, 181*n*.73; in *Prioress's Tale,* 68, 74–82, 91, 100; race and, 16, 139; reading by, 28–29, 39–44, 47; relationship to Gentiles, 22–23; relative tolerance toward, 36–37, 62; ritual murder attributed to, 58, 108, 110, 150, 209*n*.74; separating from Christians, 77–78; sins (depicted) of, 45–46, 98–99; in Spain, 108–12; spiritual blindness (depicted) of, 28–29, 37–38, 43–46, 81–82, 88–89, 119, 121–22, 133, 147, 194*n*.105, 195*n*.106; spirituality of, 34–35, 37–38; subjugation of, 47–48; supersession and, 10–11, 24–27, 33–35; symbolic boundaries, 11; trade and, 14–15, 112–14; usury and, 12, 69, 147–49; vilified, at the time of Christ, 38, 66; violence against, 10–11; Virgin birth and, 37; as wandering exiles, 114–15; witches and, 178*n*.45
John, 43
Johnson, Lesley, 123
John the Baptist, 130, 131
Jones, W. R., 89–90, 203*n*.9
Joseph, 45, 124, 127–28, 130
Judenfeindschaft, 182*n*.80
Julian of Norwich, 62

Kelly, Joan, 16
Kempe, Margery, 63

Kimḥi, Joseph, 50, 53
Kinservik, Matthew, 133, 135
knowledge, 28–29
Kolve, V. A., 127–28
Kristeva, Julia, 55, 56
Kruger, Steven, 3, 51, 53, 79–80, 139, 189*n*.53, 211*n*.89

Laclau, Ernesto, 4–7, 9, 54, 170
Langmuir, Gavin, 17, 209*n*.74
Lasker, Daniel, 50
Latin, 212*n*.95, 213*n*.101; Wycliffite movement and, 64–65
Leclerq, Jean, 29
Lee, Becky, 130
Legenda Aurea (Jacobus a Voragine), 83
letter: Jews as, 48; spirit and, 38–43, 102; veil of, 48
Levinas, Emmanuel, 168
Leviticus, 41, 42, 48, 193*n*.97
Lewalski, Barbara, 139–40
Libelle of Englyshe Polycye, The (Warner, ed.), 111, 220*n*.40
Liber consolationis et consilii (Albertanus of Brescia), 93
Life of Our Lady (Lydgate), 131
Little, Lester, 17
Living Letters of the Law: Ideas of the Jew in Medieval Christianity (Cohen), 9
Livre de Melibée et de Dame Prudence (Renaud de Louens), 93
Lloyd, Genevieve, 32
Lollardy, 12, 13, 203*n*.9; in *Canterbury Tales,* 59, 60–61, 63; Christian universal and, 63; Croxton *Play of the Sacrament* and, 108, 218*n*.27; openness in, 63–64; sacred texts and, 63–64; *Second Nun's Tale* and, 89–90; in *Thopas/Melibee* sequence, 94; women of, 213*n*.111; Wycliffite movement and, 64–68
Loomba, Ania, 3, 140
Lopez, Roderigo, 138
Lotter, Friedrich, 25
Louens, Renaud de, 93
Lubac, Henri de, 28, 183*n*.4
Ludus de Nativitate, 37
Luke, 147
Lupton, Julia Reinhard, 140
Lydgate, John, 131

Mandeville's Travels, 62
Manichaeism, 5

Man of Law's Endlink (Chaucer), 12, 89, 99, 203*n*.11; Lollards in, 59, 60–61; positioning in *Canterbury Tales,* 60

Marlowe, Christopher, 144

marranos, 109–10, 144

marriage, 71–72

martyrdom: masculinized women, 213*n*.104; in the *Prioress's Tale,* 83; in the *Second Nun's Tale,* 83, 85–86

Mary: assaults to, 123–24, 133–37; Assumption of, 133, 225*n*.111; bifurcated view of women and, 35–36; bodily boundaries, 54–55; body of, 11, 49–55, 80, 123–25, 133–37; carnality and, 29; doubted by Jews, 106; doubted by midwife, in N-Town "Nativity," 13–14; incarnation and, 46, 49–55; in medieval drama, 102; medieval representations of, 49; menstruation of, 49, 50; in N-Town "Nativity," 123–32; in the *Prioress's Tale,* 73–75, 78, 83; purity of, 49, 123–24, 126, 135; sexual morality and, 74; as transition between Judaism and Christianity, 48–49; virgin birth, 49–55; womb of, 50, 124–28

Mary Magdalene, 46–47

Massacre of the Innocents, 95

masturbation, 207*n*.51

Matthew, 95

Maurus, Rabanus, 34

McClintock, Anne, 3, 19

medieval drama, 101–37; audience reaction to, 106–7, 118–19, 127–28, 136–37; construction of Christian identity through, 105–6; functions of, 102; social and economic context of, 107. *See also* Croxton *Play of the Sacrament;* N-Town "Nativity"

Medieval Misogyny (Bloch), 36

medieval period: bifurcated representations of Jews and women in, 2, 35–38, 169–70; gender, 2, 16–17; Jews, 2, 16–20; Middle Ages/Renaissance division, 16, 139; race, 16–20

Melibee (Chaucer), 92–94, 97

menstruation, 49, 50, 199*n*.136, 211*n*.88

Merchant of Venice (Shakespeare), 3, 14–15, 19, 54, 71, 116, 123, 136, 138–67, 172; courtroom scene, 149–51; patrimony and, 145, 147–50, 154–55, 160–66; setting, 227*n*.18; supersession and, 33, 141, 144; usury in, 146–49

Merchant's Tale (Chaucer), 71

Metzger, Mary Janell, 140

Mézières, Phillipe de, 102

midwives: control over reproduction, 103, 130–32; doubter, in N-Town "Nativity," 13–14, 103–4, 123–32, 136; examination of Mary's womb by, 124–28; functions of, 125–28; licensed by church, 129–30; symbolism of, 130–32; witches and, 224*n*.108

Mill, Anna, 106

Minh-ha, Trinh T., 2

Mirk, John, 129

Mirk's Festial, 135

miscegenation, 141–42, 155–66, 232*n*.65; use of term, 227*n*.17

Mohammed, 113

Monk's Tale (Chaucer), 94

Moore, R. I., 17

Moraga, Cherríe, 2

Moralia in Job (Gregory the Great), 45

Morrison, Toni, 168–69

Moses, 10

mothers: Christian, 95–96; patrimony and, 231*n*.62

Mouffe, Chantal, 4, 7

multiculturalism, 3–4

murder: of child, in the *Prioress's Tale,* 74–82, 91, 209*n*.71; of Jews, 181–82*n*.74; ritual, 58, 76, 96, 108, 110, 150, 209*n*.74

New Christians, 110, 162

New Testament: bifurcated view of Jews and, 36; early interpretations of, 5; Old Testament and, 10, 23, 28, 33, 58–59

Nirenberg, David, 18

Nissé, Ruth, 66, 67, 204*n*.19

N-Town "Assumption," 13, 133–37, 225*n*.114

N-Town cycle, 3, 13, 101, 172

N-Town "Joseph's Doubt," 124

N-Town "Nativity," 13, 38, 102–8, 122–32; Christian universalism and, 101; humor in, 127–29, 132; stricken hand in, 126–28; supersession in, 104; topos of the stricken hand in, 102–3

N-Town "Trial of Mary and Joseph," 124

Odo of Tournai, 51, 52, 53

Old Testament: bifurcated view of Jews and, 37; Christian perspective of, 28; Jewish particularity and, 170–71; Jewish understanding of, 28, 33–34; literal sense of, 65; New Testament and, 10, 23, 28, 33, 58–59; Wycliffite movement and, 65

olive tree symbolism, 22–24, 26, 171, 184*n*.10, 185*n*.16

Ordo Prophetarum, 38

Origen, 23, 27, 41–42, 48, 55, 184*n*.10

Othello (Shakespeare), 155

Other, the: abjection and, 55–56; Christian identity and, 1, 97–98, 116–17; foreigners as, 142–43; "intercourse" with, 155; pagans as, 87–90

pagans: blindness of, 88–89; Christianity and, 66; as Other, 87–90; represented by fallen woman, 47

pagan texts, Christian reading of, 40–42

Palmer, Thomas, 67

parent-child relationship, 214*n*.116

Parson's Tale (Chaucer), 13; Jews in, 98–100

particularity: supersession and, 10–11; universalism and, 4–7, 22, 26

Passion: depiction of Jews in, 215*n*.131; in *Melibee,* 93–94; in *Parson's Tale,* 98

patriarchal control, 160

patrimony: Jewish identity and, 147–50, 154–55; in *Merchant of Venice,* 145, 147–50, 154–55, 160–66; supersession and, 147, 149–50; women's desires and, 159–62

Patterson, Lee, 94, 95, 98

Paul, 10, 64, 147, 170–71; allegorical method, 28; Christian identity and, 22–23; supersession and, 38; universal salvation, 28

Pauline Epistles, 5, 12, 65, 164, 170–71; Christian definition, 13

Pecock, Reginald, 67, 68

Penitence, 98

performativity theory, 5, 56

Peter the Venerable, 43

Philo, 30, 32, 187*n*.40

Piers Plowman (Langland), 62

piety: of children, 81–82; gender and, 12–13, 75–76, 80; in *Prioress's Tale* (Chaucer), 59, 75–76, 80–83, 91, 211*n*.92; in *Second Nun's Tale* (Chaucer), 59, 85; of women, 12–13, 75–76, 80, 88

Pius IX, pope, 49

Play Called Corpus Christi (Kolve), 127–28, 221*n*.54

Playing in the Dark: Whiteness and the Literary Imagination (Morrison), 168–69

Power, Eileen, 36, 72–73, 84, 213*n*.101

Powers of Horror (Kristeva), 55

Preus, James Samuel, 27

Prioress's Tale (Chaucer), 11–13, 54, 58, 72–83, 104, 142, 159; Jews in, 68, 74–82, 91, 100; Mary's role in, 73–75, 78, 83; piety in, 59, 75–76, 80–83, 91; Prioress's rank and responsibilities, 72–73; women in, 80

profit, 69–70

prostitution, 71–72

purity, of Mary, 49, 123–24, 126, 135

Purity and Danger (Douglas), 54–55

race: academic feminist theory and, 2–3; defined, 19; gender and, 2–3; inner and outer worth and, 155–59; Jews and, 16, 139; medieval context of, 16–20; miscegenation, 141–42, 155–66, 232*n*.65; skin color, 168–69, 230*n*.52, 233*n*.8

"Race" (Appiah), 16

Rachel, 95, 147, 214*n*.121

Ragussis, Michael, 116, 172

reading: by Christians, 39–43, 47, 49, 97, 141; faith and, 43; gender and, 194*n*.101; by Jews, 28–29, 39–44, 47; layered meaning in, 39; letter and spirit, 38–43; pagan texts, 40–42; spirituality and, 43; by women, 39, 42–43

redemption, 51

reproduction: Incarnation as, 73–74; midwives' control over, 103, 130–32; sterility, 207*n*.55; unnatural, usury as, 69–70, 146, 206*n*.47, 207*n*.55; by women, 30

Resurrection, 103

Rieder, Paula, 130

ritual murder: attributed to Jews, 58, 76, 96, 108, 110, 150, 209*n*.74; defined, 209*n*.74

Robbins, Jill, 33, 214*n*.120

Robertson, D. W., Jr., 97, 140

Roman de la Rose, 69–70

Romans, 22, 26, 33, 147

Rubin, Miri, 116, 123, 227*n*.22

Ruether, Rosemary, 36

sacramental theology, 216*n*.5

Sal/ège of Toulouse, cardinal, 21–22, 183*n*.4

Salomé, 130–31

salvation, 62

Samson, 196*n*.114

Sandoval, Fray Prudencio de, 155

Sartre, Jean-Paul, 168

Scale of Perfection (Hilton), 62

Schor, Naomi, 4, 6–9, 170

Scott, Joan, 8, 171

Scriptural language, 64–65

Second Nun's Tale (Chaucer), 12–13, 83–90; idealized Christian identity in, 86–87; Jewish blindness in, 88–89; Lollardy and, 89–90; pagan blindness in, 88–89; piety in, 59, 85, 91

Second Sex, The (de Beauvoir), 1, 2, 169, 175n.3

Seidel, Linda, 130, 131

"sentence": in *Canterbury Tales,* 59; child's understanding of, 95; in Fragment VII, 96–97; in *Thopas/Melibee* sequence, 93–94

Sermones super Cantica Canticorum (Bernard of Clairvaux), 24–25, 37, 46

sexuality, 159

Shahar, Shulamith, 81, 208n.68, 212n.93

Shakespeare, William, 3, 19, 116, 123, 136

Shakespeare and the Jews (Shapiro), 138

Shapiro, James, 138, 139, 140, 164

Sheingorn, Pamela, 123, 134

Shell, Marc, 71

Shem Tov, Joseph ben, 50

Sherman, Gail Berkeley, 86

Shipman's Tale (Chaucer), 12, 60, 80, 91, 203n.11, 211n.88; corruption in, 69–72, 77; usury in, 69, 91

Showings (Julian of Norwich), 62

Simon of Trent, 96

sin: of Jews, 45–46, 98–99; original, Mary's freedom from, 49; women and, 72

Sir Thopas (Chaucer), 92–94, 97

skin color, 168–69, 230n.52, 233n.8

Smith, Barbara, 2

societal order, body imagery and, 11, 78–80, 120–21

sodomy, 206n.47, 227–28n.30

song schools, 74

Spain: Christian identity in, 109–12; Jews in, 109–12; as setting for Croxton *Play of the Sacrament,* 108; trade with England, 110–11, 220n.40

Spector, Stephen, 79, 109, 219n.32

Spenser, Edmund, 156

spirit, letter and, 38–43, 102

spirituality: blindness of Jews to, 119; Chris-

tian identity and, 140–41, 211n.91; gender and, 30–32; immature, 190n.63; Jews and, 34–35, 37–38; masculine, 42–43; reading and, 43; Scriptural language and, 64–65; women and, 30, 91

Spivak, Gayatri, 21

Sponsler, Claire, 107

Stacey, Robert, 17, 19

sterility, 207n.55

Stock, Brian, 39

stricken hand, topos of: in Croxton *Play of the Sacrament,* 103; in East Anglian drama, 102–4; England and, 136; in N-Town "Nativity," 102–3, 126–28; restoration through faith, 103, 128; "zone of uninhabitability" and, 107

Summit, Jennifer, 16

supersession: of child, in the *Prioress's Tale,* 95; Christianity and Judaism and, 10–11, 24–26; in Croxton *Play of the Sacrament,* 104, 172; double, 67; gender and, 30–31, 33; hermeneutical divide and, 27–28; Incarnation and, 53–54, 134–35; in *Merchant of Venice,* 141, 144, 164, 167; in N-Town "Nativity," 104, 172; paradoxes of, 24, 26–27; patrimony and, 147, 149–50; Paul and, 38; Synagogue and, 47–48; youth and, 33–35, 95, 144, 214n.120

Sutcliffe, Adam, 7, 9

Synagoga, 195n.112, 227n.22; depicted Jewish blindness and, 44–48

Tale of Melibee (Chaucer), 60

Tertullian, 48–49, 51

Toledot Yeshu tradition, 50

Tractatus Adversus Iudaeos (Augustine), 23

Tractatus de Incarnatione contra Judaeos (Guibert of Nogent), 52–53

trade: corruption and, 120–21; England and Spain, 111, 220n.40; Jews and, 14–15, 112–14, 120–21. *See also* commerce

"Transitus" (York), 105–7

transubstantiation, 13–14

Treatise on the Astrolabe (Chaucer), 68

Tretise of Miraclis Pleyinge, The, 67

Trevisa, 68

uncanny, the, 55–56

universalism: in *Canterbury Tales,* 61–62; Enlightenment and, 7–8; false universal,

4; feminist thought and, 7; gender and, 29–30, 33; growth of, 4; heterogeneity of, 62; Jews and, 2, 7, 35, 36–38, 54, 62–63; Mary and Jesus and, 54; in medieval drama, 101; National Socialism and, 22; particularity and, 4–7, 22, 26; salvation and, 62; use of term, 177n.29; women and, 2, 7, 35–36

usury: in *Canterbury Tales,* 12; Jews and, 12, 69, 147–49; justification of, 146–47; in *Merchant of Venice,* 146–49; obsession with, 70–71; in *Prioress's Tale,* 77; in *Shipman's Tale,* 69–70, 77, 91; sodomy and, 206n.47, 227–28n.30; as unnatural reproduction, 69–70, 146, 206n.47, 207n.55

van Court, Elisa Narin, 35

vernacular, 62, 212n.95; in *Thopas/Melibee* sequence, 93–94

View of the Present State of Ireland, A (Spenser), 156

virginal children, 78–79

virginal women, 36

Virgin birth: debate over, 49–55; Jews and, 37

Virgin Mary. *See* Mary

Voltaire, 7

Voragine, Jacobus a, 83

Warner, Marina, 79

Watson, Nicholas, 62

wealth: bodily harm and, 117; corruption by, 113–14, 120–21. *See also* commerce; trade

whiteness: Africanist presence and, 168–69; normative, 233n.8

William of St. Thierry, 25

witches: Jews and, 178n.45; midwives and, 224n.108

Wogan-Browne, Jocelyn, 88, 123

women: bifurcated views of, 2, 35–36, 169–70; in *Canterbury Tales,* 12–13, 58, 71–72; captive foreign bride (Deut. 21:10–13), 40–42, 55, 158, 193n.91; carnality of, 29, 30, 31–32, 44–45; Christian universalism and, 2, 7, 27, 33, 35–36, 169–72; commerce and, 158–62, 227n.29; conversion of, 103–4, 160–66; doubting, 101, 102–3; education of, 84–85; Enlightenment attitudes toward, 10; erotic desire, 158–59, 165, 231n.62; fallen, Jews and, 44–45, 47; fascist depiction of, 231n.57; incompleteness of, 34; Jews, 123–37, 143–44; marginalized and central, 56; martyrs, 83, 85–86, 213n.104; midwives, 103; mothers, 95–96, 231n.62; paradoxical roles of, 55–56; patrimony and, 159–62; piety of, 12–13, 75–76, 80, 88, 91; portrayal of, in medieval drama, 101, 128, 216n.1; in *Prioress's Tale,* 80; prostitutes, 71–72; reading by, 39, 42–43; reproductive capacities, 30; sin and, 49, 72; spirituality and, 30–32, 91; transcendence of bodily sex by, 30–31, 32. *See also* gender

Wood, Charles, 49

World War II, Christian response to, 183n.4

Wyclif, John, 64, 89–90, 203n.9

Wycliffite Bible, *General Prologue* to, 63–64, 66, 93–94

Wycliffite movement, 61, 63–68, 89–90

Yerushalmi, Yosef, 17, 179n.57

York "Funeral of the Virgin" or "Transitus," 105–7

youth: Christian identity and, 96; supersession and, 33–35, 95, 144, 214n.120. *See also* children

Zerilli, Linda, 4–5

Žižek, Slavoj, 170

"zone of uninhabitability," 55, 107, 118–19

Acknowledgments

It is a great pleasure to have the opportunity to thank those who have helped so generously with this book. Any reader will immediately recognize my debts to Carolyn Dinshaw, whose approach to literature and to politics long ago captivated my interest. Her scholarship, teaching, and engagement with the world outside the academy continue to serve as models for me. Anne Middleton, always a generous and insightful reader, challenged me to think in new directions and to question my assumptions at an early stage in this work. Daniel Boyarin's influence on the project and my great debt to his work are also obvious. I am grateful to him for his comments and for his continuous support. Although this book focuses on English literature, it has been deeply enriched by my experiences with German literature and culture, none of which I would have had without the help of Elaine Tennant, an inspirational scholar, teacher, and mentor, as well as a very dear friend. Elaine introduced me to Edith Wenzel, who acted as my advisor during my periods of research and study in Berlin and whose scholarship and teaching have also inspired and influenced my work. Numerous other individuals at the University of California, Berkeley, provided support, advice, and inspiration. I would like particularly to thank Paul Alpers, Joel Altman, Geoffrey Koziol, Steven Justice, and Alan Nelson. Reaching back further, three wonderful professors from my undergraduate days at the University of California, Los Angeles, have continued to offer support and guidance as I completed this project: V. A. Kolve, Vincent Pecora, and Ross Shideler.

The early phases of this work were generously supported by the University of California, Berkeley, the American Association of University Women, the Deutscher Akademischer Austausch Dienst, the Leo Baeck Institute, and the Alexander von Humboldt Stiftung. In addition to this generous financial support, while at Berkeley, I also had the benefit of a wonderful intellectual community. I would like particularly to thank Mary Becker, Andrew Escobedo, Frank Grady, Willis Johnson, Donna Kaiser, Ann-Marie Karlsson, Laura Severt King, Mary Ann Koory, Elisa Narin van

Court, Nancy Nenno, Ruth Nissé, Beth Quitsland, Wendy Roth, Kathryn Starkey, and Katherine Zieman.

At the University of Illinois, Urbana-Champaign, where I worked from 1997 until 2002, I found not only a rich intellectual community but also a kind of second family. I would like particularly to thank Nina Baym, Matti Bunzl, Juliana Chang, Jed Esty, Karen Fresco, Dara Goldman, Achsah Guibbory, Stephen Hartnett, Anne D. Hedeman, David A. H. Hirsch, Stephen Jaeger, Marianne Kalinke, Brett Kaplan, Suvir Kaul, Ania Loomba, Martin Manalansan, Bill Maxwell, Carol Neely, Lori Newcomb, Gary Porton, Catherine Prendergast, Elizabeth Shapiro, Michael Shapiro, Jack Stillinger, Zoreh Sullivan, Adam Sutcliffe, Billy Vaughn, and Julia Walker. Charlie Wright read and reread this manuscript; his insight and his generosity as a mentor cannot be adequately acknowledged. Among my students at Illinois, I would like particularly to thank Rebecca Brackmann, Carlee Bradbury, Nathan Breen, Dana Katz, Tara Lyons, Robyn Niesmann, and especially my research assistant, Jennifer Munroe. At the English library, Bill Brockman, Kathleen Kluegel, and Bill Ogg greatly facilitated my work. I also owe thanks to the staff of the English department, especially Christine Clark, Cathy Harney, and Rene Wahlfeldt. The Research Board at the University of Illinois provided a semester's release from teaching and research funds to aid in the completion of this project.

During the 2000–2001 academic year, I was a fellow at the Erasmus Institute at the University of Notre Dame, which generously supported this project in numerous ways, especially by providing a congenial, supportive, and stimulating intellectual environment. I would like to thank the Institute's director, James Turner, and senior associate director, Robert Sullivan, as well as the Institute staff, Kathleen Sobieralski, and Terri O'Reilly, and the other members of our fellowship group, especially Mary Keys, Paul Kollman, C.S.C., Michael Peletz, Patrick Provost-Smith, and Kristen Schwain. I also benefited greatly from the insights and generosity of other members of the vibrant community at Notre Dame. I felt particularly welcomed by the faculty and staff of the Medieval Institute, headed by Tom Noble, and by the staff at the Hesburgh Library. I would also like to thank David Bachrach, Kathleen Biddick, Joseph Blenkinsopp, Graham Hammill, Daniel Hobbins, Angela Kim, Theresa Krier, Jill Mann, Betty Signer, Michael Signer and especially Maura Nolan.

I have not been long at my new home at the University of California, San Diego, but I am already grateful to the faculty and staff of the Literature department for their warm welcome and their help with making the transition back to California during the final crucial stages of revising this manuscript. This work would have been impossible without the assistance of the wonderful staff at the Geisel Library, especially the interlibrary loan department. I would also like to thank Dylan Sailor for graciously sharing his Latin expertise. The Academic Senate also provided funding for final manuscript preparation.

Numerous other colleagues have generously read and commented on this manuscript, have shared work and ideas, and have provided opportunities for me to present my work. I would like to thank Suzanne Conklin Akbari, Thomas Bestul, Robert L. A. Clark, Denise Despres, Jutta Eming, Jill C. Havens, Ingrid Kasten, Patricia Larash, Helga Neumann, Christina von Nolcken, Derrick Pitard, Elizabeth Scala, Kerstin Schmitt, Kenneth Stow, Jennifer Summit, Sylvia Tomasch, Nancy Bradley Warren, and George Williamson. I am especially grateful to Steven F. Kruger and Julia Reinhard Lupton, who read the manuscript for the press. At the University of Pennsylvania Press, I would also like to thank Jerry Singerman for his guidance and support, as well as Rebecca Rich, Erica Ginsburg, Ted Mann, and the members of the editorial staff.

Finally there are family and friends who have helped me to complete this project, sometimes by reading and commenting, sometimes by just listening. I wish to thank Christian von Goetze, Romy Kozak, Andreas Krausz, Zsuzsanna Lipták, and Darlene Routh. For their support, I also thank my aunt and uncle, Sylvia and Robert Tapper, and my brother-in-law, Andrew Diekmann. My sister, Lynn Lampert, has saved me many a time, not only through her talents as reader, librarian, and title-coiner but also through her amazing sense of humor. To my mother, Frances Lampert, I owe more than I can figure out how to say, so I'll just say, "thanks."